SAYONARA, ZETSUBOU-SENSEI

The Power of Negative Thinking

10

Koji Kumeta

D1210499

Translated and adapted by Joshua Weeks
Lettered by North Market Street Graphics

KC
KODANSHA
COMICS

A Kodansha Comics Trade Paperback Original.

Sayonara, Zetsubou-sensei: The Power of Negative Thinking volume 10 copyright © 2007 Koji Kumeta. English translation copyright © 2011 Koji Kumeta.

Published in the United States by Kodansha Comics, an imprint of Kodansha USA Publishing, LLC., New York.

Publication rights for this English edition arranged through Kodansha Ltd., Tokyo.

First published in Japan in 2007 by Kodansha Ltd., Tokyo, as *Sayonara, Zetsubou-Sensei*, volume 10.

ISBN 978-1-935-42980-7

Printed in the United States of America.

www.kodanshacomics.com

1 2 3 4 5 6 7 8 9

Translator/Adapter: Joshua Weeks
Lettering: North Market Street Graphics

SAYONARA, ZETSUBOU-SENSEI

The Power of Negative Thinking 10

CONTENTS

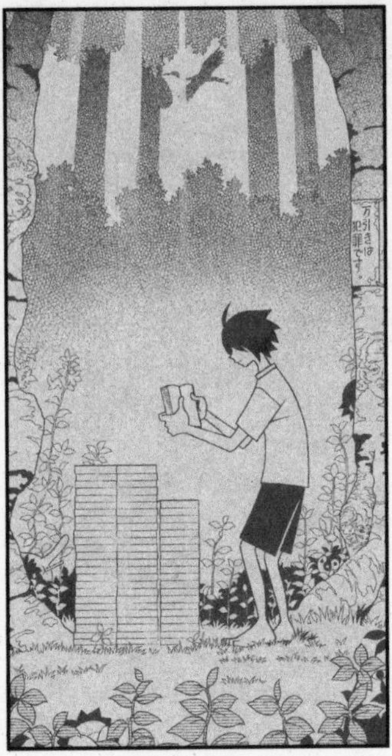
万引きは犯罪です。

THE STORY SO FAR

Our hero takes the stage, unable to totally brush off the pressing request from John Mazzo as a senseless pipe dream. However, he is forced to sing the boy soprano part, ruining his vocal cords, and in two minutes is booed off stage. He snubs the chanson concert he had been planning for the following week, retreating in disappointment to the forest of pianos (which was actually Manga no Mori). He is forced to take a numbered ticket and wait in line at a signing event, and immediately the man in front of him strikes up a conversation. He grows weary of the man's endless barrage of (the recently trendy) "otaku pride." For example, comments like: "I've heard that in France, manga is the ninth art form!" When the conversation turned to the viewer rates of Grendizer, it was finally his turn, and before him stood none other than Shiina-sensei, who had changed his name to "Maple Pinpin."

"What on earth are you doing?"

"Err... it's a long story..." And with that, he began telling a story of a clock tower of darkness, made of rejected manuscripts and raw meat, which informs him of his deadlines. At that moment, our hero hears an otherworldly bell toll in the distance.

"Run! The green people are coming!"

Honorifics Explained

Throughout the Kodansha Comics books, you will find Japanese honorifics left intact in the translations. For those not familiar with how the Japanese use honorifics and, more important, how they differ from American honorifics, we present this brief overview.

Politeness has always been a critical facet of Japanese culture. Ever since the feudal era, when Japan was a highly stratified society, use of honorifics—which can be defined as polite speech that indicates relationship or status—has played an essential role in the Japanese language. When addressing someone in Japanese, an honorific usually takes the form of a suffix attached to one's name (example: "Asuna-san"), is used as a title at the end of one's name, or appears in place of the name itself (example: "Negi-sensei," or simply "Sensei!").

Honorifics can be expressions of respect or endearment. In the context of manga and anime, honorifics give insight into the nature of the relationship between characters. Many English translations leave out these important honorifics and therefore distort the feel of the original Japanese. Because Japanese honorifics contain nuances that English honorifics lack, it is our policy at Kodansha Comics not to translate them. Here, instead, is a guide to some of the honorifics you may encounter in Kodansha Comics books.

-san: This is the most common honorific and is equivalent to Mr., Miss, Ms., or Mrs. It is the all-purpose honorific and can be used in any situation where politeness is required.

-sama: This is one level higher than "-san" and is used to confer great respect.

-dono: This comes from the word "tono," which means "lord." It is an even higher level than "-sama" and confers utmost respect.

-kun: This suffix is used at the end of boys' names to express familiarity or endearment. It is also sometimes used by men among friends, or when addressing someone younger or of a lower station.

-chan: This is used to express endearment, mostly toward girls. It is also used for little boys, pets, and even among lovers. It gives a sense of childish cuteness.

Bozu: This is an informal way to refer to a boy, similar to the English terms "kid" and "squirt."

Sempai/
Senpai: This title suggests that the addressee is one's senior in a group or organization. It is most often used in a school setting, where underclassmen refer to their upperclassmen as "sempai." It can also be used in the workplace, such as when a newer employee addresses an employee who has seniority in the company.

Kohai: This is the opposite of "sempai" and is used toward underclassmen in school or newcomers in the workplace. It connotes that the addressee is of a lower station.

Sensei: Literally meaning "one who has come before," this title is used for teachers, doctors, or masters of any profession or art.

-[blank]: This is usually forgotten in these lists, but it is perhaps the most significant difference between Japanese and English. The lack of honorific means that the speaker has permission to address the person in a very intimate way. Usually, only family, spouses, or very close friends have this kind of permission. Known as *yobisute*, it can be gratifying when someone who has earned the intimacy starts to call one by one's name without an honorific. But when that intimacy hasn't been earned, it can be very insulting.

Koji Kumeta

SAYONARA, ZETSUBOU-SENSEI 10

The Power of Negative Thinking

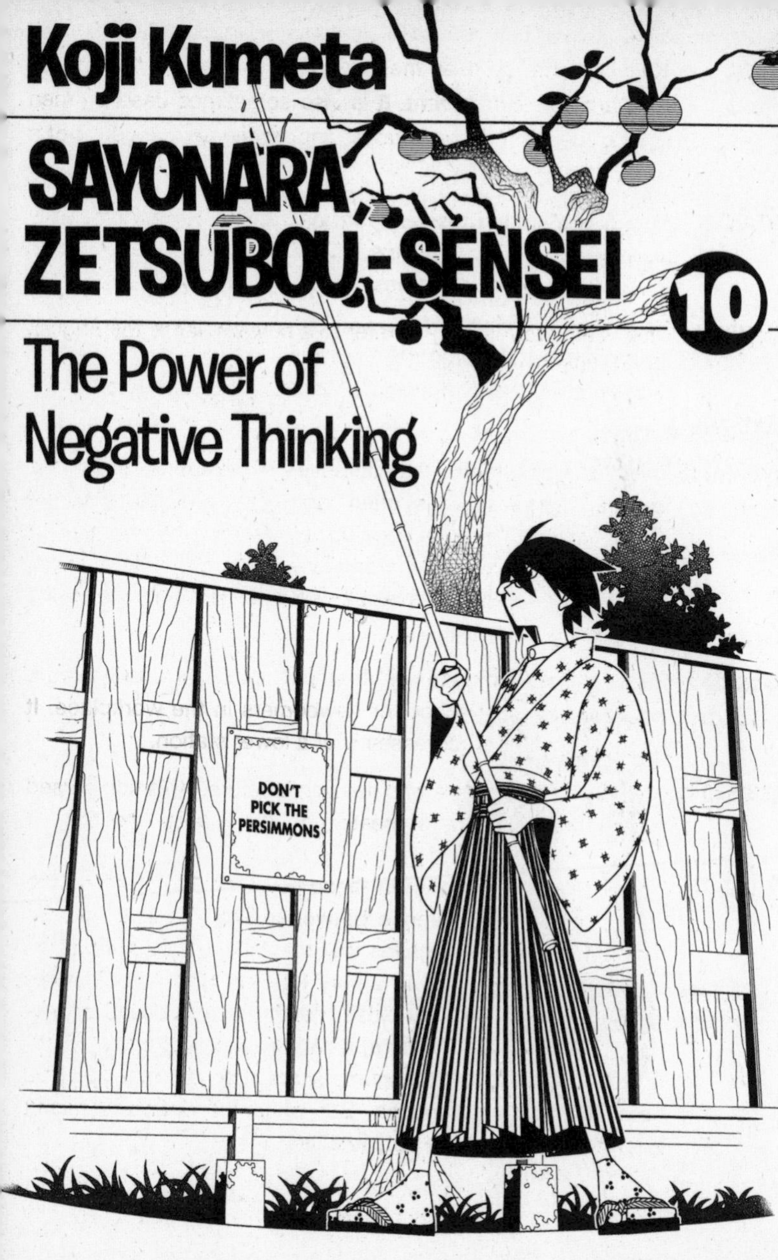
DON'T PICK THE PERSIMMONS

Contents

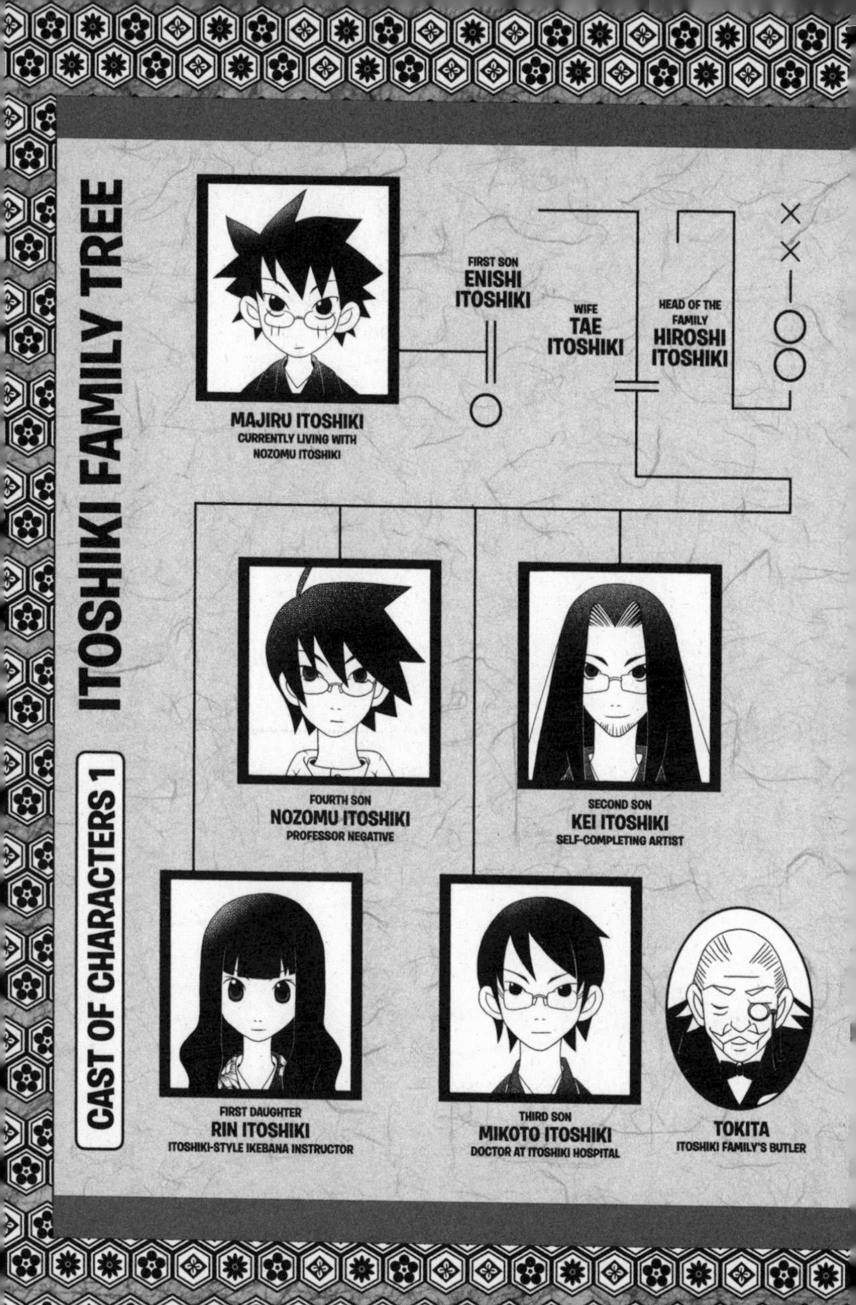
CAST OF CHARACTERS 1
ITOSHIKI FAMILY TREE
FIRST SON
ENISHI ITOSHIKI
WIFE
TAE ITOSHIKI
HEAD OF THE FAMILY
HIROSHI ITOSHIKI
MAJIRU ITOSHIKI
CURRENTLY LIVING WITH NOZOMU ITOSHIKI
SECOND SON
KEI ITOSHIKI
SELF-COMPLETING ARTIST
FOURTH SON
NOZOMU ITOSHIKI
PROFESSOR NEGATIVE
TOKITA
ITOSHIKI FAMILY'S BUTLER
THIRD SON
MIKOTO ITOSHIKI
DOCTOR AT ITOSHIKI HOSPITAL
FIRST DAUGHTER
RIN ITOSHIKI
ITOSHIKI-STYLE IKEBANA INSTRUCTOR

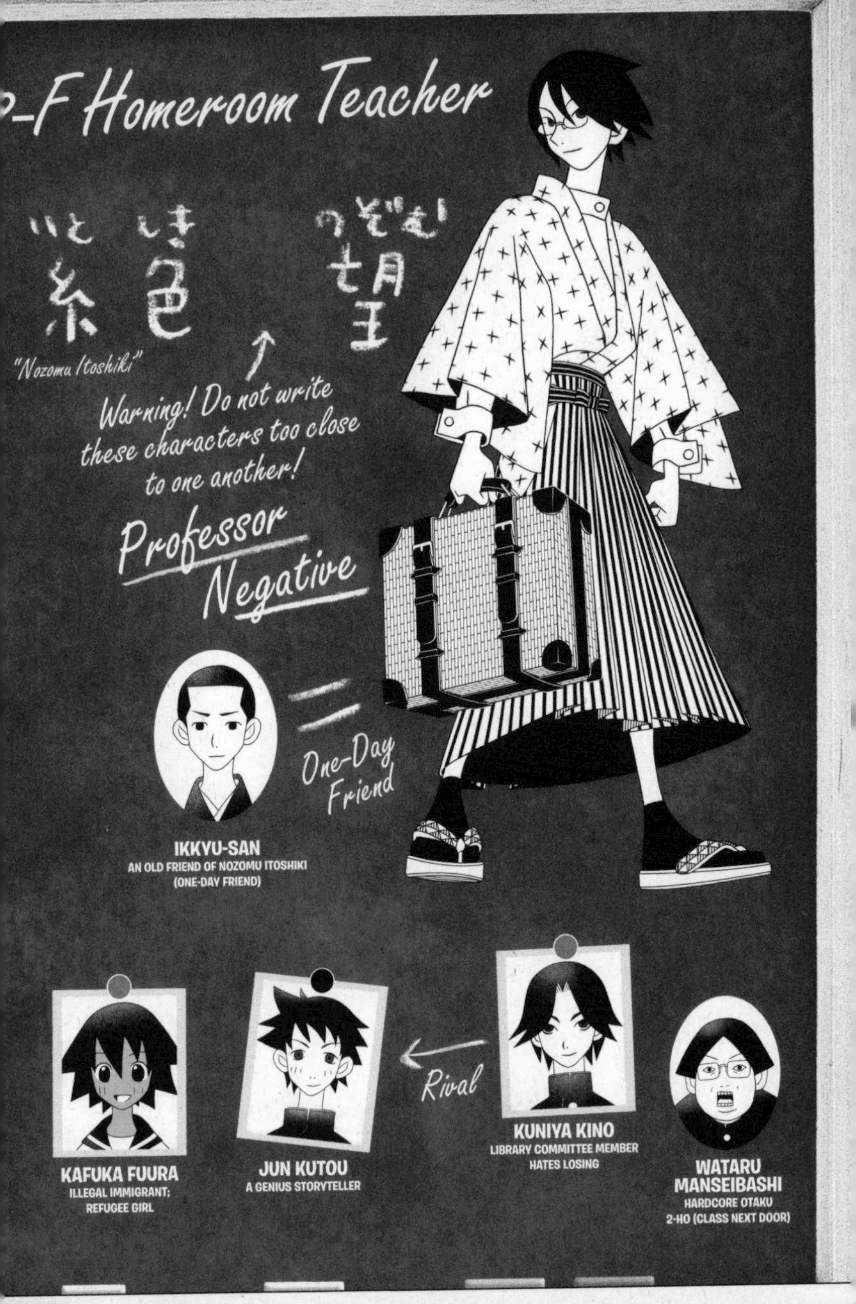
-F Homeroom Teacher
いと しき のぞむ
糸 色 望
"Nozomu Itoshiki"
Warning! Do not write these characters too close to one another!
Professor Negative
One-Day Friend
IKKYU-SAN
AN OLD FRIEND OF NOZOMU ITOSHIKI
(ONE-DAY FRIEND)
Rival
KAFUKA FUURA
ILLEGAL IMMIGRANT; REFUGEE GIRL
JUN KUTOU
A GENIUS STORYTELLER
KUNIYA KINO
LIBRARY COMMITTEE MEMBER
HATES LOSING
WATARU MANSEIBASHI
HARDCORE OTAKU
2-HO (CLASS NEXT DOOR)

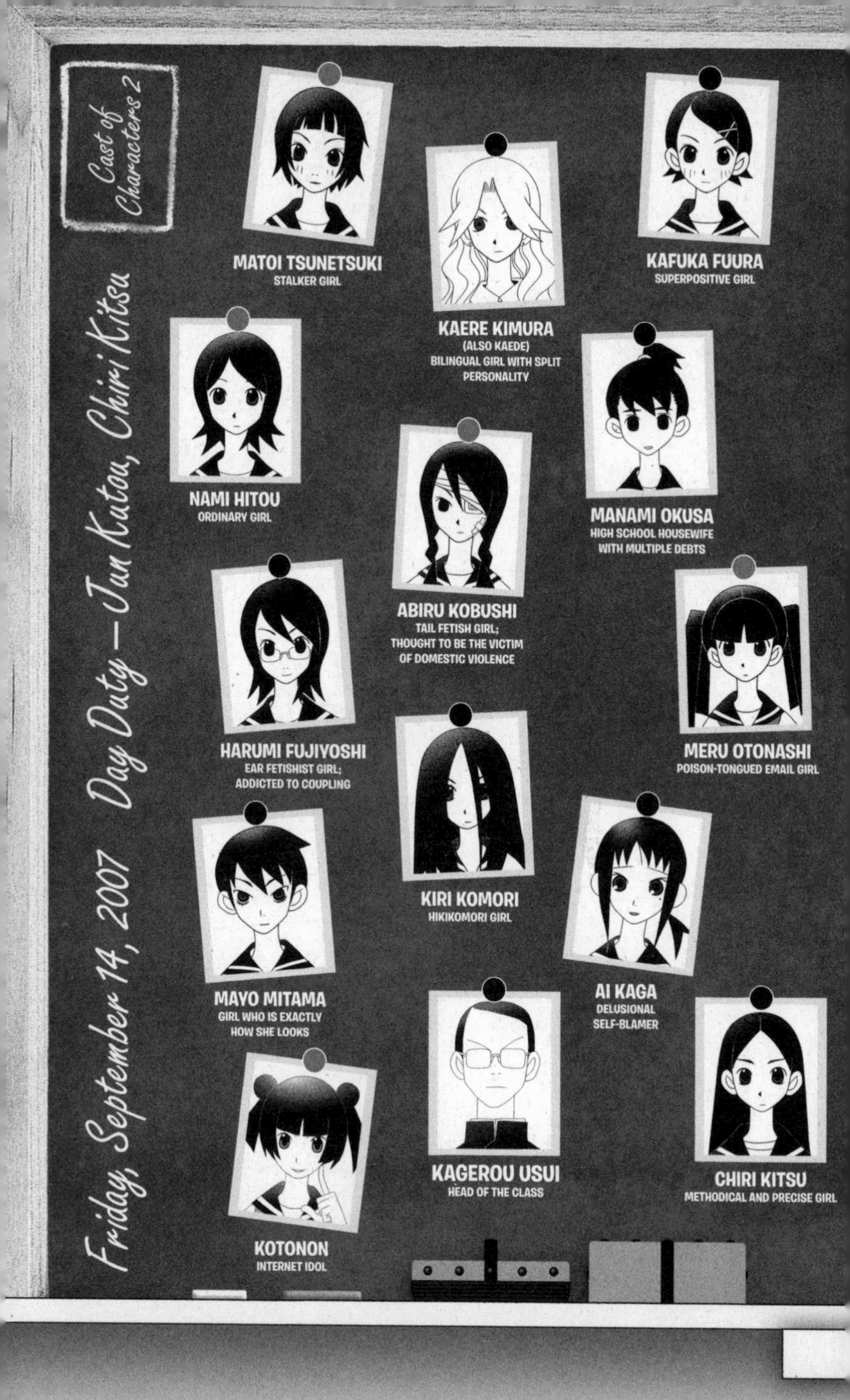
Cast of Characters 2
Friday, September 14, 2007 Day Duty — Jun Kutou, Chiri Kitsu
KAFUKA FUURA
SUPERPOSITIVE GIRL
KAERE KIMURA
(ALSO KAEDE)
BILINGUAL GIRL WITH SPLIT PERSONALITY
MATOI TSUNETSUKI
STALKER GIRL
MANAMI OKUSA
HIGH SCHOOL HOUSEWIFE WITH MULTIPLE DEBTS
ABIRU KOBUSHI
TAIL FETISH GIRL; THOUGHT TO BE THE VICTIM OF DOMESTIC VIOLENCE
NAMI HITOU
ORDINARY GIRL
MERU OTONASHI
POISON-TONGUED EMAIL GIRL
HARUMI FUJIYOSHI
EAR FETISHIST GIRL; ADDICTED TO COUPLING
AI KAGA
DELUSIONAL SELF-BLAMER
KIRI KOMORI
HIKIKOMORI GIRL
MAYO MITAMA
GIRL WHO IS EXACTLY HOW SHE LOOKS
CHIRI KITSU
METHODICAL AND PRECISE GIRL
KAGEROU USUI
HEAD OF THE CLASS
KOTONON
INTERNET IDOL

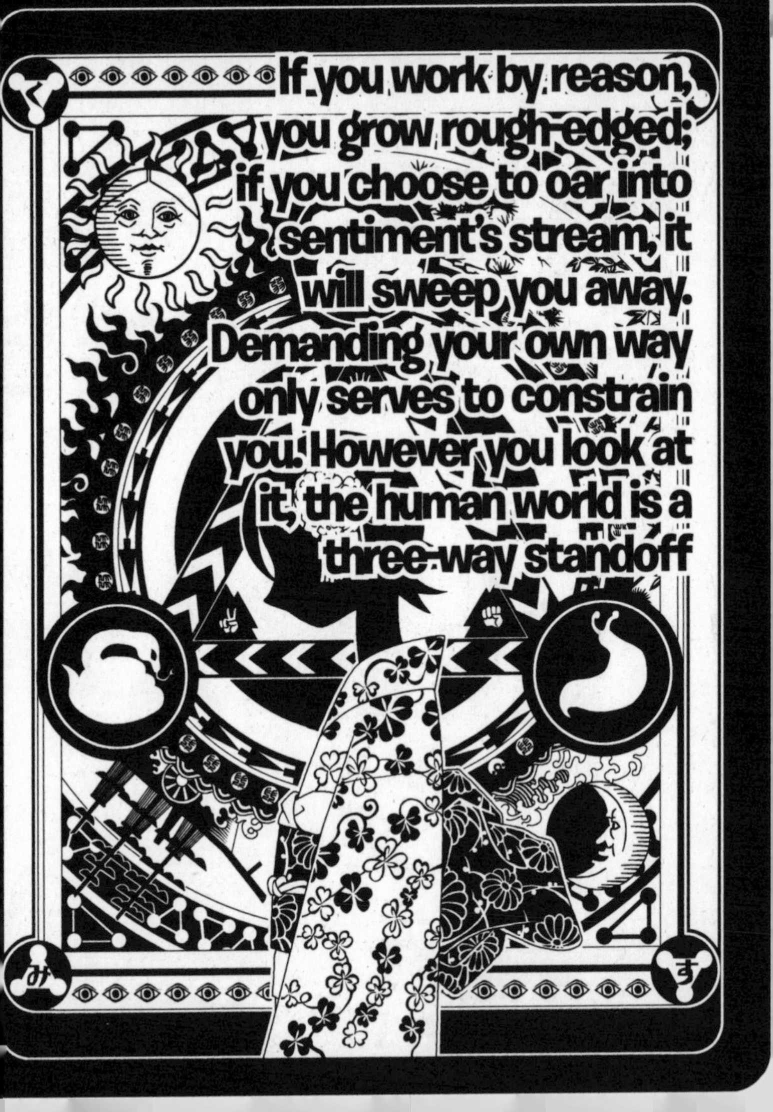

If you work by reason, you grow rough-edged; if you choose to oar into sentiment's stream, it will sweep you away. Demanding your own way only serves to constrain you. However you look at it, the human world is a three-way standoff
く
み
す

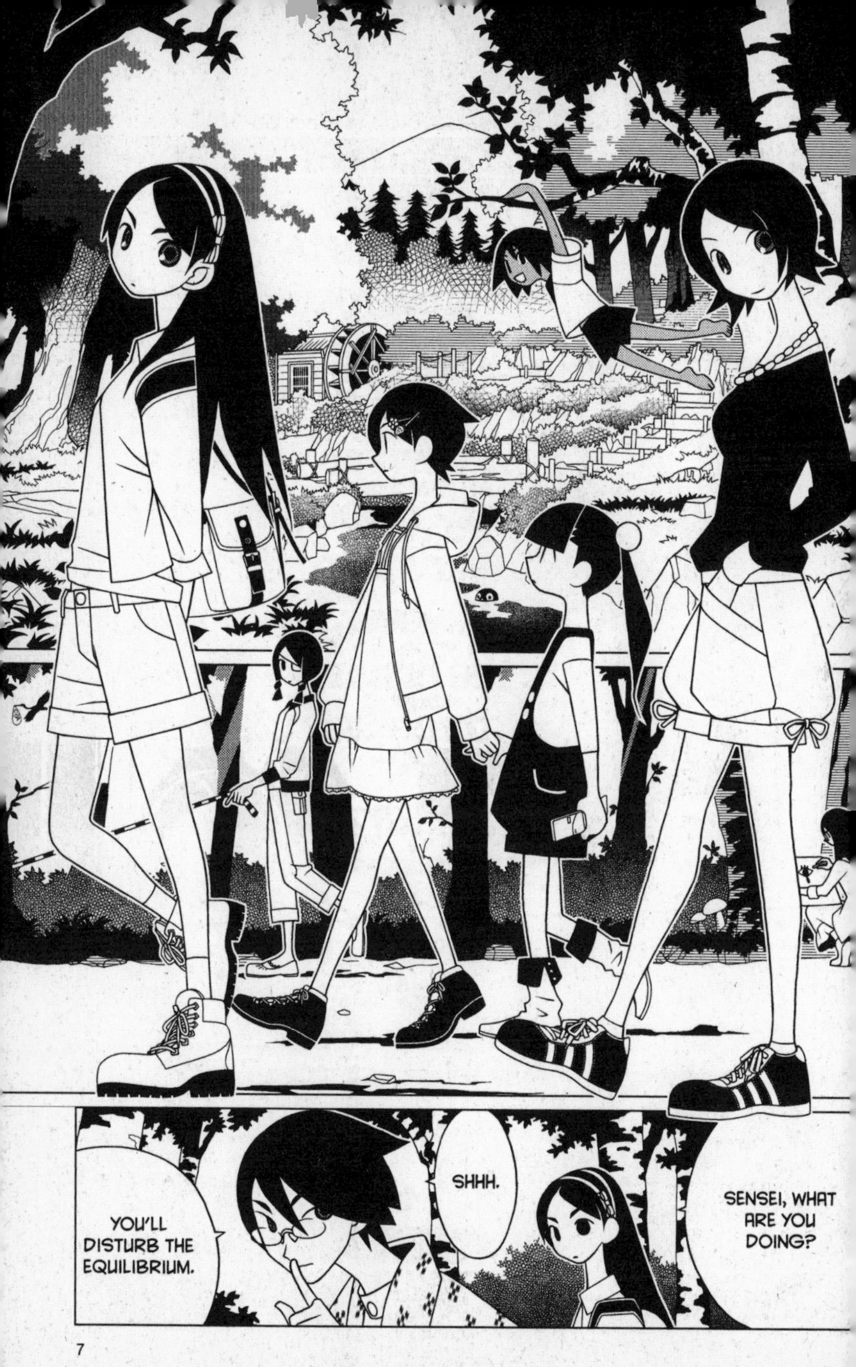
SENSEI, WHAT ARE YOU DOING?
SHHH.
YOU'LL DISTURB THE EQUILIBRIUM.

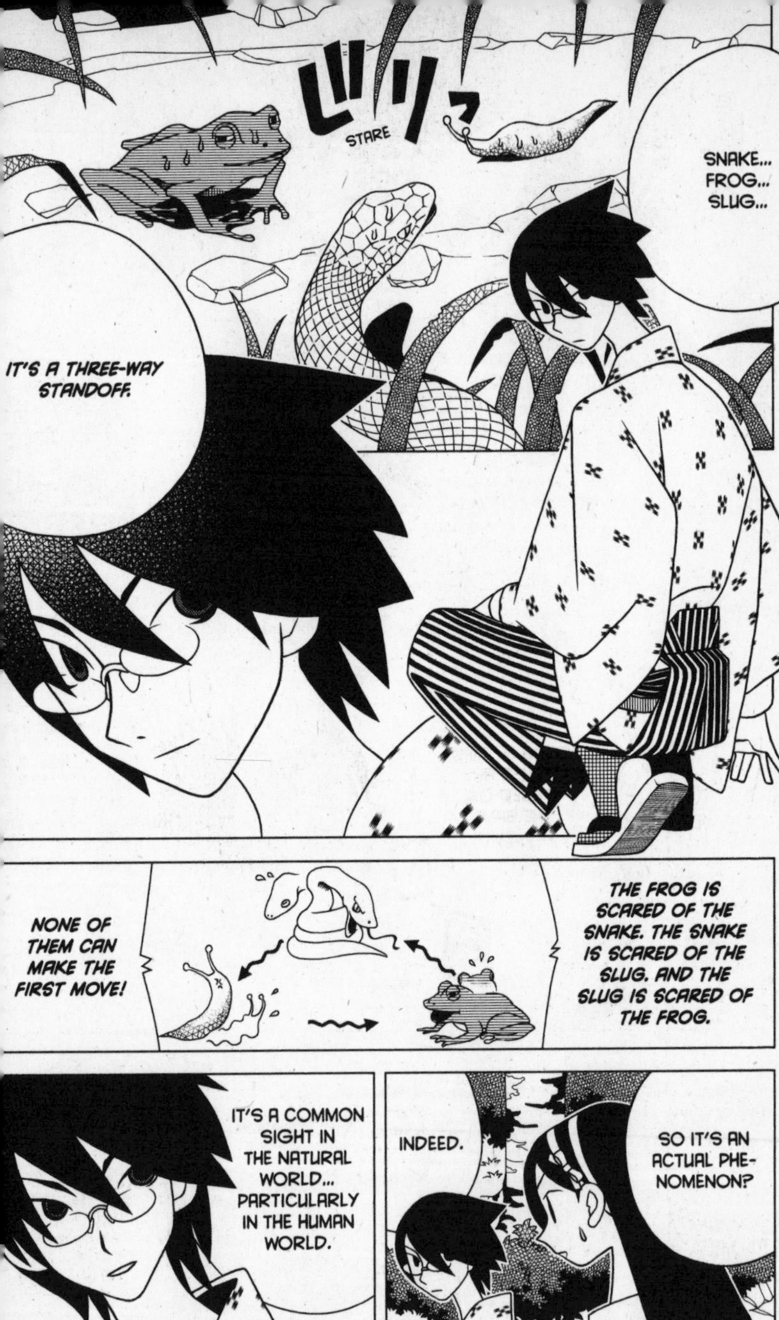
STARE
SNAKE... FROG... SLUG...
IT'S A THREE-WAY STANDOFF.
THE FROG IS SCARED OF THE SNAKE. THE SNAKE IS SCARED OF THE SLUG. AND THE SLUG IS SCARED OF THE FROG.
NONE OF THEM CAN MAKE THE FIRST MOVE!
SO IT'S AN ACTUAL PHE-NOMENON?
INDEED.
IT'S A COMMON SIGHT IN THE NATURAL WORLD... PARTICULARLY IN THE HUMAN WORLD.

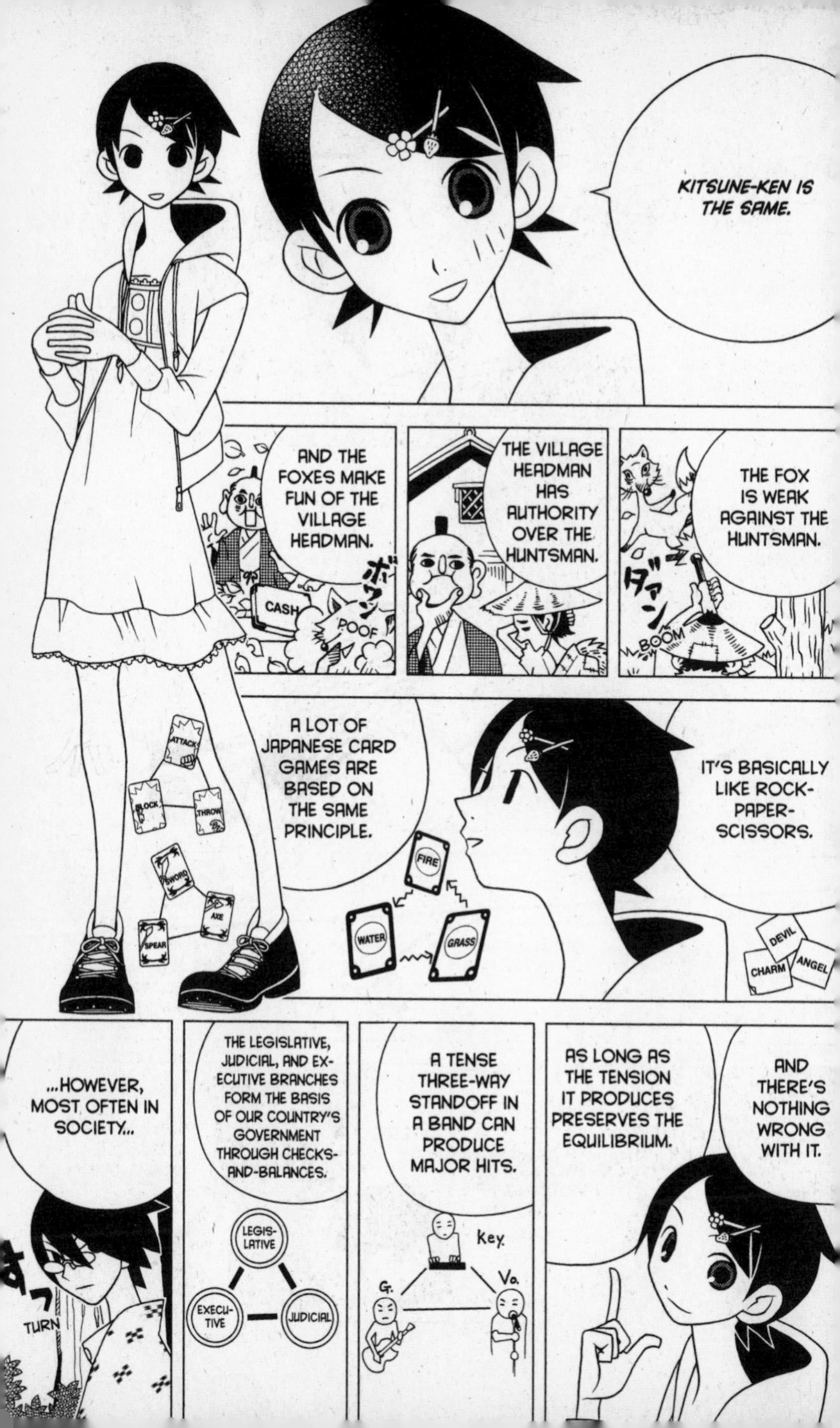
KITSUNE-KEN IS THE SAME.
THE FOX IS WEAK AGAINST THE HUNTSMAN.
BOOM
THE VILLAGE HEADMAN HAS AUTHORITY OVER THE HUNTSMAN.
AND THE FOXES MAKE FUN OF THE VILLAGE HEADMAN.
CASH
POOF
IT'S BASICALLY LIKE ROCK-PAPER-SCISSORS.
DEVIL
CHARM
ANGEL
A LOT OF JAPANESE CARD GAMES ARE BASED ON THE SAME PRINCIPLE.
FIRE
WATER
GRASS
ATTACK
BLOCK
THROW
SWORD
AXE
SPEAR
AND THERE'S NOTHING WRONG WITH IT.
AS LONG AS THE TENSION IT PRODUCES PRESERVES THE EQUILIBRIUM.
A TENSE THREE-WAY STANDOFF IN A BAND CAN PRODUCE MAJOR HITS.
Key.
G.
Vo.
THE LEGISLATIVE, JUDICIAL, AND EX-ECUTIVE BRANCHES FORM THE BASIS OF OUR COUNTRY'S GOVERNMENT THROUGH CHECKS-AND-BALANCES.
LEGIS-LATIVE
EXECU-TIVE
JUDICIAL
...HOWEVER, MOST OFTEN IN SOCIETY...
TURN

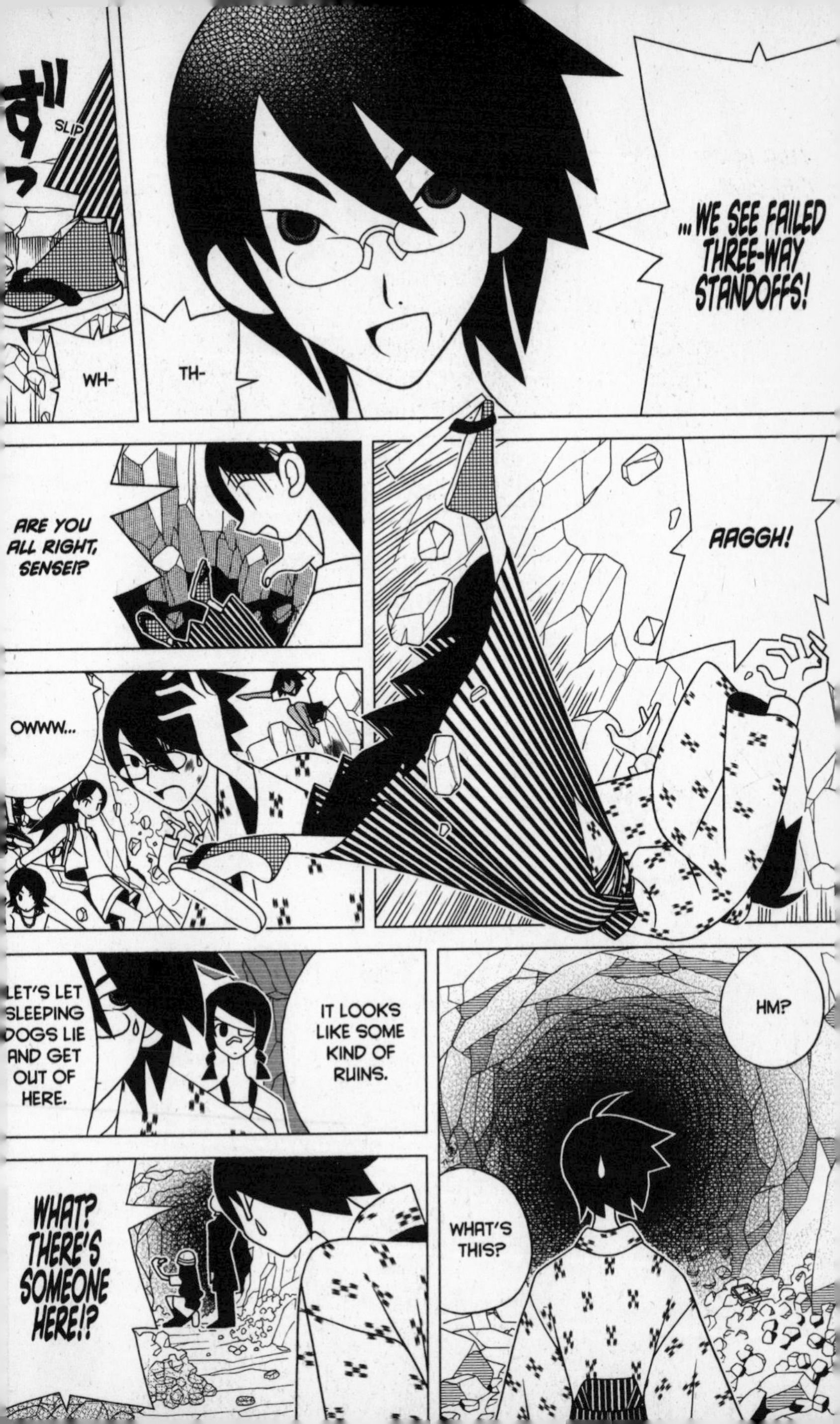

...WE SEE FAILED THREE-WAY STANDOFFS!
TH-
ずっ
SLIP
WH-
AAGGH!
ARE YOU ALL RIGHT, SENSEI?
OWWW...
HM?
WHAT'S THIS?
IT LOOKS LIKE SOME KIND OF RUINS.
LET'S LET SLEEPING DOGS LIE AND GET OUT OF HERE.
WHAT? THERE'S SOMEONE HERE!?

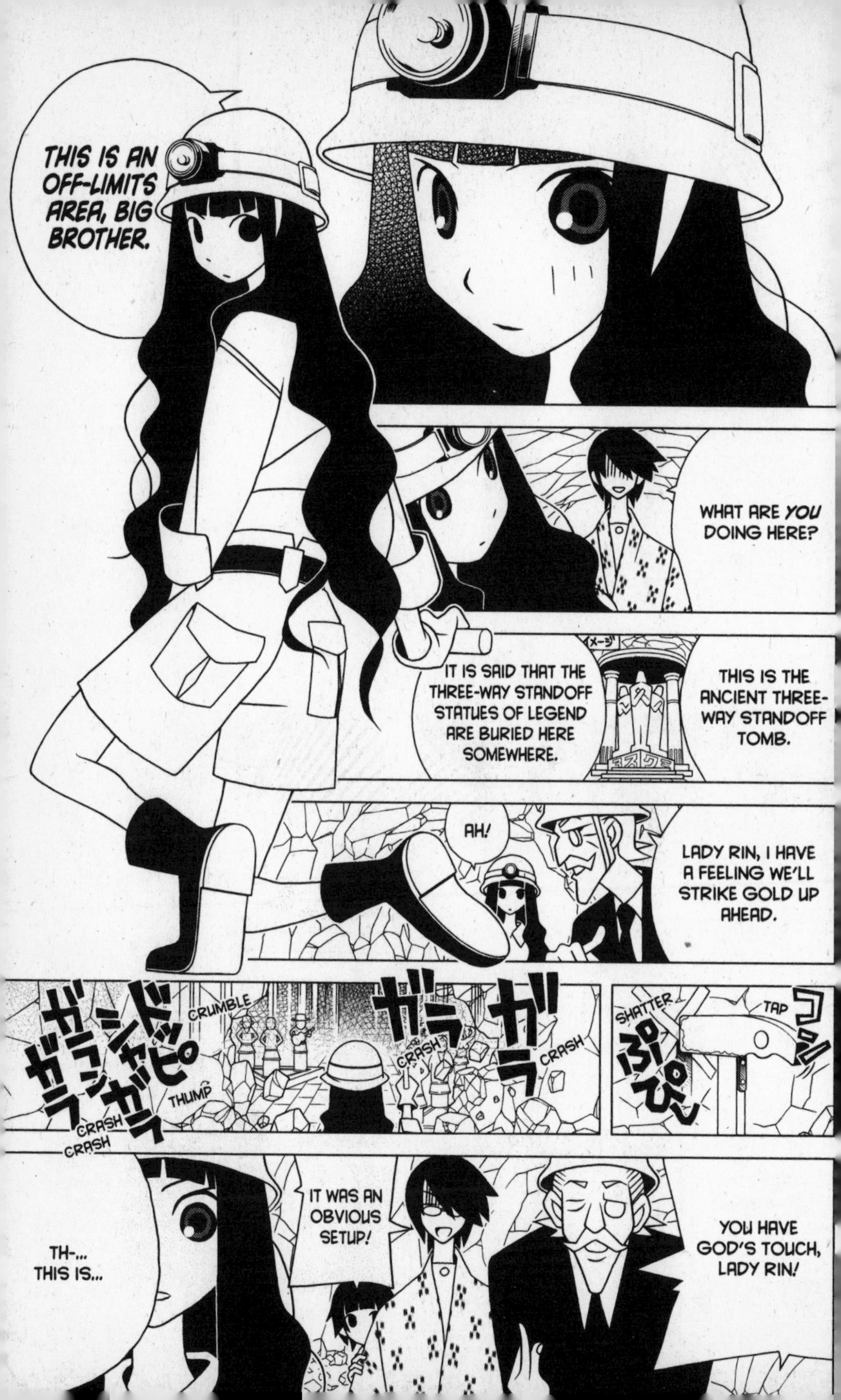
WHAT ARE *YOU* DOING HERE?
THIS IS THE ANCIENT THREE-WAY STANDOFF TOMB.
イメージ
IT IS SAID THAT THE THREE-WAY STANDOFF STATUES OF LEGEND ARE BURIED HERE SOMEWHERE.
LADY RIN, I HAVE A FEELING WE'LL STRIKE GOLD UP AHEAD.
AH!
THIS IS AN OFF-LIMITS AREA, BIG BROTHER.
TAP
SHATTER
ガラ
ガラ
CRASH
CRASH
CRUMBLE
THUMP
CRASH
CRASH
YOU HAVE GOD'S TOUCH, LADY RIN!
IT WAS AN OBVIOUS SETUP!
TH-... THIS IS...

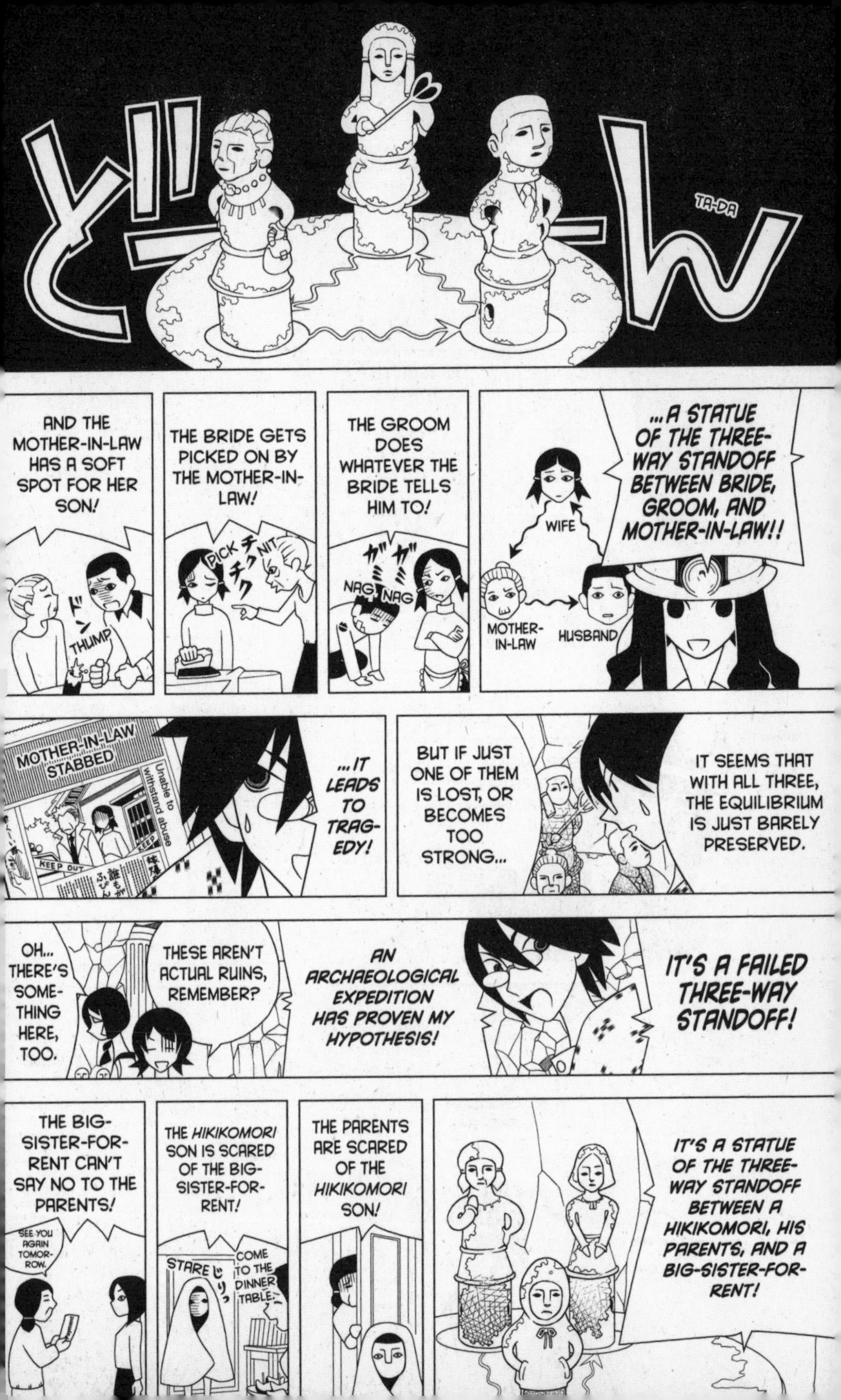
TA-DA
...A STATUE OF THE THREE-WAY STANDOFF BETWEEN BRIDE, GROOM, AND MOTHER-IN-LAW!!
WIFE
MOTHER-IN-LAW
HUSBAND
THE GROOM DOES WHATEVER THE BRIDE TELLS HIM TO!
NAG NAG
THE BRIDE GETS PICKED ON BY THE MOTHER-IN-LAW!
PICK NIT
AND THE MOTHER-IN-LAW HAS A SOFT SPOT FOR HER SON!
THUMP
IT SEEMS THAT WITH ALL THREE, THE EQUILIBRIUM IS JUST BARELY PRESERVED.
BUT IF JUST ONE OF THEM IS LOST, OR BECOMES TOO STRONG...
...IT LEADS TO TRAG-EDY!
MOTHER-IN-LAW STABBED
Unable to withstand abuse
KEEP OUT
IT'S A FAILED THREE-WAY STANDOFF!
AN ARCHAEOLOGICAL EXPEDITION HAS PROVEN MY HYPOTHESIS!
THESE AREN'T ACTUAL RUINS, REMEMBER?
OH... THERE'S SOME-THING HERE, TOO.
IT'S A STATUE OF THE THREE-WAY STANDOFF BETWEEN A HIKIKOMORI, HIS PARENTS, AND A BIG-SISTER-FOR-RENT!
THE PARENTS ARE SCARED OF THE HIKIKOMORI SON!
THE HIKIKOMORI SON IS SCARED OF THE BIG-SISTER-FOR-RENT!
COME TO THE DINNER TABLE
STARE
THE BIG-SISTER-FOR-RENT CAN'T SAY NO TO THE PARENTS!
SEE YOU AGAIN TOMOR-ROW.

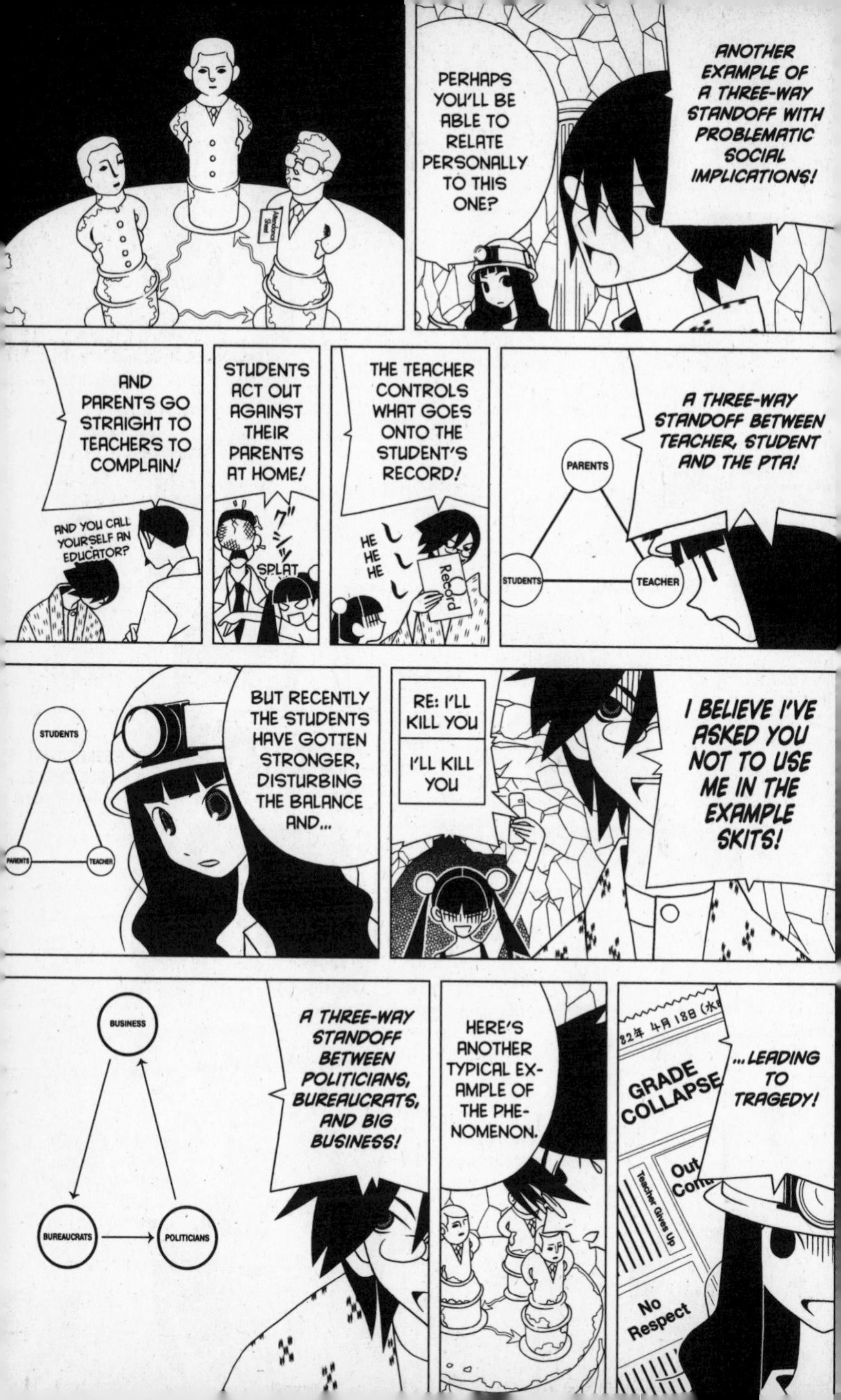
ANOTHER EXAMPLE OF A THREE-WAY STANDOFF WITH PROBLEMATIC SOCIAL IMPLICATIONS!
PERHAPS YOU'LL BE ABLE TO RELATE PERSONALLY TO THIS ONE?
A THREE-WAY STANDOFF BETWEEN TEACHER, STUDENT AND THE PTA!
PARENTS
STUDENTS
TEACHER
THE TEACHER CONTROLS WHAT GOES ONTO THE STUDENT'S RECORD!
HE HE HE
Record
STUDENTS ACT OUT AGAINST THEIR PARENTS AT HOME!
グシッ
SPLAT
AND PARENTS GO STRAIGHT TO TEACHERS TO COMPLAIN!
AND YOU CALL YOURSELF AN EDUCATOR?
I BELIEVE I'VE ASKED YOU NOT TO USE ME IN THE EXAMPLE SKITS!
RE: I'LL KILL YOU
I'LL KILL YOU
BUT RECENTLY THE STUDENTS HAVE GOTTEN STRONGER, DISTURBING THE BALANCE AND...
STUDENTS
PARENTS
TEACHER
...LEADING TO TRAGEDY!
82年 4月18日
GRADE COLLAPSE
Teacher Gives Up
No Respect
HERE'S ANOTHER TYPICAL EXAMPLE OF THE PHENOMENON.
A THREE-WAY STANDOFF BETWEEN POLITICIANS, BUREAUCRATS, AND BIG BUSINESS!
BUSINESS
BUREAUCRATS
POLITICIANS

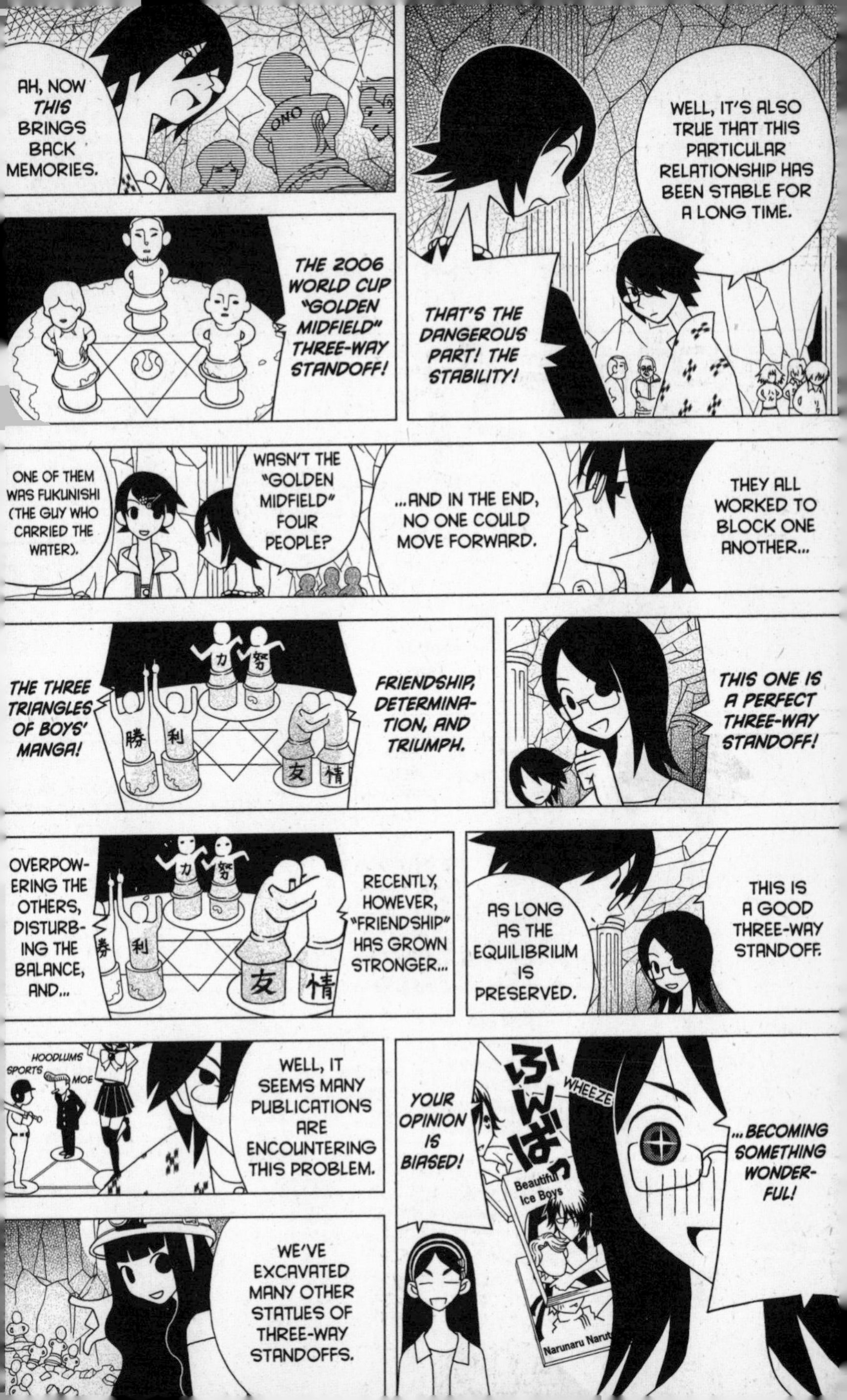
WELL, IT'S ALSO TRUE THAT THIS PARTICULAR RELATIONSHIP HAS BEEN STABLE FOR A LONG TIME.
THAT'S THE DANGEROUS PART! THE STABILITY!
AH, NOW THIS BRINGS BACK MEMORIES.
ONO
THE 2006 WORLD CUP "GOLDEN MIDFIELD" THREE-WAY STANDOFF!
THEY ALL WORKED TO BLOCK ONE ANOTHER...
...AND IN THE END, NO ONE COULD MOVE FORWARD.
WASN'T THE "GOLDEN MIDFIELD" FOUR PEOPLE?
ONE OF THEM WAS FUKUNISHI (THE GUY WHO CARRIED THE WATER).
THIS ONE IS A PERFECT THREE-WAY STANDOFF!
FRIENDSHIP, DETERMINATION, AND TRIUMPH.
力 努
勝 利
友 情
THE THREE TRIANGLES OF BOYS' MANGA!
THIS IS A GOOD THREE-WAY STANDOFF.
AS LONG AS THE EQUILIBRIUM IS PRESERVED.
RECENTLY, HOWEVER, "FRIENDSHIP" HAS GROWN STRONGER...
力 努
勝 利
友 情
OVERPOW-ERING THE OTHERS, DISTURB-ING THE BALANCE, AND...
...BECOMING SOMETHING WONDER-FUL!
WHEEZE
ふんばっ
YOUR OPINION IS BIASED!
Beautiful Ice Boys
Narunaru Narut
WELL, IT SEEMS MANY PUBLICATIONS ARE ENCOUNTERING THIS PROBLEM.
HOODLUMS
SPORTS
MOE
WE'VE EXCAVATED MANY OTHER STATUES OF THREE-WAY STANDOFFS.

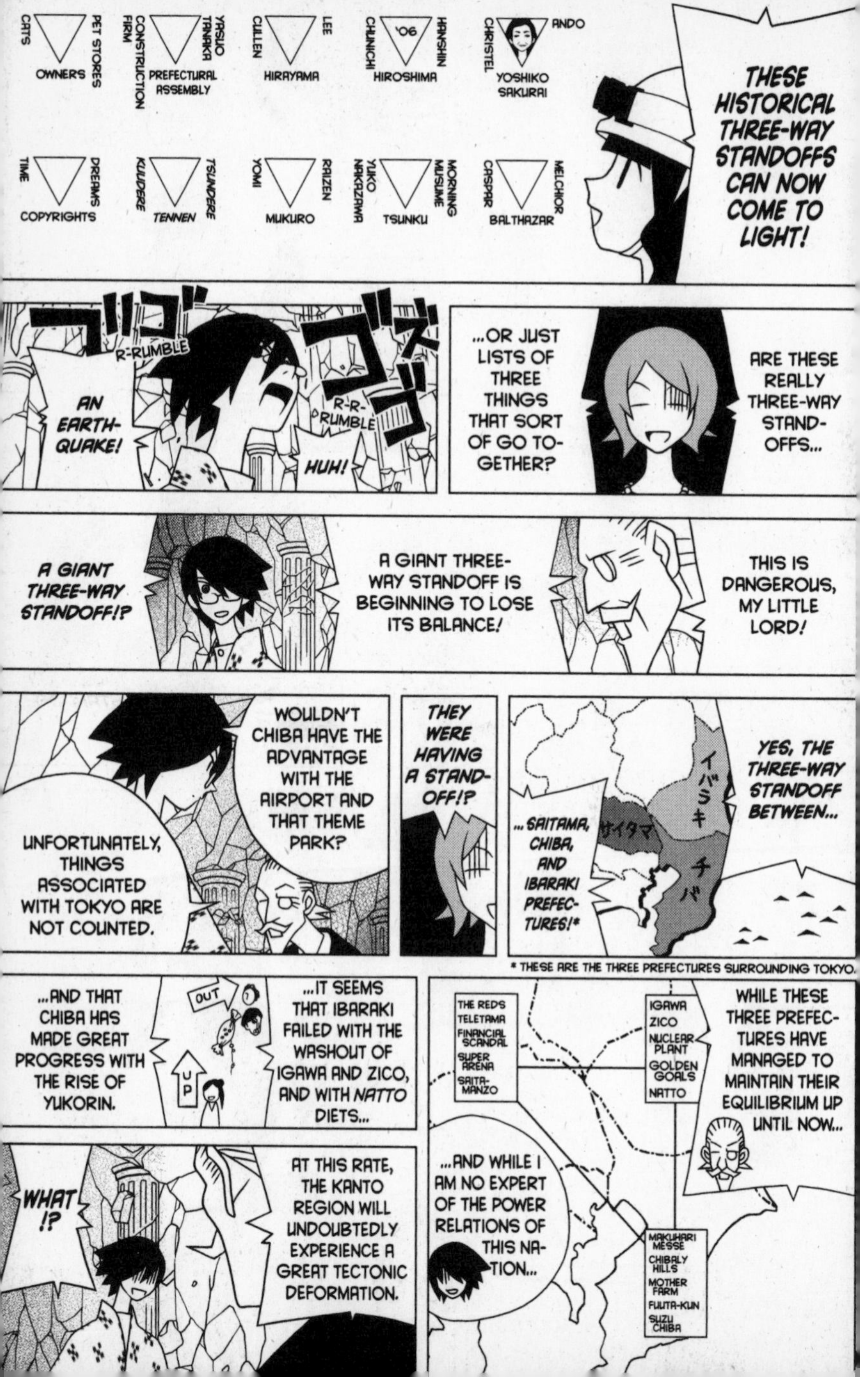
THESE HISTORICAL THREE-WAY STANDOFFS CAN NOW COME TO LIGHT!
ANDO
CHRISTEL
YOSHIKO SAKURAI
HANSHIN
CHUNICHI
'06
HIROSHIMA
LEE
CULLEN
HIRAYAMA
YASUO TANAKA
CONSTRUCTION FIRM
PREFECTURAL ASSEMBLY
PET STORES
CATS
OWNERS
MELCHIOR
CASPAR
BALTHAZAR
MORNING MUSUME
YUKO NAKAZAWA
TSUNKU
RAIZEN
YOMI
MUKURO
TSUNDERE
KUUDERE
TENNEN
DREAMS
TIME
COPYRIGHTS
ARE THESE REALLY THREE-WAY STAND-OFFS...
...OR JUST LISTS OF THREE THINGS THAT SORT OF GO TO-GETHER?
R-R-RUMBLE
HUH!
R-RUMBLE
AN EARTH-QUAKE!
THIS IS DANGEROUS, MY LITTLE LORD!
A GIANT THREE-WAY STANDOFF IS BEGINNING TO LOSE ITS BALANCE!
A GIANT THREE-WAY STANDOFF!?
YES, THE THREE-WAY STANDOFF BETWEEN...
イバラキ
サイタマ
チバ
...SAITAMA, CHIBA, AND IBARAKI PREFECTURES!*
THEY WERE HAVING A STAND-OFF!?
WOULDN'T CHIBA HAVE THE ADVANTAGE WITH THE AIRPORT AND THAT THEME PARK?
UNFORTUNATELY, THINGS ASSOCIATED WITH TOKYO ARE NOT COUNTED.
WHILE THESE THREE PREFEC-TURES HAVE MANAGED TO MAINTAIN THEIR EQUILIBRIUM UP UNTIL NOW...
IGAWA
ZICO
NUCLEAR PLANT
GOLDEN GOALS
NATTO
THE REDS
TELETAMA
FINANCIAL SCANDAL
SUPER ARENA
SAITA-MANZO
MAKUHARI MESSE
CHIBALY HILLS
MOTHER FARM
FUUTA-KUN
SUZU CHIBA
...AND WHILE I AM NO EXPERT OF THE POWER RELATIONS OF THIS NA-TION...
...IT SEEMS THAT IBARAKI FAILED WITH THE WASHOUT OF IGAWA AND ZICO, AND WITH NATTO DIETS...
OUT
UP
...AND THAT CHIBA HAS MADE GREAT PROGRESS WITH THE RISE OF YUKORIN.
AT THIS RATE, THE KANTO REGION WILL UNDOUBTEDLY EXPERIENCE A GREAT TECTONIC DEFORMATION.
WHAT!?

* THESE ARE THE THREE PREFECTURES SURROUNDING TOKYO.

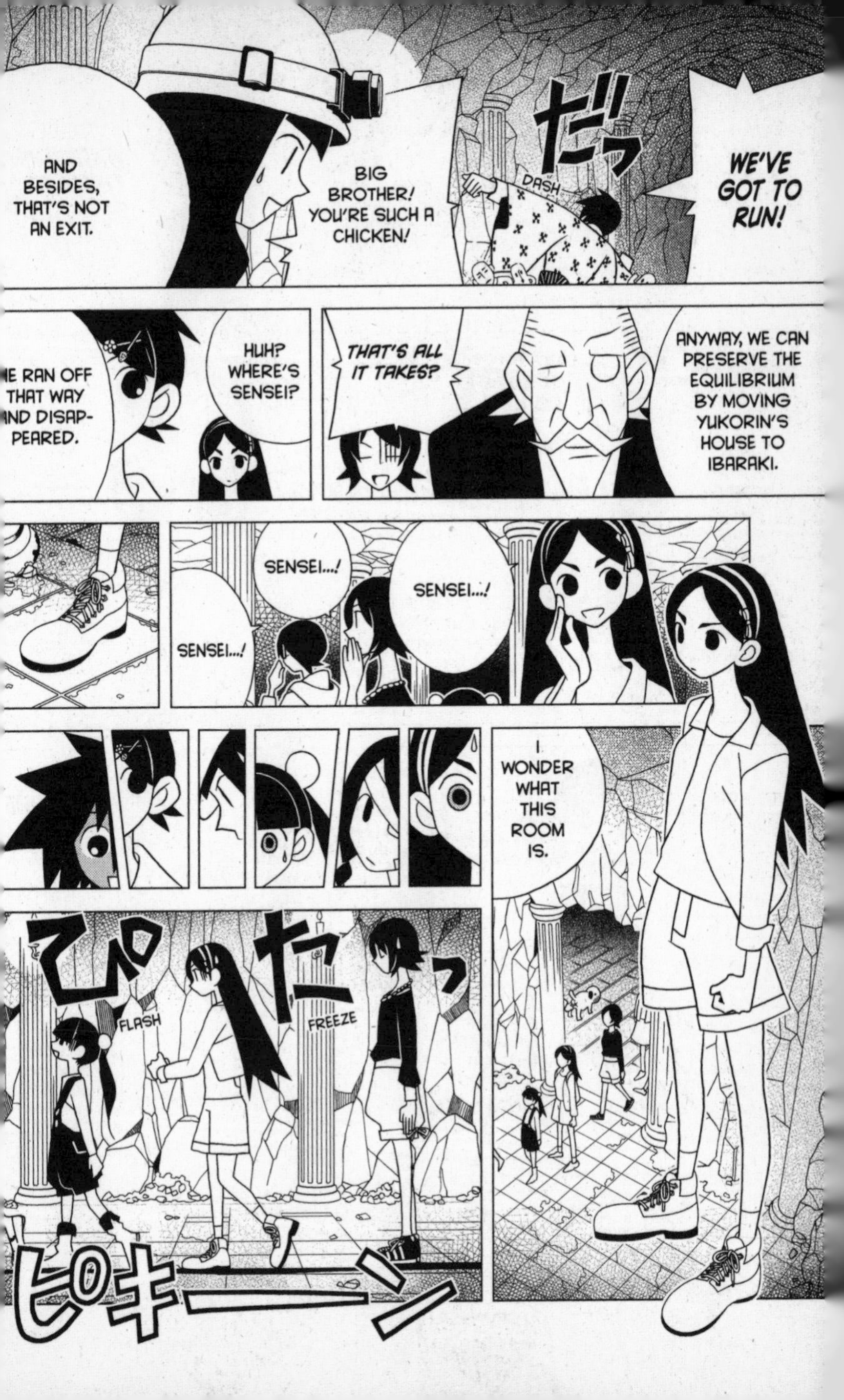
WE'VE GOT TO RUN!
だっ
DASH
BIG BROTHER! YOU'RE SUCH A CHICKEN!
AND BESIDES, THAT'S NOT AN EXIT.
ANYWAY, WE CAN PRESERVE THE EQUILIBRIUM BY MOVING YUKORIN'S HOUSE TO IBARAKI.
THAT'S ALL IT TAKES?
HUH? WHERE'S SENSEI?
E RAN OFF THAT WAY ND DISAP-PEARED.
SENSEI...!
SENSEI...!
SENSEI...!
I WONDER WHAT THIS ROOM IS.
ぴたーっ
FREEZE
FLASH
ピキーン

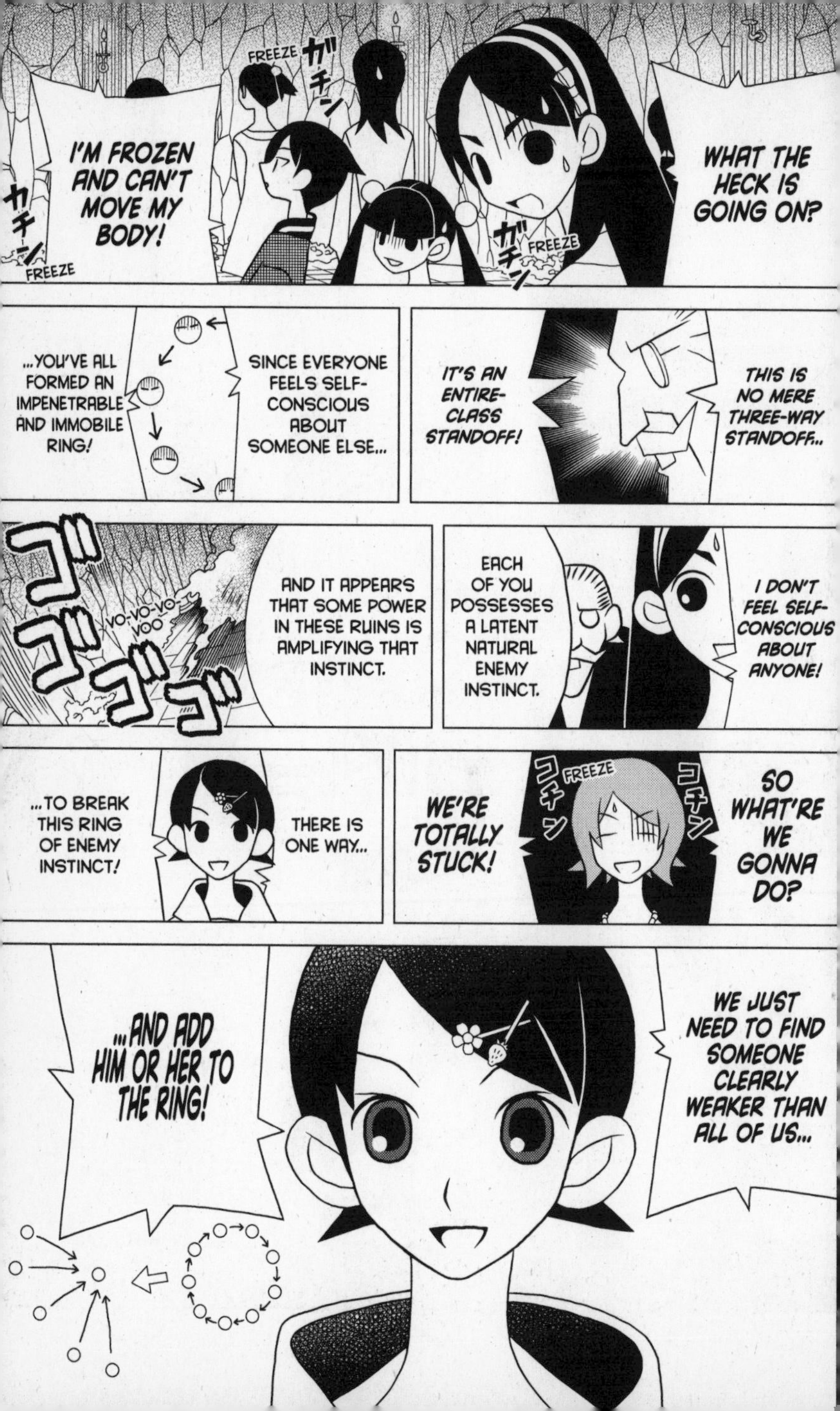
WHAT THE HECK IS GOING ON?
ガチン
FREEZE
ガチン
FREEZE
I'M FROZEN AND CAN'T MOVE MY BODY!
ガチーン
FREEZE
THIS IS NO MERE THREE-WAY STANDOFF...
IT'S AN ENTIRE-CLASS STANDOFF!
SINCE EVERYONE FEELS SELF-CONSCIOUS ABOUT SOMEONE ELSE...
...YOU'VE ALL FORMED AN IMPENETRABLE AND IMMOBILE RING!
I DON'T FEEL SELF-CONSCIOUS ABOUT ANYONE!
EACH OF YOU POSSESSES A LATENT NATURAL ENEMY INSTINCT.
AND IT APPEARS THAT SOME POWER IN THESE RUINS IS AMPLIFYING THAT INSTINCT.
VO-VO-VO-VOO
ゴゴゴゴ
SO WHAT'RE WE GONNA DO?
コチン
FREEZE
コチン
WE'RE TOTALLY STUCK!
THERE IS ONE WAY...
...TO BREAK THIS RING OF ENEMY INSTINCT!
WE JUST NEED TO FIND SOMEONE CLEARLY WEAKER THAN ALL OF US...
...AND ADD HIM OR HER TO THE RING!

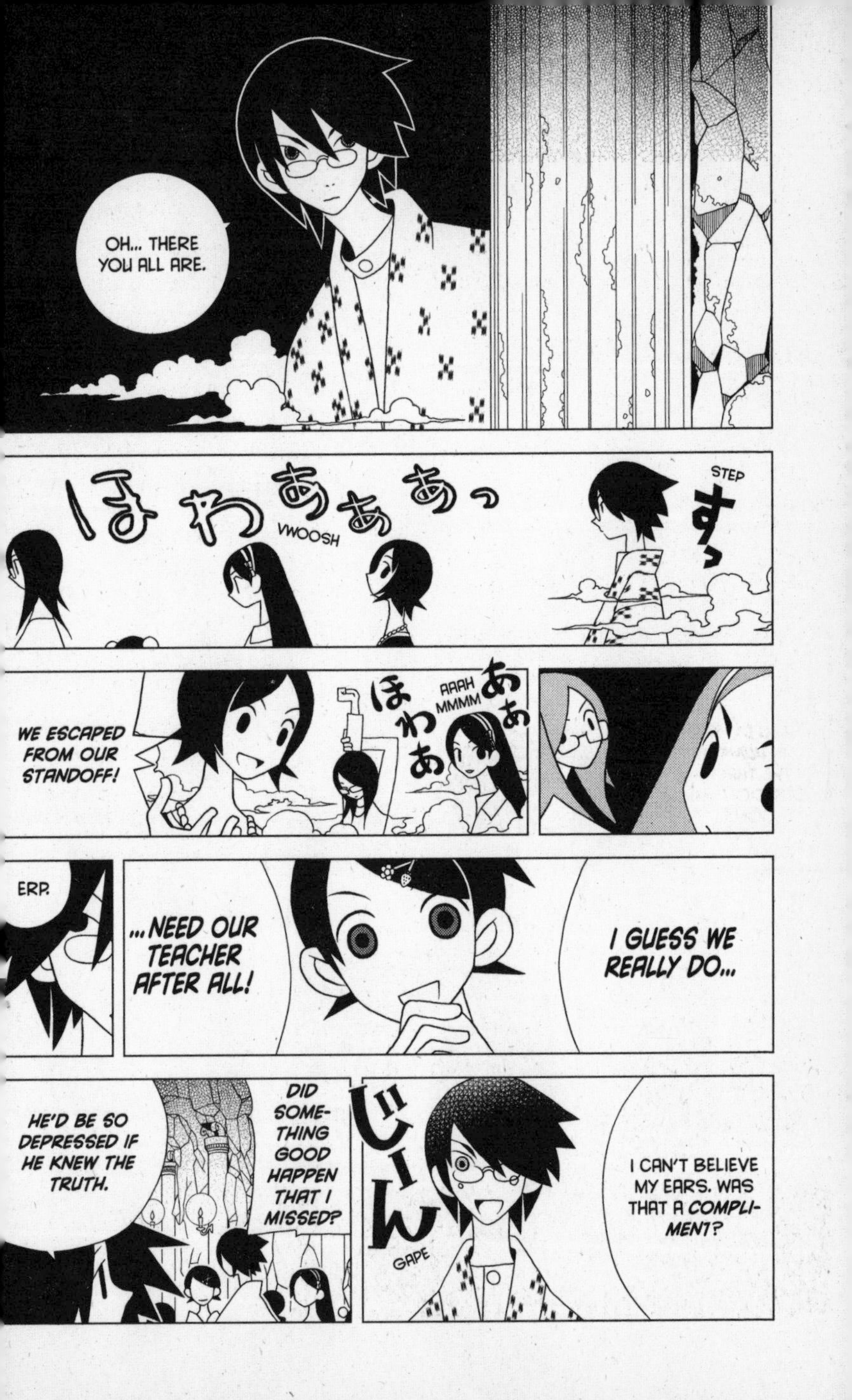
OH... THERE YOU ALL ARE.
STEP
すっ
ほわあぁあっ
VWOOSH
ほわあ
AAAH MMMM
ああ
WE ESCAPED FROM OUR STANDOFF!
I GUESS WE REALLY DO...
...NEED OUR TEACHER AFTER ALL!
ERP.
I CAN'T BELIEVE MY EARS. WAS THAT A *COMPLIMENT*?
じーん
GAPE
DID SOMETHING GOOD HAPPEN THAT I MISSED?
HE'D BE SO DEPRESSED IF HE KNEW THE TRUTH.

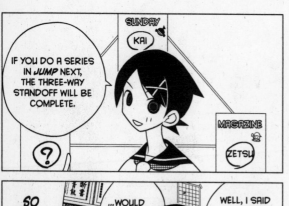

SUNDAY
KAI
MAGAZINE
ZETSU
IF YOU DO A SERIES IN *JUMP* NEXT, THE THREE-WAY STANDOFF WILL BE COMPLETE.
?
WELL, I SAID IT... THOUGH I DOUBT MY CHARACTER, AS SUPER-POSITIVE AS SHE IS...
...WOULD EVER SAY THAT LINE.
SO WHY'D YOU SAY IT THEN, HUH!?

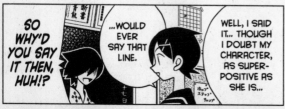

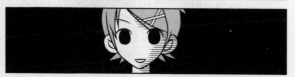

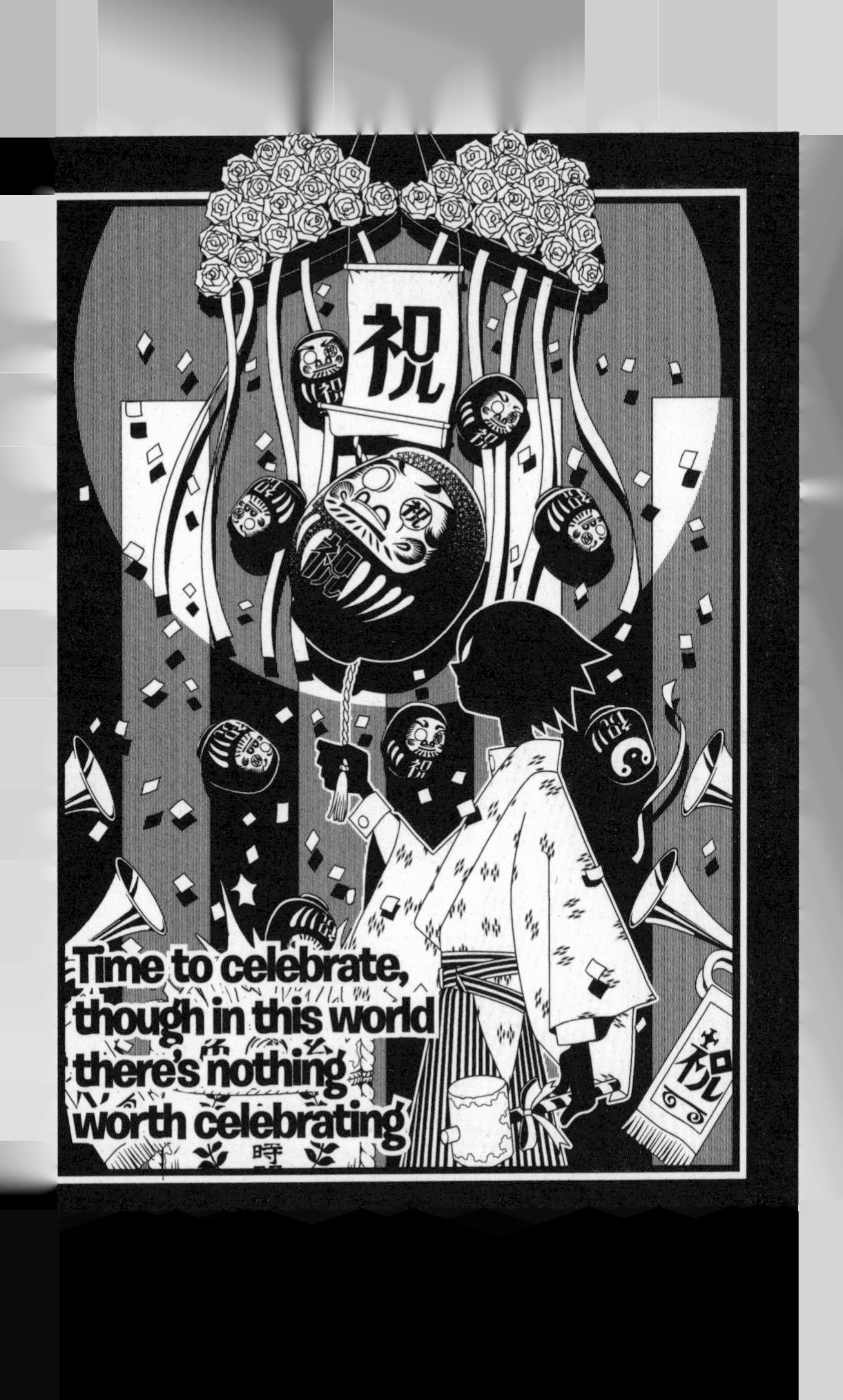
祝
Time to celebrate,
though in this world
there's nothing
worth celebrating

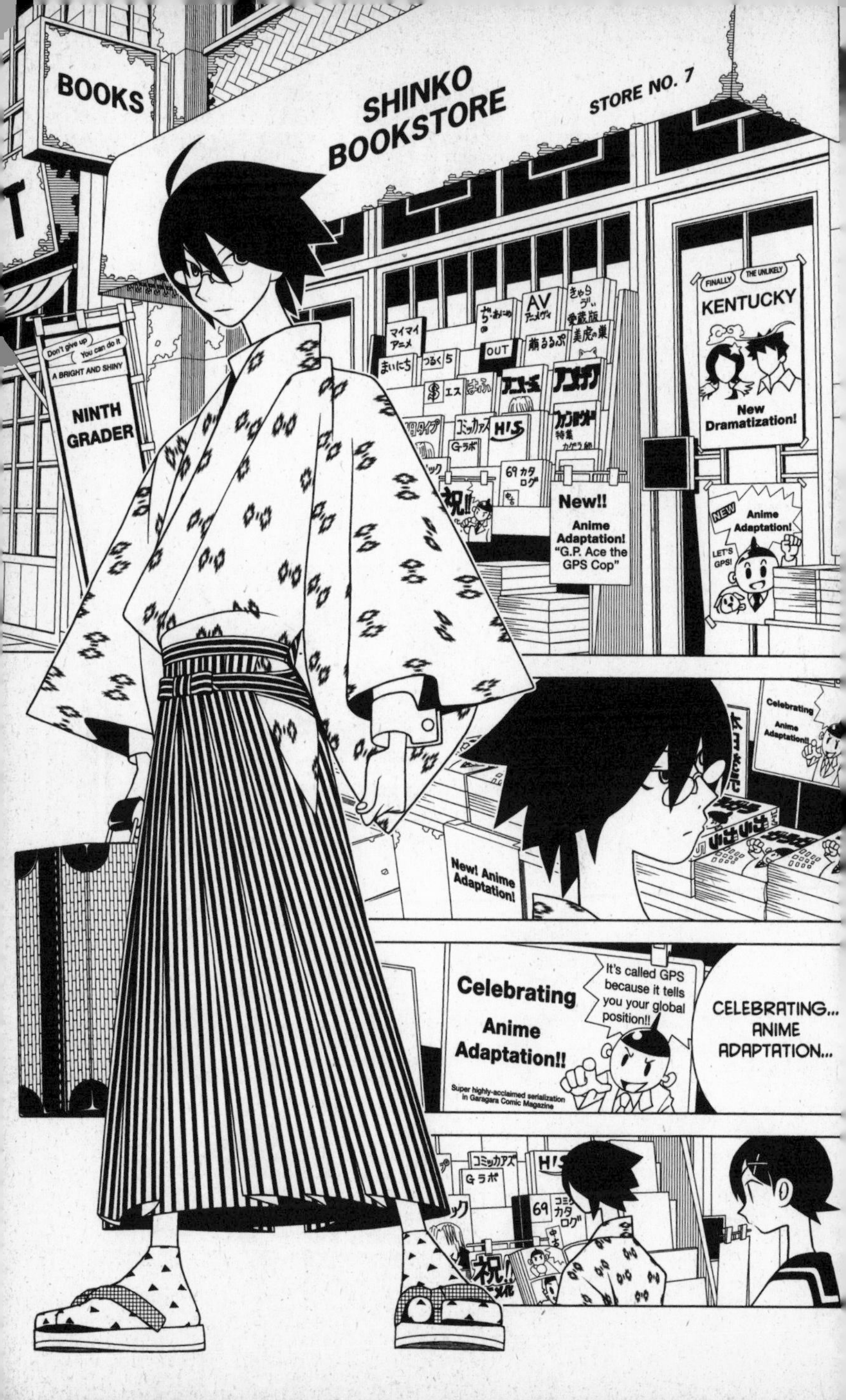

STORE NO. 7
SHINKO BOOKSTORE
BOOKS
FINALLY THE UNLIKELY KENTUCKY New Dramatization!
New!! Anime Adaptation! "G.P. Ace the GPS Cop"
Don't give up You can do it A BRIGHT AND SHINY NINTH GRADER
NEW Anime Adaptation! LET'S GPS!
Celebrating Anime Adaptation!!
New! Anime Adaptation!
CELEBRATING... ANIME ADAPTATION...
It's called GPS because it tells you your global position!!
Celebrating Anime Adaptation!!
Super highly-acclaimed serialization in Garagara Comic Magazine

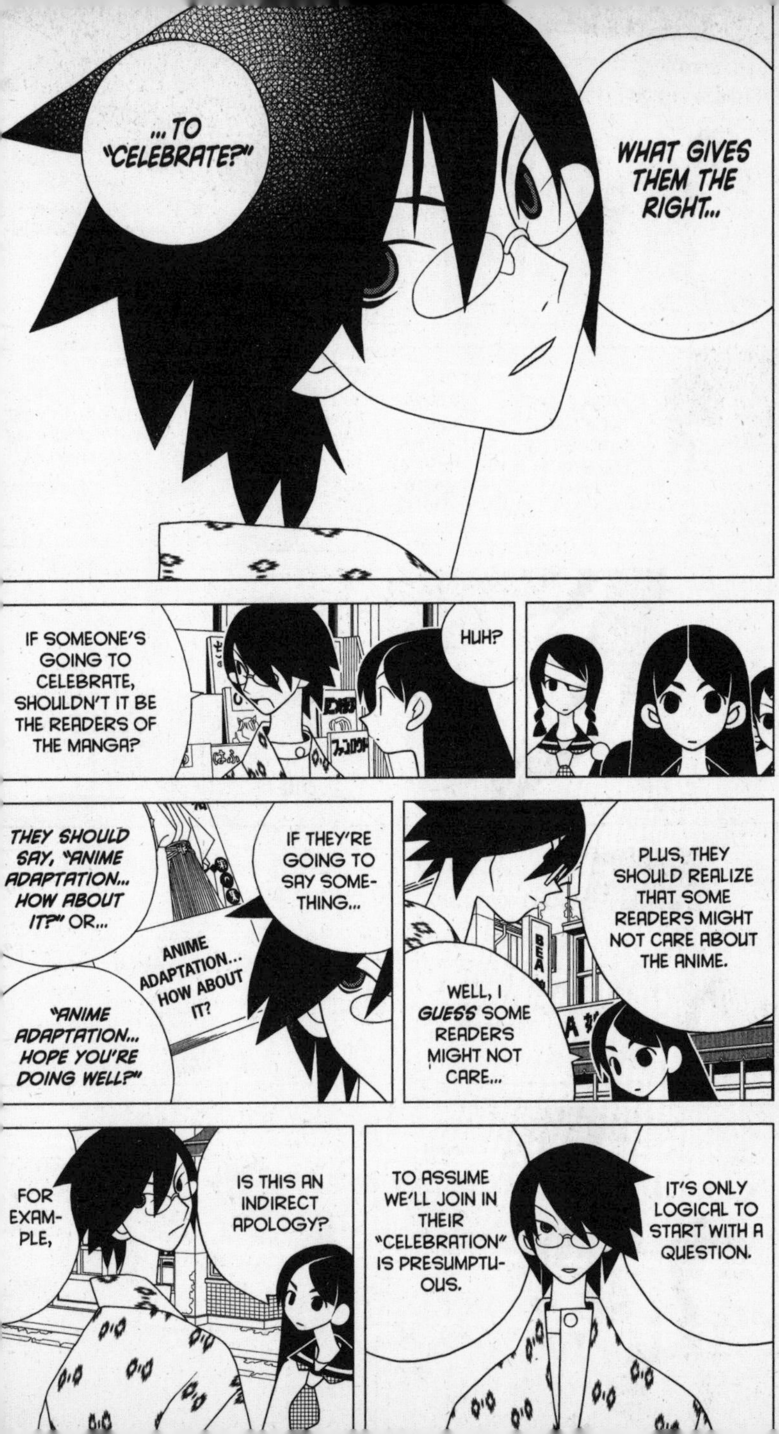
WHAT GIVES THEM THE RIGHT...
...TO "CELEBRATE?"
HUH?
IF SOMEONE'S GOING TO CELEBRATE, SHOULDN'T IT BE THE READERS OF THE MANGA?
PLUS, THEY SHOULD REALIZE THAT SOME READERS MIGHT NOT CARE ABOUT THE ANIME.
WELL, I *GUESS* SOME READERS MIGHT NOT CARE...
IF THEY'RE GOING TO SAY SOME-THING...
THEY SHOULD SAY, "ANIME ADAPTATION... HOW ABOUT IT?" OR...
ANIME ADAPTATION... HOW ABOUT IT?
"ANIME ADAPTATION... HOPE YOU'RE DOING WELL?"
IT'S ONLY LOGICAL TO START WITH A QUESTION.
TO ASSUME WE'LL JOIN IN THEIR "CELEBRATION" IS PRESUMPTU-OUS.
IS THIS AN INDIRECT APOLOGY?
FOR EXAM-PLE,

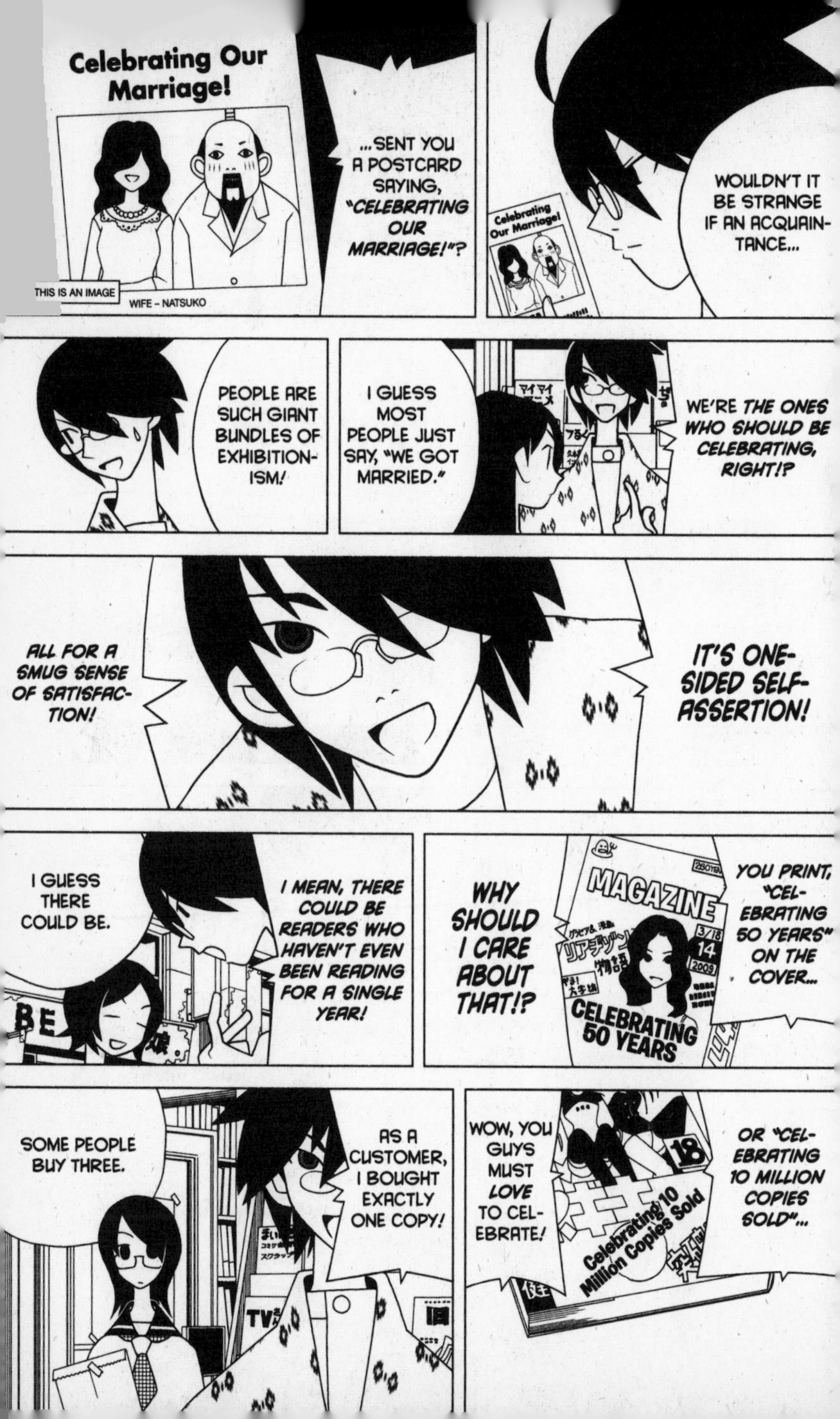
WOULDN'T IT BE STRANGE IF AN ACQUAINTANCE...
Celebrating Our Marriage!
...SENT YOU A POSTCARD SAYING, "CELEBRATING OUR MARRIAGE!"?
Celebrating Our Marriage!
THIS IS AN IMAGE
WIFE – NATSUKO
WE'RE THE ONES WHO SHOULD BE CELEBRATING, RIGHT!?
I GUESS MOST PEOPLE JUST SAY, "WE GOT MARRIED."
PEOPLE ARE SUCH GIANT BUNDLES OF EXHIBITIONISM!
IT'S ONE-SIDED SELF-ASSERTION!
ALL FOR A SMUG SENSE OF SATISFACTION!
YOU PRINT, "CELEBRATING 50 YEARS" ON THE COVER...
MAGAZINE
3/18 14 2009
CELEBRATING 50 YEARS
WHY SHOULD I CARE ABOUT THAT!?
I MEAN, THERE COULD BE READERS WHO HAVEN'T EVEN BEEN READING FOR A SINGLE YEAR!
I GUESS THERE COULD BE.
OR "CELEBRATING 10 MILLION COPIES SOLD"...
18
Celebrating 10 Million Copies Sold
WOW, YOU GUYS MUST LOVE TO CELEBRATE!
AS A CUSTOMER, I BOUGHT EXACTLY ONE COPY!
SOME PEOPLE BUY THREE.

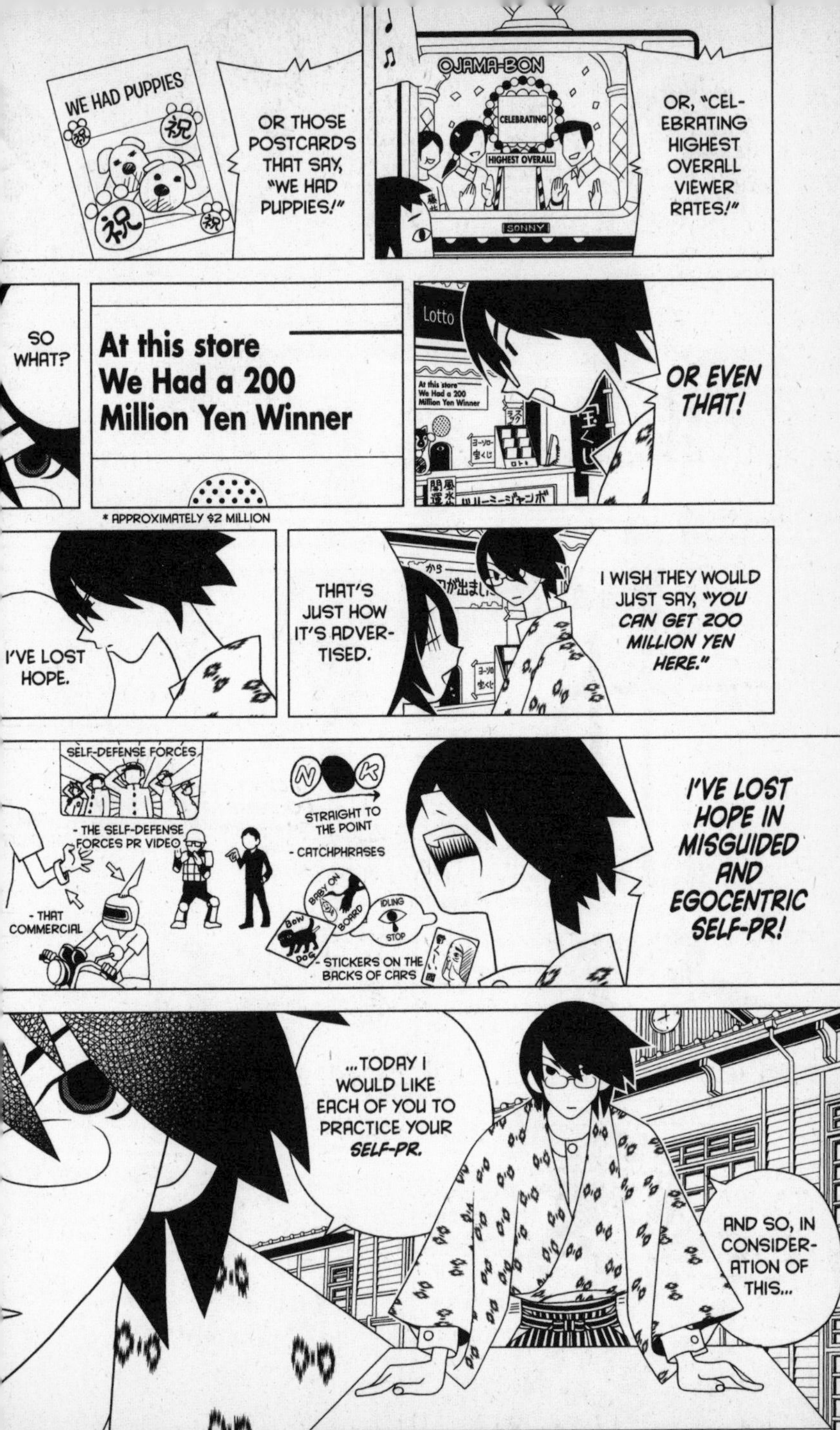
OJAMA-BON
CELEBRATING
HIGHEST OVERALL
SONNY
OR, "CELEBRATING HIGHEST OVERALL VIEWER RATES!"
WE HAD PUPPIES
祝
OR THOSE POSTCARDS THAT SAY, "WE HAD PUPPIES!"
Lotto
OR EVEN THAT!
At this store We Had a 200 Million Yen Winner
SO WHAT?
* APPROXIMATELY $2 MILLION
I WISH THEY WOULD JUST SAY, "*YOU CAN GET 200 MILLION YEN HERE.*"
THAT'S JUST HOW IT'S ADVERTISED.
I'VE LOST HOPE.
I'VE LOST HOPE IN MISGUIDED AND EGOCENTRIC SELF-PR!
STRAIGHT TO THE POINT
- CATCHPHRASES
SELF-DEFENSE FORCES
- THE SELF-DEFENSE FORCES PR VIDEO
- THAT COMMERCIAL
BABY ON BOARD
IDLING STOP
BOW DOG
- STICKERS ON THE BACKS OF CARS
AND SO, IN CONSIDERATION OF THIS...
...TODAY I WOULD LIKE EACH OF YOU TO PRACTICE YOUR *SELF-PR.*

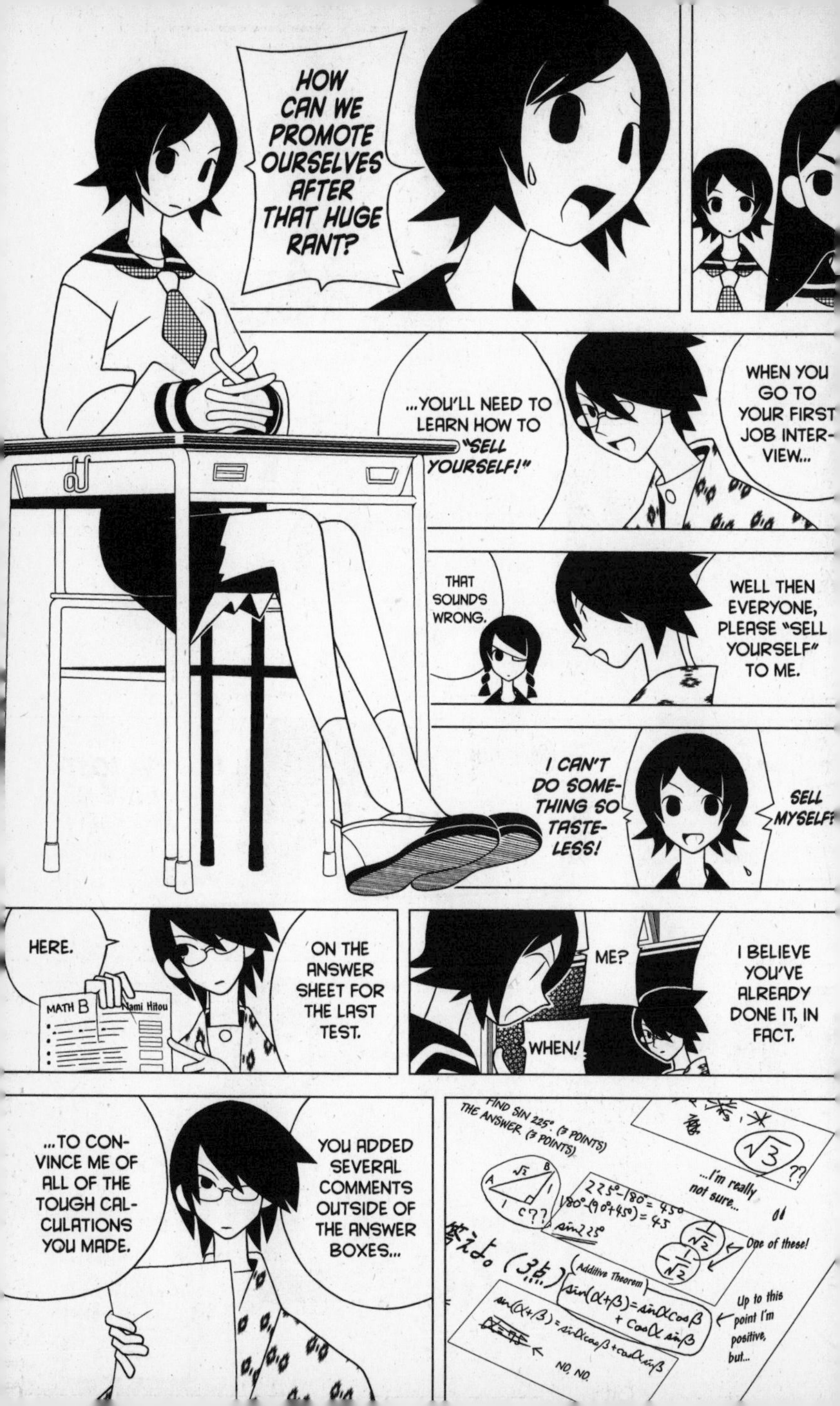

HOW CAN WE PROMOTE OURSELVES AFTER THAT HUGE RANT?
WHEN YOU GO TO YOUR FIRST JOB INTER-VIEW...
...YOU'LL NEED TO LEARN HOW TO "SELL YOURSELF!"
WELL THEN EVERYONE, PLEASE "SELL YOURSELF" TO ME.
THAT SOUNDS WRONG.
SELL MYSELF!?
I CAN'T DO SOME-THING SO TASTE-LESS!
I BELIEVE YOU'VE ALREADY DONE IT, IN FACT.
ME?
WHEN!
ON THE ANSWER SHEET FOR THE LAST TEST.
HERE.
MATH B
Nami Hitou
YOU ADDED SEVERAL COMMENTS OUTSIDE OF THE ANSWER BOXES...
...TO CON-VINCE ME OF ALL OF THE TOUGH CAL-CULATIONS YOU MADE.
FIND SIN 225°. (3 POINTS)
THE ANSWER. (3 POINTS)
√2
A B C??
1
225°-180°=45°
180°-(90°+45°)=45
sin 225°
√3 ??
...I'm really not sure...
1/√2
-1/√2
One of these!
答えよ。(3点)
(Additive Theorem)
sin(α+β)=sinαcosβ + cosαsinβ
sin(α+β)=sinαcosβ+cosαsinβ
Up to this point I'm positive, but...
NO, NO.

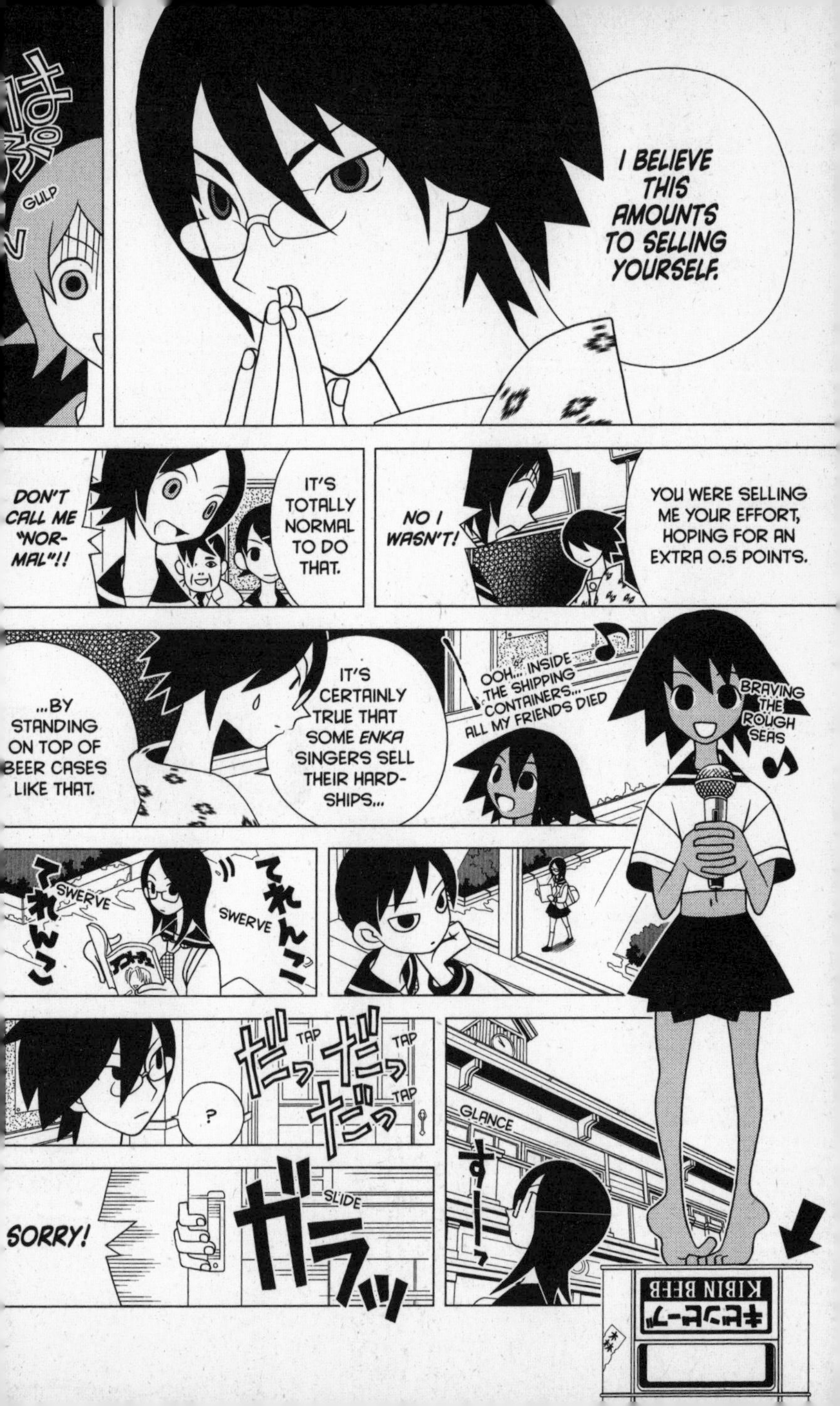

I BELIEVE THIS AMOUNTS TO SELLING YOURSELF.
はっ
GULP
YOU WERE SELLING ME YOUR EFFORT, HOPING FOR AN EXTRA 0.5 POINTS.
NO I WASN'T!
IT'S TOTALLY NORMAL TO DO THAT.
DON'T CALL ME "NOR-MAL"!!
BRAVING THE ROUGH SEAS
OOH... INSIDE THE SHIPPING CONTAINERS... ALL MY FRIENDS DIED
キビンビール
KIBIN BEER
IT'S CERTAINLY TRUE THAT SOME *ENKA* SINGERS SELL THEIR HARD-SHIPS...
...BY STANDING ON TOP OF BEER CASES LIKE THAT.
てれんこ
SWERVE
てれんこ
SWERVE
GLANCE
すーっ
だっ だっ だっ
TAP TAP TAP
?
ガラッ
SLIDE
SORRY!

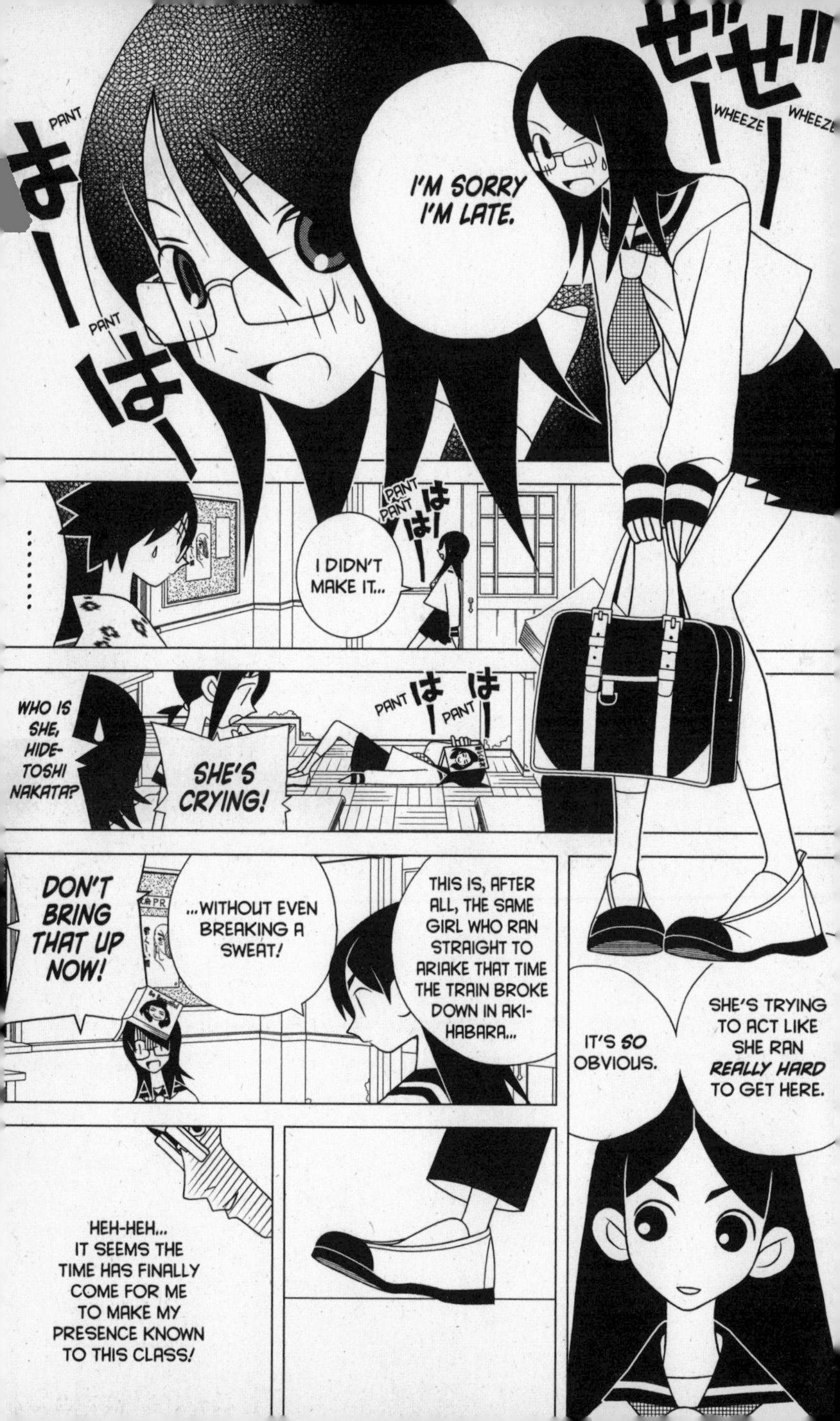
ぜー ぜー
WHEEZE WHEEZE
I'M SORRY I'M LATE.
はー はー
PANT PANT
はーはー
PANT PANT
I DIDN'T MAKE IT...
......
はー はー
PANT PANT
SHE'S CRYING!
WHO IS SHE, HIDE-TOSHI NAKATA?
SHE'S TRYING TO ACT LIKE SHE RAN *REALLY HARD* TO GET HERE.
IT'S *SO* OBVIOUS.
THIS IS, AFTER ALL, THE SAME GIRL WHO RAN STRAIGHT TO ARIAKE THAT TIME THE TRAIN BROKE DOWN IN AKI-HABARA...
...WITHOUT EVEN BREAKING A SWEAT!
DON'T BRING THAT UP NOW!
HEH-HEH... IT SEEMS THE TIME HAS FINALLY COME FOR ME TO MAKE MY PRESENCE KNOWN TO THIS CLASS!

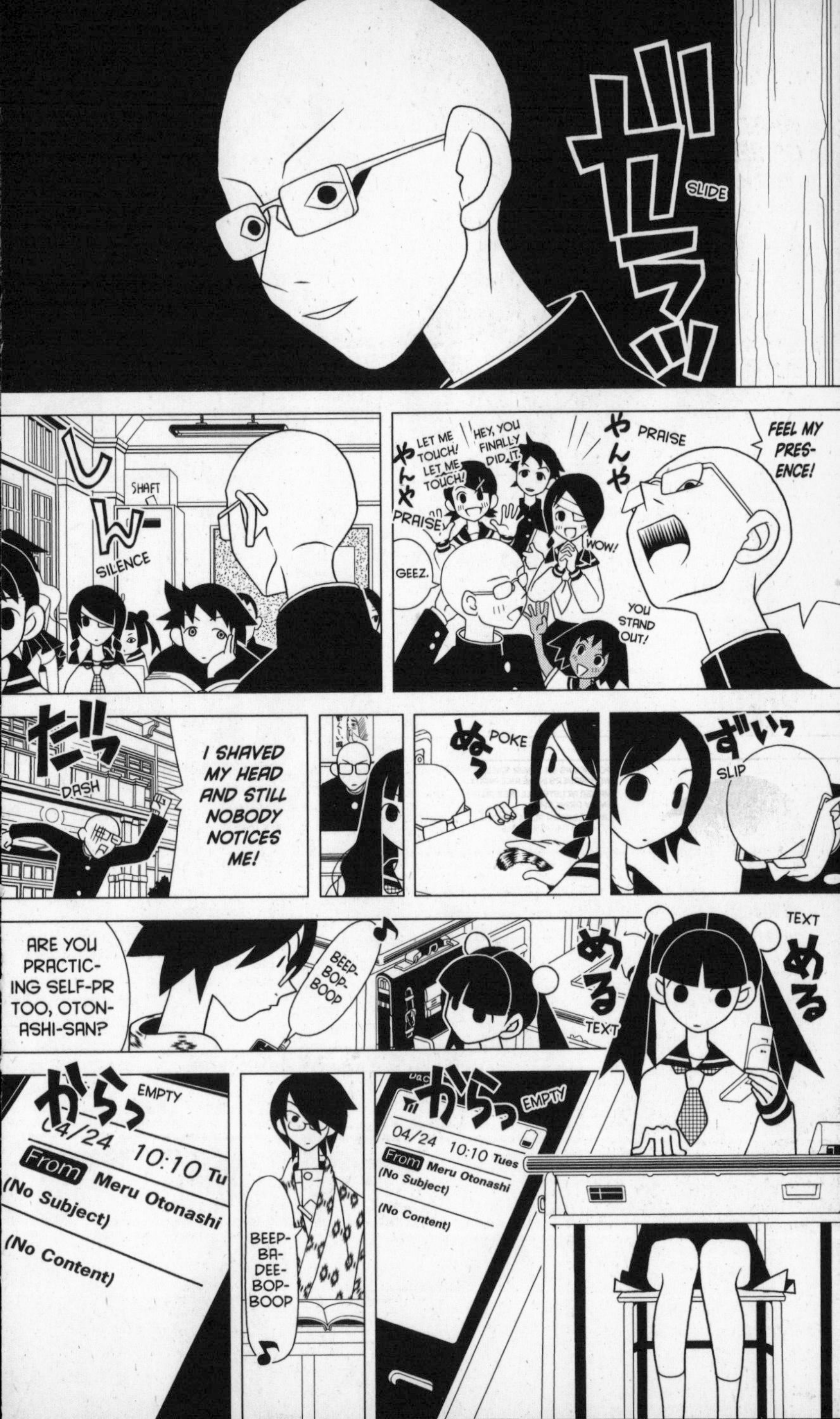

ガラッ
SLIDE
やんや
PRAISE
FEEL MY PRES-ENCE!
HEY, YOU FINALLY DID IT.
LET ME TOUCH! LET ME TOUCH!
やんや
PRAISE
WOW!
GEEZ.
YOU STAND OUT!
しーん
SHAFT
SILENCE
ずいっ
SLIP
ぬっ
POKE
I SHAVED MY HEAD AND STILL NOBODY NOTICES ME!
だっ
DASH
TEXT
める
める
める
TEXT
BEEP-BOP-BOOP
ARE YOU PRACTIC-ING SELF-PR TOO, OTON-ASHI-SAN?
がらっ
EMPTY
04/24 10:10 Tues
From Meru Otonashi
(No Subject)
(No Content)
BEEP-BA-DEE-BOP-BOOP
がらっ
EMPTY
04/24 10:10 Tu
From Meru Otonashi
(No Subject)
(No Content)

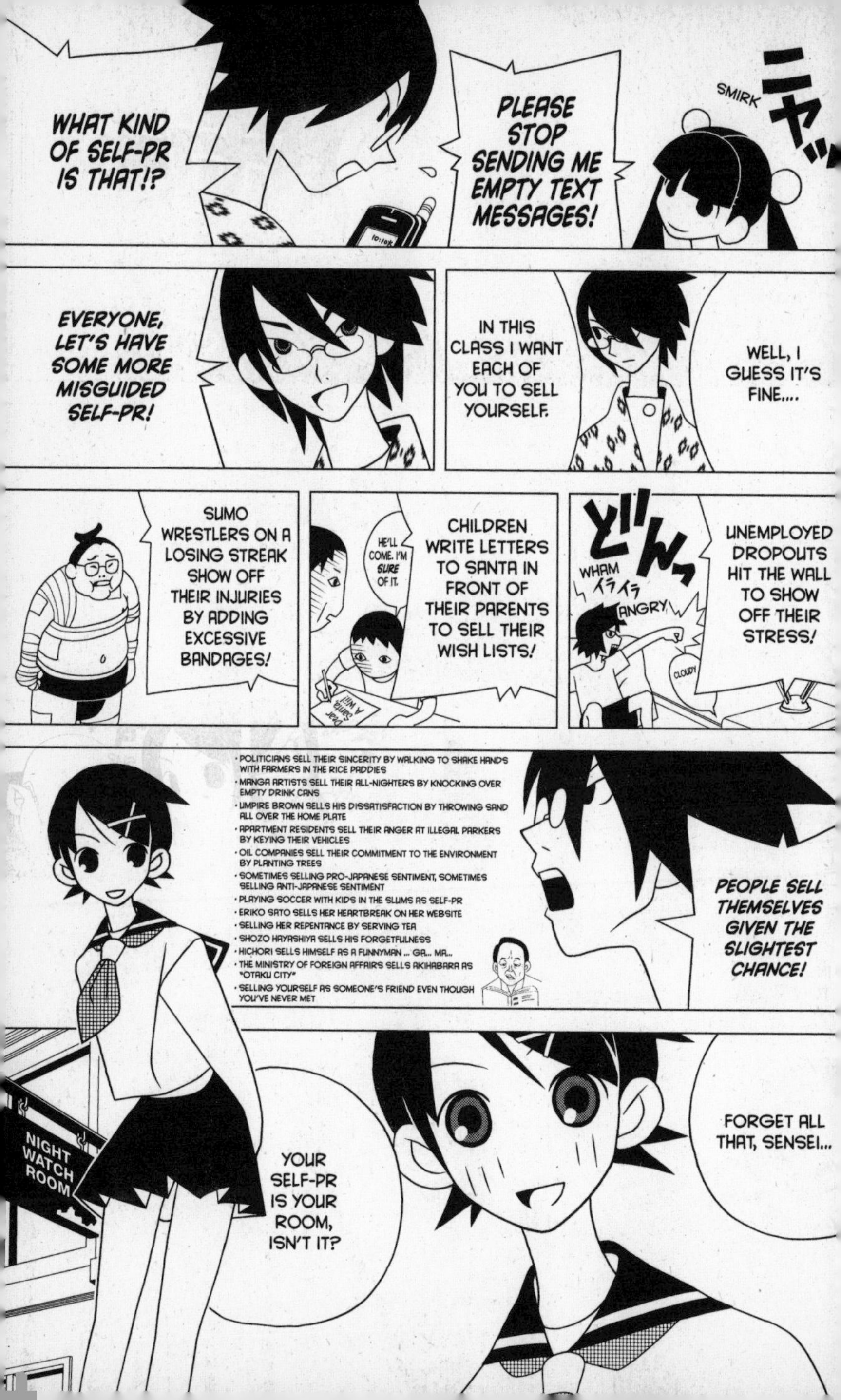

SMIRK
ニヤッ
PLEASE STOP SENDING ME EMPTY TEXT MESSAGES!
WHAT KIND OF SELF-PR IS THAT!?
WELL, I GUESS IT'S FINE....
IN THIS CLASS I WANT EACH OF YOU TO SELL YOURSELF.
EVERYONE, LET'S HAVE SOME MORE MISGUIDED SELF-PR!
UNEMPLOYED DROPOUTS HIT THE WALL TO SHOW OFF THEIR STRESS!
どんっ
WHAM
イライラ
ANGRY
CLOUDY
CHILDREN WRITE LETTERS TO SANTA IN FRONT OF THEIR PARENTS TO SELL THEIR WISH LISTS!
HE'LL COME. I'M SURE OF IT.
Dear Santa, A Wii!
SUMO WRESTLERS ON A LOSING STREAK SHOW OFF THEIR INJURIES BY ADDING EXCESSIVE BANDAGES!
PEOPLE SELL THEMSELVES GIVEN THE SLIGHTEST CHANCE!
• POLITICIANS SELL THEIR SINCERITY BY WALKING TO SHAKE HANDS WITH FARMERS IN THE RICE PADDIES
• MANGA ARTISTS SELL THEIR ALL-NIGHTERS BY KNOCKING OVER EMPTY DRINK CANS
• UMPIRE BROWN SELLS HIS DISSATISFACTION BY THROWING SAND ALL OVER THE HOME PLATE
• APARTMENT RESIDENTS SELL THEIR ANGER AT ILLEGAL PARKERS BY KEYING THEIR VEHICLES
• OIL COMPANIES SELL THEIR COMMITMENT TO THE ENVIRONMENT BY PLANTING TREES
• SOMETIMES SELLING PRO-JAPANESE SENTIMENT, SOMETIMES SELLING ANTI-JAPANESE SENTIMENT
• PLAYING SOCCER WITH KIDS IN THE SLUMS AS SELF-PR
• ERIKO SATO SELLS HER HEARTBREAK ON HER WEBSITE
• SELLING HER REPENTANCE BY SERVING TEA
• SHOZO HAYASHIYA SELLS HIS FORGETFULNESS
• HICHORI SELLS HIMSELF AS A FUNNYMAN ... GA... MA...
• THE MINISTRY OF FOREIGN AFFAIRS SELLS AKIHABARA AS "OTAKU CITY"
• SELLING YOURSELF AS SOMEONE'S FRIEND EVEN THOUGH YOU'VE NEVER MET
FORGET ALL THAT, SENSEI...
YOUR SELF-PR IS YOUR ROOM, ISN'T IT?
NIGHT WATCH ROOM

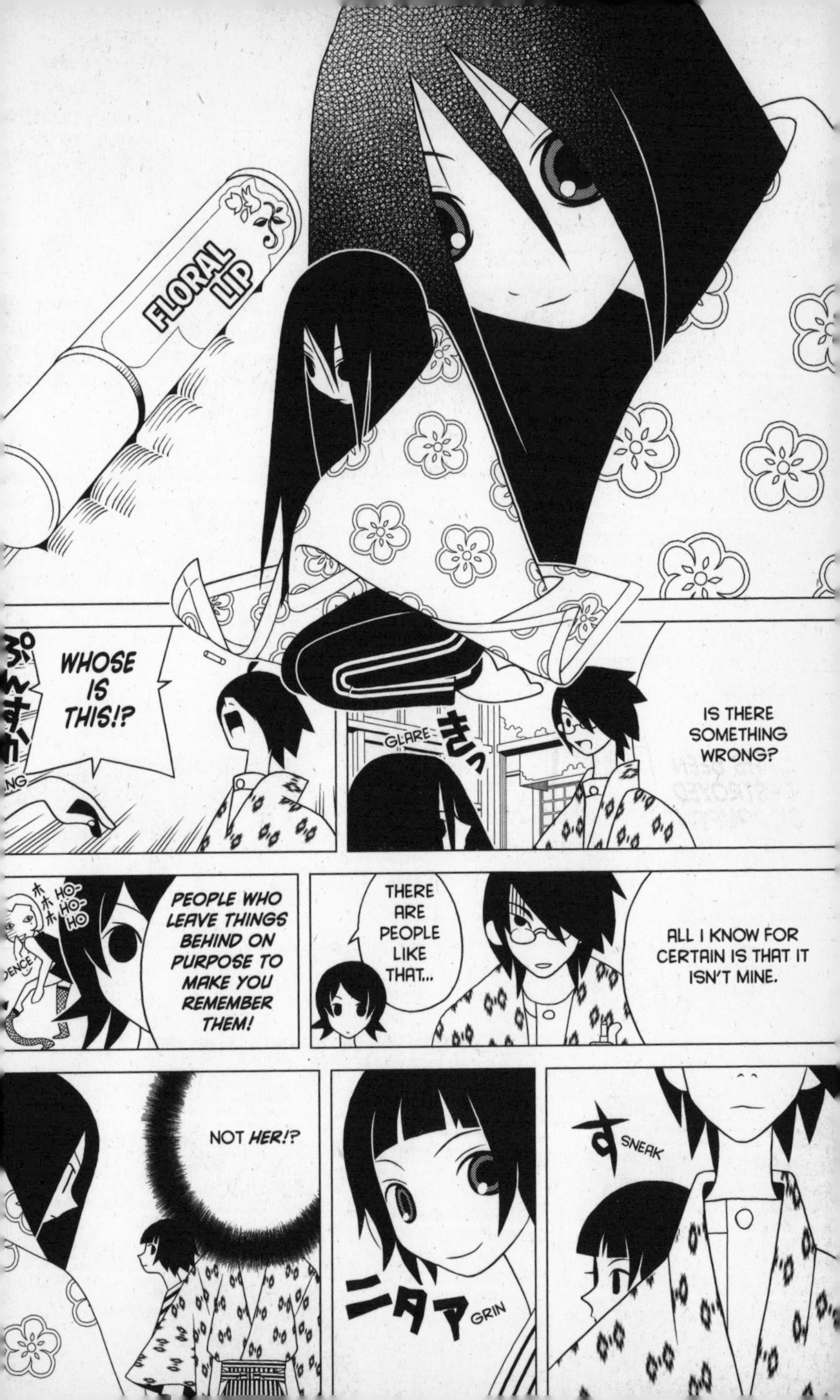
FLORAL LIP
IS THERE SOMETHING WRONG?
きっ
GLARE
WHOSE IS THIS!?
ALL I KNOW FOR CERTAIN IS THAT IT ISN'T MINE.
THERE ARE PEOPLE LIKE THAT...
PEOPLE WHO LEAVE THINGS BEHIND ON PURPOSE TO MAKE YOU REMEMBER THEM!
ホホホ
HO-HO-HO
す
SNEAK
ニタァ
GRIN
NOT HER!?

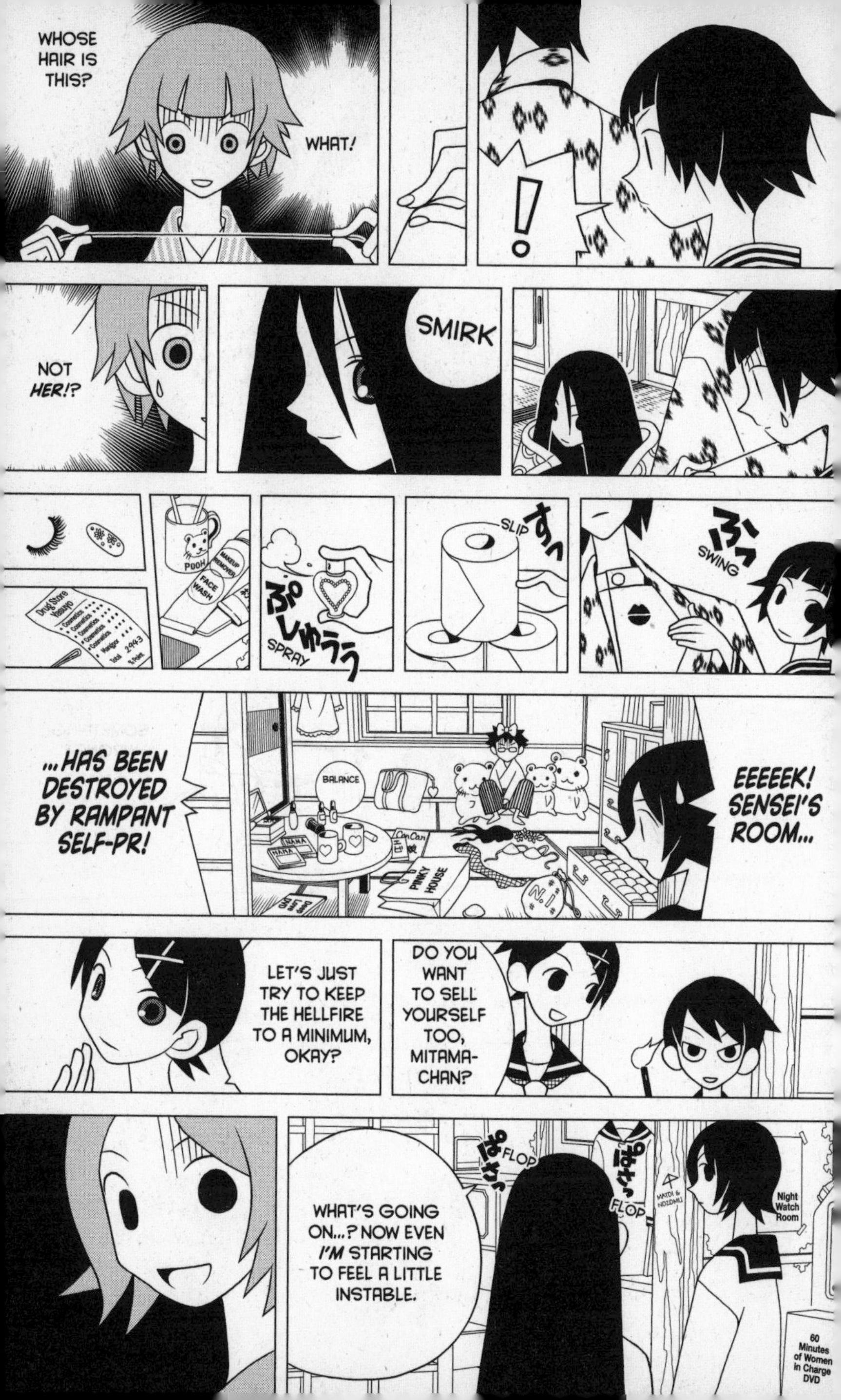
!
WHOSE HAIR IS THIS?
WHAT!
SMIRK
NOT HER!?
ふっ SWING
すっ SLIP
ぷしゅううう SPRAY
POOH
MAKEUP REMOVER
FACE WASH
EEEEEK! SENSEI'S ROOM...
...HAS BEEN DESTROYED BY RAMPANT SELF-PR!
BALANCE
CanCan
NANA
PINKY HOUSE
DO YOU WANT TO SELL YOURSELF TOO, MITAMA-CHAN?
LET'S JUST TRY TO KEEP THE HELLFIRE TO A MINIMUM, OKAY?
ぱさっ FLOP
ぱさっ FLOP
Night Watch Room
60 Minutes of Women in Charge DVD
WHAT'S GOING ON...? NOW EVEN I'M STARTING TO FEEL A LITTLE INSTABLE.

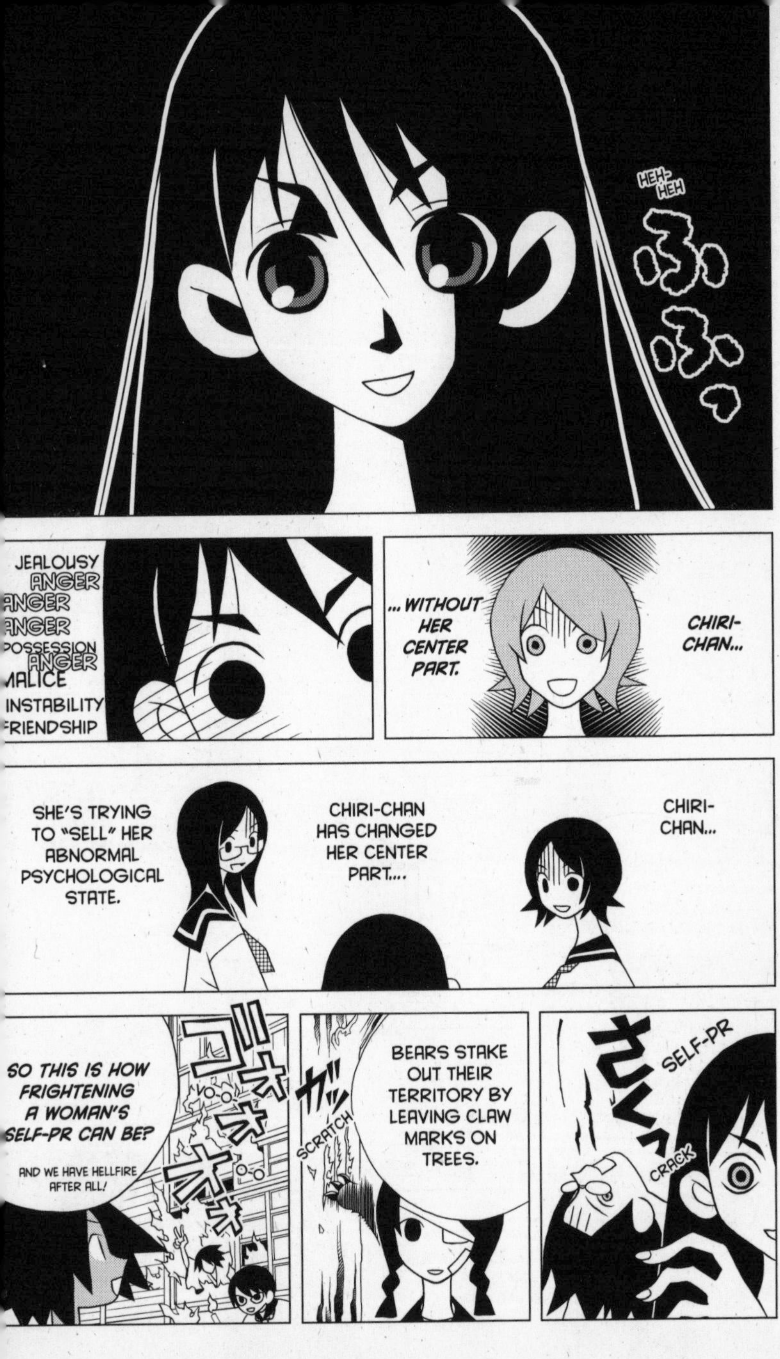
HEH-HEH
ふふっ
CHIRI-CHAN...
...WITHOUT HER CENTER PART.
JEALOUSY
ANGER
ANGER
ANGER
POSSESSION
ANGER
MALICE
INSTABILITY
FRIENDSHIP
CHIRI-CHAN...
CHIRI-CHAN HAS CHANGED HER CENTER PART....
SHE'S TRYING TO "SELL" HER ABNORMAL PSYCHOLOGICAL STATE.
さくっ
CRACK
SELF-PR
BEARS STAKE OUT THEIR TERRITORY BY LEAVING CLAW MARKS ON TREES.
ガッ
SCRATCH
ゴォォォ
SO THIS IS HOW FRIGHTENING A WOMAN'S SELF-PR CAN BE?
AND WE HAVE HELLFIRE AFTER ALL!

RETURNED COPIES
RETURNED COPIES
RETURNED COPIES
I THINK AT THIS POINT YOU'RE SELLING SOMETHING BESIDES HARDSHIP....
RETURNED COPIES
RETURNED COPIES
RETURNED COPIES
RETURNED COPIES

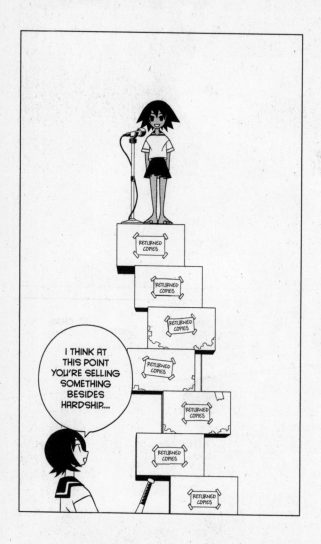

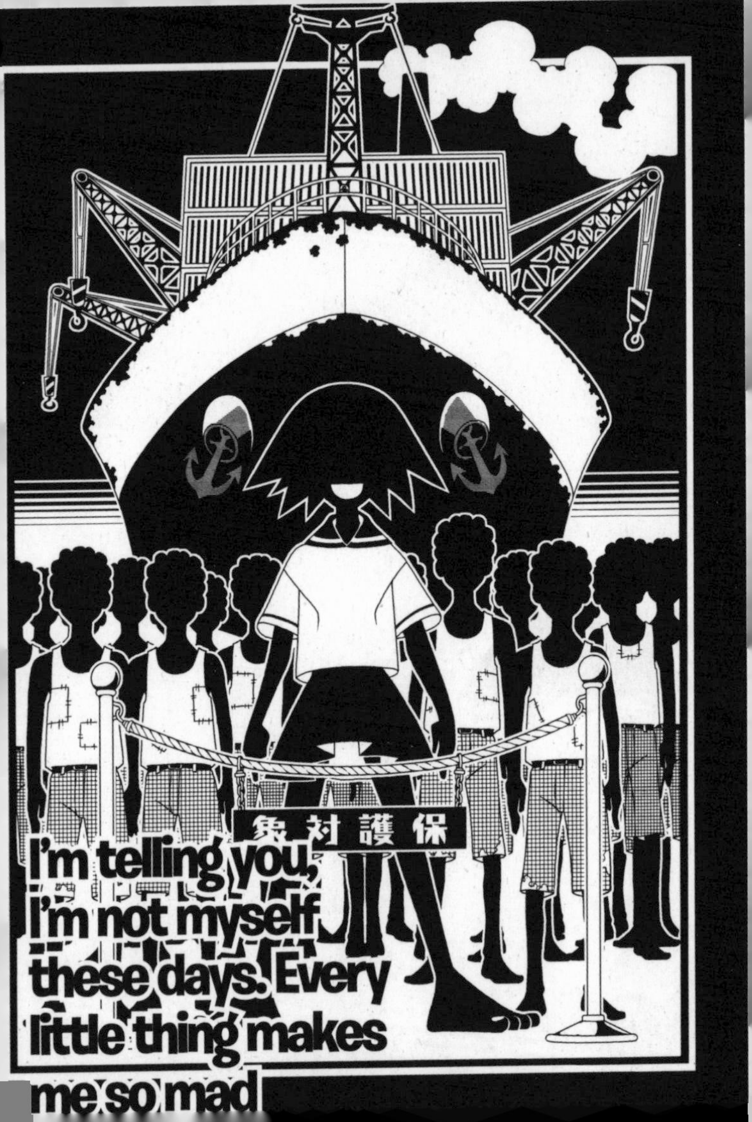
保護対象
I'm telling you, I'm not myself these days. Every little thing makes me so mad

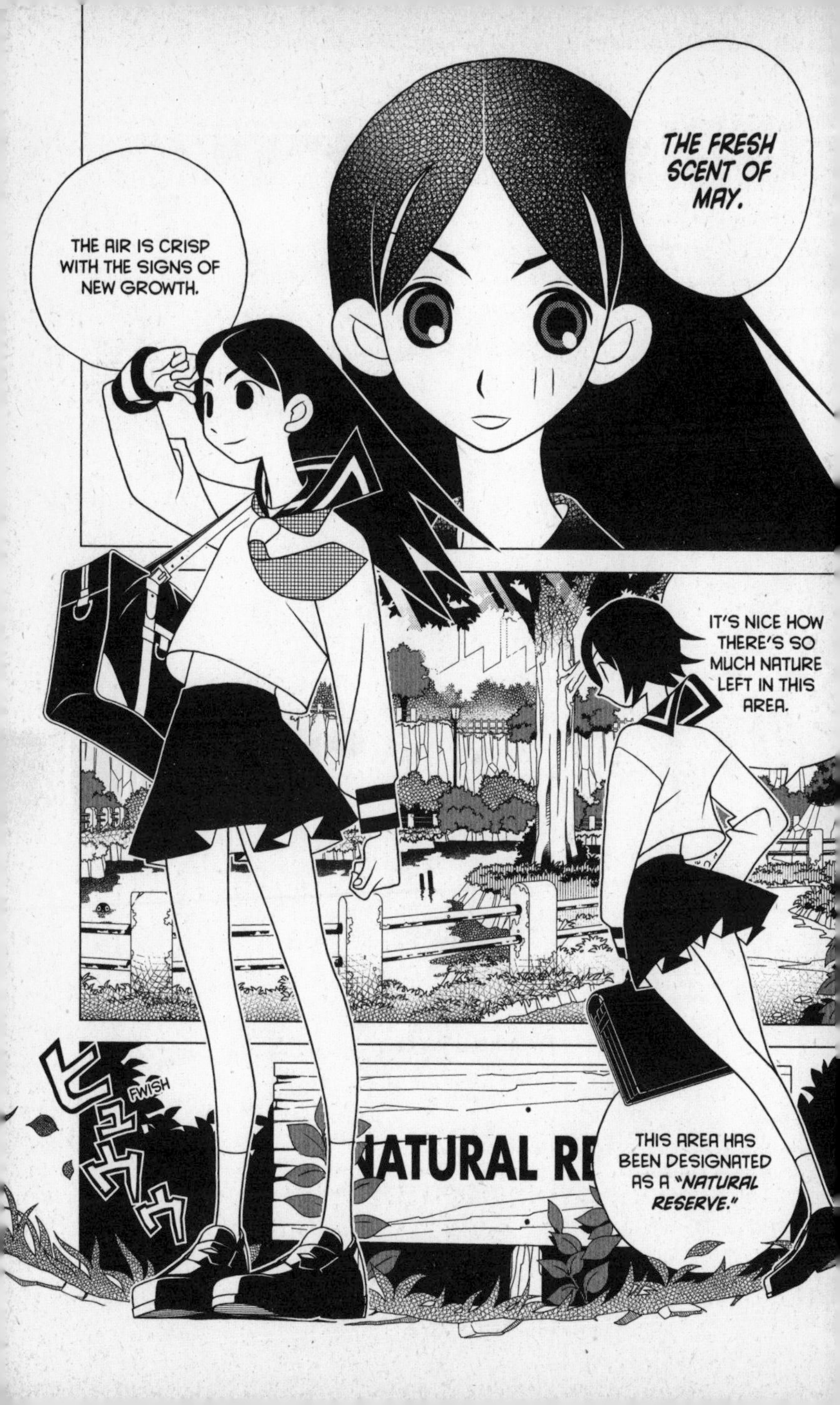
THE FRESH SCENT OF MAY.
THE AIR IS CRISP WITH THE SIGNS OF NEW GROWTH.
IT'S NICE HOW THERE'S SO MUCH NATURE LEFT IN THIS AREA.
FWISH
NATURAL RE
THIS AREA HAS BEEN DESIGNATED AS A *"NATURAL RESERVE."*

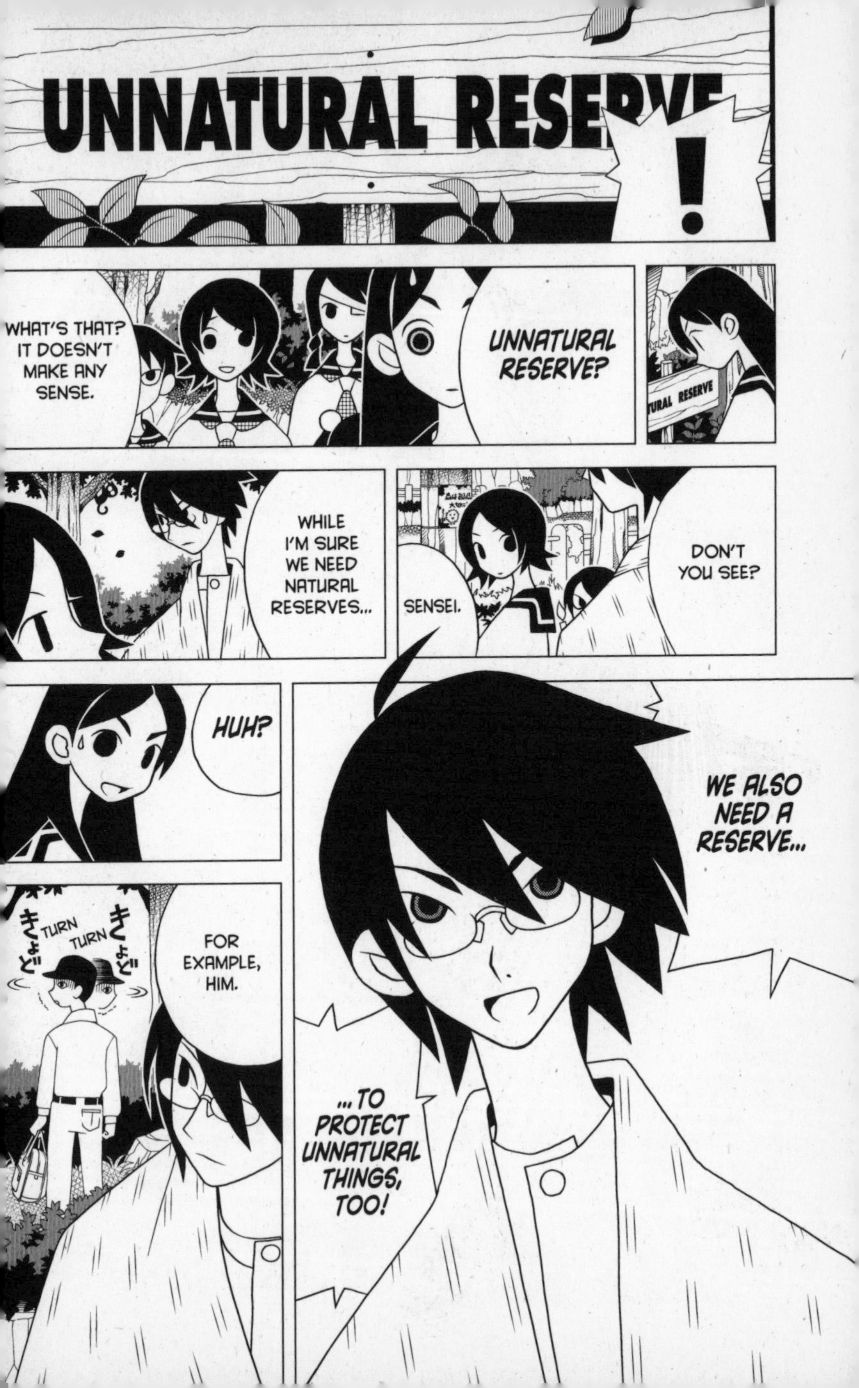
UNNATURAL RESERVE!
UNNATURAL RESERVE?
WHAT'S THAT? IT DOESN'T MAKE ANY SENSE.
DON'T YOU SEE?
SENSEI.
WHILE I'M SURE WE NEED NATURAL RESERVES...
WE ALSO NEED A RESERVE...
...TO PROTECT UNNATURAL THINGS, TOO!
HUH?
FOR EXAMPLE, HIM.
きょど TURN
きょど TURN

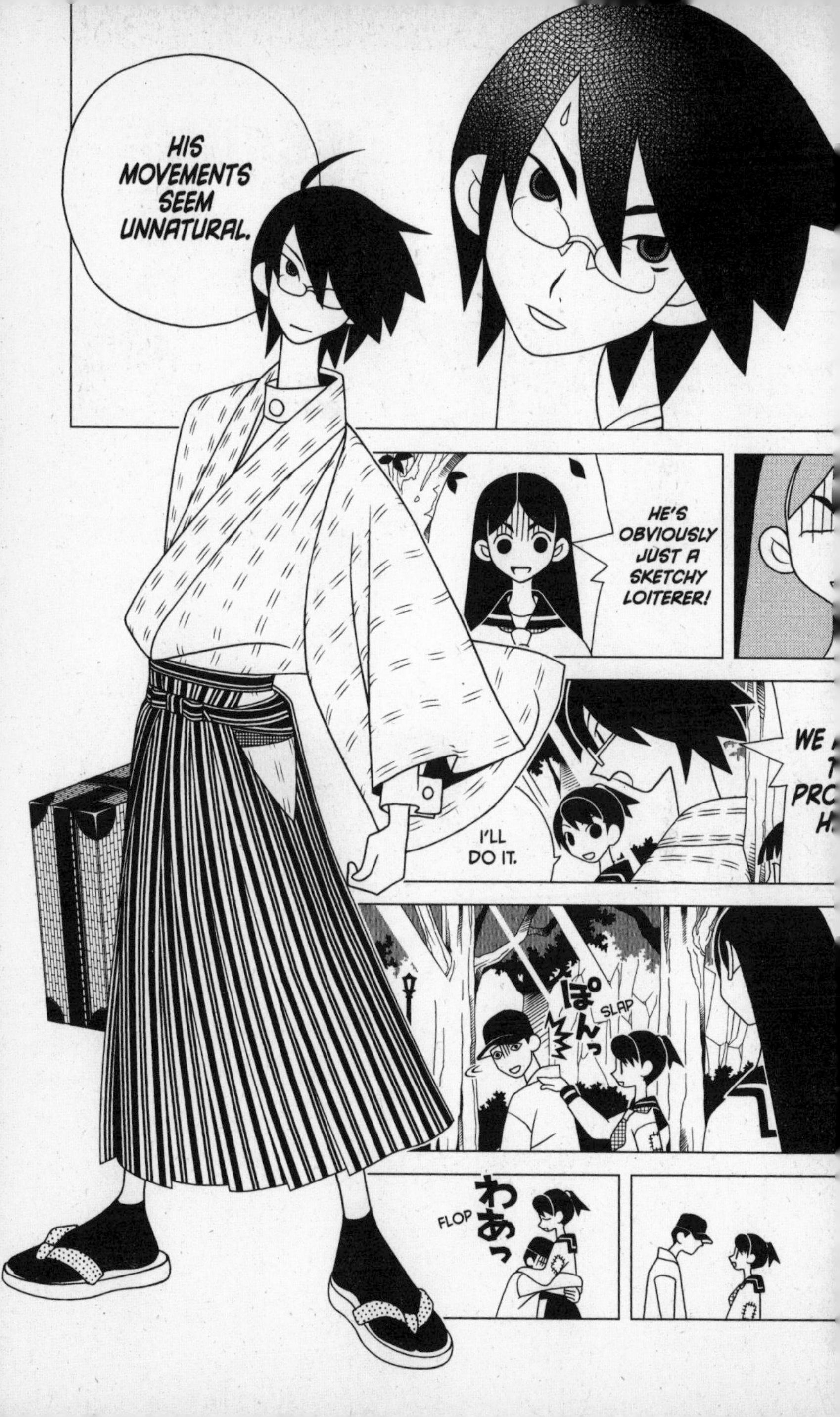
HIS MOVEMENTS SEEM UNNATURAL.
HE'S OBVIOUSLY JUST A SKETCHY LOITERER!
WE
I'LL DO IT.
ぽんっ
SLAP
わあっ
FLOP

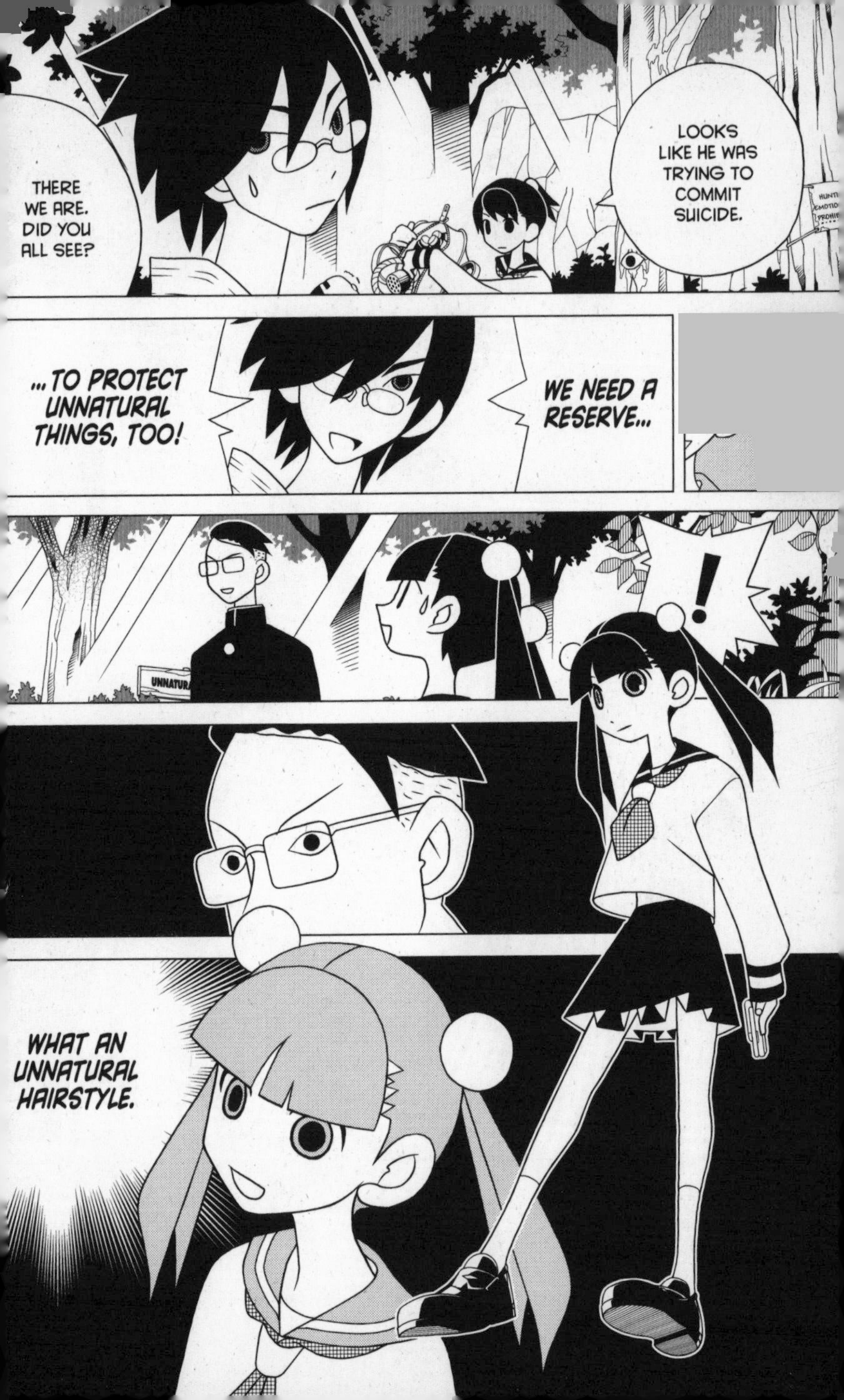
LOOKS LIKE HE WAS TRYING TO COMMIT SUICIDE.
THERE WE ARE. DID YOU ALL SEE?
WE NEED A RESERVE...
...TO PROTECT UNNATURAL THINGS, TOO!
!
WHAT AN UNNATURAL HAIRSTYLE.

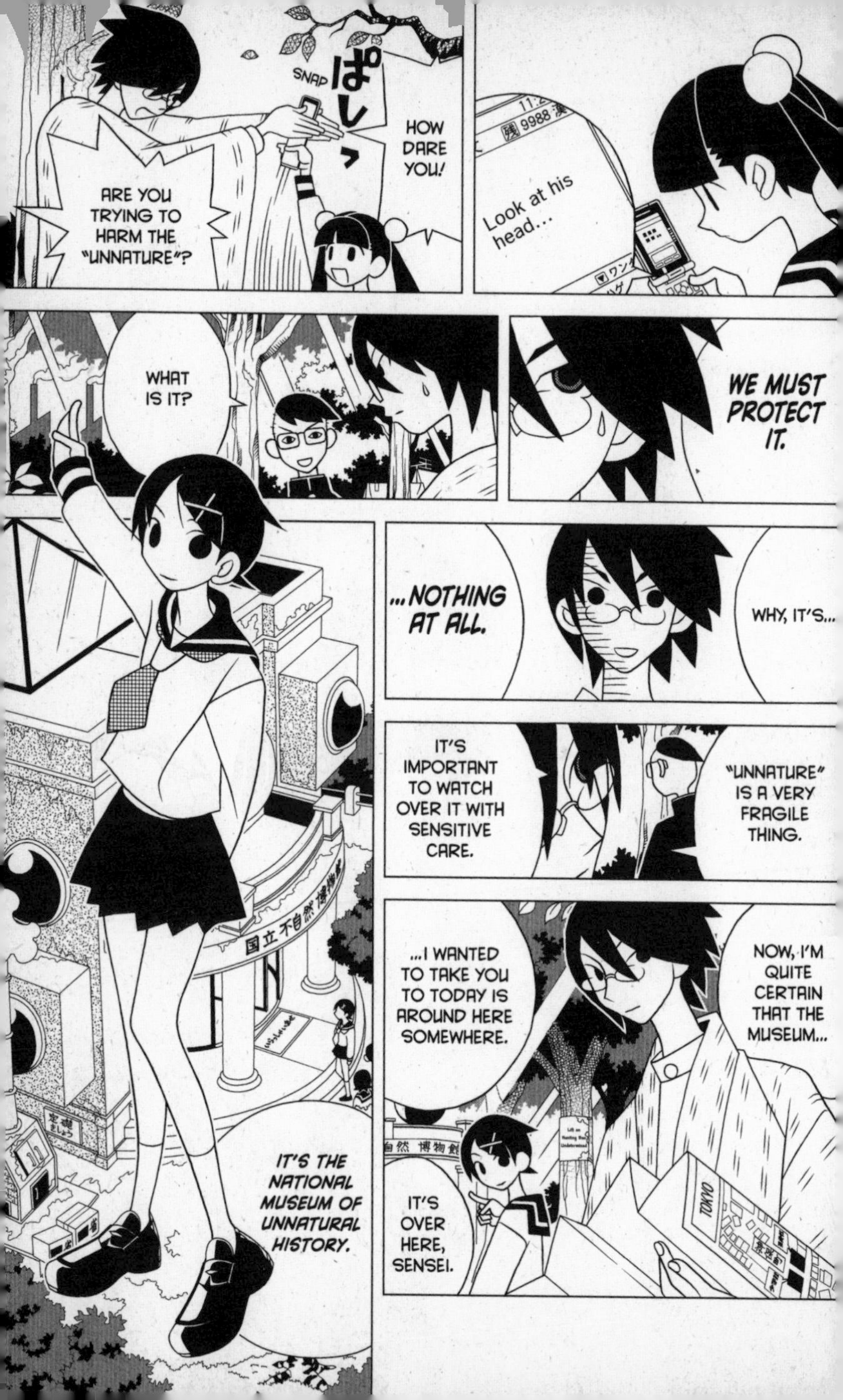
Look at his head...
ぱしっ
SNAP
HOW DARE YOU!
ARE YOU TRYING TO HARM THE "UNNATURE"?
WE MUST PROTECT IT.
WHAT IS IT?
WHY, IT'S...
...NOTHING AT ALL.
"UNNATURE" IS A VERY FRAGILE THING.
IT'S IMPORTANT TO WATCH OVER IT WITH SENSITIVE CARE.
NOW, I'M QUITE CERTAIN THAT THE MUSEUM...
...I WANTED TO TAKE YOU TO TODAY IS AROUND HERE SOMEWHERE.
IT'S OVER HERE, SENSEI.
TOKYO
国立不自然博物館
IT'S THE NATIONAL MUSEUM OF UNNATURAL HISTORY.

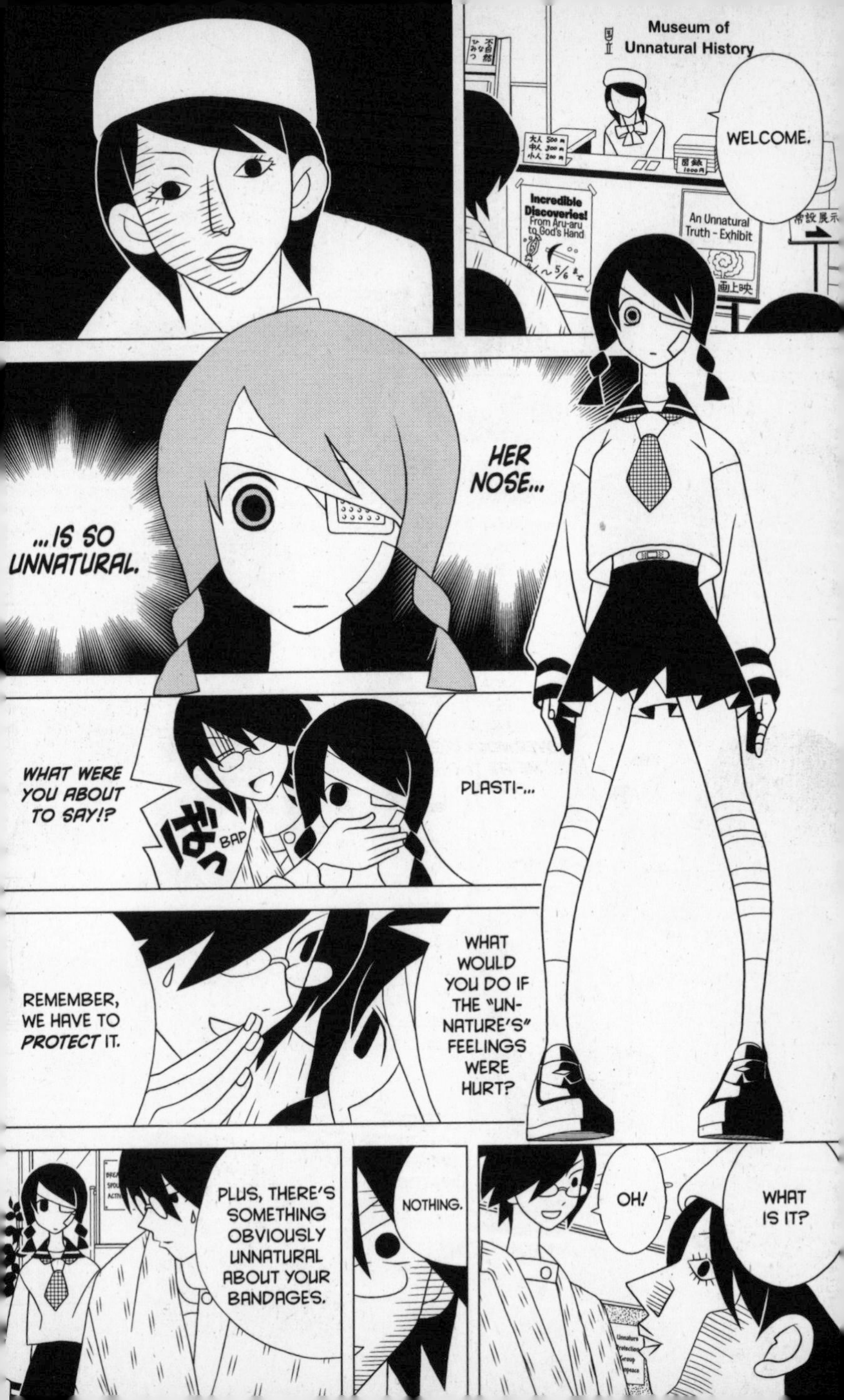
Museum of Unnatural History
WELCOME.
Incredible Discoveries! From Aru-aru to God's Hand
An Unnatural Truth - Exhibit
HER NOSE...
...IS SO UNNATURAL.
PLASTI-...
WHAT WERE YOU ABOUT TO SAY!?
BAP
WHAT WOULD YOU DO IF THE "UN-NATURE'S" FEELINGS WERE HURT?
REMEMBER, WE HAVE TO PROTECT IT.
WHAT IS IT?
OH!
NOTHING.
PLUS, THERE'S SOMETHING OBVIOUSLY UNNATURAL ABOUT YOUR BANDAGES.

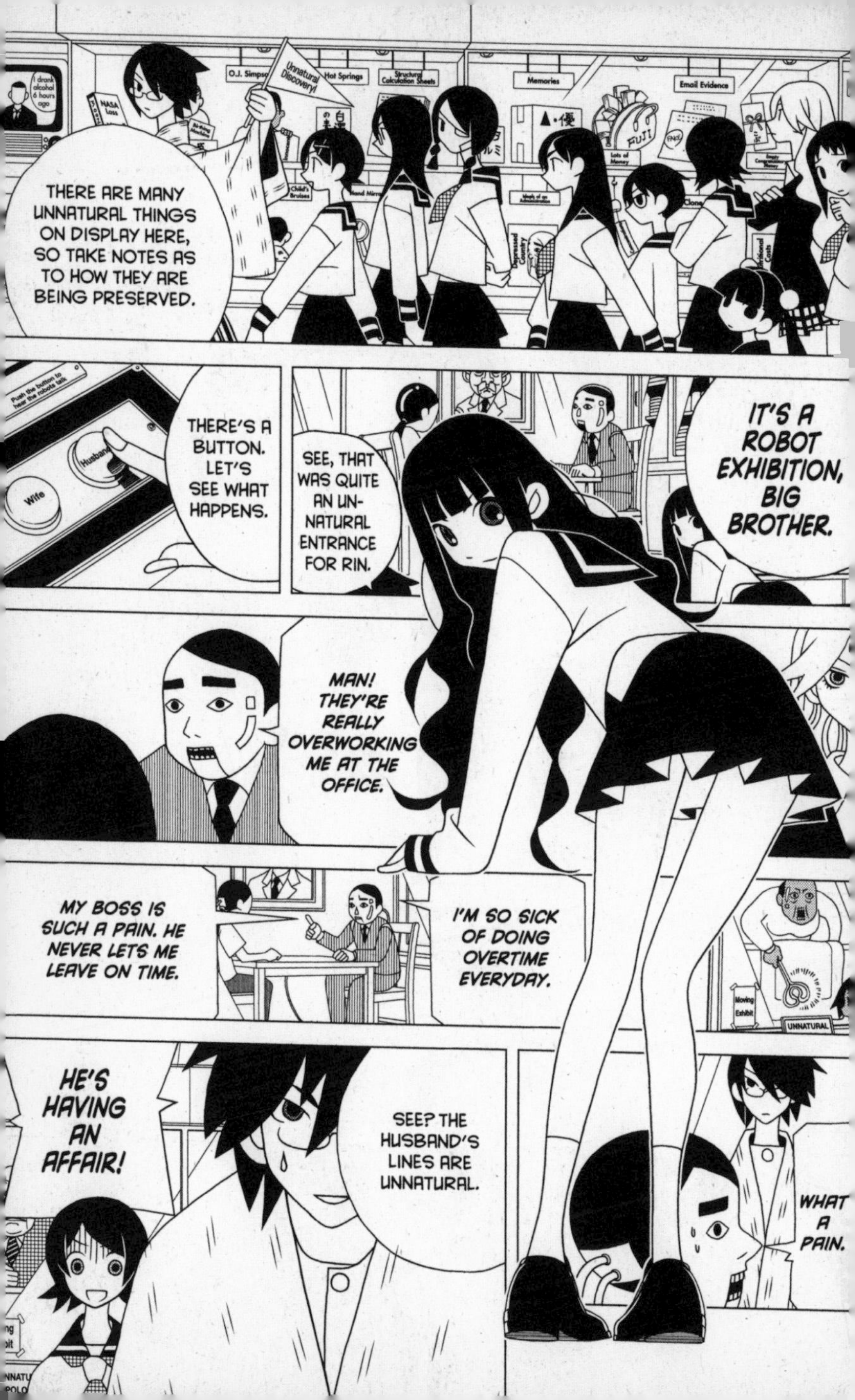
Email Evidence
Memories
Structural Calculation Sheets
Hot Springs
Unnatural Discovery!
O.J. Simpson
NASA Loss
I drank alcohol 6 hours ago
Lots of Money
Clone
Hand Mirror
Child's Bruises
THERE ARE MANY UNNATURAL THINGS ON DISPLAY HERE, SO TAKE NOTES AS TO HOW THEY ARE BEING PRESERVED.
IT'S A ROBOT EXHIBITION, BIG BROTHER.
SEE, THAT WAS QUITE AN UN-NATURAL ENTRANCE FOR RIN.
Push the button to hear the robots talk
Husband
Wife
THERE'S A BUTTON. LET'S SEE WHAT HAPPENS.
MAN! THEY'RE REALLY OVERWORKING ME AT THE OFFICE.
Moving Exhibit
UNNATURAL
I'M SO SICK OF DOING OVERTIME EVERYDAY.
MY BOSS IS SUCH A PAIN. HE NEVER LETS ME LEAVE ON TIME.
WHAT A PAIN.
SEE? THE HUSBAND'S LINES ARE UNNATURAL.
HE'S HAVING AN AFFAIR!

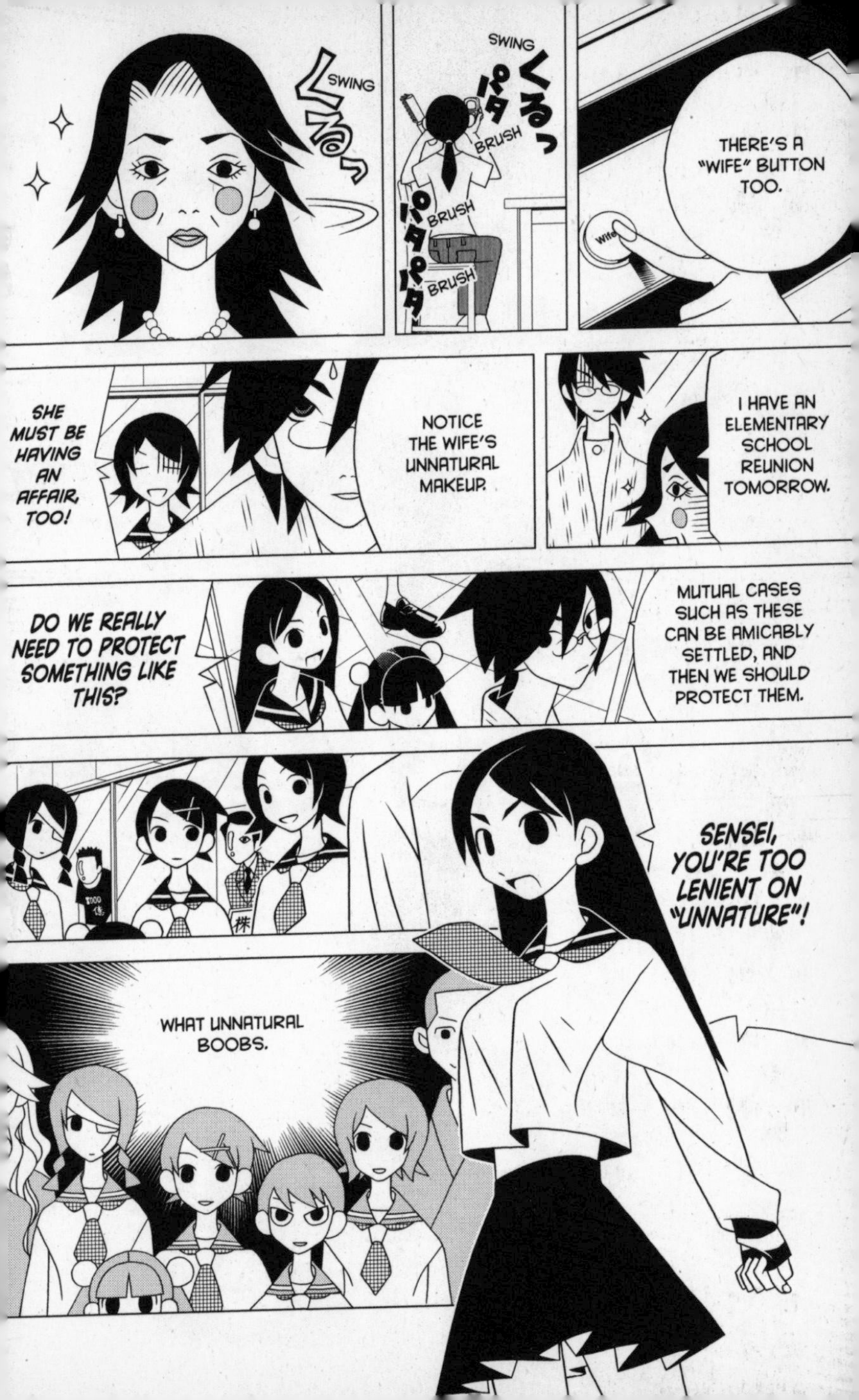
THERE'S A "WIFE" BUTTON TOO.
Wife
SWING
くるっ
パタ
BRUSH
パタパタ
BRUSH
BRUSH
SWING
くるっ
I HAVE AN ELEMENTARY SCHOOL REUNION TOMORROW.
NOTICE THE WIFE'S UNNATURAL MAKEUP.
SHE MUST BE HAVING AN AFFAIR, TOO!
MUTUAL CASES SUCH AS THESE CAN BE AMICABLY SETTLED, AND THEN WE SHOULD PROTECT THEM.
DO WE REALLY NEED TO PROTECT SOMETHING LIKE THIS?
SENSEI, YOU'RE TOO LENIENT ON "UNNATURE"!
WHAT UNNATURAL BOOBS.

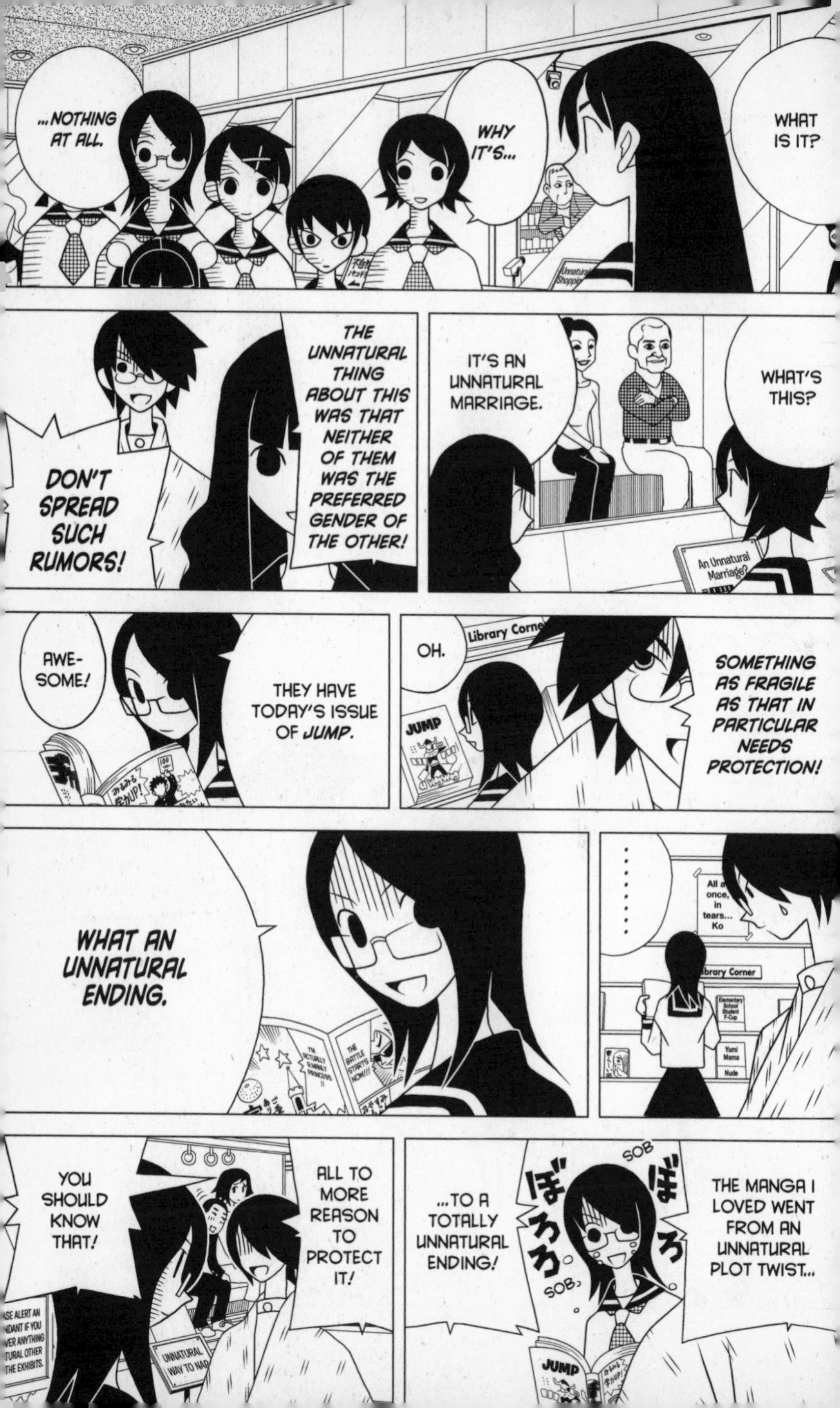
WHAT IS IT?
WHY IT'S...
...NOTHING AT ALL.
WHAT'S THIS?
IT'S AN UNNATURAL MARRIAGE.
An Unnatural Marriage?
THE UNNATURAL THING ABOUT THIS WAS THAT NEITHER OF THEM WAS THE PREFERRED GENDER OF THE OTHER!
DON'T SPREAD SUCH RUMORS!
SOMETHING AS FRAGILE AS THAT IN PARTICULAR NEEDS PROTECTION!
OH.
JUMP
THEY HAVE TODAY'S ISSUE OF JUMP.
AWE-SOME!
......
Library Corner
Elementary School Student F-Cup
Yumi Mama
Nude
WHAT AN UNNATURAL ENDING.
I'M ACTUALLY A MANLY PRINCESS!!
THE BATTLE STARTS NOW!!!
THE MANGA I LOVED WENT FROM AN UNNATURAL PLOT TWIST...
ぼろ
SOB
ぼろろ
SOB
...TO A TOTALLY UNNATURAL ENDING!
JUMP
ALL TO MORE REASON TO PROTECT IT!
YOU SHOULD KNOW THAT!

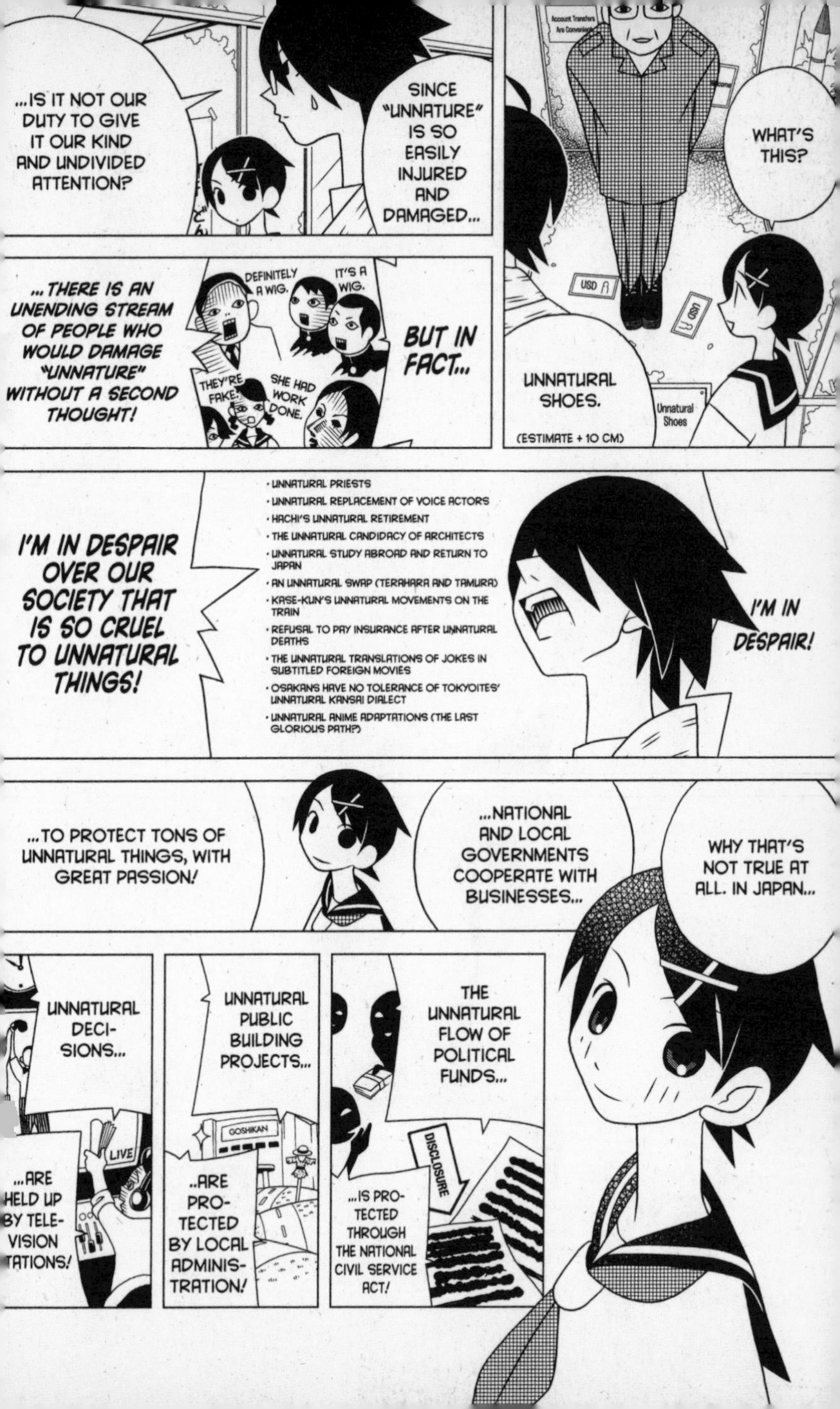
WHAT'S THIS?
USD
UNNATURAL SHOES.
(ESTIMATE + 10 CM)
Unnatural Shoes
SINCE "UNNATURE" IS SO EASILY INJURED AND DAMAGED...
...IS IT NOT OUR DUTY TO GIVE IT OUR KIND AND UNDIVIDED ATTENTION?
BUT IN FACT...
IT'S A WIG.
DEFINITELY A WIG.
SHE HAD WORK DONE.
THEY'RE FAKE!
...THERE IS AN UNENDING STREAM OF PEOPLE WHO WOULD DAMAGE "UNNATURE" WITHOUT A SECOND THOUGHT!
I'M IN DESPAIR!
• UNNATURAL PRIESTS
• UNNATURAL REPLACEMENT OF VOICE ACTORS
• HACHI'S UNNATURAL RETIREMENT
• THE UNNATURAL CANDIDACY OF ARCHITECTS
• UNNATURAL STUDY ABROAD AND RETURN TO JAPAN
• AN UNNATURAL SWAP (TERAHARA AND TAMURA)
• KASE-KUN'S UNNATURAL MOVEMENTS ON THE TRAIN
• REFUSAL TO PAY INSURANCE AFTER UNNATURAL DEATHS
• THE UNNATURAL TRANSLATIONS OF JOKES IN SUBTITLED FOREIGN MOVIES
• OSAKANS HAVE NO TOLERANCE OF TOKYOITES' UNNATURAL KANSAI DIALECT
• UNNATURAL ANIME ADAPTATIONS (THE LAST GLORIOUS PATH?)
I'M IN DESPAIR OVER OUR SOCIETY THAT IS SO CRUEL TO UNNATURAL THINGS!
WHY THAT'S NOT TRUE AT ALL. IN JAPAN...
...NATIONAL AND LOCAL GOVERNMENTS COOPERATE WITH BUSINESSES...
...TO PROTECT TONS OF UNNATURAL THINGS, WITH GREAT PASSION!
THE UNNATURAL FLOW OF POLITICAL FUNDS...
DISCLOSURE
...IS PROTECTED THROUGH THE NATIONAL CIVIL SERVICE ACT!
UNNATURAL PUBLIC BUILDING PROJECTS...
GOSHIKAN
..ARE PROTECTED BY LOCAL ADMINISTRATION!
UNNATURAL DECISIONS...
LIVE
...ARE HELD UP BY TELEVISION TATIONS!

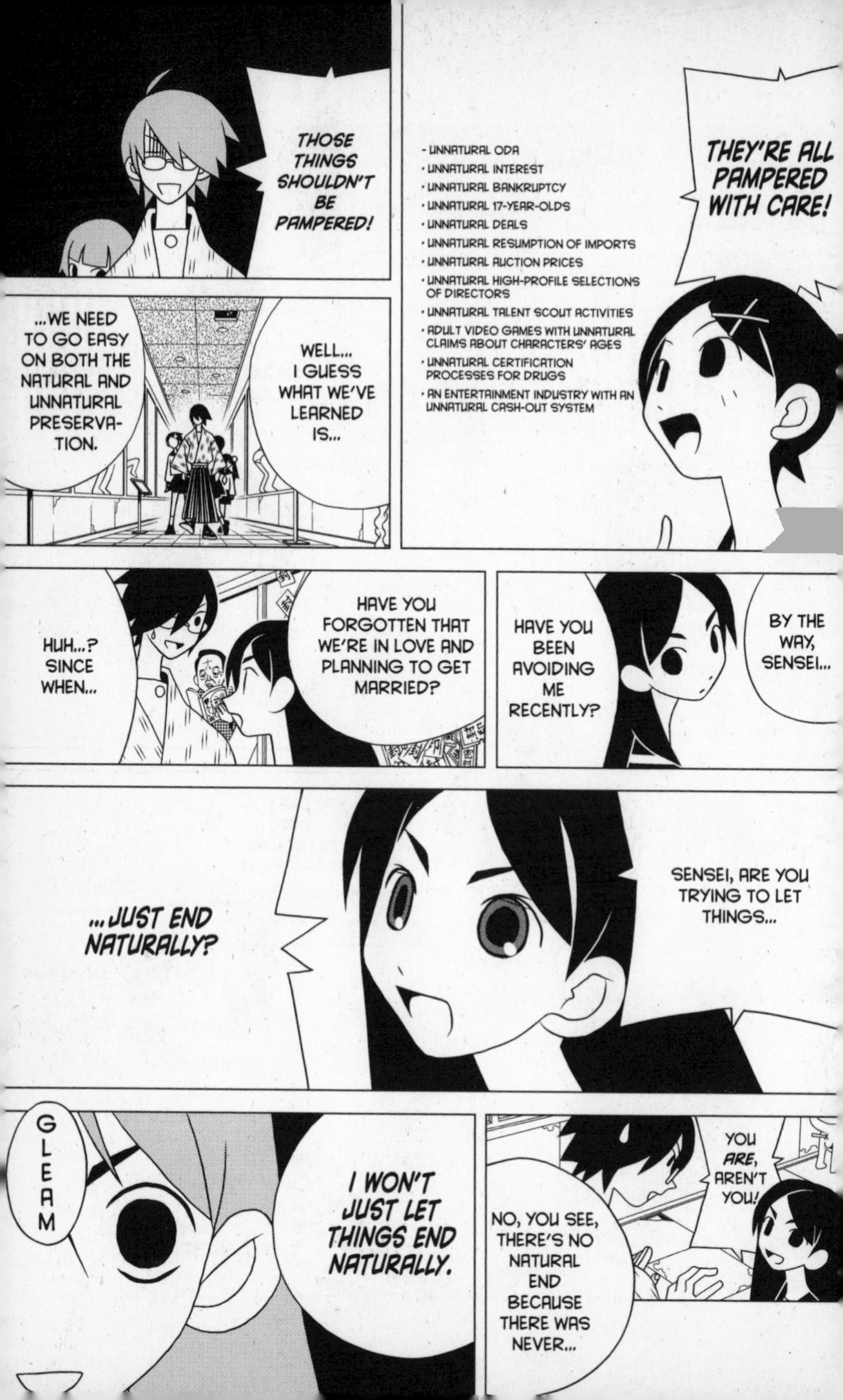
THEY'RE ALL PAMPERED WITH CARE!
- UNNATURAL ODA
- UNNATURAL INTEREST
- UNNATURAL BANKRUPTCY
- UNNATURAL 17-YEAR-OLDS
- UNNATURAL DEALS
- UNNATURAL RESUMPTION OF IMPORTS
- UNNATURAL AUCTION PRICES
- UNNATURAL HIGH-PROFILE SELECTIONS OF DIRECTORS
- UNNATURAL TALENT SCOUT ACTIVITIES
- ADULT VIDEO GAMES WITH UNNATURAL CLAIMS ABOUT CHARACTERS' AGES
- UNNATURAL CERTIFICATION PROCESSES FOR DRUGS
- AN ENTERTAINMENT INDUSTRY WITH AN UNNATURAL CASH-OUT SYSTEM
THOSE THINGS SHOULDN'T BE PAMPERED!
WELL... I GUESS WHAT WE'VE LEARNED IS...
...WE NEED TO GO EASY ON BOTH THE NATURAL AND UNNATURAL PRESERVATION.
BY THE WAY, SENSEI...
HAVE YOU BEEN AVOIDING ME RECENTLY?
HAVE YOU FORGOTTEN THAT WE'RE IN LOVE AND PLANNING TO GET MARRIED?
HUH...? SINCE WHEN...
SENSEI, ARE YOU TRYING TO LET THINGS...
...JUST END NATURALLY?
YOU ARE, AREN'T YOU!
NO, YOU SEE, THERE'S NO NATURAL END BECAUSE THERE WAS NEVER...
I WON'T JUST LET THINGS END NATURALLY.
GLEAM

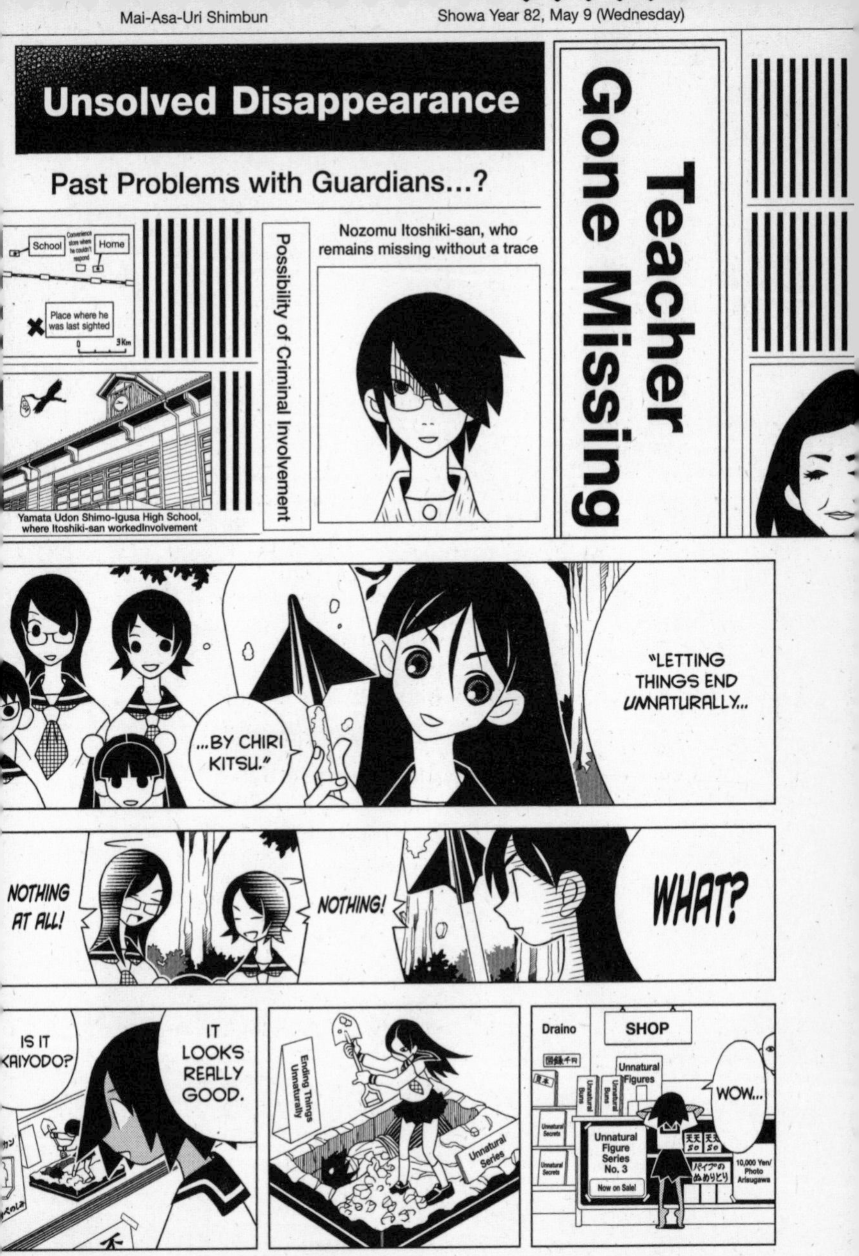
Mai-Asa-Uri Shimbun
Showa Year 82, May 9 (Wednesday)
Teacher Gone Missing
Unsolved Disappearance
Past Problems with Guardians...?
Nozomu Itoshiki-san, who remains missing without a trace
Possibility of Criminal Involvement
Home
School
Place where he was last sighted
0 3Km
Yamata Udon Shimo-Igusa High School, where Itoshiki-san workedInvolvement
"LETTING THINGS END UNNATURALLY...
...BY CHIRI KITSU."
WHAT?
NOTHING!
NOTHING AT ALL!
SHOP
Draino
Unnatural Figures
Unnatural Buns
Unnatural Secrets
Unnatural Figure Series No. 3
Now on Sale!
パイプの ぬめりとり
10,000 Yen/ Photo Arisugawa
WOW...
Ending Things Unnaturally
Unnatural Series
IT LOOKS REALLY GOOD.
IS IT KAIYODO?

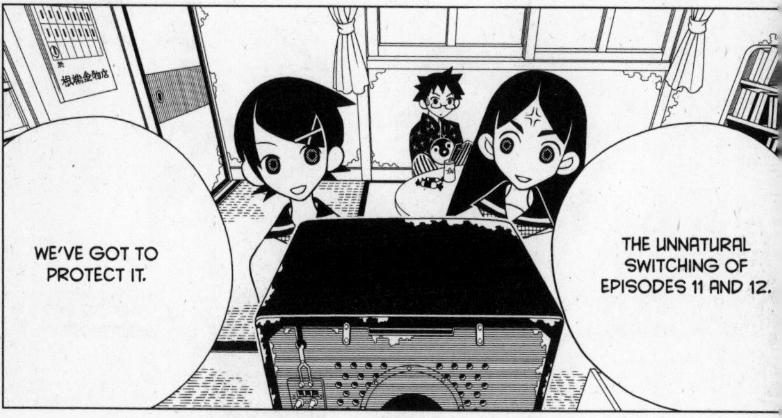
THE UNNATURAL SWITCHING OF EPISODES 11 AND 12.
WE'VE GOT TO PROTECT IT.

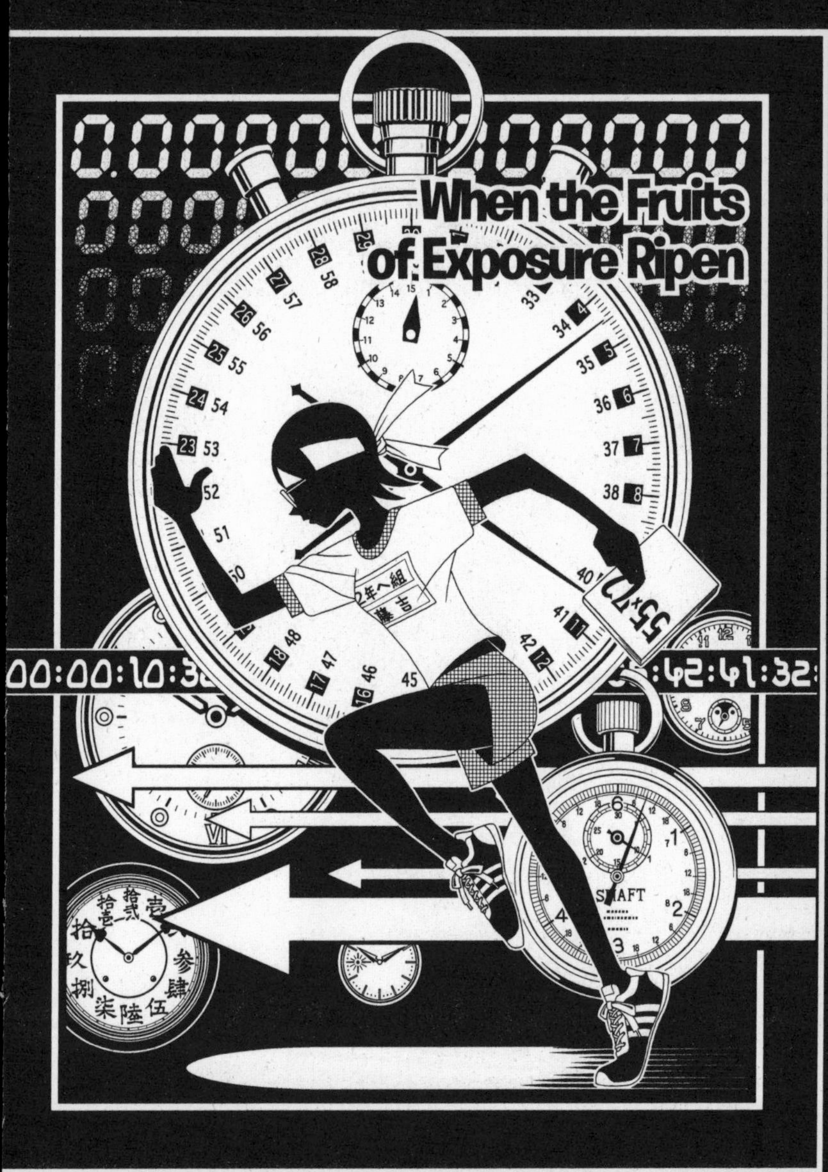
When the Fruits of Exposure Ripen
2年へ組
藤吉
SHAFT

CHAPTER 94

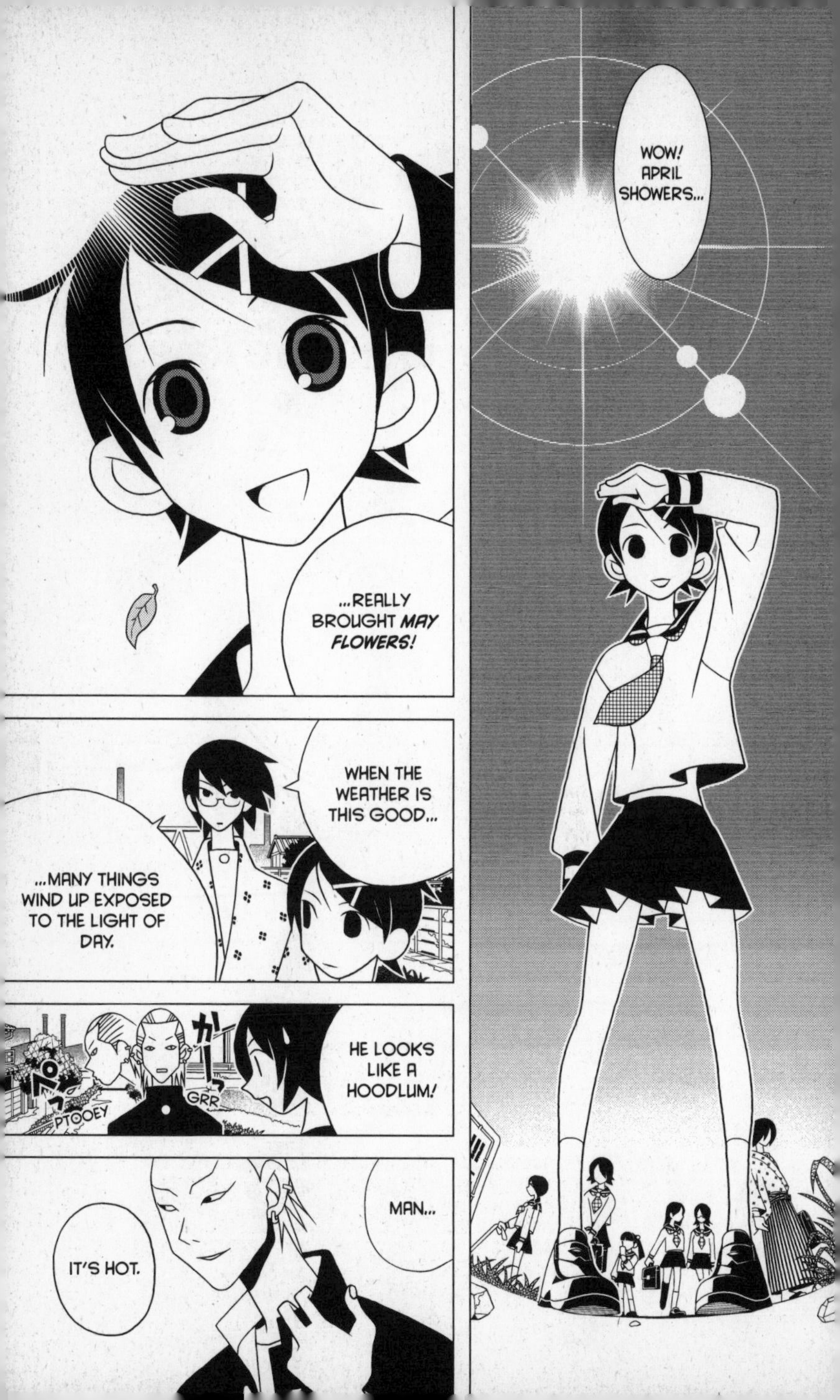
WOW! APRIL SHOWERS...
...REALLY BROUGHT MAY FLOWERS!
WHEN THE WEATHER IS THIS GOOD...
...MANY THINGS WIND UP EXPOSED TO THE LIGHT OF DAY.
HE LOOKS LIKE A HOODLUM!
GRR
PTOOEY
MAN...
IT'S HOT.

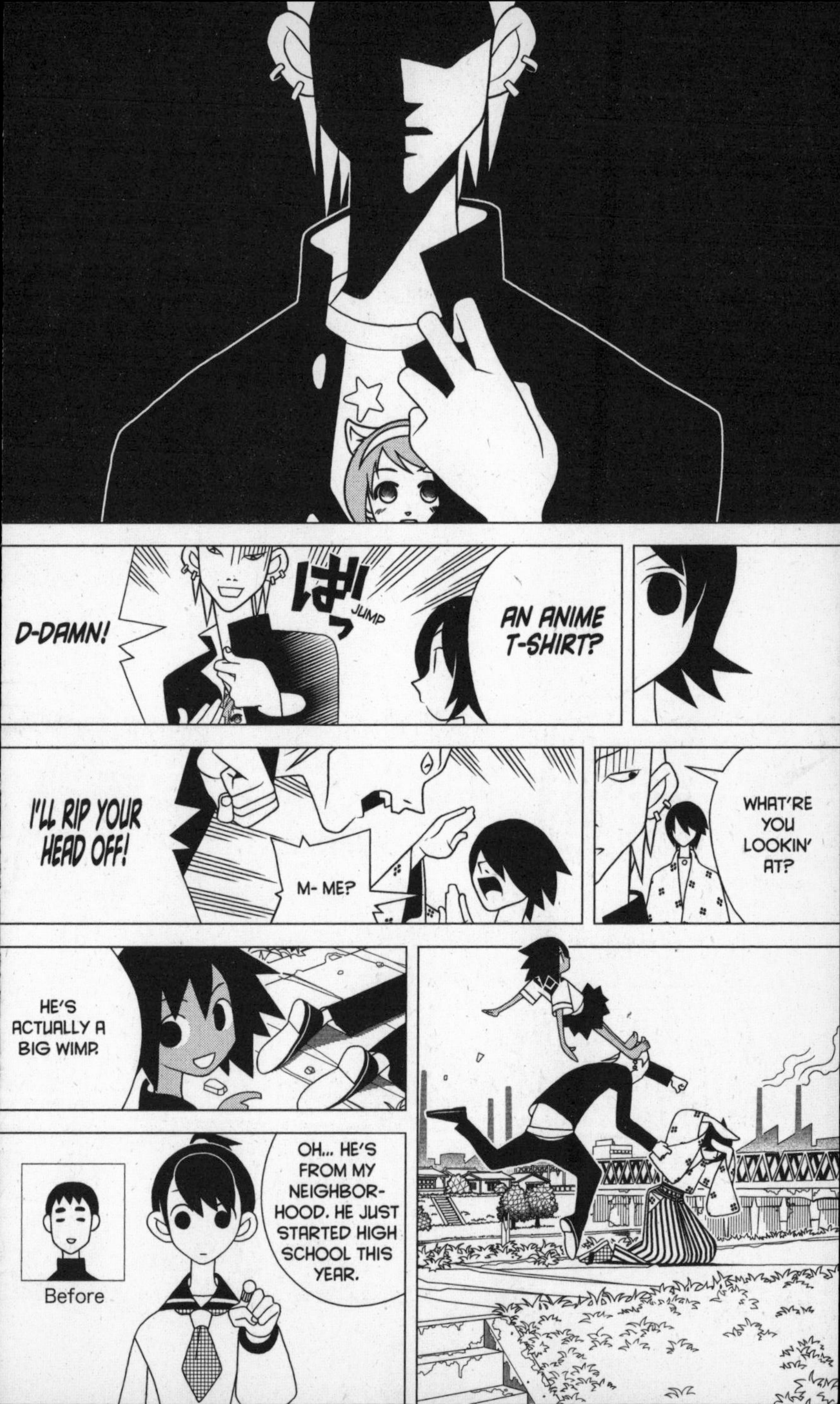
AN ANIME T-SHIRT?
ぱっ
JUMP
D-DAMN!
WHAT'RE YOU LOOKIN' AT?
I'LL RIP YOUR HEAD OFF!
M- ME?
HE'S ACTUALLY A BIG WIMP.
OH... HE'S FROM MY NEIGHBOR-HOOD. HE JUST STARTED HIGH SCHOOL THIS YEAR.
Before

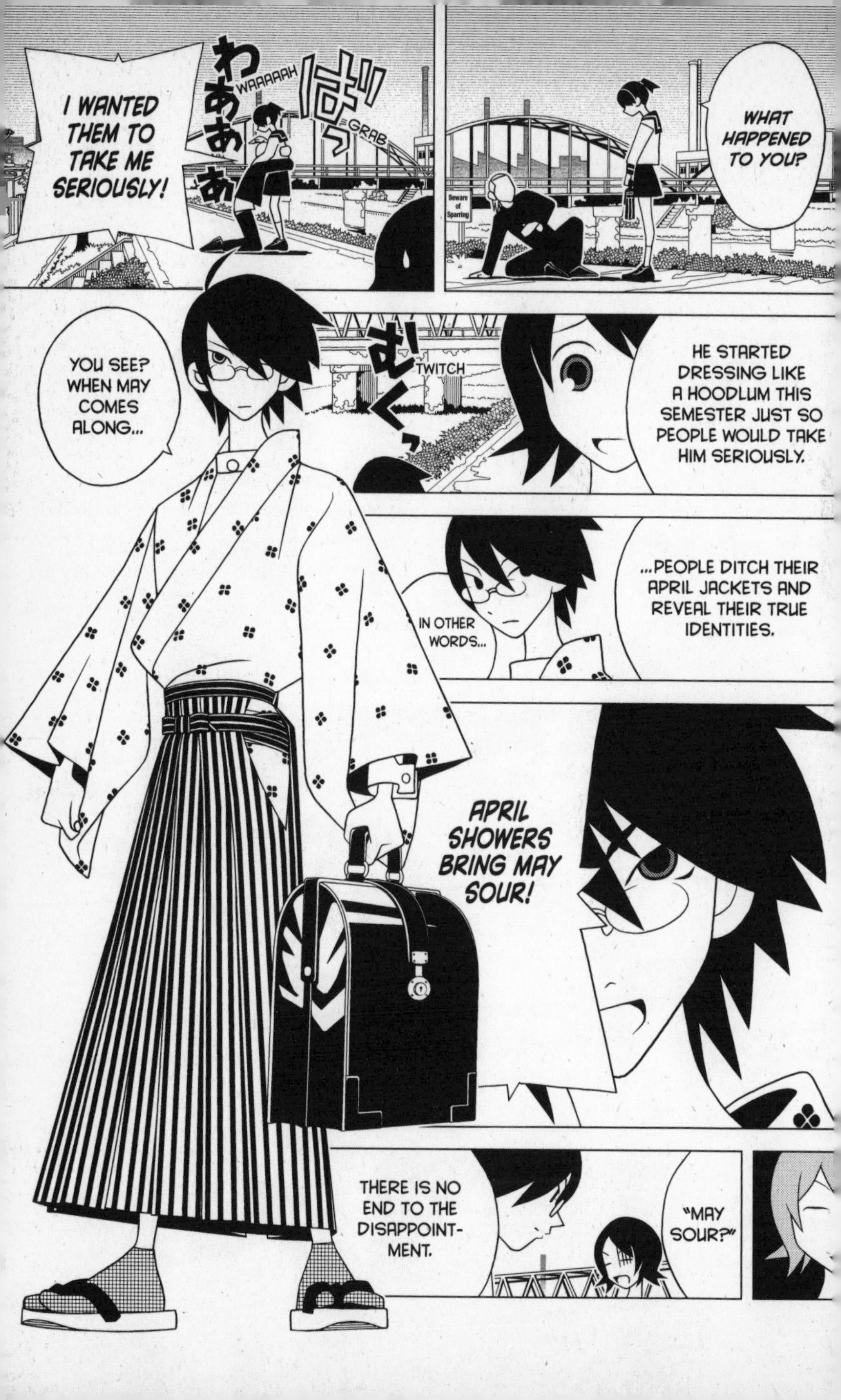
WHAT HAPPENED TO YOU?
Beware of Sparring
ばっ GRAB
わあああ WAAAAAH
I WANTED THEM TO TAKE ME SERIOUSLY!
HE STARTED DRESSING LIKE A HOODLUM THIS SEMESTER JUST SO PEOPLE WOULD TAKE HIM SERIOUSLY.
むくっ TWITCH
YOU SEE? WHEN MAY COMES ALONG...
...PEOPLE DITCH THEIR APRIL JACKETS AND REVEAL THEIR TRUE IDENTITIES.
IN OTHER WORDS...
APRIL SHOWERS BRING MAY SOUR!
"MAY SOUR?"
THERE IS NO END TO THE DISAPPOINT-MENT.

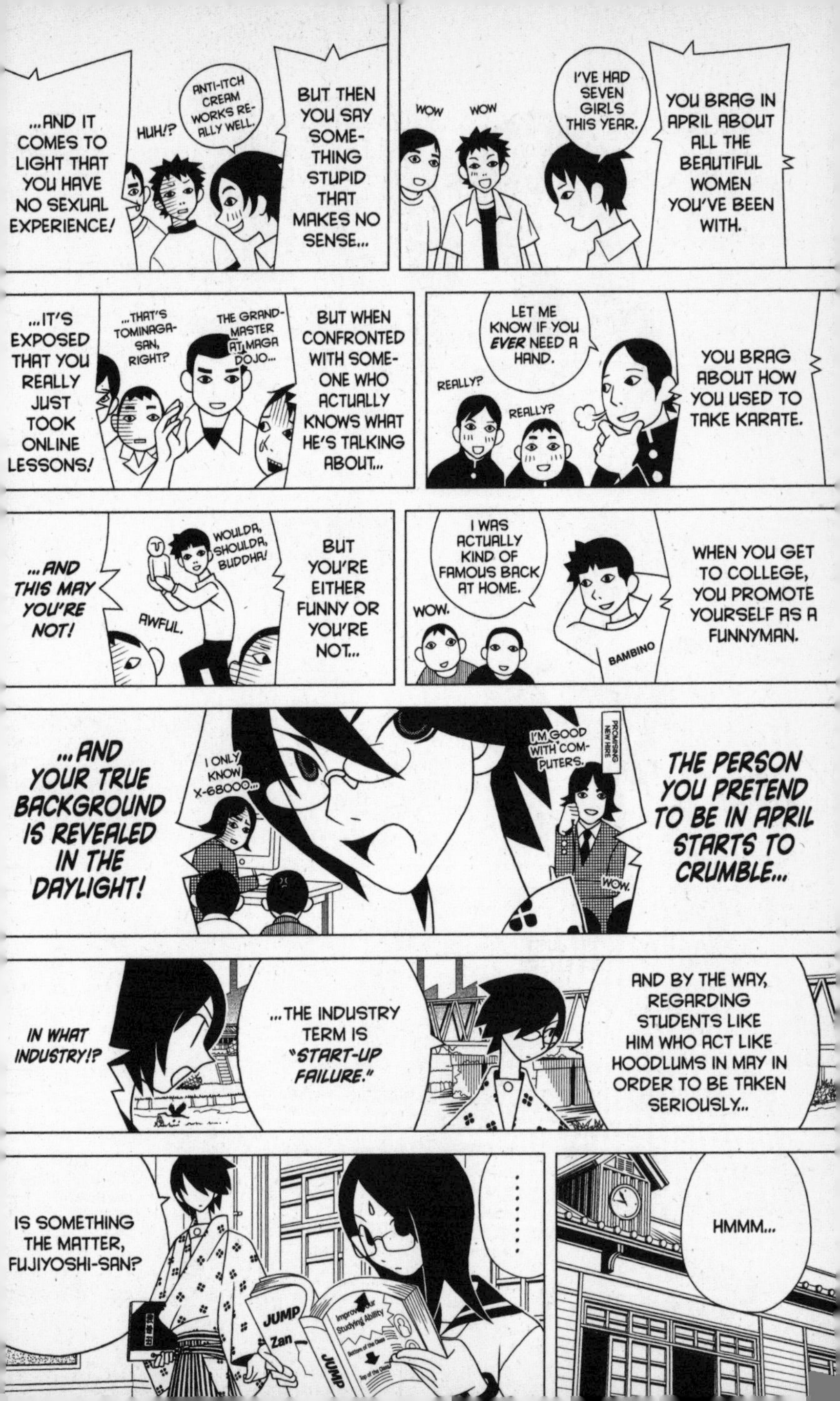
YOU BRAG IN APRIL ABOUT ALL THE BEAUTIFUL WOMEN YOU'VE BEEN WITH.
I'VE HAD SEVEN GIRLS THIS YEAR.
WOW
WOW
BUT THEN YOU SAY SOMETHING STUPID THAT MAKES NO SENSE...
ANTI-ITCH CREAM WORKS REALLY WELL.
HUH!?
...AND IT COMES TO LIGHT THAT YOU HAVE NO SEXUAL EXPERIENCE!
YOU BRAG ABOUT HOW YOU USED TO TAKE KARATE.
LET ME KNOW IF YOU *EVER* NEED A HAND.
REALLY?
REALLY?
BUT WHEN CONFRONTED WITH SOMEONE WHO ACTUALLY KNOWS WHAT HE'S TALKING ABOUT...
THE GRANDMASTER AT MAGA DOJO...
...THAT'S TOMINAGA-SAN, RIGHT?
...IT'S EXPOSED THAT YOU REALLY JUST TOOK ONLINE LESSONS!
WHEN YOU GET TO COLLEGE, YOU PROMOTE YOURSELF AS A FUNNYMAN.
BAMBINO
I WAS ACTUALLY KIND OF FAMOUS BACK AT HOME.
WOW.
BUT YOU'RE EITHER FUNNY OR YOU'RE NOT...
WOULDA, SHOULDA, BUDDHA!
AWFUL.
...AND THIS MAY YOU'RE NOT!
THE PERSON YOU PRETEND TO BE IN APRIL STARTS TO CRUMBLE...
PROMISING NEW HIRE
I'M GOOD WITH COMPUTERS.
WOW.
I ONLY KNOW X-68000...
...AND YOUR TRUE BACKGROUND IS REVEALED IN THE DAYLIGHT!
AND BY THE WAY, REGARDING STUDENTS LIKE HIM WHO ACT LIKE HOODLUMS IN MAY IN ORDER TO BE TAKEN SERIOUSLY...
...THE INDUSTRY TERM IS "START-UP FAILURE."
IN WHAT INDUSTRY!?
HMMM...
......
IS SOMETHING THE MATTER, FUJIYOSHI-SAN?
JUMP
Zan
Studying Ability
Bottom of the Class
Top of the Class
JUMP

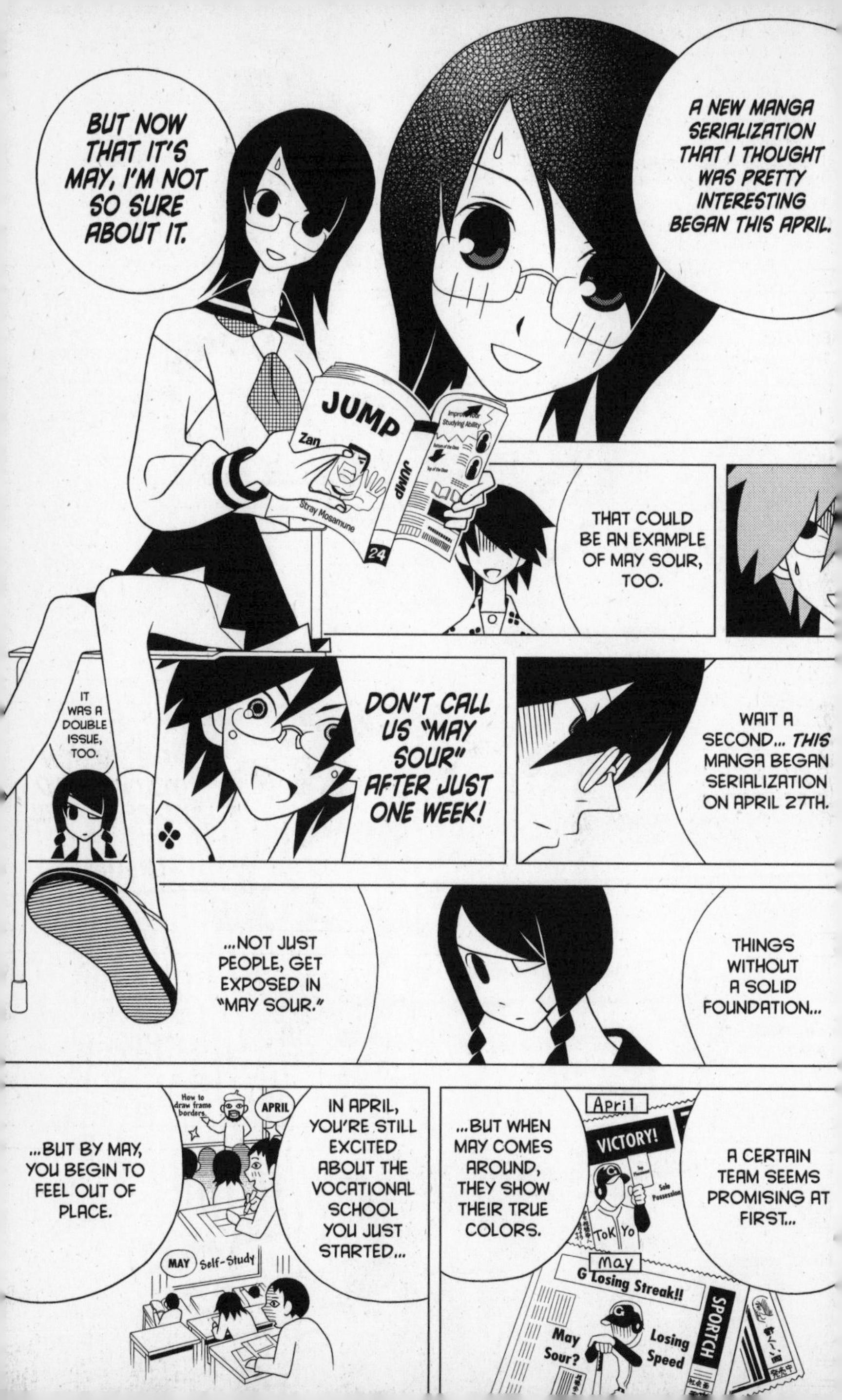
A NEW MANGA SERIALIZATION THAT I THOUGHT WAS PRETTY INTERESTING BEGAN THIS APRIL.
BUT NOW THAT IT'S MAY, I'M NOT SO SURE ABOUT IT.
JUMP
Zan
Stray Mosamune
24
THAT COULD BE AN EXAMPLE OF MAY SOUR, TOO.
WAIT A SECOND... THIS MANGA BEGAN SERIALIZATION ON APRIL 27TH.
DON'T CALL US "MAY SOUR" AFTER JUST ONE WEEK!
IT WAS A DOUBLE ISSUE, TOO.
THINGS WITHOUT A SOLID FOUNDATION...
...NOT JUST PEOPLE, GET EXPOSED IN "MAY SOUR."
A CERTAIN TEAM SEEMS PROMISING AT FIRST...
April
VICTORY!
Sole Possession
TOKYO
...BUT WHEN MAY COMES AROUND, THEY SHOW THEIR TRUE COLORS.
May
G Losing Streak!!
SPORTCH
May Sour?
Losing Speed
IN APRIL, YOU'RE STILL EXCITED ABOUT THE VOCATIONAL SCHOOL YOU JUST STARTED...
APRIL
How to draw frame borders
...BUT BY MAY, YOU BEGIN TO FEEL OUT OF PLACE.
MAY
Self-Study

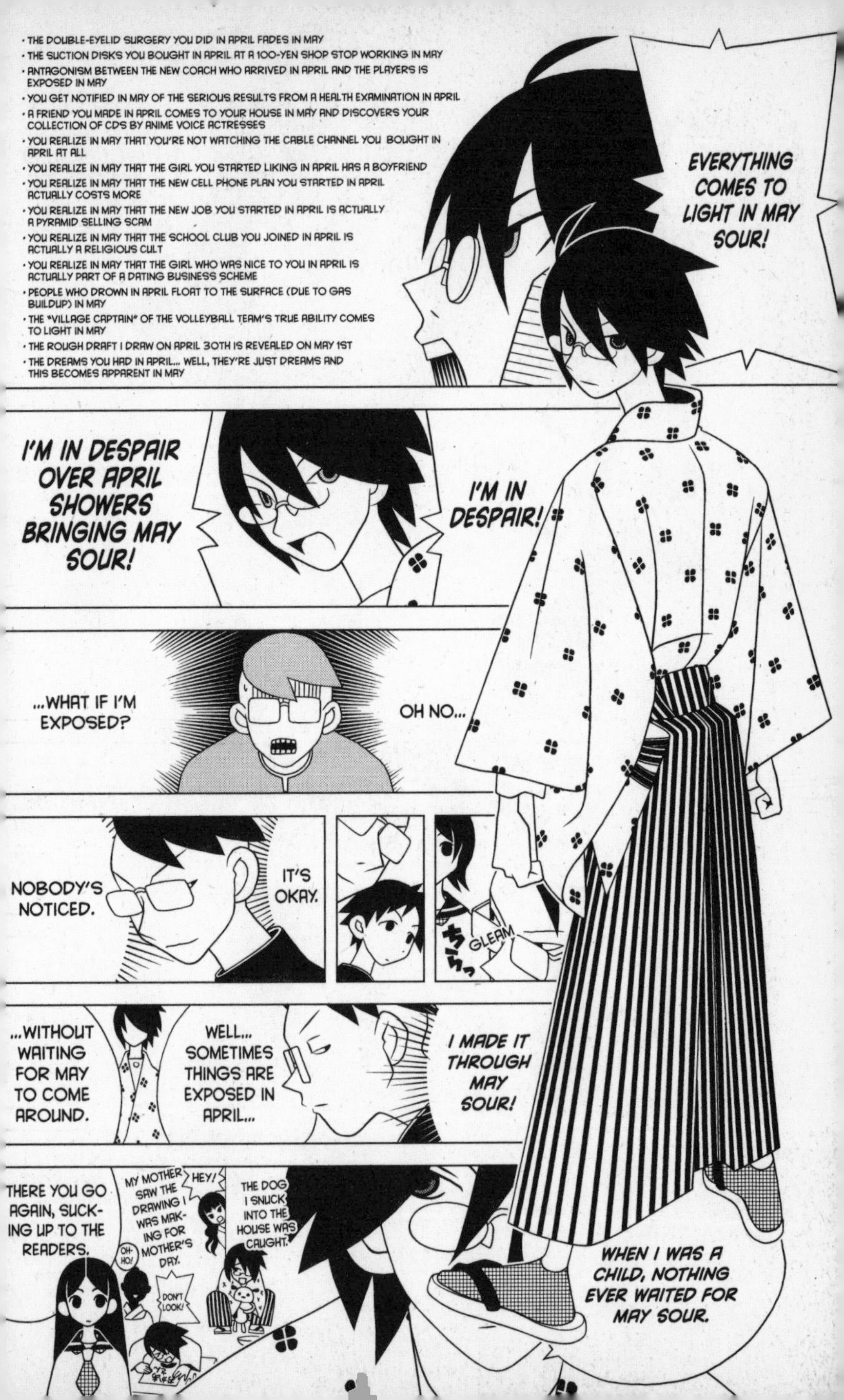
EVERYTHING COMES TO LIGHT IN MAY SOUR!
• THE DOUBLE-EYELID SURGERY YOU DID IN APRIL FADES IN MAY
• THE SUCTION DISKS YOU BOUGHT IN APRIL AT A 100-YEN SHOP STOP WORKING IN MAY
• ANTAGONISM BETWEEN THE NEW COACH WHO ARRIVED IN APRIL AND THE PLAYERS IS EXPOSED IN MAY
• YOU GET NOTIFIED IN MAY OF THE SERIOUS RESULTS FROM A HEALTH EXAMINATION IN APRIL
• A FRIEND YOU MADE IN APRIL COMES TO YOUR HOUSE IN MAY AND DISCOVERS YOUR COLLECTION OF CDS BY ANIME VOICE ACTRESSES
• YOU REALIZE IN MAY THAT YOU'RE NOT WATCHING THE CABLE CHANNEL YOU BOUGHT IN APRIL AT ALL
• YOU REALIZE IN MAY THAT THE GIRL YOU STARTED LIKING IN APRIL HAS A BOYFRIEND
• YOU REALIZE IN MAY THAT THE NEW CELL PHONE PLAN YOU STARTED IN APRIL ACTUALLY COSTS MORE
• YOU REALIZE IN MAY THAT THE NEW JOB YOU STARTED IN APRIL IS ACTUALLY A PYRAMID SELLING SCAM
• YOU REALIZE IN MAY THAT THE SCHOOL CLUB YOU JOINED IN APRIL IS ACTUALLY A RELIGIOUS CULT
• YOU REALIZE IN MAY THAT THE GIRL WHO WAS NICE TO YOU IN APRIL IS ACTUALLY PART OF A DATING BUSINESS SCHEME
• PEOPLE WHO DROWN IN APRIL FLOAT TO THE SURFACE (DUE TO GAS BUILDUP) IN MAY
• THE "VILLAGE CAPTAIN" OF THE VOLLEYBALL TEAM'S TRUE ABILITY COMES TO LIGHT IN MAY
• THE ROUGH DRAFT I DRAW ON APRIL 30TH IS REVEALED ON MAY 1ST
• THE DREAMS YOU HAD IN APRIL... WELL, THEY'RE JUST DREAMS AND THIS BECOMES APPARENT IN MAY
I'M IN DESPAIR!
I'M IN DESPAIR OVER APRIL SHOWERS BRINGING MAY SOUR!
OH NO...
...WHAT IF I'M EXPOSED?
GLEAM
IT'S OKAY.
NOBODY'S NOTICED.
I MADE IT THROUGH MAY SOUR!
WELL... SOMETIMES THINGS ARE EXPOSED IN APRIL...
...WITHOUT WAITING FOR MAY TO COME AROUND.
WHEN I WAS A CHILD, NOTHING EVER WAITED FOR MAY SOUR.
THE DOG I SNUCK INTO THE HOUSE WAS CAUGHT.
HEY!
MY MOTHER SAW THE DRAWING I WAS MAKING FOR MOTHER'S DAY.
DON'T LOOK!
OH-HO!
THERE YOU GO AGAIN, SUCKING UP TO THE READERS.

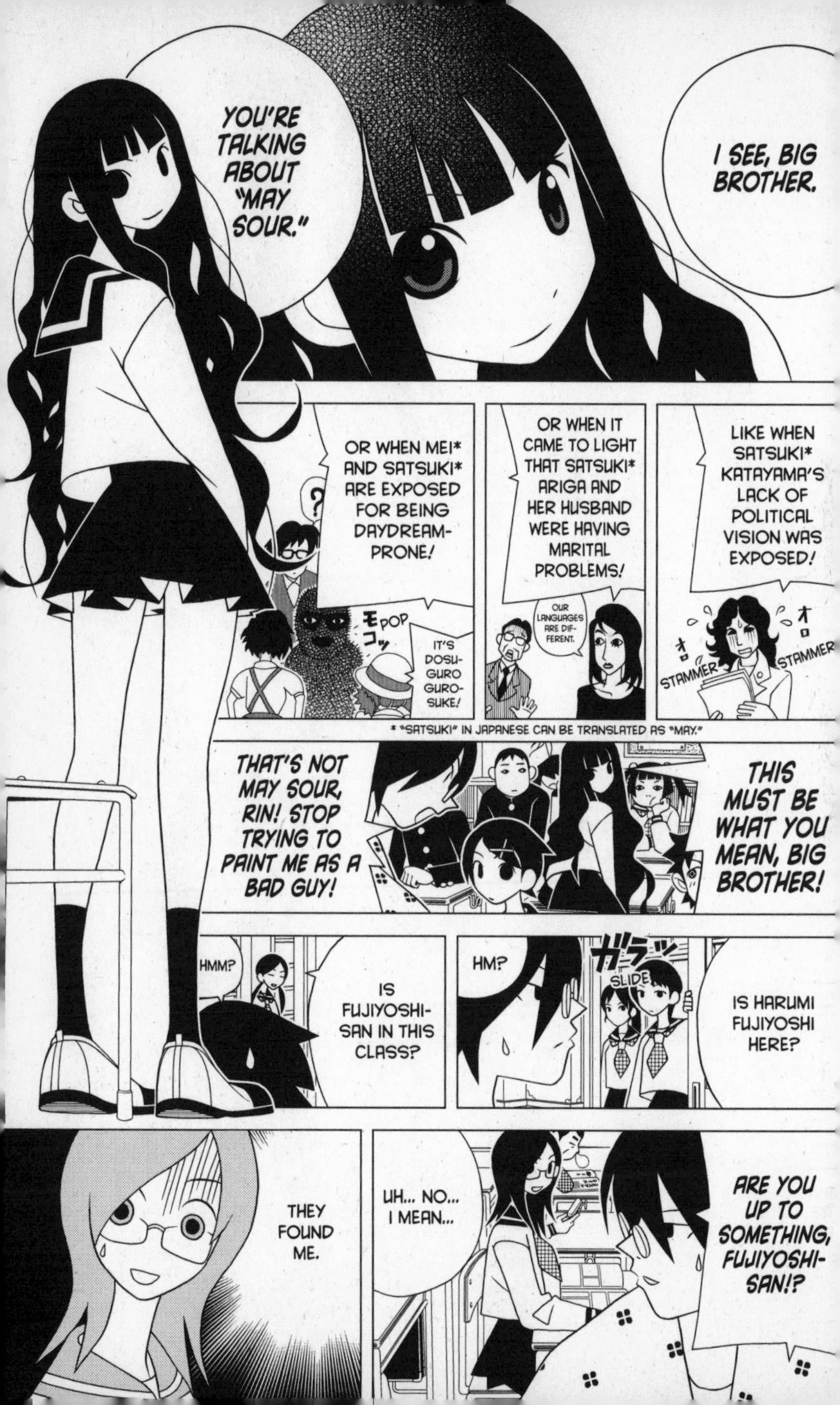
I SEE, BIG BROTHER.
YOU'RE TALKING ABOUT "MAY SOUR."
LIKE WHEN SATSUKI* KATAYAMA'S LACK OF POLITICAL VISION WAS EXPOSED!
STAMMER
STAMMER
OR WHEN IT CAME TO LIGHT THAT SATSUKI* ARIGA AND HER HUSBAND WERE HAVING MARITAL PROBLEMS!
OUR LANGUAGES ARE DIFFERENT.
OR WHEN MEI* AND SATSUKI* ARE EXPOSED FOR BEING DAYDREAM-PRONE!
?
POP
IT'S DOSUGURO GUROSUKE!
* "SATSUKI" IN JAPANESE CAN BE TRANSLATED AS "MAY."
THIS MUST BE WHAT YOU MEAN, BIG BROTHER!
THAT'S NOT MAY SOUR, RIN! STOP TRYING TO PAINT ME AS A BAD GUY!
IS HARUMI FUJIYOSHI HERE?
SLIDE
HM?
IS FUJIYOSHI-SAN IN THIS CLASS?
HMM?
ARE YOU UP TO SOMETHING, FUJIYOSHI-SAN!?
UH... NO... I MEAN...
THEY FOUND ME.

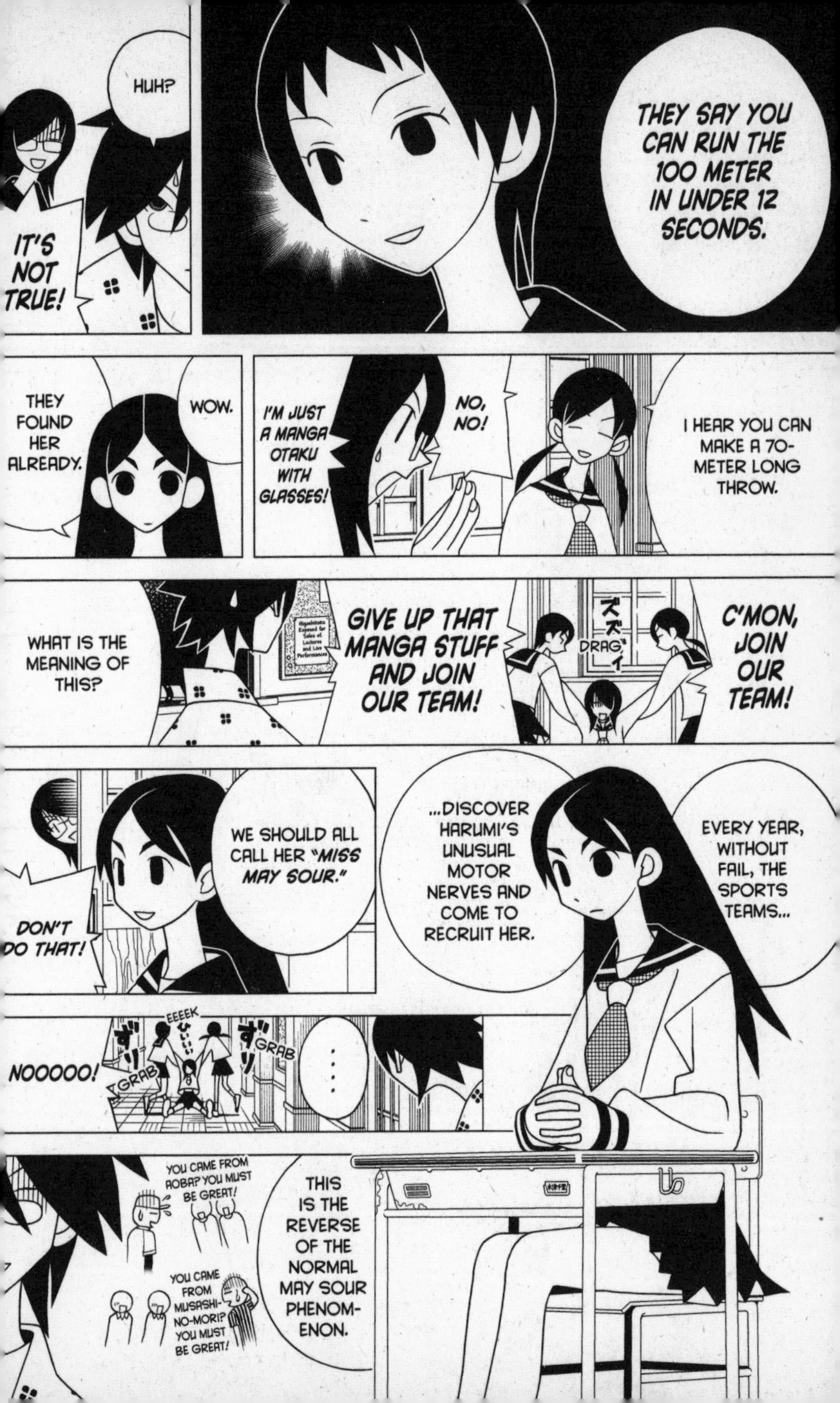
THEY SAY YOU CAN RUN THE 100 METER IN UNDER 12 SECONDS.
HUH?
IT'S NOT TRUE!
I HEAR YOU CAN MAKE A 70-METER LONG THROW.
NO, NO!
I'M JUST A MANGA OTAKU WITH GLASSES!
WOW.
THEY FOUND HER ALREADY.
C'MON, JOIN OUR TEAM!
ズズイ
DRAG
GIVE UP THAT MANGA STUFF AND JOIN OUR TEAM!
WHAT IS THE MEANING OF THIS?
EVERY YEAR, WITHOUT FAIL, THE SPORTS TEAMS...
...DISCOVER HARUMI'S UNUSUAL MOTOR NERVES AND COME TO RECRUIT HER.
WE SHOULD ALL CALL HER "MISS MAY SOUR."
DON'T DO THAT!
.....
ずり
GRAB
EEEEK
ひぃぃぃ
ずり
GRAB
NOOOOO!
THIS IS THE REVERSE OF THE NORMAL MAY SOUR PHENOM-ENON.
YOU CAME FROM AOBA? YOU MUST BE GREAT!
YOU CAME FROM MUSASHI-NO-MORI? YOU MUST BE GREAT!

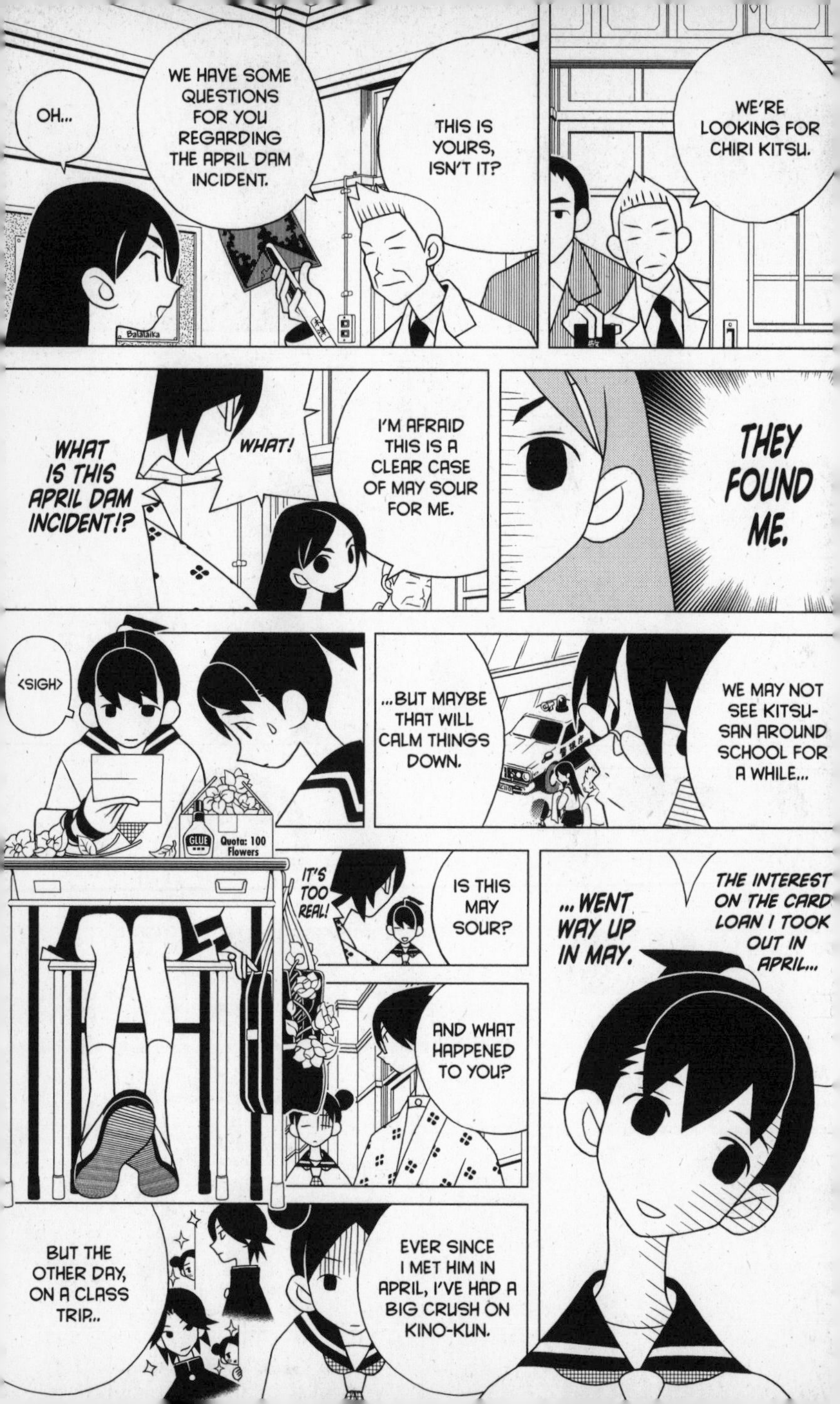
WE'RE LOOKING FOR CHIRI KITSU.
THIS IS YOURS, ISN'T IT?
WE HAVE SOME QUESTIONS FOR YOU REGARDING THE APRIL DAM INCIDENT.
OH...
Balalaika
THEY FOUND ME.
I'M AFRAID THIS IS A CLEAR CASE OF MAY SOUR FOR ME.
WHAT!
WHAT IS THIS APRIL DAM INCIDENT!?
WE MAY NOT SEE KITSU-SAN AROUND SCHOOL FOR A WHILE...
...BUT MAYBE THAT WILL CALM THINGS DOWN.
<SIGH>
GLUE
Quota: 100 Flowers
IS THIS MAY SOUR?
IT'S TOO REAL!
AND WHAT HAPPENED TO YOU?
THE INTEREST ON THE CARD LOAN I TOOK OUT IN APRIL...
...WENT WAY UP IN MAY.
EVER SINCE I MET HIM IN APRIL, I'VE HAD A BIG CRUSH ON KINO-KUN.
BUT THE OTHER DAY, ON A CLASS TRIP..

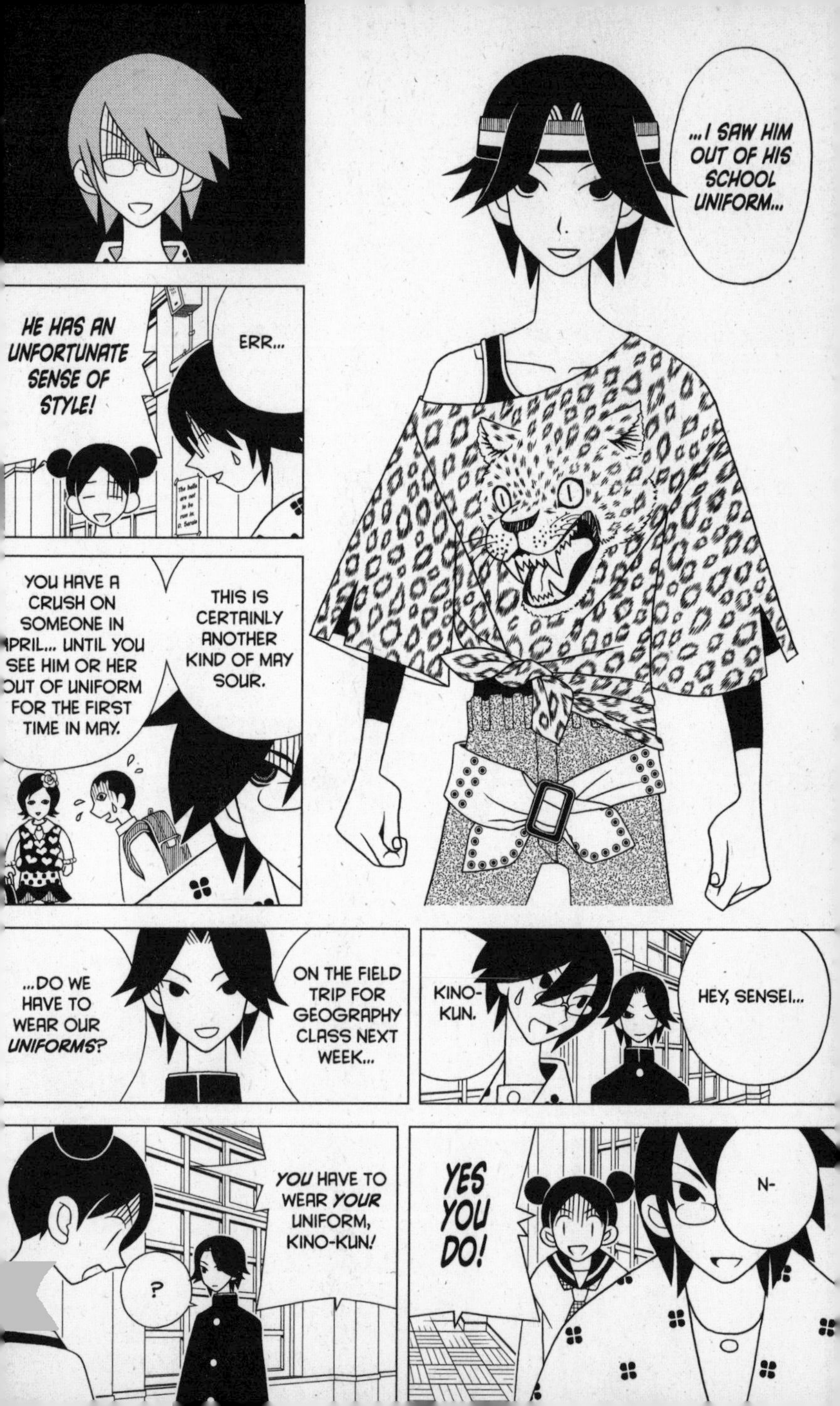

...I SAW HIM OUT OF HIS SCHOOL UNIFORM...
ERR...
HE HAS AN UNFORTUNATE SENSE OF STYLE!
THIS IS CERTAINLY ANOTHER KIND OF MAY SOUR.
YOU HAVE A CRUSH ON SOMEONE IN APRIL... UNTIL YOU SEE HIM OR HER OUT OF UNIFORM FOR THE FIRST TIME IN MAY.
HEY, SENSEI...
KINO-KUN.
ON THE FIELD TRIP FOR GEOGRAPHY CLASS NEXT WEEK...
...DO WE HAVE TO WEAR OUR UNIFORMS?
N-
YES YOU DO!
YOU HAVE TO WEAR YOUR UNIFORM, KINO-KUN!
?

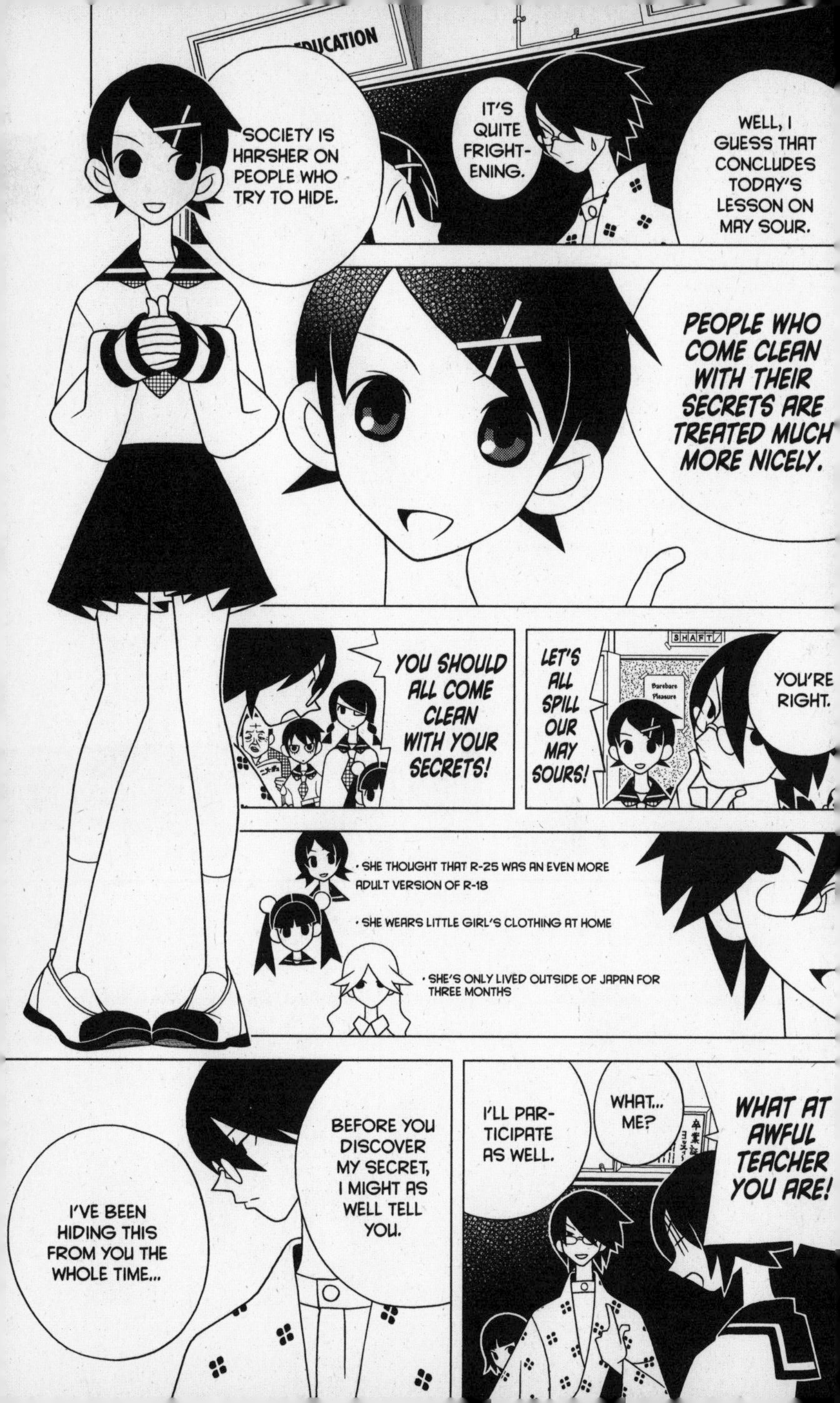

WELL, I GUESS THAT CONCLUDES TODAY'S LESSON ON MAY SOUR.
IT'S QUITE FRIGHT- ENING.
PEOPLE WHO COME CLEAN WITH THEIR SECRETS ARE TREATED MUCH MORE NICELY.
YOU'RE RIGHT.
LET'S ALL SPILL OUR MAY SOURS!
YOU SHOULD ALL COME CLEAN WITH YOUR SECRETS!
· SHE THOUGHT THAT R-25 WAS AN EVEN MORE ADULT VERSION OF R-18
· SHE WEARS LITTLE GIRL'S CLOTHING AT HOME
· SHE'S ONLY LIVED OUTSIDE OF JAPAN FOR THREE MONTHS
SOCIETY IS HARSHER ON PEOPLE WHO TRY TO HIDE.
WHAT AT AWFUL TEACHER YOU ARE!
WHAT... ME?
I'LL PAR- TICIPATE AS WELL.
BEFORE YOU DISCOVER MY SECRET, I MIGHT AS WELL TELL YOU.
I'VE BEEN HIDING THIS FROM YOU THE WHOLE TIME...

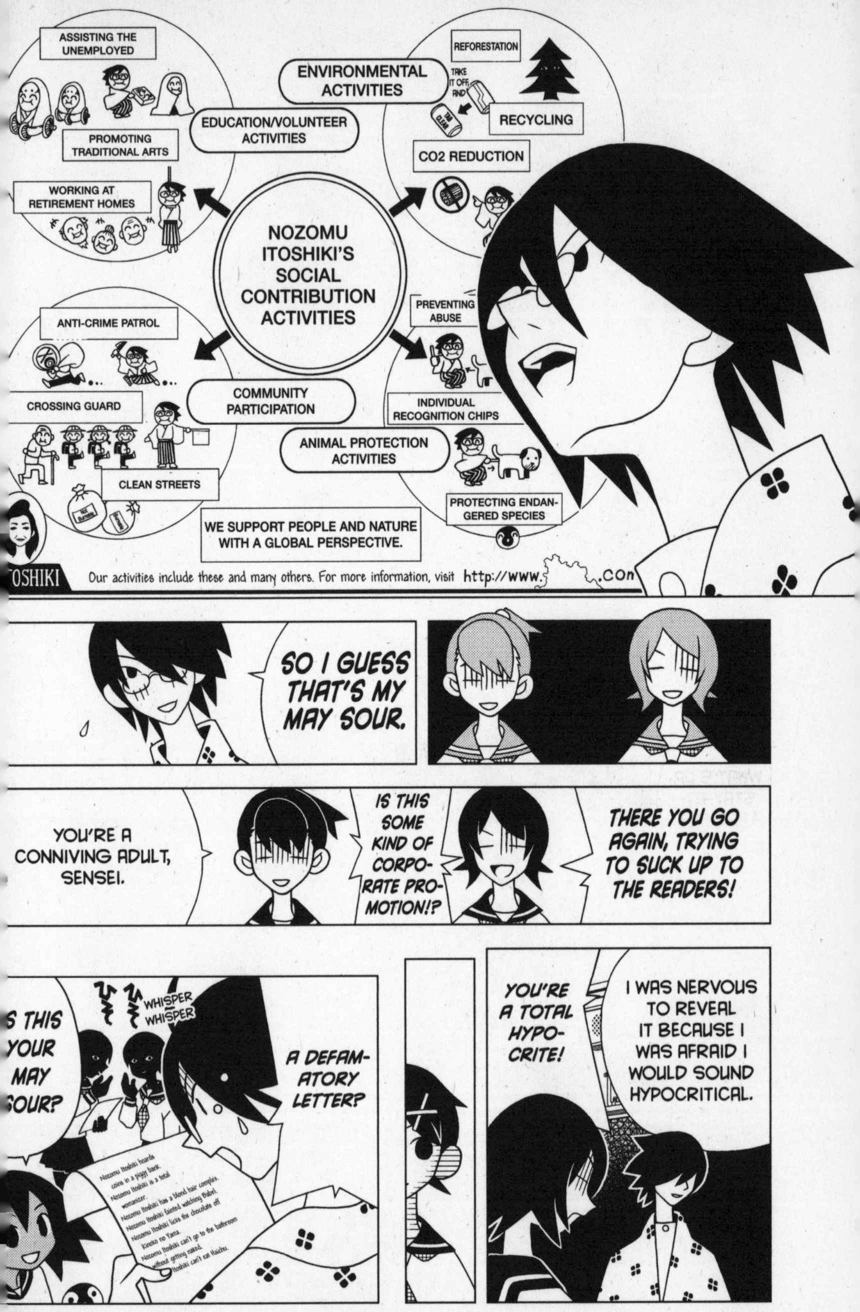
NOZOMU ITOSHIKI'S SOCIAL CONTRIBUTION ACTIVITIES
EDUCATION/VOLUNTEER ACTIVITIES
ASSISTING THE UNEMPLOYED
PROMOTING TRADITIONAL ARTS
WORKING AT RETIREMENT HOMES
ENVIRONMENTAL ACTIVITIES
REFORESTATION
TAKE IT OFF, AND
RECYCLING
CO2 REDUCTION
COMMUNITY PARTICIPATION
ANTI-CRIME PATROL
CROSSING GUARD
CLEAN STREETS
ANIMAL PROTECTION ACTIVITIES
PREVENTING ABUSE
INDIVIDUAL RECOGNITION CHIPS
PROTECTING ENDANGERED SPECIES
WE SUPPORT PEOPLE AND NATURE WITH A GLOBAL PERSPECTIVE.
TOSHIKI
Our activities include these and many others. For more information, visit http://www. .com
SO I GUESS THAT'S MY MAY SOUR.
THERE YOU GO AGAIN, TRYING TO SUCK UP TO THE READERS!
IS THIS SOME KIND OF CORPORATE PROMOTION!?
YOU'RE A CONNIVING ADULT, SENSEI.
I WAS NERVOUS TO REVEAL IT BECAUSE I WAS AFRAID I WOULD SOUND HYPOCRITICAL.
YOU'RE A TOTAL HYPOCRITE!
A DEFAMATORY LETTER?
WHISPER WHISPER
S THIS YOUR MAY SOUR?
Nozomu Itoshiki hoards coins in a piggy bank.
Nozomu Itoshiki is a total womanizer.
Nozomu Itoshiki has a blond hair complex.
Nozomu Itoshiki fainted watching Babel.
Nozomu Itoshiki licks the chocolate off Kinoko no Yama.
Nozomu Itoshiki can't go to the bathroom without getting naked.
Itoshiki can't eat Haichu.

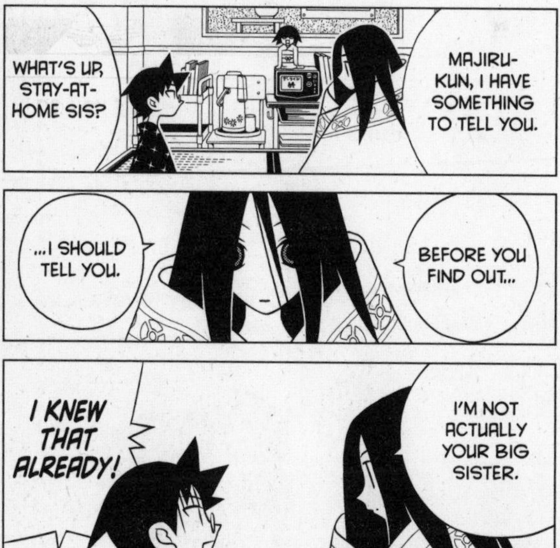
MAJIRU-KUN, I HAVE SOMETHING TO TELL YOU.
WHAT'S UP, STAY-AT-HOME SIS?
BEFORE YOU FIND OUT...
...I SHOULD TELL YOU.
I'M NOT ACTUALLY YOUR BIG SISTER.
I KNEW THAT ALREADY!

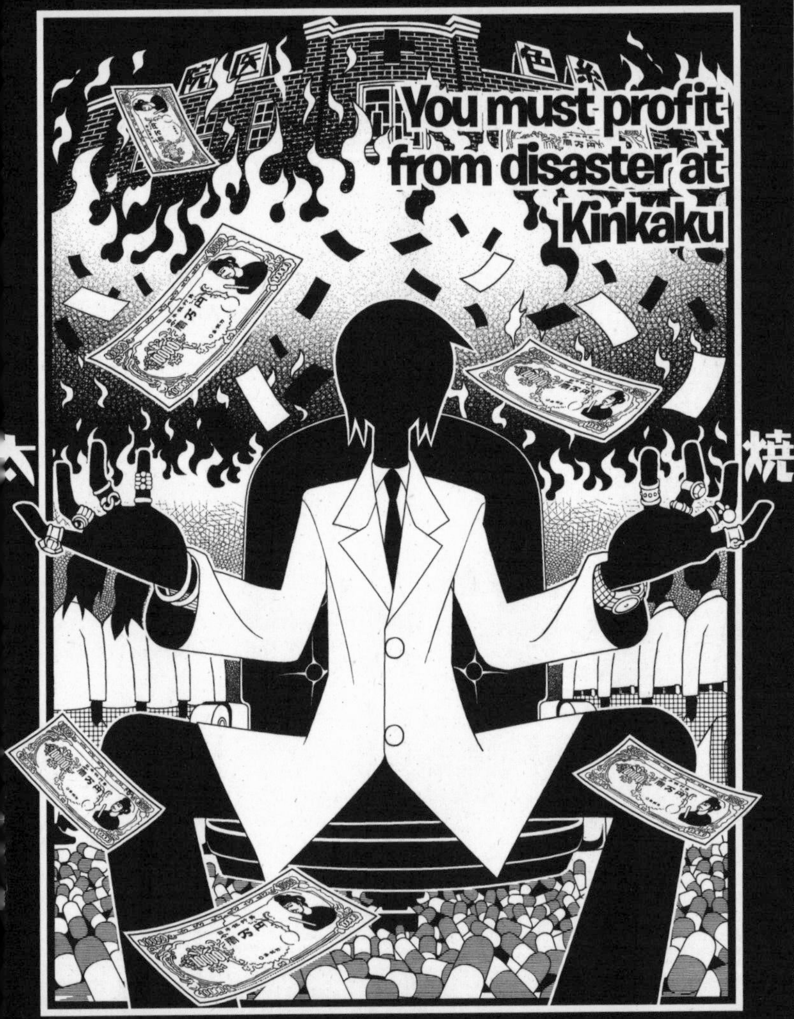
You must profit from disaster at Kinkaku

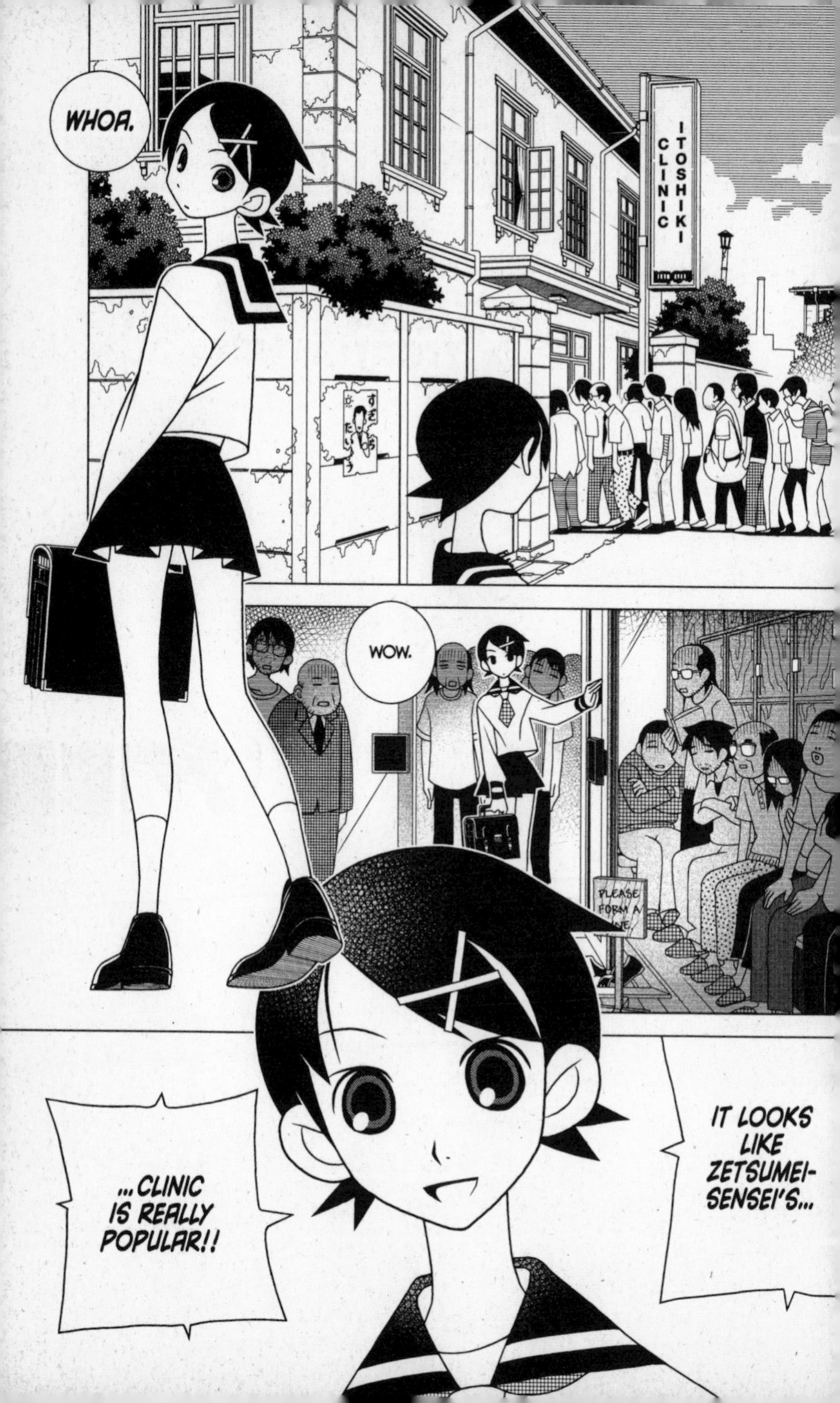
ITOSHIKI CLINIC
WOW.
PLEASE FORM A
WHOA.
IT LOOKS LIKE ZETSUMEI-SENSEI'S...
...CLINIC IS REALLY POPULAR!!

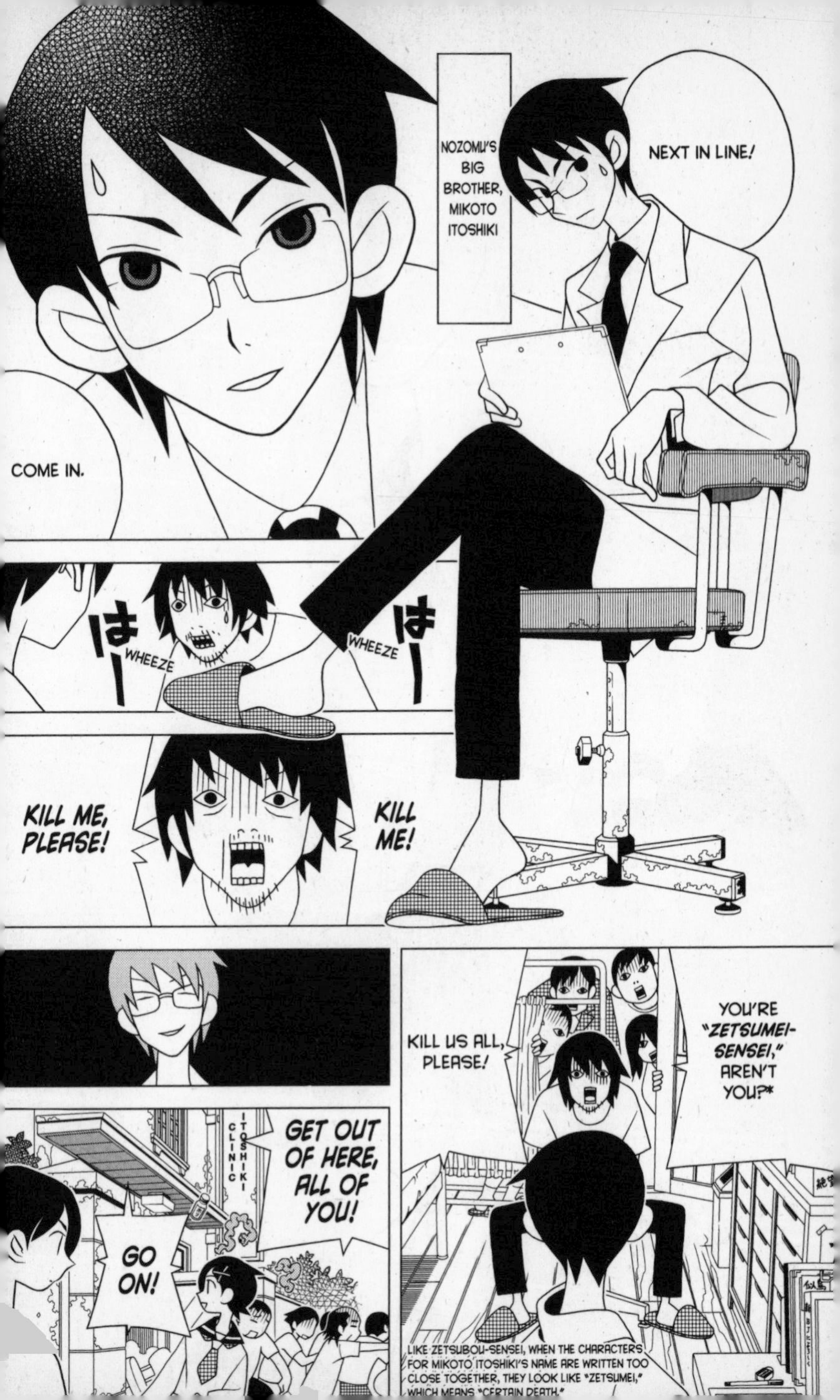
NEXT IN LINE!
NOZOMU'S BIG BROTHER, MIKOTO ITOSHIKI
COME IN.
はー WHEEZE
はー WHEEZE
KILL ME!
KILL ME, PLEASE!
YOU'RE "ZETSUMEI-SENSEI," AREN'T YOU?*
KILL US ALL, PLEASE!
LIKE ZETSUBOU-SENSEI, WHEN THE CHARACTERS FOR MIKOTO ITOSHIKI'S NAME ARE WRITTEN TOO CLOSE TOGETHER, THEY LOOK LIKE "ZETSUMEI," WHICH MEANS "CERTAIN DEATH."
ITOSHIKI CLINIC
GET OUT OF HERE, ALL OF YOU!
GO ON!

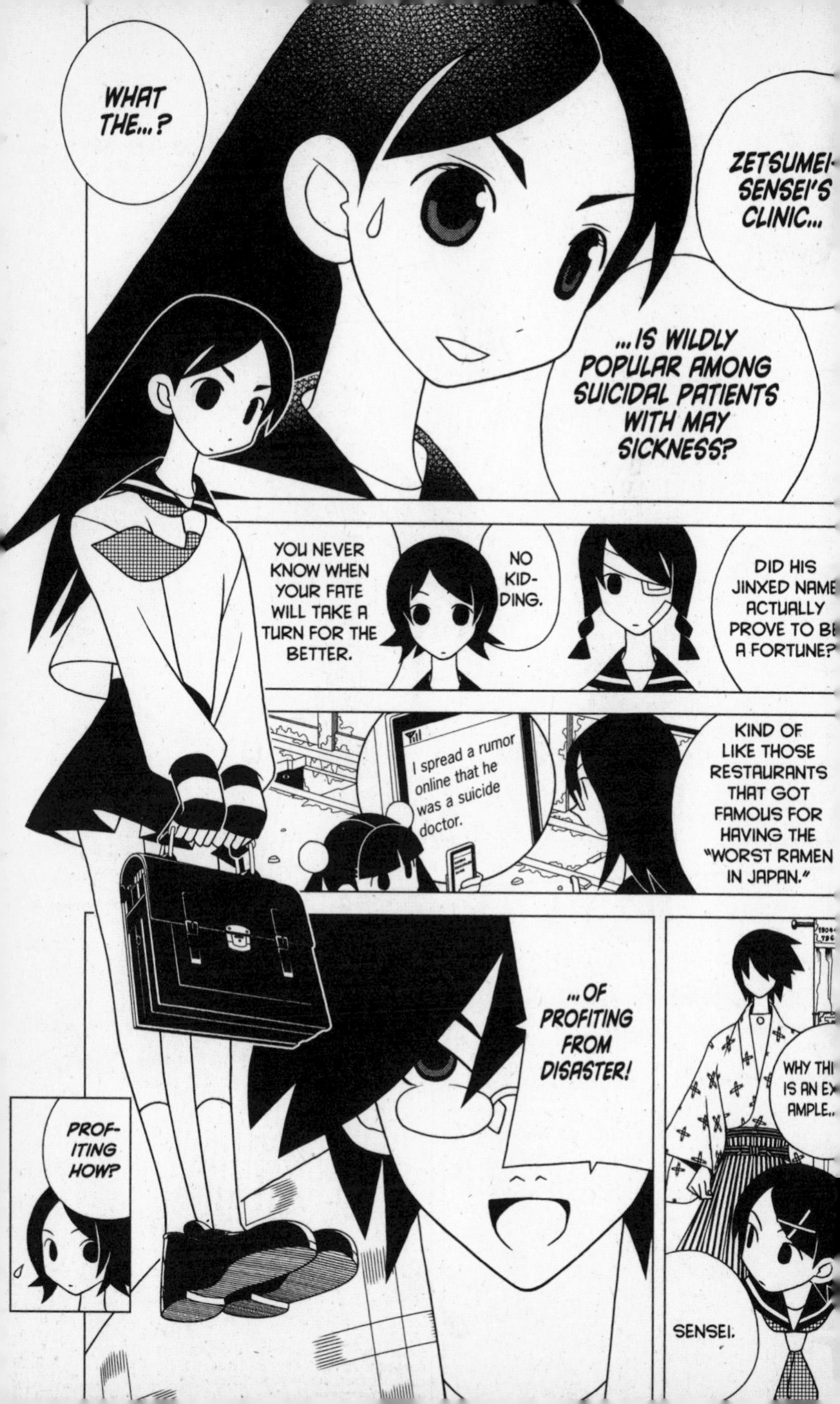
ZETSUMEI-SENSEI'S CLINIC...
WHAT THE...?
...IS WILDLY POPULAR AMONG SUICIDAL PATIENTS WITH MAY SICKNESS?
DID HIS JINXED NAM ACTUALLY PROVE TO B A FORTUNE?
NO KID-DING.
YOU NEVER KNOW WHEN YOUR FATE WILL TAKE A TURN FOR THE BETTER.
KIND OF LIKE THOSE RESTAURANTS THAT GOT FAMOUS FOR HAVING THE "WORST RAMEN IN JAPAN."
I spread a rumor online that he was a suicide doctor.
WHY THI IS AN EX AMPLE..
SENSEI.
...OF PROFITING FROM DISASTER!
PROF-ITING HOW?

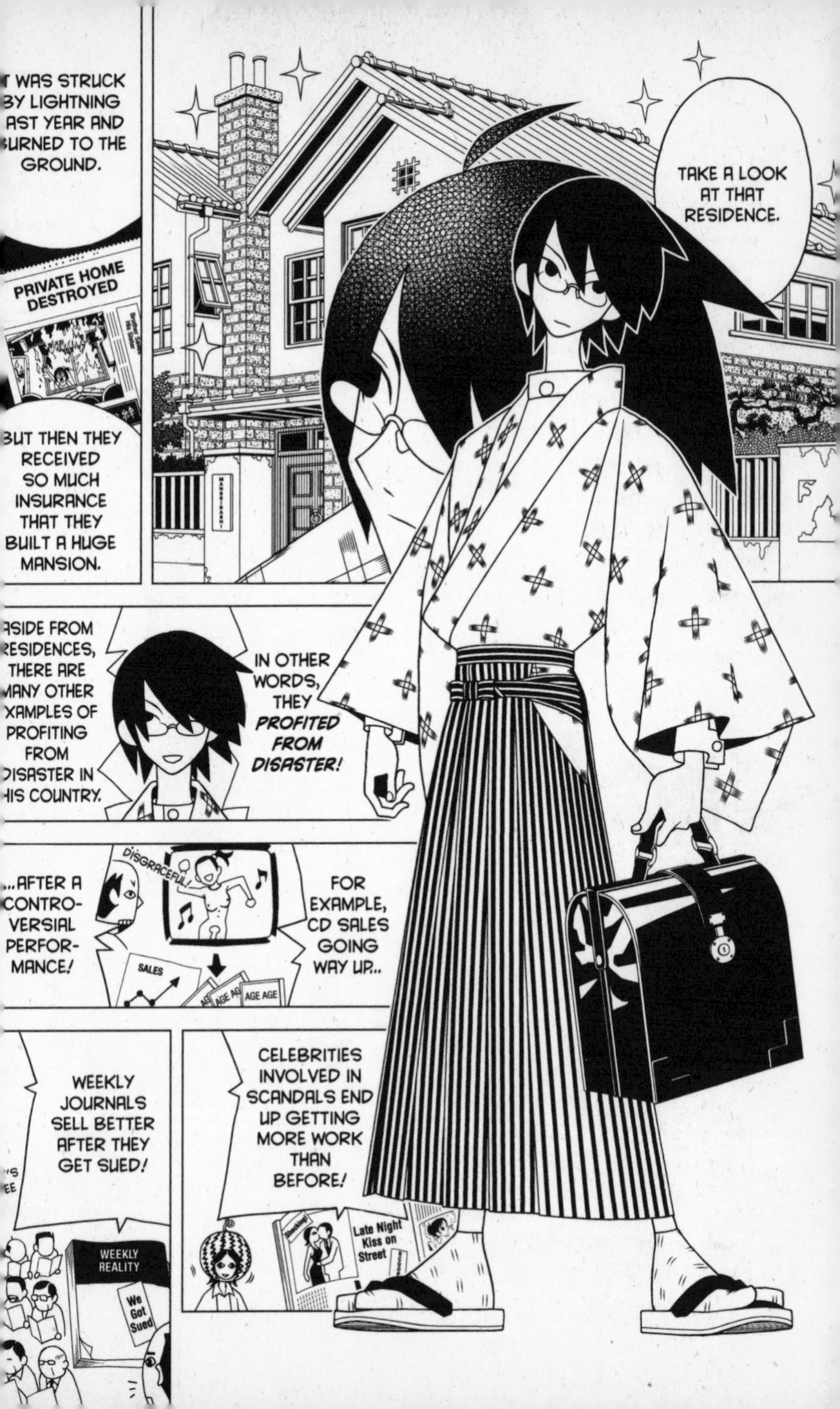
TAKE A LOOK AT THAT RESIDENCE.
T WAS STRUCK BY LIGHTNING AST YEAR AND URNED TO THE GROUND.
PRIVATE HOME DESTROYED
UT THEN THEY RECEIVED SO MUCH INSURANCE THAT THEY BUILT A HUGE MANSION.
IN OTHER WORDS, THEY PROFITED FROM DISASTER!
ASIDE FROM RESIDENCES, THERE ARE ANY OTHER XAMPLES OF PROFITING FROM ISASTER IN HIS COUNTRY.
FOR EXAMPLE, CD SALES GOING WAY UP...
DISGRACEFUL!
SALES
AGE AGE
...AFTER A CONTROVERSIAL PERFORMANCE!
CELEBRITIES INVOLVED IN SCANDALS END UP GETTING MORE WORK THAN BEFORE!
Shocking!
Late Night Kiss on Street
WEEKLY JOURNALS SELL BETTER AFTER THEY GET SUED!
WEEKLY REALITY
We Got Sued

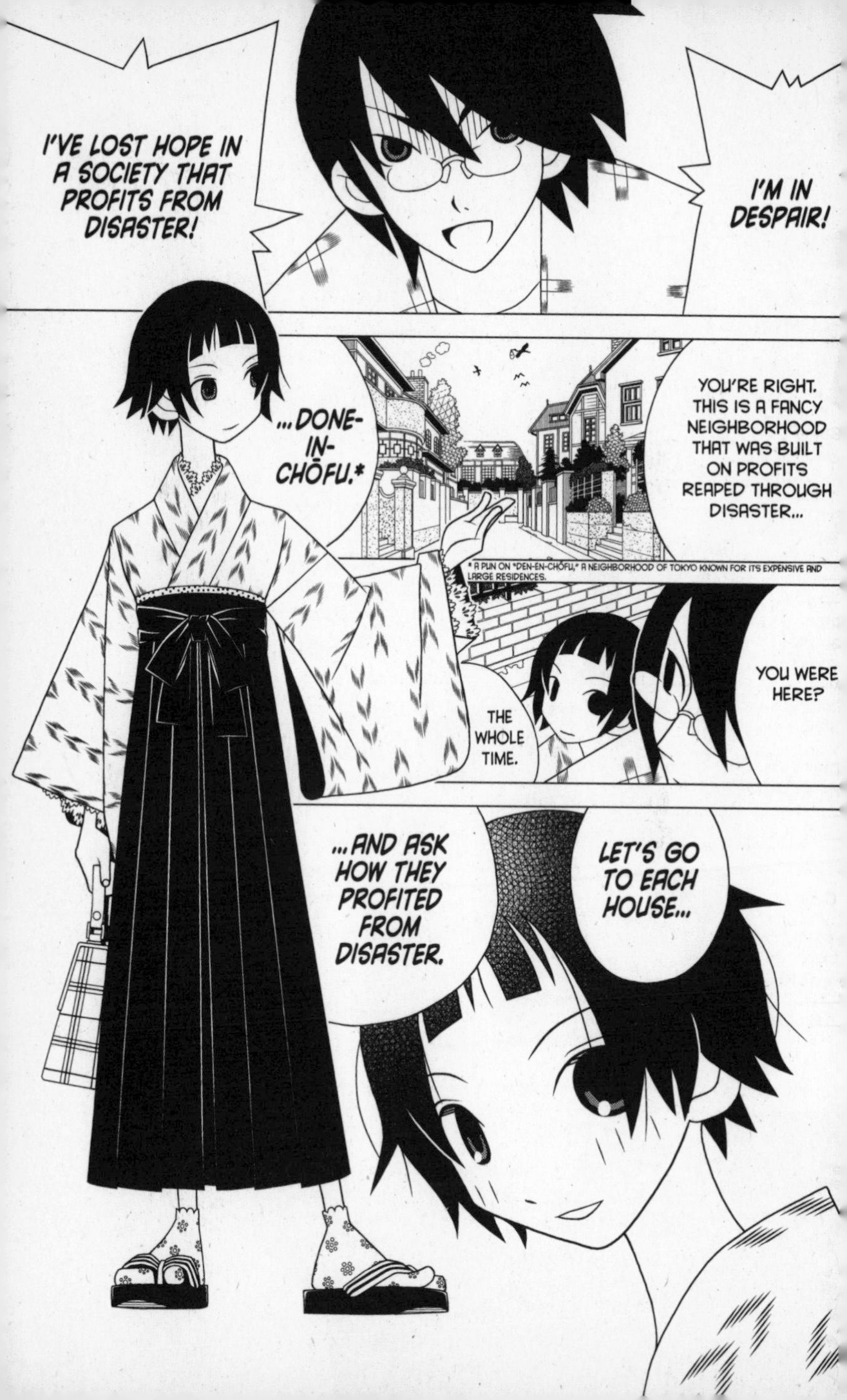
I'M IN DESPAIR!
I'VE LOST HOPE IN A SOCIETY THAT PROFITS FROM DISASTER!
YOU'RE RIGHT. THIS IS A FANCY NEIGHBORHOOD THAT WAS BUILT ON PROFITS REAPED THROUGH DISASTER...
...DONE-IN-CHŌFU.*
* A PUN ON "DEN-EN-CHŌFU," A NEIGHBORHOOD OF TOKYO KNOWN FOR ITS EXPENSIVE AND LARGE RESIDENCES.
YOU WERE HERE?
THE WHOLE TIME.
LET'S GO TO EACH HOUSE...
...AND ASK HOW THEY PROFITED FROM DISASTER.

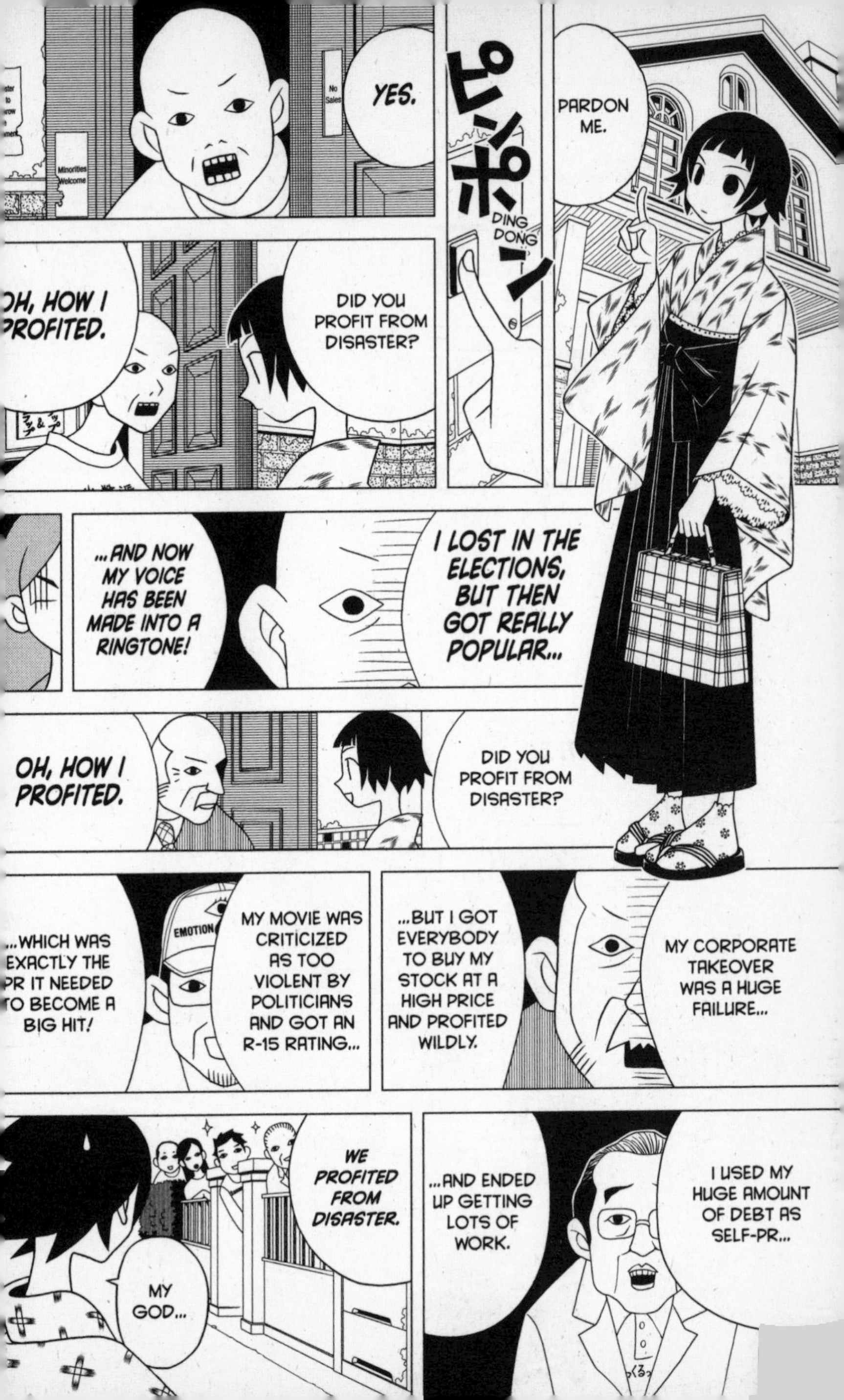
PARDON ME.
ピンポーン
DING DONG
No Sales
YES.
Minorities Welcome
DID YOU PROFIT FROM DISASTER?
OH, HOW I PROFITED.
I LOST IN THE ELECTIONS, BUT THEN GOT REALLY POPULAR...
...AND NOW MY VOICE HAS BEEN MADE INTO A RINGTONE!
DID YOU PROFIT FROM DISASTER?
OH, HOW I PROFITED.
MY CORPORATE TAKEOVER WAS A HUGE FAILURE...
...BUT I GOT EVERYBODY TO BUY MY STOCK AT A HIGH PRICE AND PROFITED WILDLY.
EMOTION
MY MOVIE WAS CRITICIZED AS TOO VIOLENT BY POLITICIANS AND GOT AN R-15 RATING...
...WHICH WAS EXACTLY THE PR IT NEEDED TO BECOME A BIG HIT!
I USED MY HUGE AMOUNT OF DEBT AS SELF-PR...
...AND ENDED UP GETTING LOTS OF WORK.
WE PROFITED FROM DISASTER.
MY GOD...

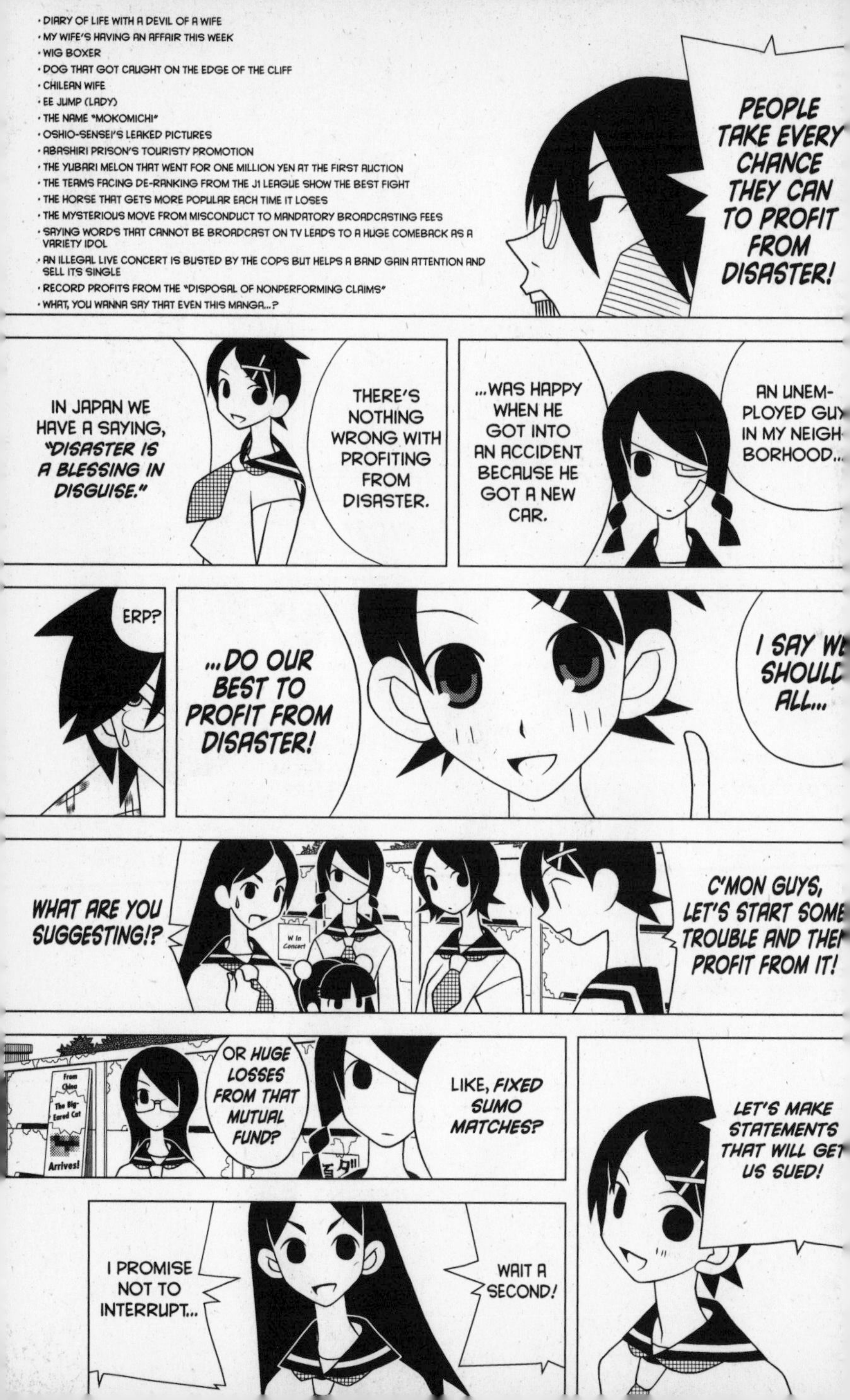

PEOPLE TAKE EVERY CHANCE THEY CAN TO PROFIT FROM DISASTER!
• DIARY OF LIFE WITH A DEVIL OF A WIFE
• MY WIFE'S HAVING AN AFFAIR THIS WEEK
• WIG BOXER
• DOG THAT GOT CAUGHT ON THE EDGE OF THE CLIFF
• CHILEAN WIFE
• EE JUMP (LADY)
• THE NAME "MOKOMICHI"
• OSHIO-SENSEI'S LEAKED PICTURES
• ABASHIRI PRISON'S TOURISTY PROMOTION
• THE YUBARI MELON THAT WENT FOR ONE MILLION YEN AT THE FIRST AUCTION
• THE TEAMS FACING DE-RANKING FROM THE J1 LEAGUE SHOW THE BEST FIGHT
• THE HORSE THAT GETS MORE POPULAR EACH TIME IT LOSES
• THE MYSTERIOUS MOVE FROM MISCONDUCT TO MANDATORY BROADCASTING FEES
• SAYING WORDS THAT CANNOT BE BROADCAST ON TV LEADS TO A HUGE COMEBACK AS A VARIETY IDOL
• AN ILLEGAL LIVE CONCERT IS BUSTED BY THE COPS BUT HELPS A BAND GAIN ATTENTION AND SELL ITS SINGLE
• RECORD PROFITS FROM THE "DISPOSAL OF NONPERFORMING CLAIMS"
• WHAT, YOU WANNA SAY THAT EVEN THIS MANGA...?
AN UNEMPLOYED GUY IN MY NEIGHBORHOOD...
...WAS HAPPY WHEN HE GOT INTO AN ACCIDENT BECAUSE HE GOT A NEW CAR.
THERE'S NOTHING WRONG WITH PROFITING FROM DISASTER.
IN JAPAN WE HAVE A SAYING, "DISASTER IS A BLESSING IN DISGUISE."
I SAY WE SHOULD ALL...
...DO OUR BEST TO PROFIT FROM DISASTER!
ERP?
C'MON GUYS, LET'S START SOME TROUBLE AND THEN PROFIT FROM IT!
W In Concert
WHAT ARE YOU SUGGESTING!?
LET'S MAKE STATEMENTS THAT WILL GET US SUED!
LIKE, FIXED SUMO MATCHES?
OR HUGE LOSSES FROM THAT MUTUAL FUND?
From China
The Big-Eared Cat
Arrives!
WAIT A SECOND!
I PROMISE NOT TO INTERRUPT...

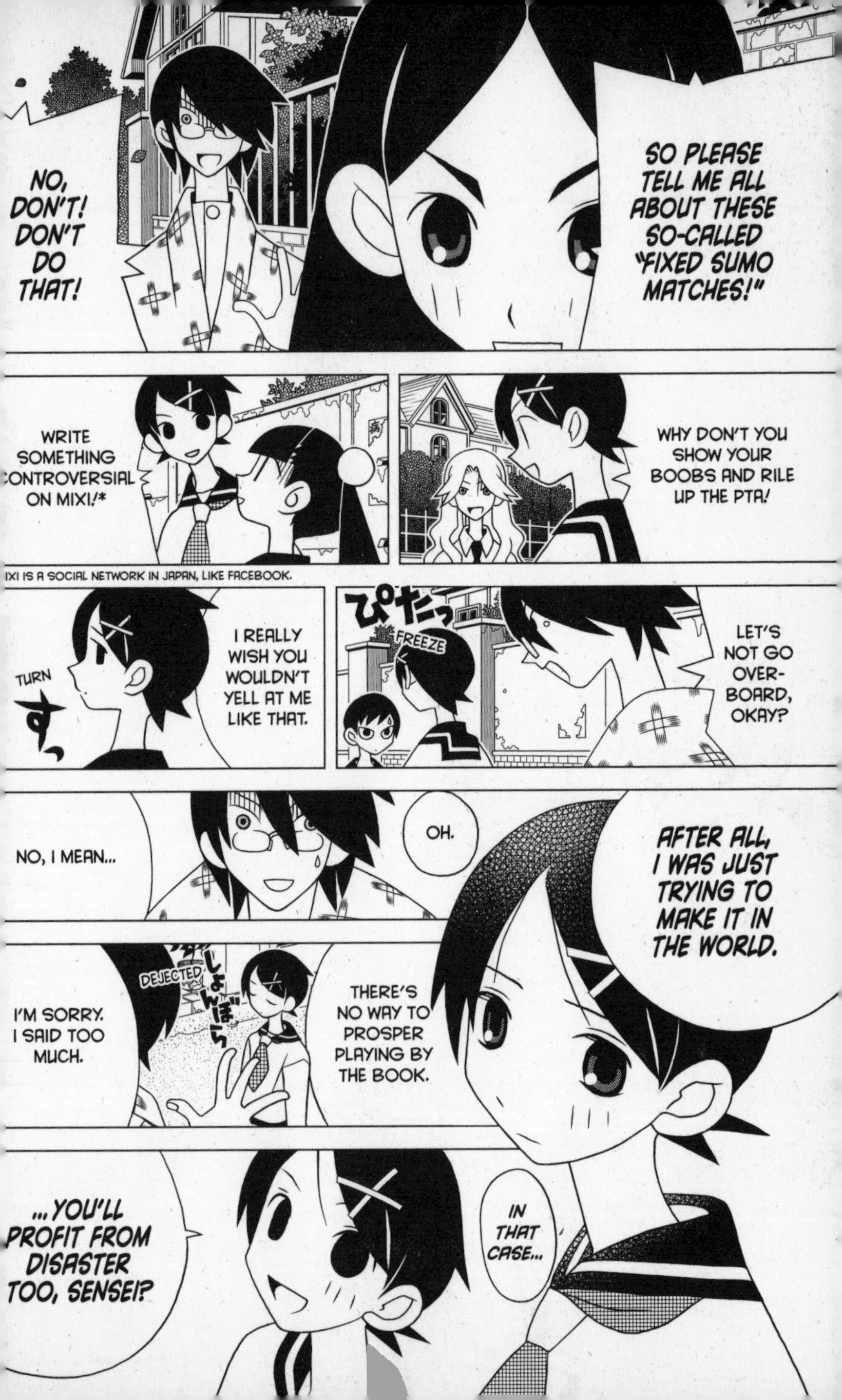
SO PLEASE TELL ME ALL ABOUT THESE SO-CALLED "FIXED SUMO MATCHES!"
NO, DON'T! DON'T DO THAT!
WHY DON'T YOU SHOW YOUR BOOBS AND RILE UP THE PTA!
WRITE SOMETHING CONTROVERSIAL ON MIXI!*
IXI IS A SOCIAL NETWORK IN JAPAN, LIKE FACEBOOK.
ぴたっ
FREEZE
LET'S NOT GO OVER-BOARD, OKAY?
I REALLY WISH YOU WOULDN'T YELL AT ME LIKE THAT.
TURN
すっ
AFTER ALL, I WAS JUST TRYING TO MAKE IT IN THE WORLD.
OH.
NO, I MEAN...
THERE'S NO WAY TO PROSPER PLAYING BY THE BOOK.
DEJECTED
しょんぼら
I'M SORRY. I SAID TOO MUCH.
IN THAT CASE...
...YOU'LL PROFIT FROM DISASTER TOO, SENSEI?

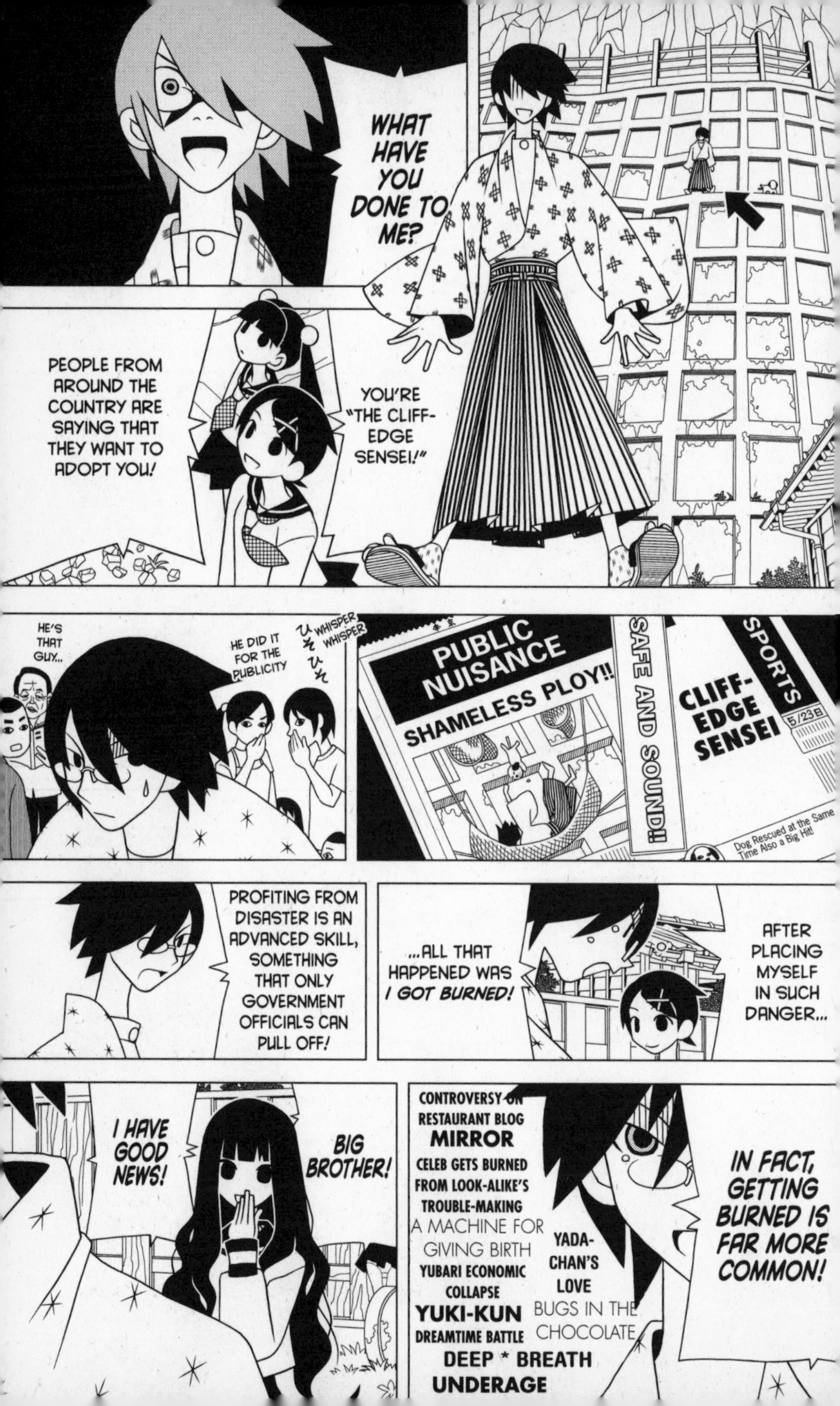
WHAT HAVE YOU DONE TO ME?
YOU'RE "THE CLIFF-EDGE SENSEI!"
PEOPLE FROM AROUND THE COUNTRY ARE SAYING THAT THEY WANT TO ADOPT YOU!
SPORTS
5/23日
CLIFF-EDGE SENSEI
SAFE AND SOUND!!
PUBLIC NUISANCE
SHAMELESS PLOY!!
Dog Rescued at the Same Time Also a Big Hit!
WHISPER WHISPER
ひそひそ
HE DID IT FOR THE PUBLICITY
HE'S THAT GUY...
AFTER PLACING MYSELF IN SUCH DANGER...
...ALL THAT HAPPENED WAS I GOT BURNED!
PROFITING FROM DISASTER IS AN ADVANCED SKILL, SOMETHING THAT ONLY GOVERNMENT OFFICIALS CAN PULL OFF!
IN FACT, GETTING BURNED IS FAR MORE COMMON!
CONTROVERSY ON RESTAURANT BLOG
MIRROR
CELEB GETS BURNED FROM LOOK-ALIKE'S
TROUBLE-MAKING
A MACHINE FOR GIVING BIRTH
YUBARI ECONOMIC COLLAPSE
YUKI-KUN
DREAMTIME BATTLE
DEEP * BREATH
UNDERAGE
YADA-CHAN'S LOVE
BUGS IN THE CHOCOLATE
BIG BROTHER!
I HAVE GOOD NEWS!

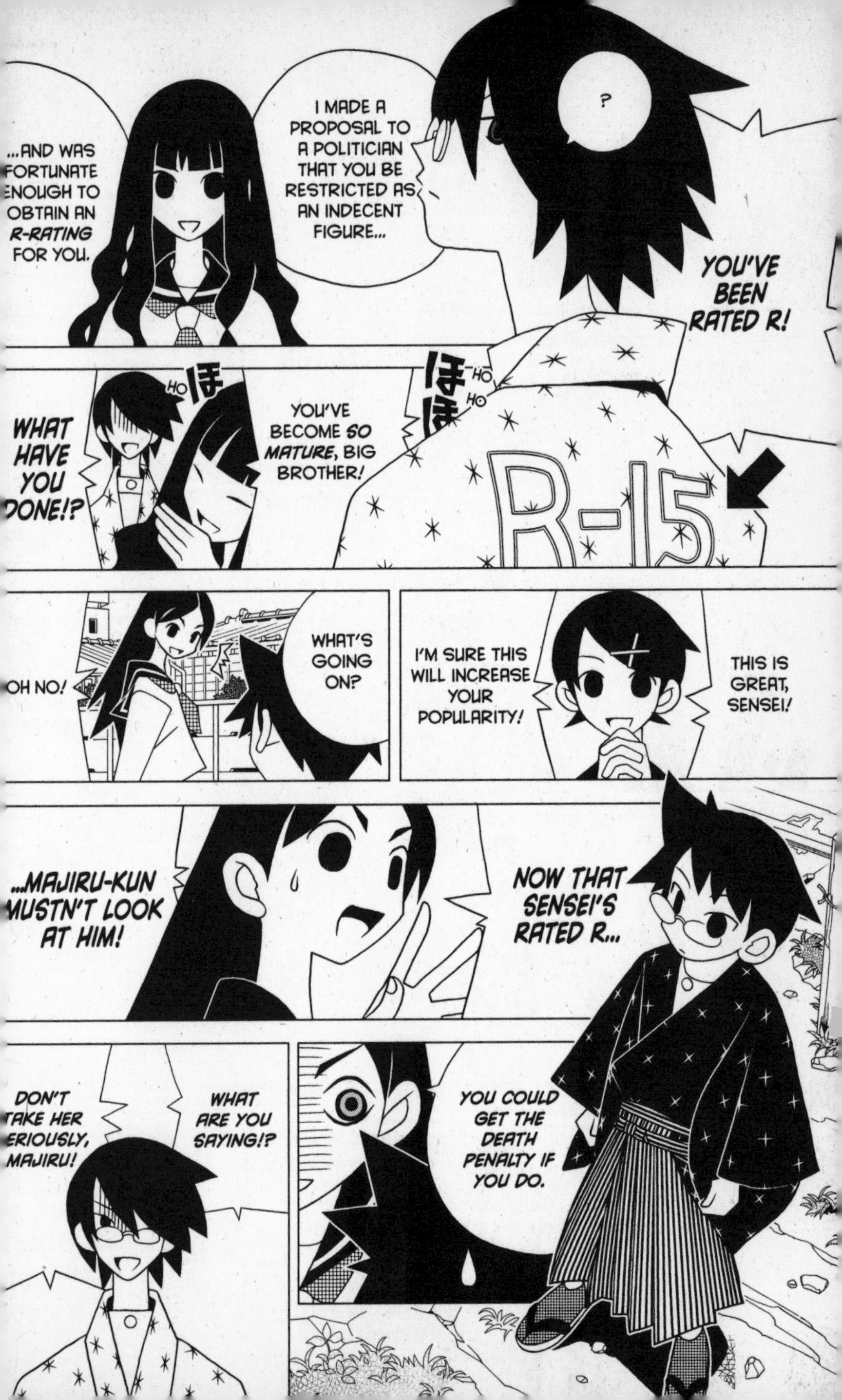
?
I MADE A PROPOSAL TO A POLITICIAN THAT YOU BE RESTRICTED AS AN INDECENT FIGURE...
...AND WAS FORTUNATE ENOUGH TO OBTAIN AN *R-RATING* FOR YOU.
YOU'VE BEEN RATED R!
R-15
ほほ HO HO
YOU'VE BECOME *SO MATURE*, BIG BROTHER!
ほ HO
WHAT HAVE YOU DONE!?
THIS IS GREAT, SENSEI!
I'M SURE THIS WILL INCREASE YOUR POPULARITY!
WHAT'S GOING ON?
OH NO!
NOW THAT SENSEI'S RATED R...
...MAJIRU-KUN MUSTN'T LOOK AT HIM!
YOU COULD GET THE DEATH PENALTY IF YOU DO.
WHAT ARE YOU SAYING!?
DON'T TAKE HER ERIOUSLY, MAJIRU!

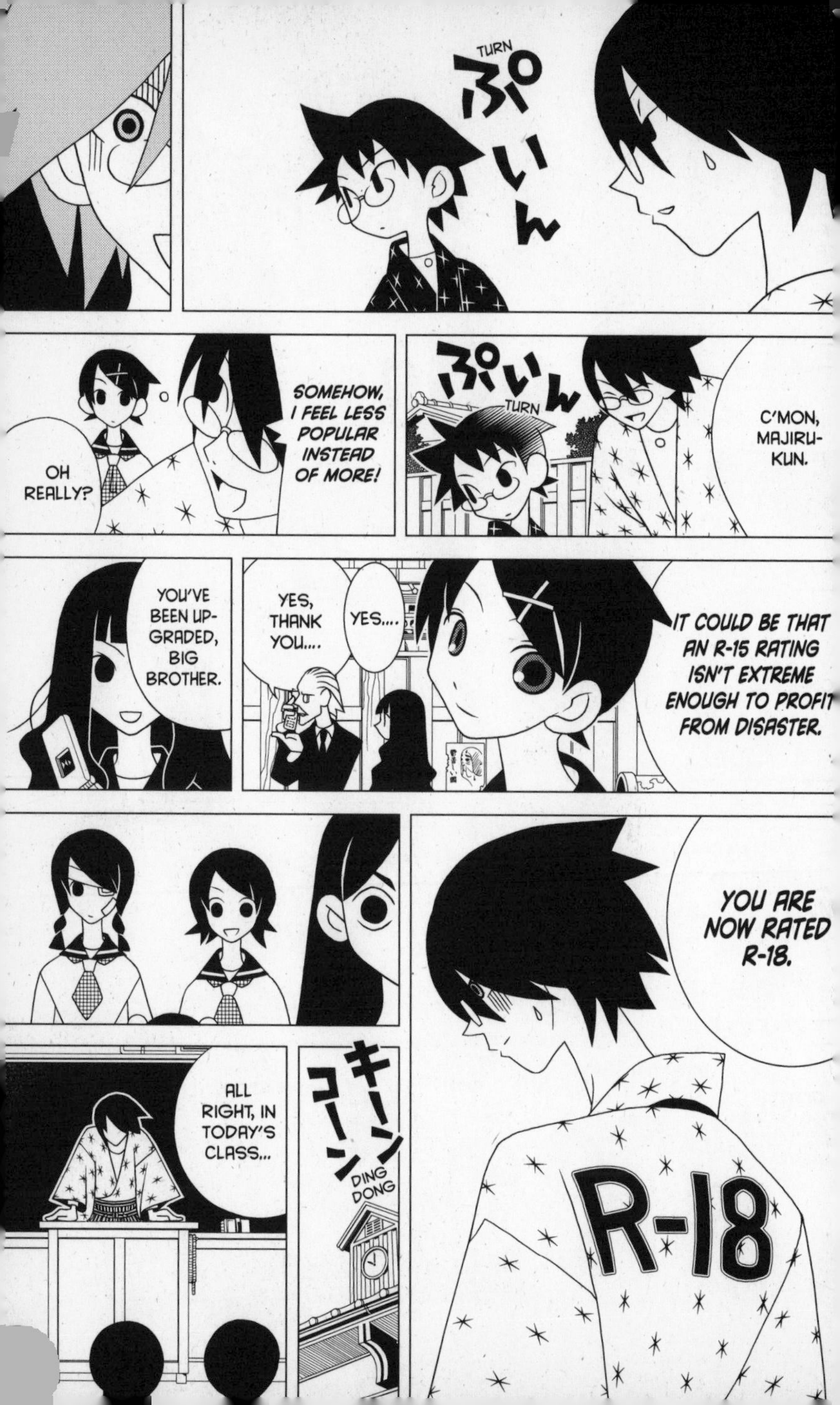
TURN
ぷいん
C'MON, MAJIRU-KUN.
ぷいん
TURN
SOMEHOW, I FEEL LESS POPULAR INSTEAD OF MORE!
OH REALLY?
IT COULD BE THAT AN R-15 RATING ISN'T EXTREME ENOUGH TO PROFIT FROM DISASTER.
YES....
YES, THANK YOU....
YOU'VE BEEN UP-GRADED, BIG BROTHER.
YOU ARE NOW RATED R-18.
R-18
キーンコーン
DING DONG
ALL RIGHT, IN TODAY'S CLASS...

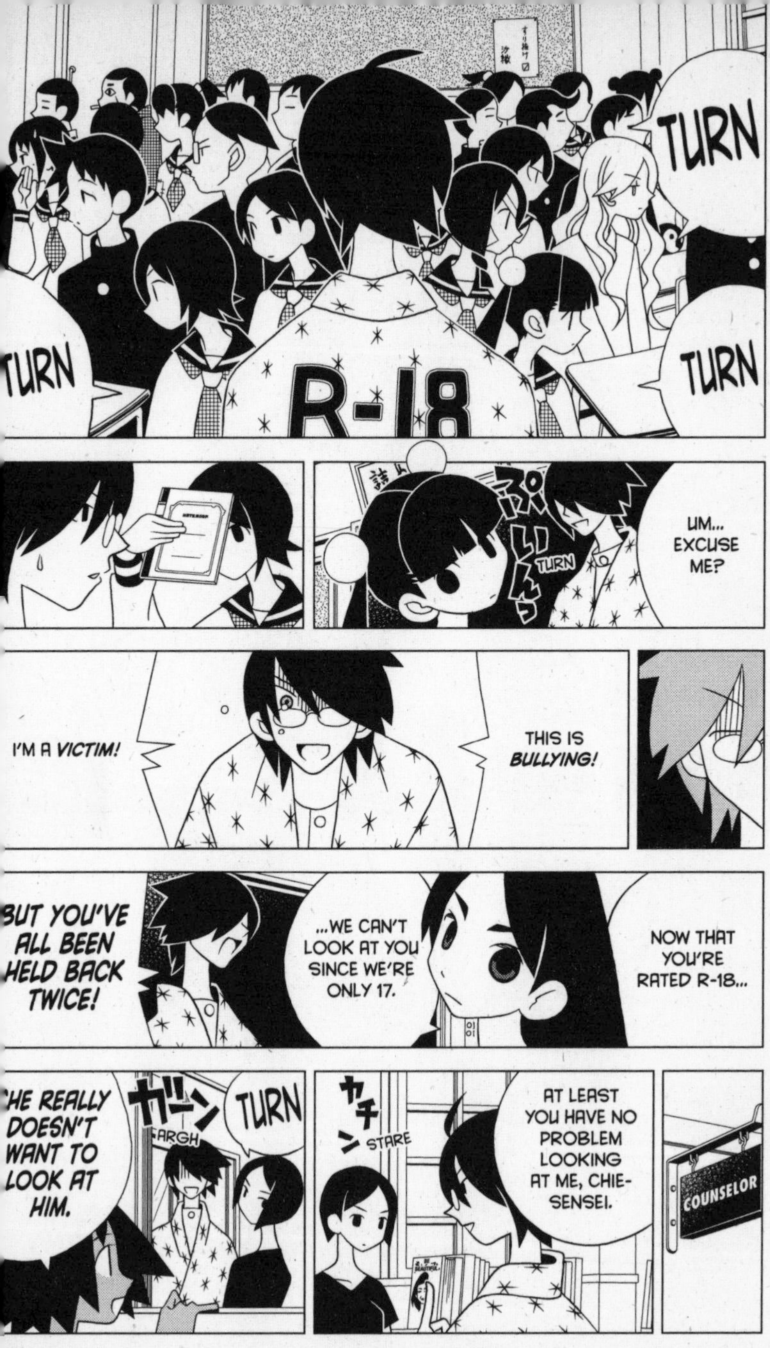

TURN
TURN
TURN
UM... EXCUSE ME?
ぷいんっ
TURN
THIS IS BULLYING!
I'M A VICTIM!
NOW THAT YOU'RE RATED R-18...
...WE CAN'T LOOK AT YOU SINCE WE'RE ONLY 17.
BUT YOU'VE ALL BEEN HELD BACK TWICE!
COUNSELOR
AT LEAST YOU HAVE NO PROBLEM LOOKING AT ME, CHIE-SENSEI.
ヤチン
STARE
TURN
ガーン
ARGH
HE REALLY DOESN'T WANT TO LOOK AT HIM.

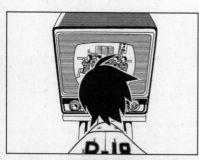

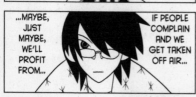

IF PEOPLE COMPLAIN AND WE GET TAKEN OFF AIR...
...MAYBE, JUST MAYBE, WE'LL PROFIT FROM...
NO! DON'T EVEN THINK ABOUT IT... DON'T EVEN!

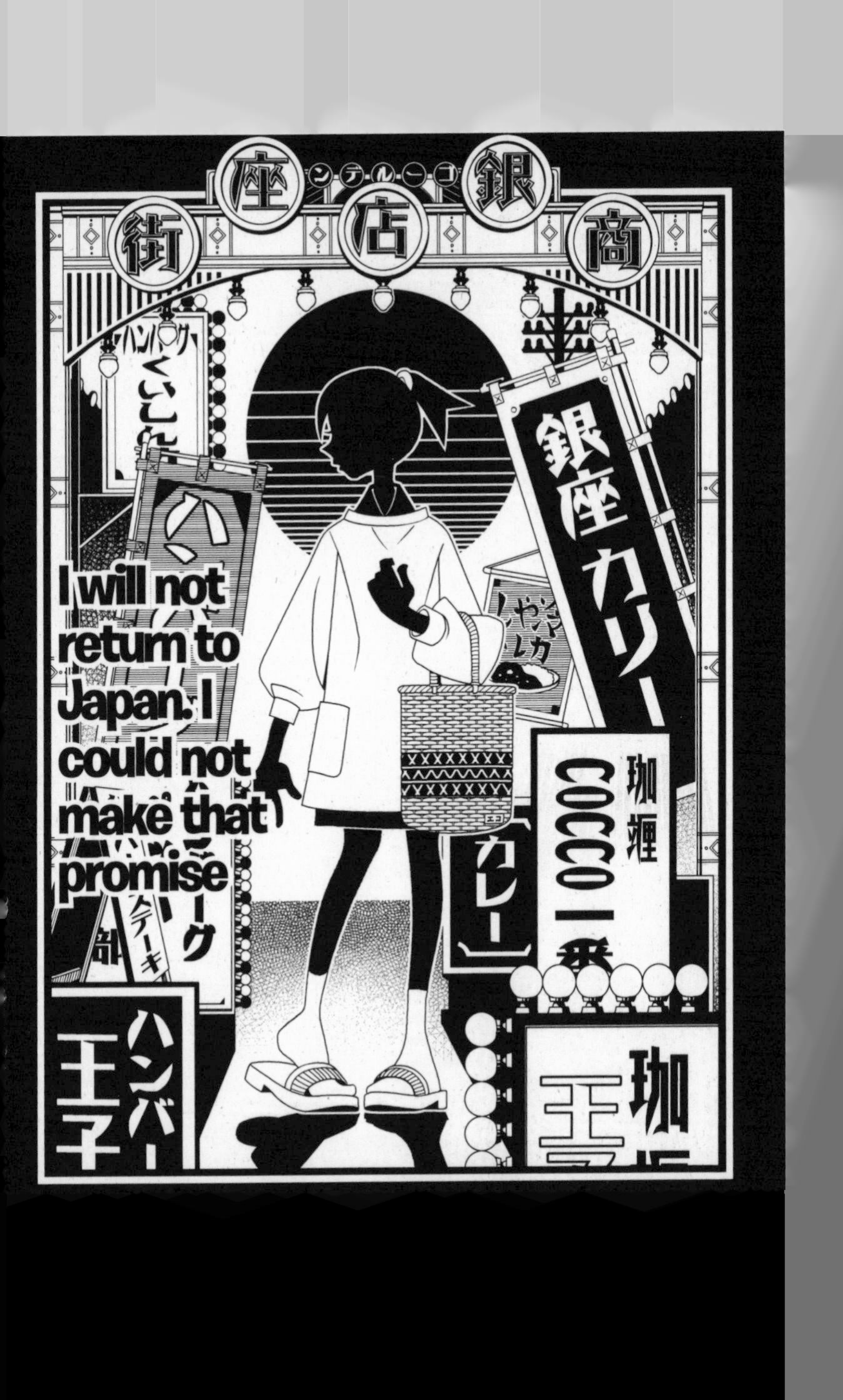

銀座商店街
ゴールデン
銀座カリー
珈琲
COCCO一番
カレー
I will not return to Japan. I could not make that promise

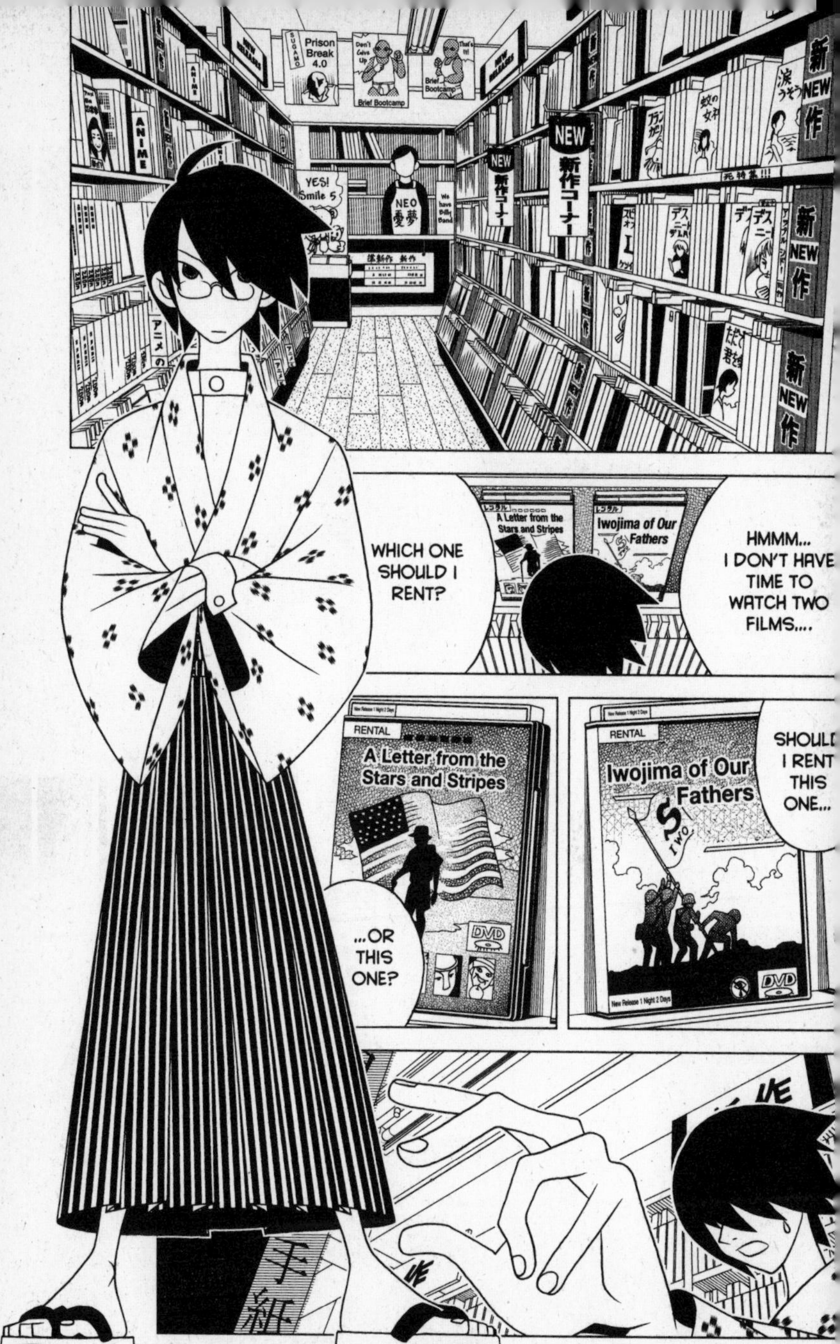
NEW
新作
NEW
新作コーナー
NEW RELEASES
Prison Break 4.0
SUGAMO
Don't Give Up
That's it!
Brief Bootcamp
Brief Bootcamp
NEO
憂夢
YES! Smile 5
ANIME
HMMM... I DON'T HAVE TIME TO WATCH TWO FILMS....
Iwojima of Our Fathers
A Letter from the Stars and Stripes
WHICH ONE SHOULD I RENT?
SHOULD I RENT THIS ONE...
RENTAL
Iwojima of Our Fathers
DVD
New Release 1 Night 2 Days
RENTAL
A Letter from the Stars and Stripes
DVD
...OR THIS ONE?

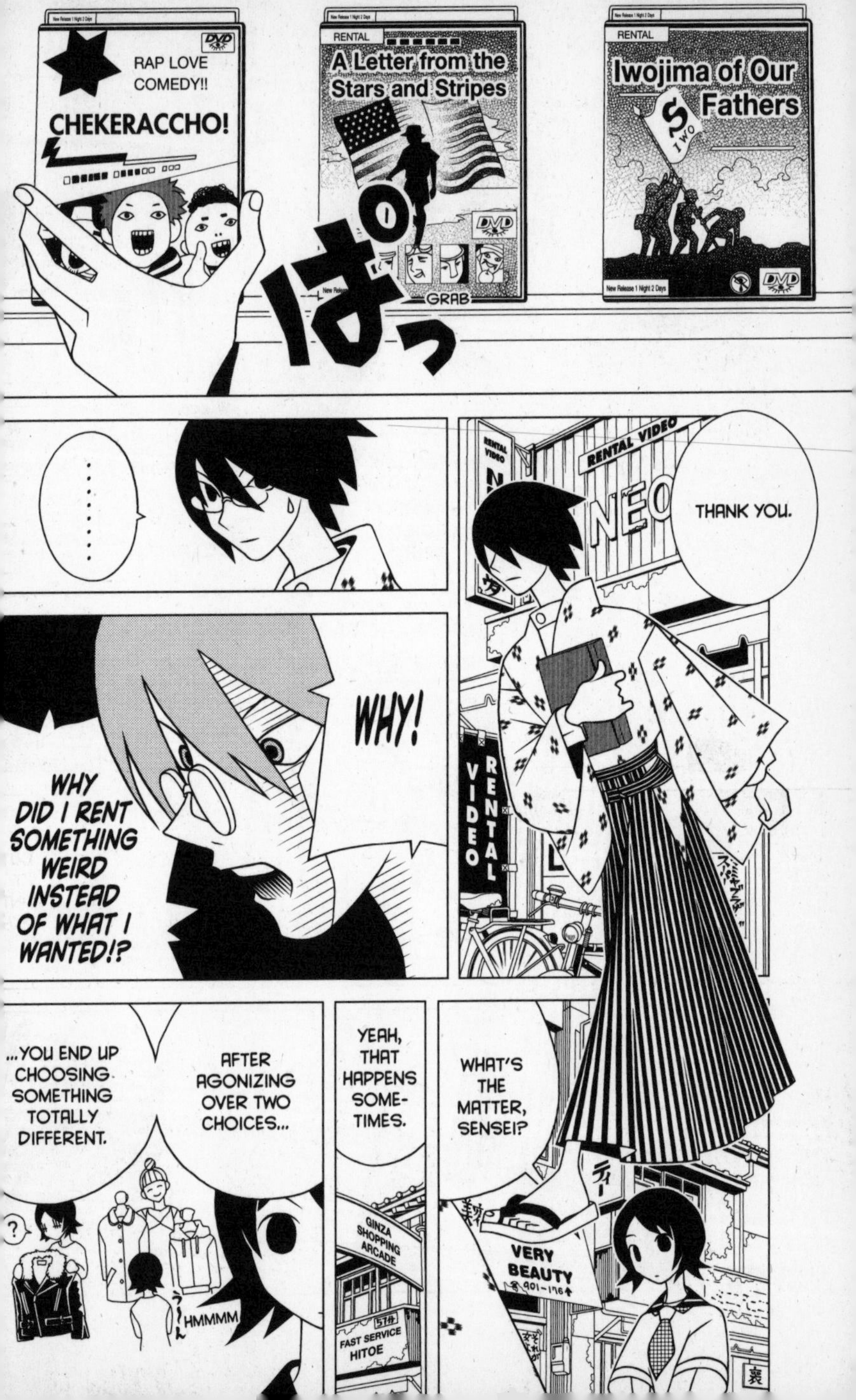

RENTAL
Iwojima of Our Fathers
New Release 1 Night 2 Days
RENTAL
A Letter from the Stars and Stripes
DVD
RAP LOVE COMEDY!!
CHEKERACCHO!
DVD
ぱっ
GRAB
RENTAL VIDEO
NEO
THANK YOU.
RENTAL VIDEO
......
WHY!
WHY DID I RENT SOMETHING WEIRD INSTEAD OF WHAT I WANTED!?
WHAT'S THE MATTER, SENSEI?
VERY BEAUTY
YEAH, THAT HAPPENS SOME-TIMES.
GINZA SHOPPING ARCADE
FAST SERVICE HITOE
AFTER AGONIZING OVER TWO CHOICES...
...YOU END UP CHOOSING SOMETHING TOTALLY DIFFERENT.
?
HMMMM

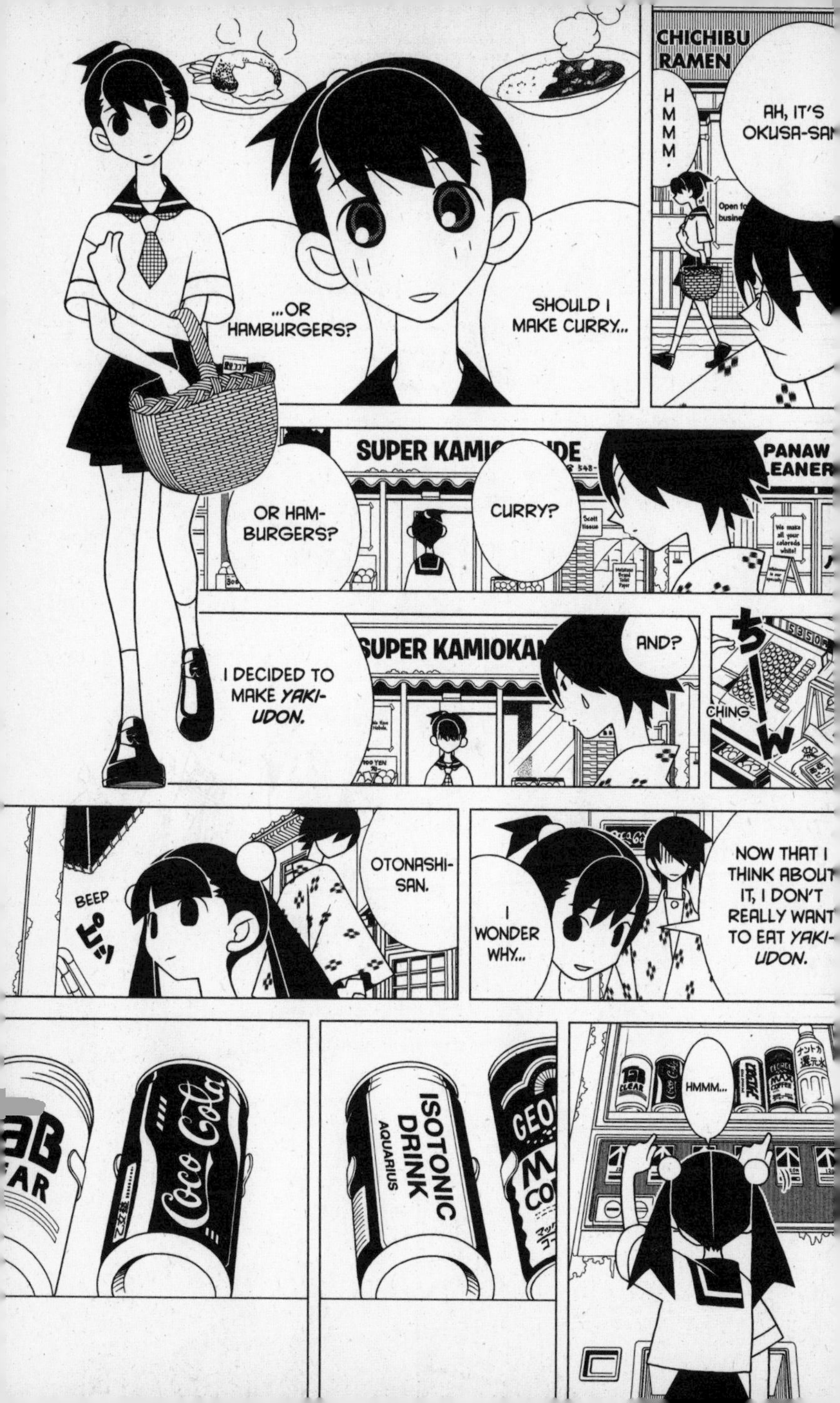
CHICHIBU RAMEN
HMMM.
AH, IT'S OKUSA-SAN
SHOULD I MAKE CURRY...
...OR HAMBURGERS?
CURRY?
OR HAM-BURGERS?
CHING
AND?
I DECIDED TO MAKE *YAKI-UDON.*
NOW THAT I THINK ABOUT IT, I DON'T REALLY WANT TO EAT *YAKI-UDON.*
I WONDER WHY...
OTONASHI-SAN.
BEEP
HMMM...
ISOTONIC DRINK
AQUARIUS
Coco Cola

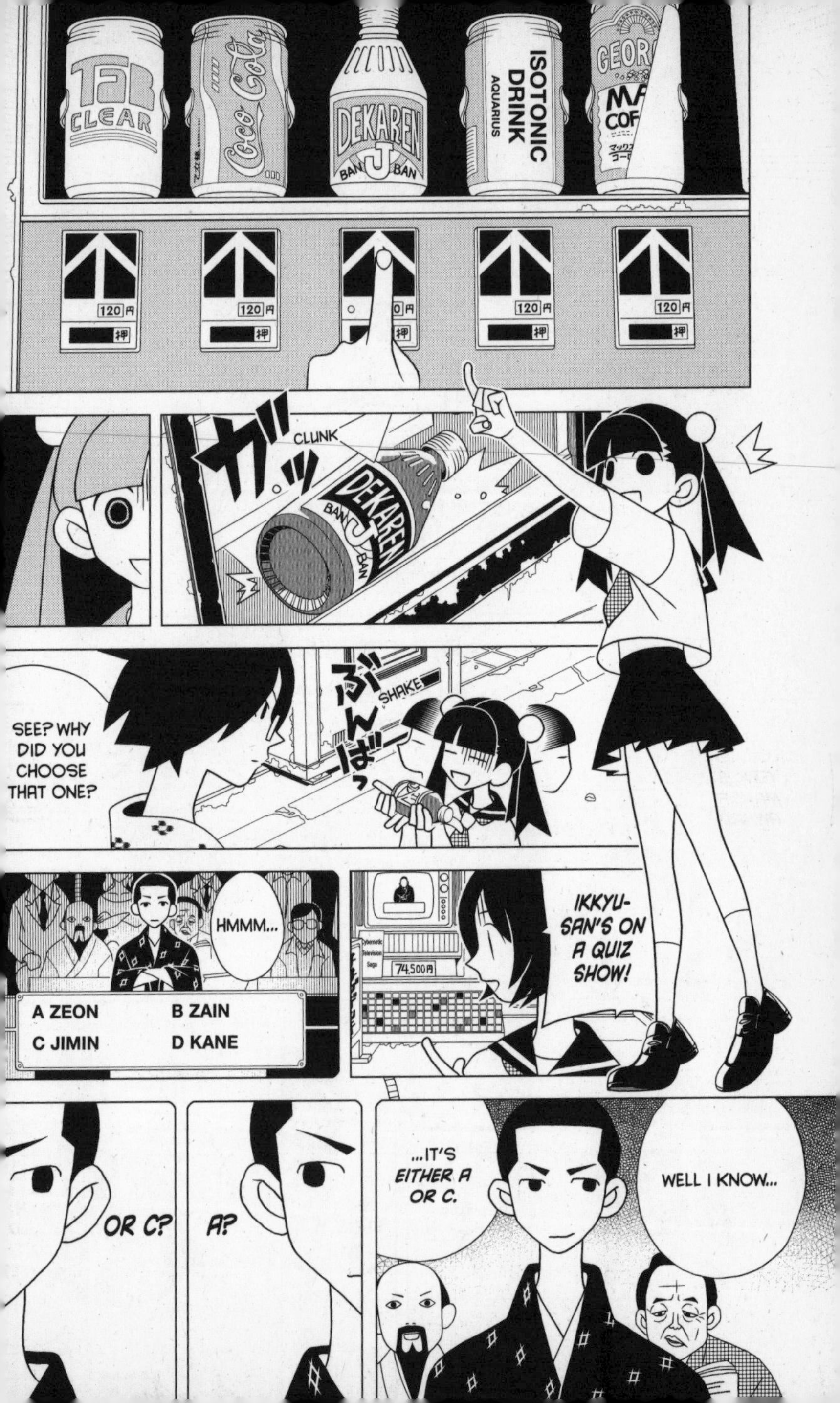

TFB CLEAR
Coca Cola
DEKAREN J BAN BAN
ISOTONIC DRINK
AQUARIUS
120円
押
ガッ
CLUNK
DEKAREN BAN J BAN
ぶんばっ
SHAKE
SEE? WHY DID YOU CHOOSE THAT ONE?
IKKYU-SAN'S ON A QUIZ SHOW!
Cybernetic Television Saga
74,500円
HMMM...
A ZEON
B ZAIN
C JIMIN
D KANE
WELL I KNOW...
...IT'S EITHER A OR C.
A?
OR C?

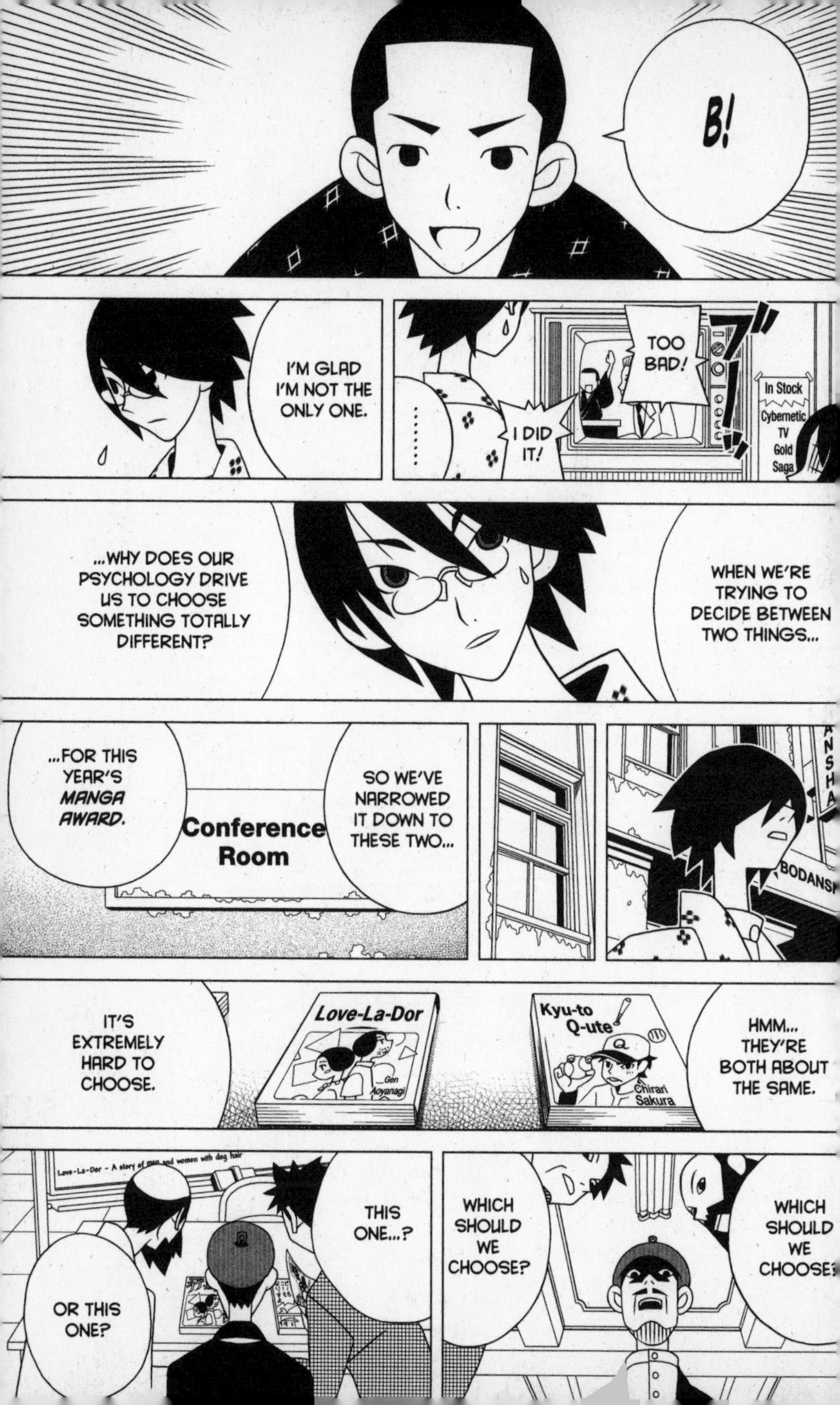
B!
In Stock
Cybernetic TV Gold Saga
TOO BAD!
I DID IT!
......
I'M GLAD I'M NOT THE ONLY ONE.
WHEN WE'RE TRYING TO DECIDE BETWEEN TWO THINGS...
...WHY DOES OUR PSYCHOLOGY DRIVE US TO CHOOSE SOMETHING TOTALLY DIFFERENT?
ANSHA
BODANSH
SO WE'VE NARROWED IT DOWN TO THESE TWO...
Conference Room
...FOR THIS YEAR'S *MANGA AWARD.*
HMM... THEY'RE BOTH ABOUT THE SAME.
Kyu-to Q-ute
Chirari Sakura
Love-La-Dor
Gen Aoyanagi
IT'S EXTREMELY HARD TO CHOOSE.
WHICH SHOULD WE CHOOSE?
WHICH SHOULD WE CHOOSE?
THIS ONE...?
Love-La-Dor - A story of man and women with dog hair
OR THIS ONE?

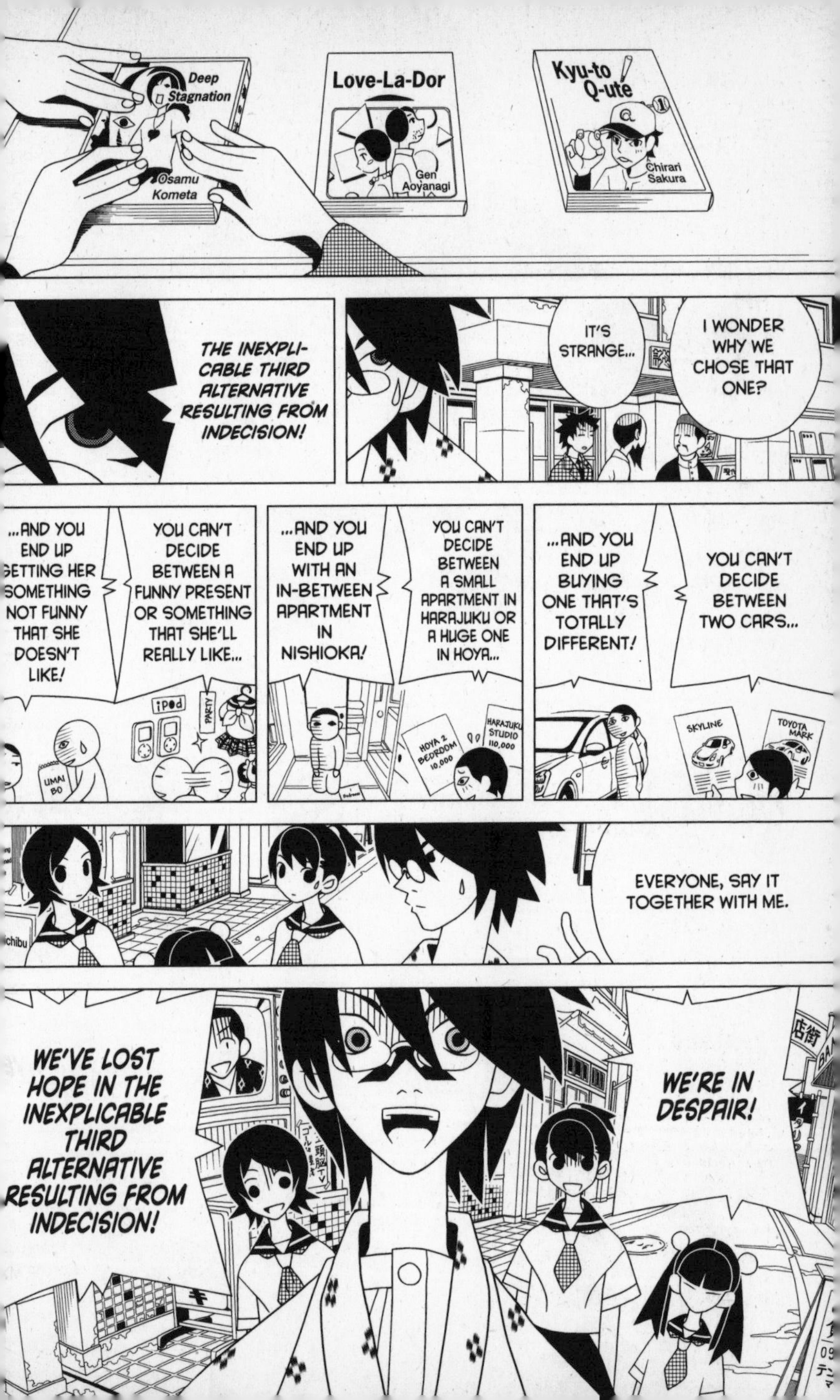
Kyu-to Q-ute
Chirari Sakura
Love-La-Dor
Gen Aoyanagi
Deep Stagnation
Osamu Kometa
I WONDER WHY WE CHOSE THAT ONE?
IT'S STRANGE...
THE INEXPLICABLE THIRD ALTERNATIVE RESULTING FROM INDECISION!
YOU CAN'T DECIDE BETWEEN TWO CARS...
...AND YOU END UP BUYING ONE THAT'S TOTALLY DIFFERENT!
SKYLINE
TOYOTA MARK
YOU CAN'T DECIDE BETWEEN A SMALL APARTMENT IN HARAJUKU OR A HUGE ONE IN HOYA...
...AND YOU END UP WITH AN IN-BETWEEN APARTMENT IN NISHIOKA!
HARAJUKU STUDIO 110,000
HOYA 2 BEDROOM 10,000
YOU CAN'T DECIDE BETWEEN A FUNNY PRESENT OR SOMETHING THAT SHE'LL REALLY LIKE...
...AND YOU END UP GETTING HER SOMETHING NOT FUNNY THAT SHE DOESN'T LIKE!
iPod
PARTY
UMAI BO
EVERYONE, SAY IT TOGETHER WITH ME.
WE'RE IN DESPAIR!
WE'VE LOST HOPE IN THE INEXPLICABLE THIRD ALTERNATIVE RESULTING FROM INDECISION!

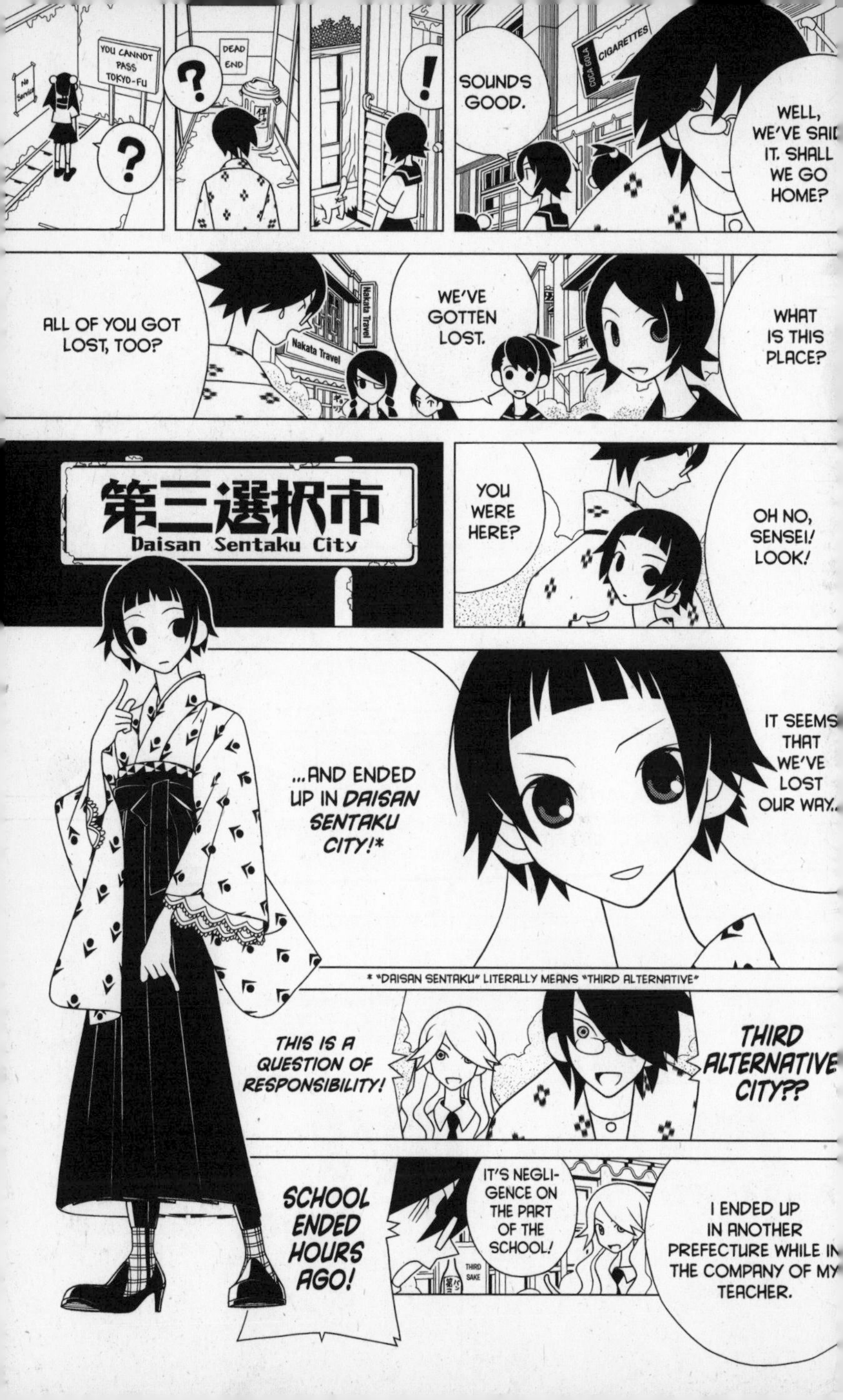

WELL, WE'VE SAID IT. SHALL WE GO HOME?
CIGARETTES
COCA COLA
SOUNDS GOOD.
!
DEAD END
?
YOU CANNOT PASS TOKYO-FU
?
WHAT IS THIS PLACE?
WE'VE GOTTEN LOST.
Nakata Travel
Nakata Travel
ALL OF YOU GOT LOST, TOO?
OH NO, SENSEI! LOOK!
YOU WERE HERE?
第三選択市
Daisan Sentaku City
IT SEEMS THAT WE'VE LOST OUR WAY..
...AND ENDED UP IN DAISAN SENTAKU CITY!*
* "DAISAN SENTAKU" LITERALLY MEANS "THIRD ALTERNATIVE"
THIRD ALTERNATIVE CITY??
THIS IS A QUESTION OF RESPONSIBILITY!
I ENDED UP IN ANOTHER PREFECTURE WHILE IN THE COMPANY OF MY TEACHER.
IT'S NEGLI-GENCE ON THE PART OF THE SCHOOL!
THIRD SAKE
SCHOOL ENDED HOURS AGO!

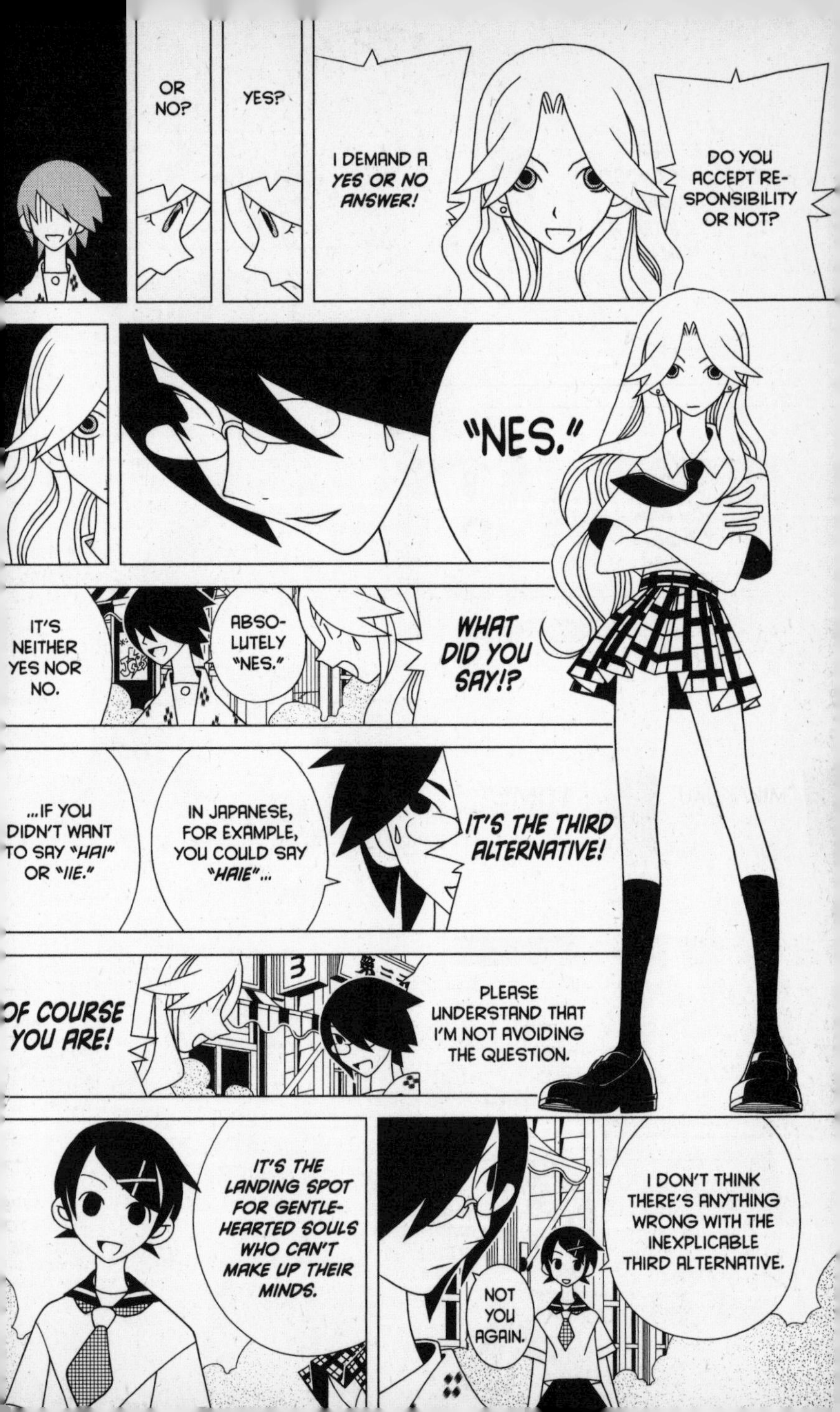
DO YOU ACCEPT RESPONSIBILITY OR NOT?
I DEMAND A YES OR NO ANSWER!
YES?
OR NO?
"NES."
WHAT DID YOU SAY!?
ABSOLUTELY "NES."
IT'S NEITHER YES NOR NO.
IT'S THE THIRD ALTERNATIVE!
IN JAPANESE, FOR EXAMPLE, YOU COULD SAY "HAIE"...
...IF YOU DIDN'T WANT TO SAY "HAI" OR "IIE."
PLEASE UNDERSTAND THAT I'M NOT AVOIDING THE QUESTION.
OF COURSE YOU ARE!
I DON'T THINK THERE'S ANYTHING WRONG WITH THE INEXPLICABLE THIRD ALTERNATIVE.
NOT YOU AGAIN.
IT'S THE LANDING SPOT FOR GENTLE-HEARTED SOULS WHO CAN'T MAKE UP THEIR MINDS.

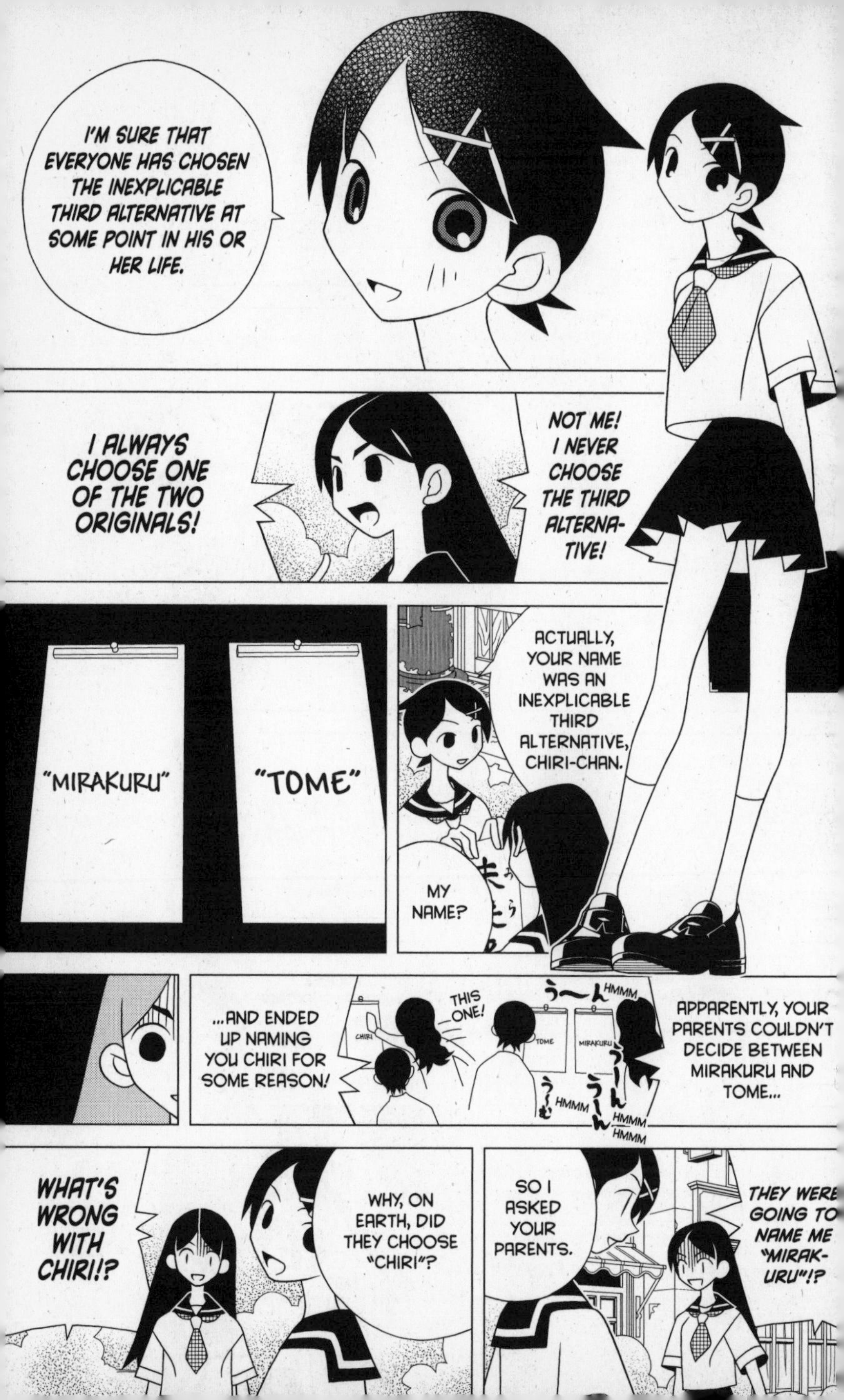
I'M SURE THAT EVERYONE HAS CHOSEN THE INEXPLICABLE THIRD ALTERNATIVE AT SOME POINT IN HIS OR HER LIFE.
NOT ME! I NEVER CHOOSE THE THIRD ALTERNA-TIVE!
I ALWAYS CHOOSE ONE OF THE TWO ORIGINALS!
ACTUALLY, YOUR NAME WAS AN INEXPLICABLE THIRD ALTERNATIVE, CHIRI-CHAN.
MY NAME?
"TOME"
"MIRAKURU"
APPARENTLY, YOUR PARENTS COULDN'T DECIDE BETWEEN MIRAKURU AND TOME...
う～ん HMMM
MIRAKURU
TOME
うーん HMMM
うーん HMMM
う～む HMMM
THIS ONE!
CHIRI
...AND ENDED UP NAMING YOU CHIRI FOR SOME REASON!
THEY WERE GOING TO NAME ME "MIRAK-URU"!?
SO I ASKED YOUR PARENTS.
WHY, ON EARTH, DID THEY CHOOSE "CHIRI"?
WHAT'S WRONG WITH CHIRI!?

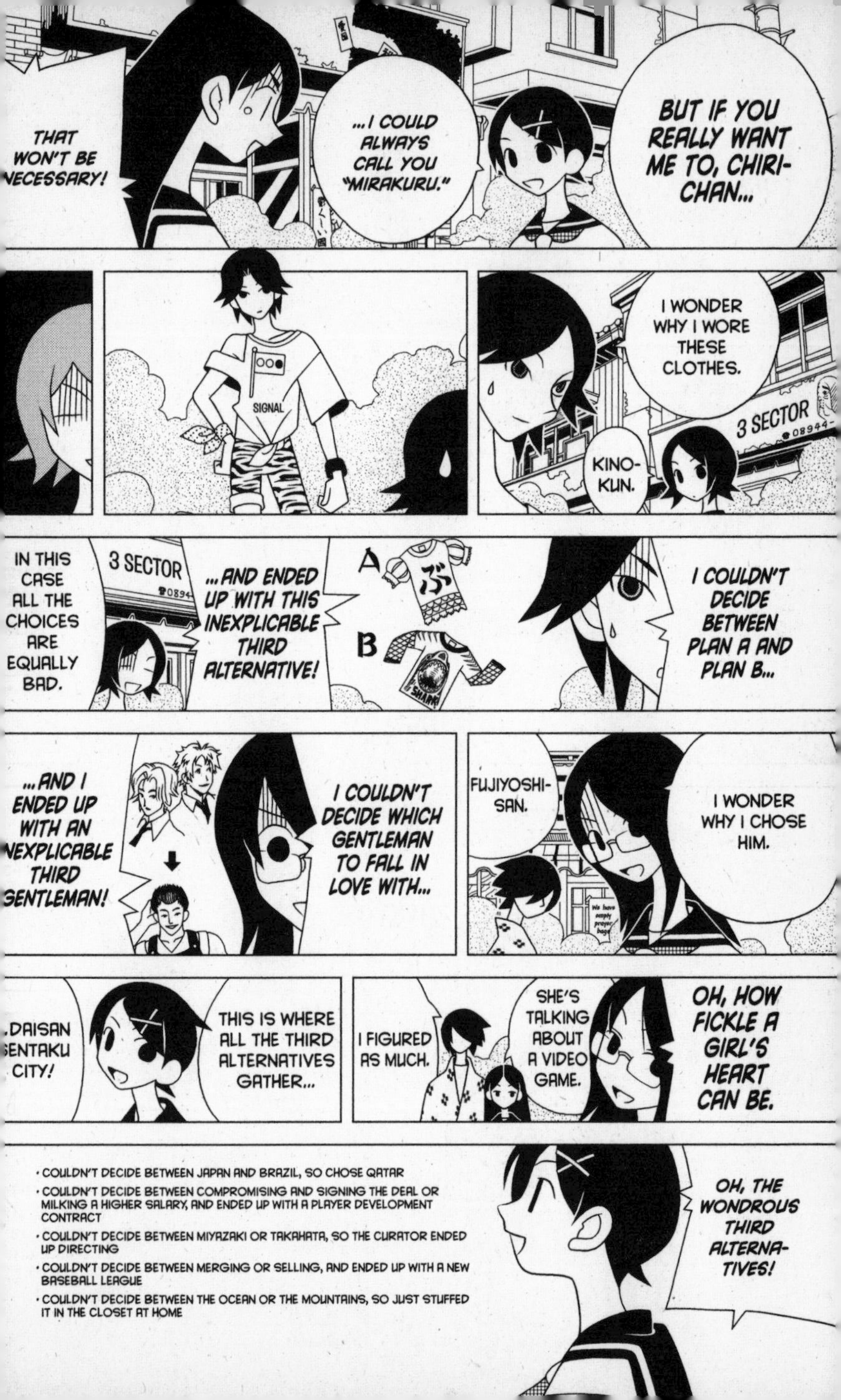
BUT IF YOU REALLY WANT ME TO, CHIRI-CHAN...
...I COULD ALWAYS CALL YOU "MIRAKURU."
THAT WON'T BE NECESSARY!
I WONDER WHY I WORE THESE CLOTHES.
3 SECTOR
KINO-KUN.
SIGNAL
I COULDN'T DECIDE BETWEEN PLAN A AND PLAN B...
A
ぶ
B
SHARK
...AND ENDED UP WITH THIS INEXPLICABLE THIRD ALTERNATIVE!
3 SECTOR
IN THIS CASE ALL THE CHOICES ARE EQUALLY BAD.
I WONDER WHY I CHOSE HIM.
FUJIYOSHI-SAN.
We have empty prayer bags
I COULDN'T DECIDE WHICH GENTLEMAN TO FALL IN LOVE WITH...
...AND I ENDED UP WITH AN INEXPLICABLE THIRD GENTLEMAN!
OH, HOW FICKLE A GIRL'S HEART CAN BE.
SHE'S TALKING ABOUT A VIDEO GAME.
I FIGURED AS MUCH.
THIS IS WHERE ALL THE THIRD ALTERNATIVES GATHER...
DAISAN SENTAKU CITY!
OH, THE WONDROUS THIRD ALTERNA-TIVES!
• COULDN'T DECIDE BETWEEN JAPAN AND BRAZIL, SO CHOSE QATAR
• COULDN'T DECIDE BETWEEN COMPROMISING AND SIGNING THE DEAL OR MILKING A HIGHER SALARY, AND ENDED UP WITH A PLAYER DEVELOPMENT CONTRACT
• COULDN'T DECIDE BETWEEN MIYAZAKI OR TAKAHATA, SO THE CURATOR ENDED UP DIRECTING
• COULDN'T DECIDE BETWEEN MERGING OR SELLING, AND ENDED UP WITH A NEW BASEBALL LEAGUE
• COULDN'T DECIDE BETWEEN THE OCEAN OR THE MOUNTAINS, SO JUST STUFFED IT IN THE CLOSET AT HOME

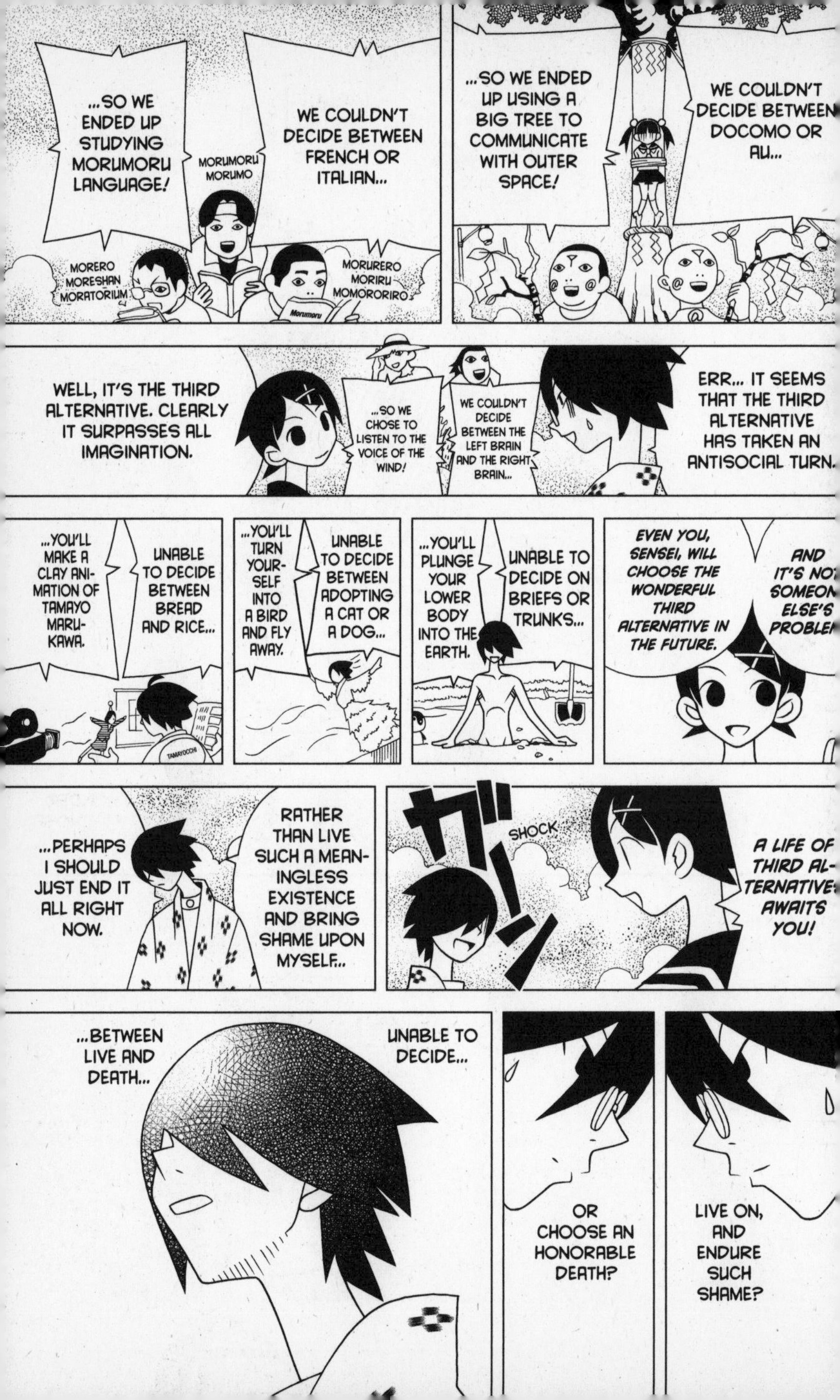
WE COULDN'T DECIDE BETWEEN DOCOMO OR AU...
...SO WE ENDED UP USING A BIG TREE TO COMMUNICATE WITH OUTER SPACE!
WE COULDN'T DECIDE BETWEEN FRENCH OR ITALIAN...
...SO WE ENDED UP STUDYING MORUMORU LANGUAGE!
MORUMORU MORUMO
MORURERO MORIRU MOMORORIRO
MORERO MORESHAN MORATORIUM
Morumoru
ERR... IT SEEMS THAT THE THIRD ALTERNATIVE HAS TAKEN AN ANTISOCIAL TURN.
WE COULDN'T DECIDE BETWEEN THE LEFT BRAIN AND THE RIGHT BRAIN...
...SO WE CHOSE TO LISTEN TO THE VOICE OF THE WIND!
WELL, IT'S THE THIRD ALTERNATIVE. CLEARLY IT SURPASSES ALL IMAGINATION.
AND IT'S NO SOMEON ELSE'S PROBLE
EVEN YOU, SENSEI, WILL CHOOSE THE WONDERFUL THIRD ALTERNATIVE IN THE FUTURE.
UNABLE TO DECIDE ON BRIEFS OR TRUNKS...
...YOU'LL PLUNGE YOUR LOWER BODY INTO THE EARTH.
UNABLE TO DECIDE BETWEEN ADOPTING A CAT OR A DOG...
...YOU'LL TURN YOURSELF INTO A BIRD AND FLY AWAY.
UNABLE TO DECIDE BETWEEN BREAD AND RICE...
...YOU'LL MAKE A CLAY ANIMATION OF TAMAYO MARUKAWA.
TAMAYOCCHI
A LIFE OF THIRD ALTERNATIVE AWAITS YOU!
SHOCK
RATHER THAN LIVE SUCH A MEANINGLESS EXISTENCE AND BRING SHAME UPON MYSELF..
...PERHAPS I SHOULD JUST END IT ALL RIGHT NOW.
LIVE ON, AND ENDURE SUCH SHAME?
OR CHOOSE AN HONORABLE DEATH?
UNABLE TO DECIDE...
...BETWEEN LIVE AND DEATH...

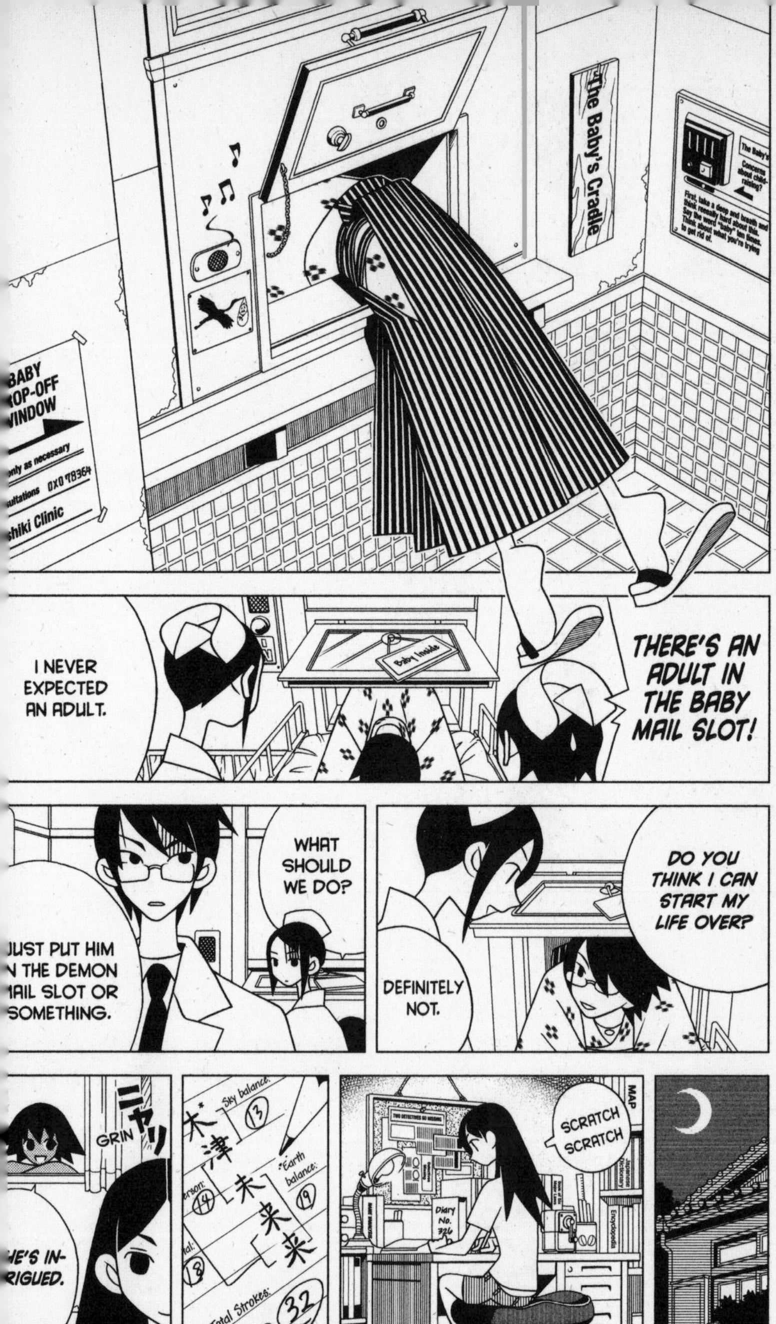
The Baby's Cradle
The Baby's
Concerns about child-raising?
First, take a deep and breath and think reeeally hard about this. Say the word "baby" ten times. Think about what you're trying to get rid of.
BABY
ROP-OFF
WINDOW
only as necessary
sultations 0X0 78364
shiki Clinic
THERE'S AN ADULT IN THE BABY MAIL SLOT!
Baby Inside
I NEVER EXPECTED AN ADULT.
DO YOU THINK I CAN START MY LIFE OVER?
DEFINITELY NOT.
WHAT SHOULD WE DO?
JUST PUT HIM
N THE DEMON
IAIL SLOT OR
SOMETHING.
MAP
TWO DETECTIVES GO MISSING
SCRATCH SCRATCH
Diary No. 326
Japanese Dictionary
Encyclopedia
木津* 未来
Sky balance: 13
Earth balance: 19
erson: 14
al: 18
Total Strokes: 32
ニヤリ
GRIN
HE'S IN-
RIGUED.

*MIRAKURU KITSU

AWW...
WHY DID I CHOOSE *THIS* ONE?
YOU NEVER REGRET YOUR CHOICES. WHAT HAPPENED?
I JUST COULDN'T DECIDE, SO I ENDED UP...
...CHOOSING THIS TOTALLY WEIRD ONE.
WHAT WERE THE OTHER CHOICES?
OHHH, WHY DID I CHOOSE *THIS* ONE?

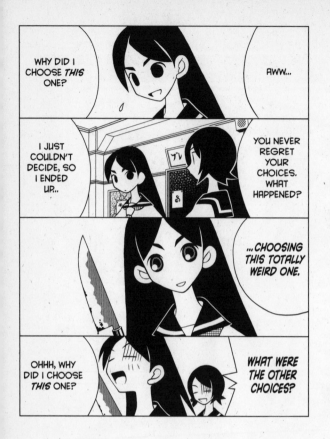

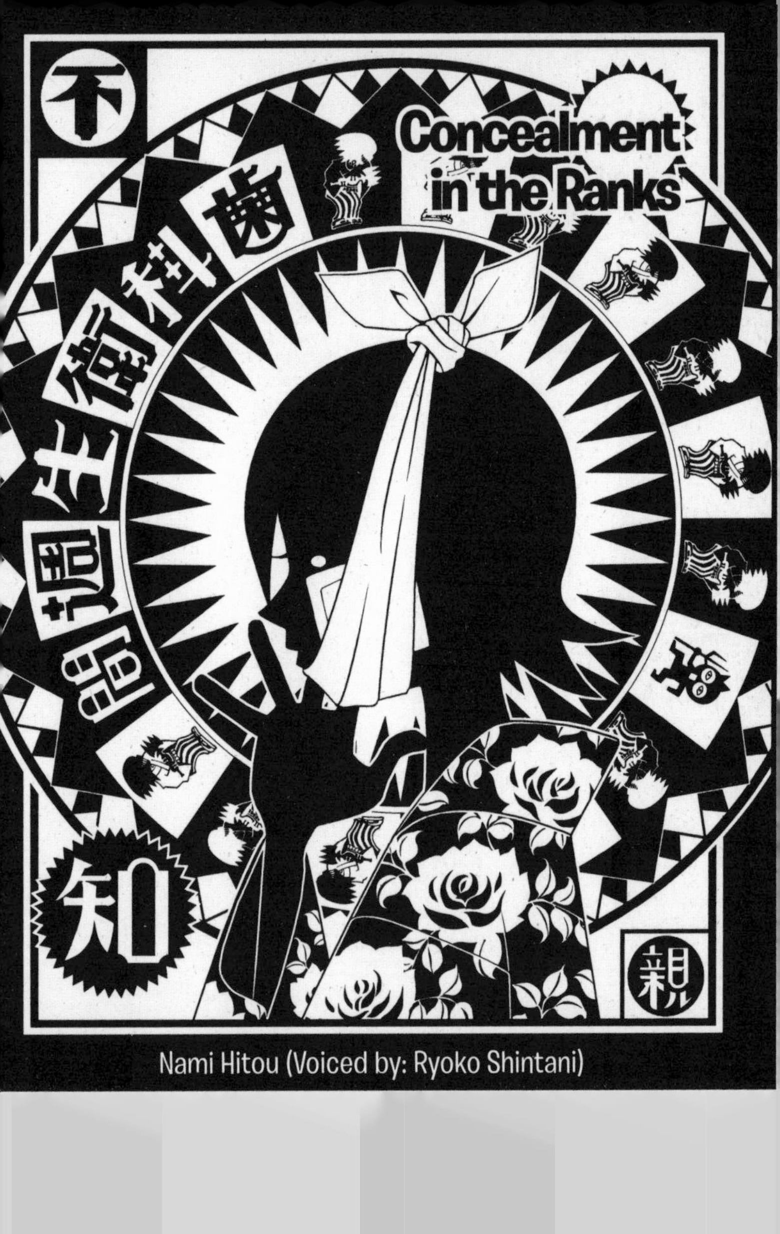
Concealment in the Ranks
歯科衛生週間

Nami Hitou (Voiced by: Ryoko Shintani)

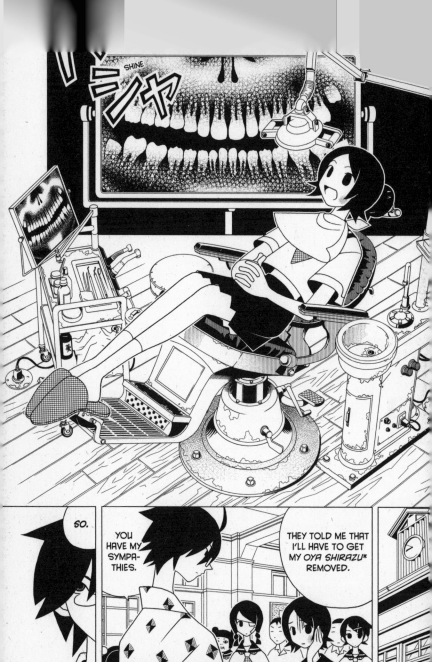

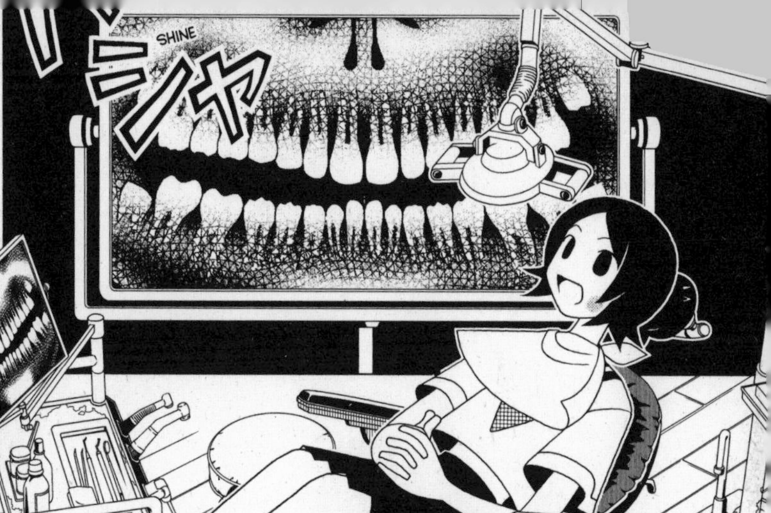
SHINE
シャ

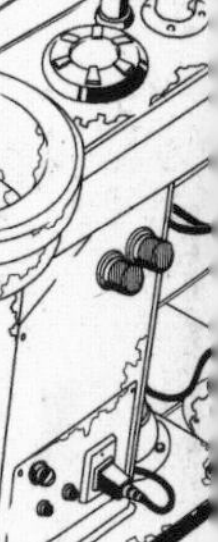

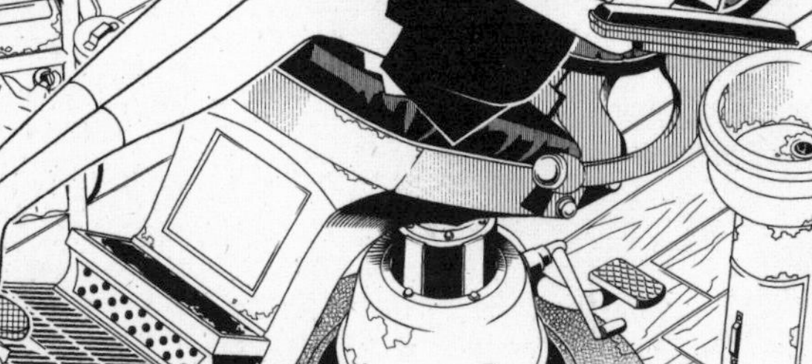
THEY TOLD ME THAT I'LL HAVE TO GET MY *OYA SHIRAZU** REMOVED.
YOU HAVE MY SYMPA-THIES.

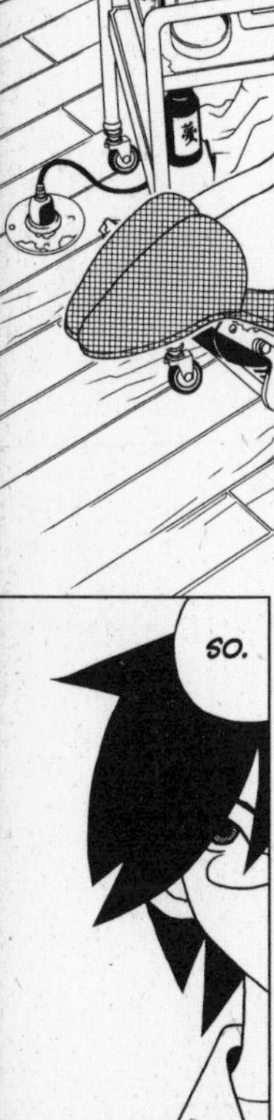
SO.

* THIS CHAPTER REVOLVES AROUND A PUN IN JAPANESE. THE JAPANESE WORD FOR "WISDOM TEETH" IS *OYA SHIRAZU*, WHICH LITERALLY TRANSLATES AS "PARENTS DON'T KNOW." THE ORIGIN OF THIS TERM COMES FROM THE FACT THAT WISDOM TEETH APPEAR LATER IN LIFE, AFTER A PERSON HAS LEFT THE CARE OF THEIR PARENTS.

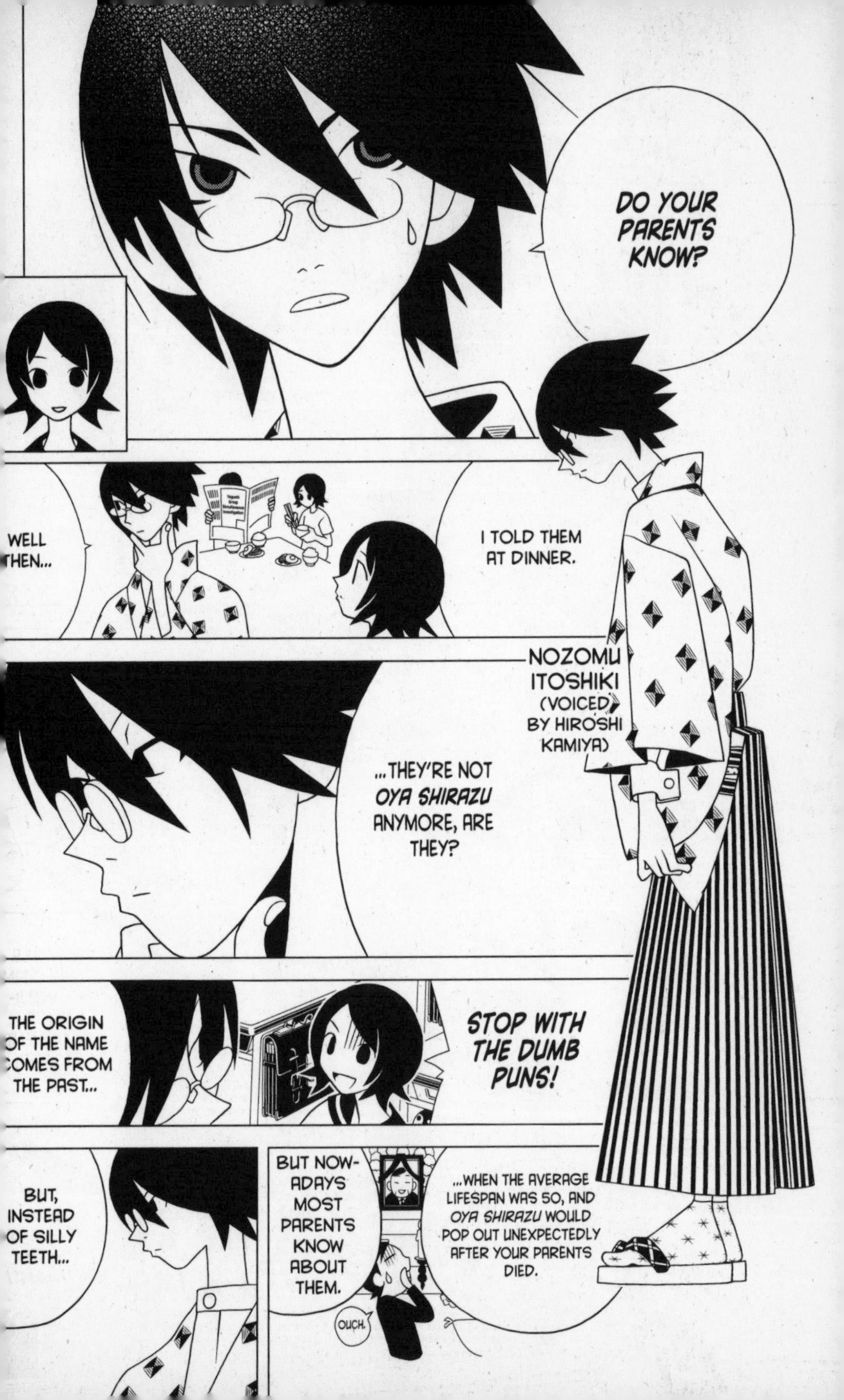
DO YOUR PARENTS KNOW?
NOZOMU ITOSHIKI (VOICED BY HIROSHI KAMIYA)
I TOLD THEM AT DINNER.
WELL THEN...
...THEY'RE NOT *OYA SHIRAZU* ANYMORE, ARE THEY?
STOP WITH THE DUMB PUNS!
THE ORIGIN OF THE NAME COMES FROM THE PAST...
...WHEN THE AVERAGE LIFESPAN WAS 50, AND *OYA SHIRAZU* WOULD POP OUT UNEXPECTEDLY AFTER YOUR PARENTS DIED.
OUCH.
BUT NOWADAYS MOST PARENTS KNOW ABOUT THEM.
BUT, INSTEAD OF SILLY TEETH...

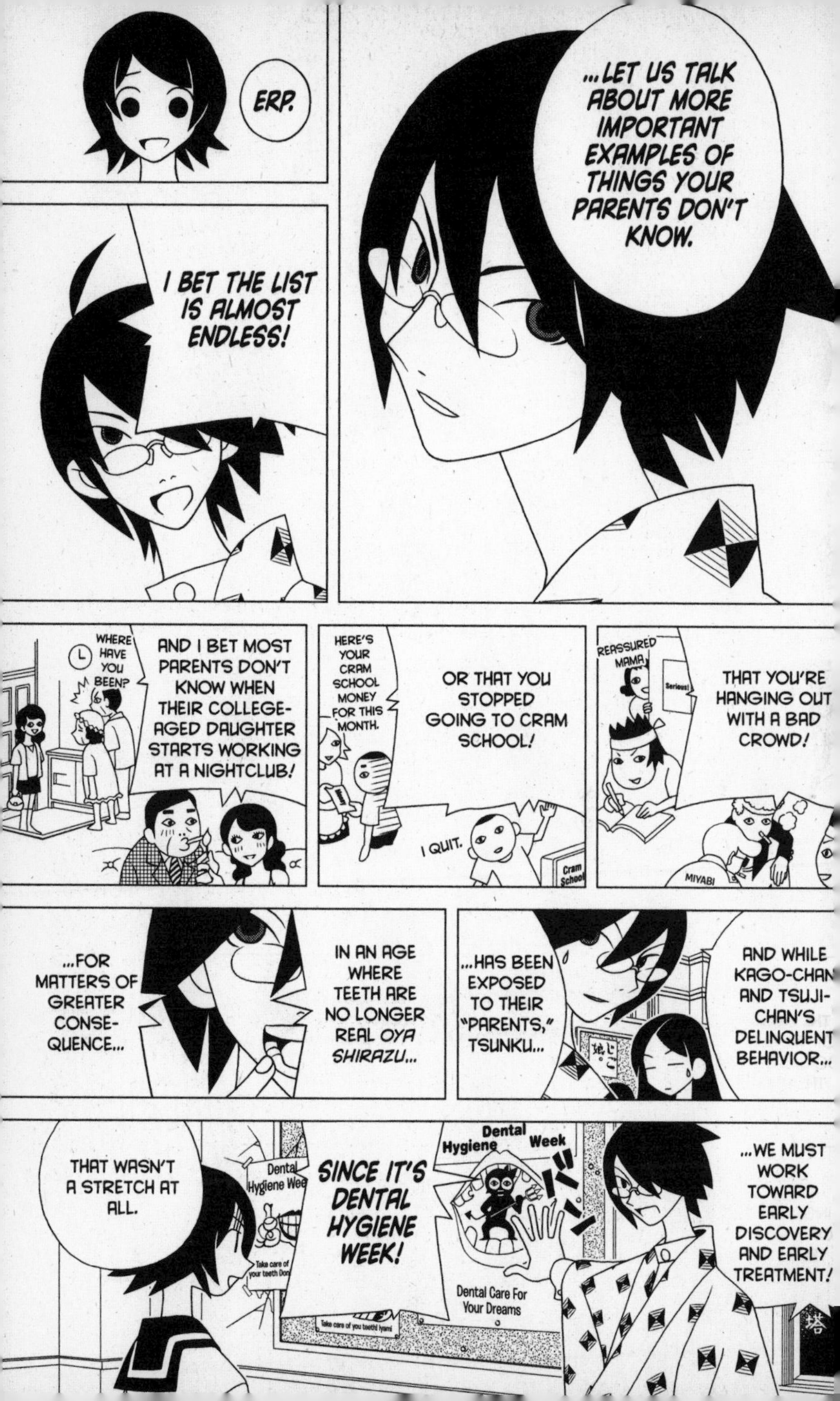
...LET US TALK ABOUT MORE IMPORTANT EXAMPLES OF THINGS YOUR PARENTS DON'T KNOW.
ERP.
I BET THE LIST IS ALMOST ENDLESS!
REASSURED MAMA
Serious!
THAT YOU'RE HANGING OUT WITH A BAD CROWD!
MIYABI
HERE'S YOUR CRAM SCHOOL MONEY FOR THIS MONTH.
OR THAT YOU STOPPED GOING TO CRAM SCHOOL!
I QUIT.
Cram School
WHERE HAVE YOU BEEN?
AND I BET MOST PARENTS DON'T KNOW WHEN THEIR COLLEGE-AGED DAUGHTER STARTS WORKING AT A NIGHTCLUB!
AND WHILE KAGO-CHAN AND TSUJI-CHAN'S DELINQUENT BEHAVIOR...
...HAS BEEN EXPOSED TO THEIR "PARENTS," TSUNKU...
IN AN AGE WHERE TEETH ARE NO LONGER REAL OYA SHIRAZU...
...FOR MATTERS OF GREATER CONSEQUENCE...
...WE MUST WORK TOWARD EARLY DISCOVERY AND EARLY TREATMENT!
Dental Hygiene Week
Dental Care For Your Dreams
SINCE IT'S DENTAL HYGIENE WEEK!
Take care of you teeth! Iyami
Dental Hygiene Wee
Take care of your teeth Don
THAT WASN'T A STRETCH AT ALL.

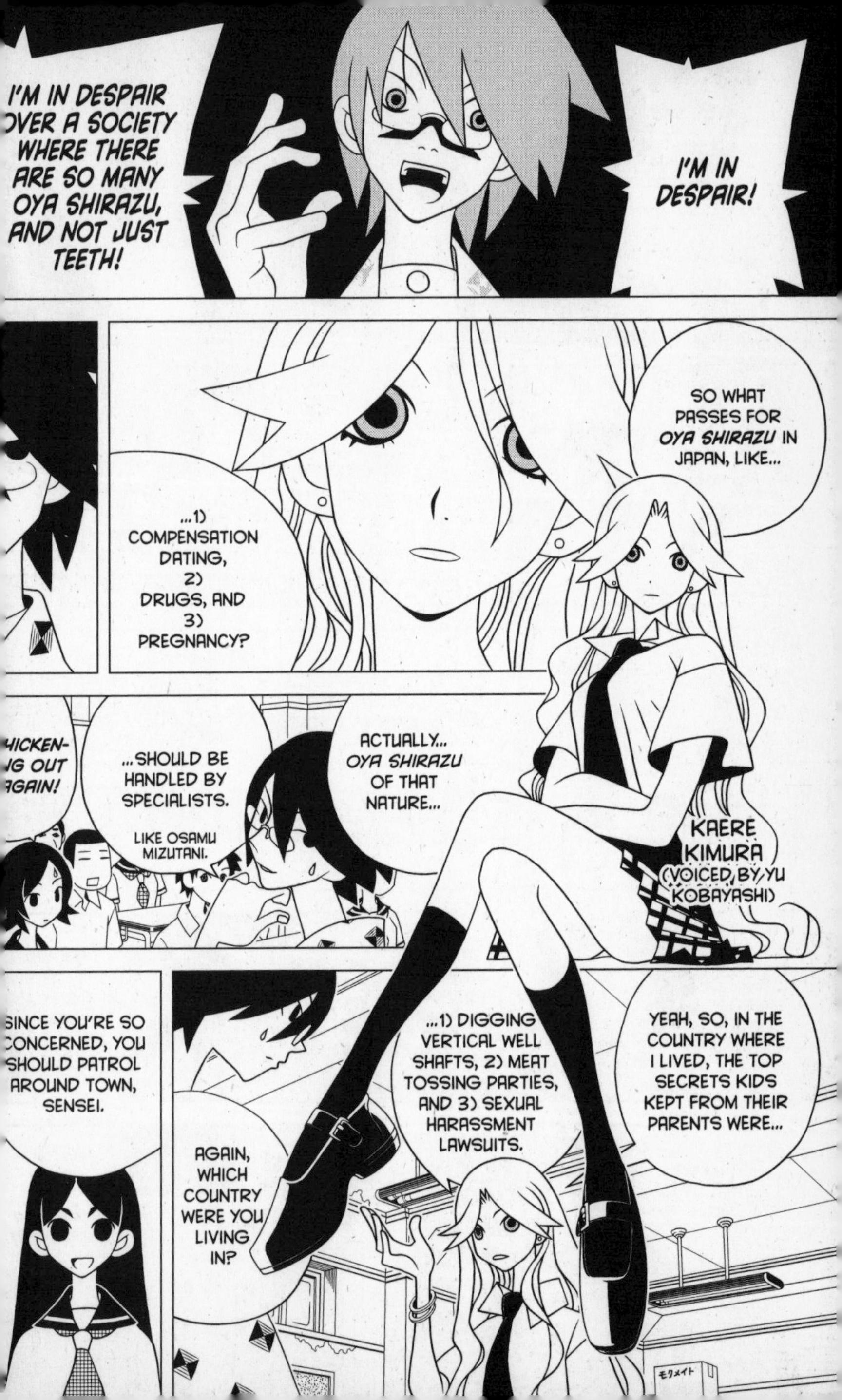
I'M IN DESPAIR!
I'M IN DESPAIR OVER A SOCIETY WHERE THERE ARE SO MANY OYA SHIRAZU, AND NOT JUST TEETH!
SO WHAT PASSES FOR OYA SHIRAZU IN JAPAN, LIKE...
...1) COMPENSATION DATING, 2) DRUGS, AND 3) PREGNANCY?
KAERE KIMURA (VOICED BY YU KOBAYASHI)
ACTUALLY... OYA SHIRAZU OF THAT NATURE...
...SHOULD BE HANDLED BY SPECIALISTS.
LIKE OSAMU MIZUTANI.
YEAH, SO, IN THE COUNTRY WHERE I LIVED, THE TOP SECRETS KIDS KEPT FROM THEIR PARENTS WERE...
...1) DIGGING VERTICAL WELL SHAFTS, 2) MEAT TOSSING PARTIES, AND 3) SEXUAL HARASSMENT LAWSUITS.
AGAIN, WHICH COUNTRY WERE YOU LIVING IN?
SINCE YOU'RE SO CONCERNED, YOU SHOULD PATROL AROUND TOWN, SENSEI.
モクメイト

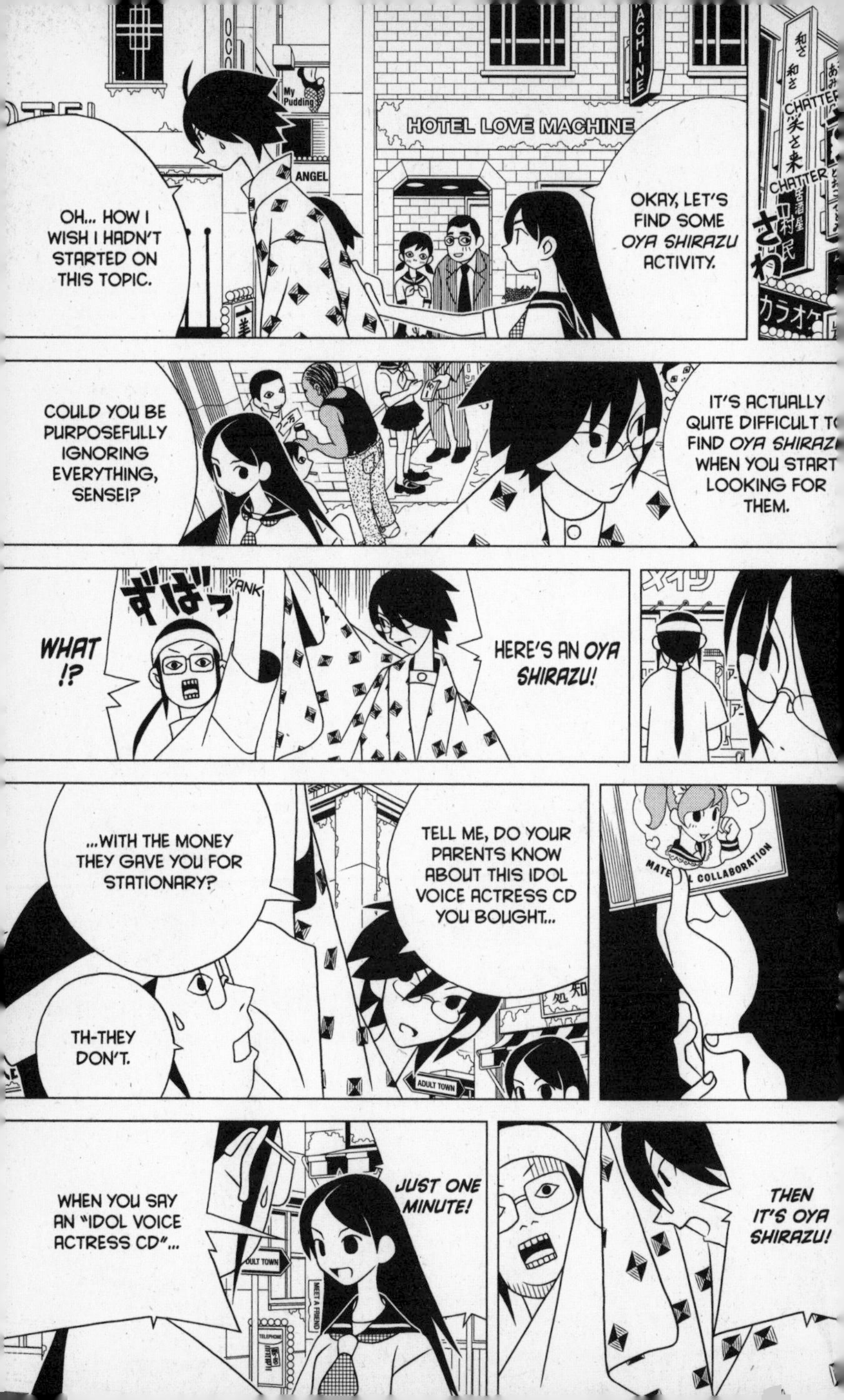
HOTEL LOVE MACHINE
CHATTER
CHATTER
My Pudding
ANGEL
OKAY, LET'S FIND SOME OYA SHIRAZU ACTIVITY.
OH... HOW I WISH I HADN'T STARTED ON THIS TOPIC.
IT'S ACTUALLY QUITE DIFFICULT T FIND OYA SHIRAZ WHEN YOU START LOOKING FOR THEM.
COULD YOU BE PURPOSEFULLY IGNORING EVERYTHING, SENSEI?
HERE'S AN OYA SHIRAZU!
ずばっ YANK
WHAT !?
MATE L COLLABORATION
TELL ME, DO YOUR PARENTS KNOW ABOUT THIS IDOL VOICE ACTRESS CD YOU BOUGHT...
...WITH THE MONEY THEY GAVE YOU FOR STATIONARY?
TH-THEY DON'T.
ADULT TOWN
THEN IT'S OYA SHIRAZU!
JUST ONE MINUTE!
WHEN YOU SAY AN "IDOL VOICE ACTRESS CD"...
ULT TOWN
MEET A FRIEND

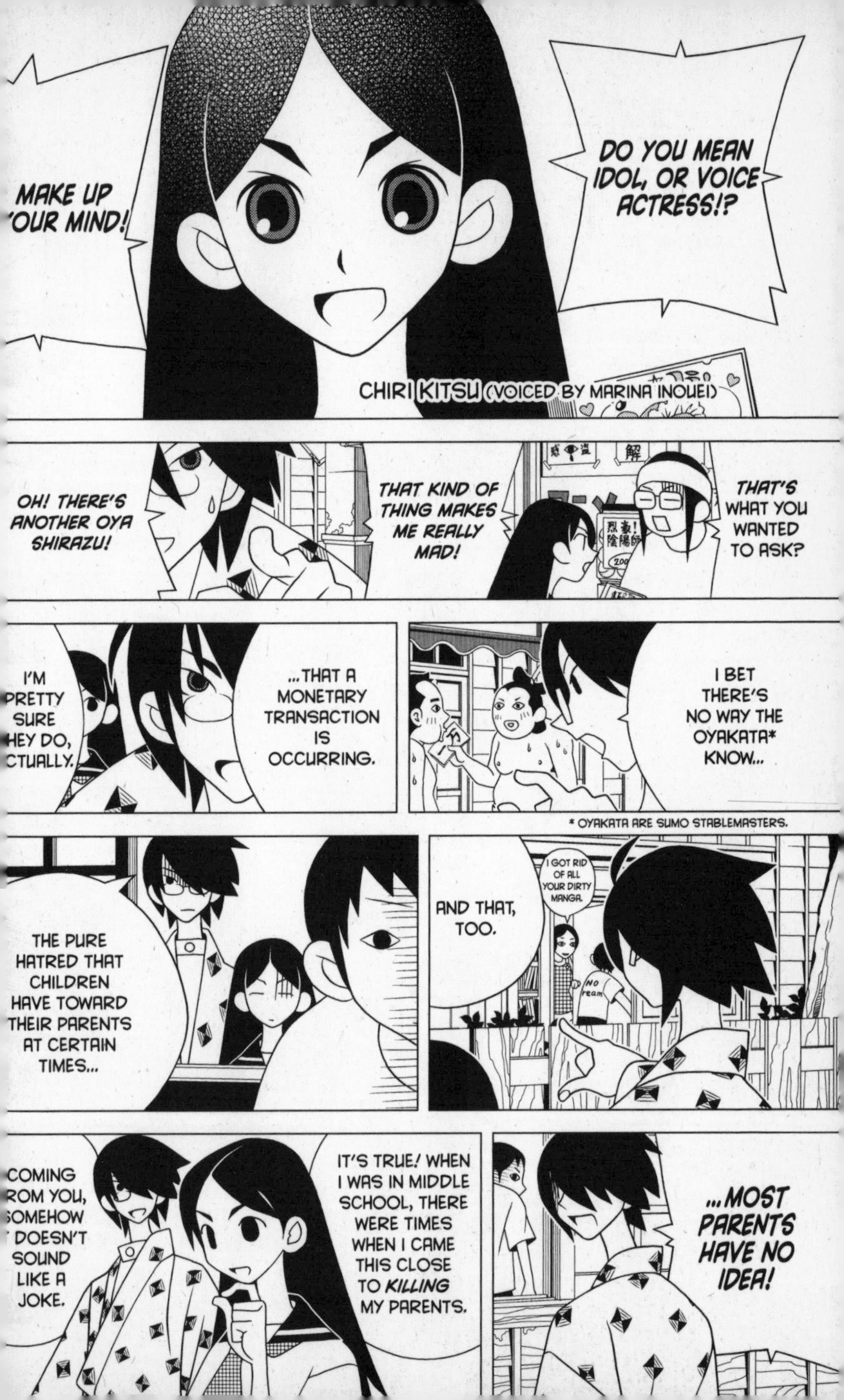
DO YOU MEAN IDOL, OR VOICE ACTRESS!?
MAKE UP 'OUR MIND!
CHIRI KITSU (VOICED BY MARINA INOUE)
THAT'S WHAT YOU WANTED TO ASK?
THAT KIND OF THING MAKES ME REALLY MAD!
OH! THERE'S ANOTHER OYA SHIRAZU!
I BET THERE'S NO WAY THE OYAKATA* KNOW...
...THAT A MONETARY TRANSACTION IS OCCURRING.
I'M PRETTY SURE HEY DO, CTUALLY.
* OYAKATA ARE SUMO STABLEMASTERS.
I GOT RID OF ALL YOUR DIRTY MANGA.
AND THAT, TOO.
THE PURE HATRED THAT CHILDREN HAVE TOWARD THEIR PARENTS AT CERTAIN TIMES...
...MOST PARENTS HAVE NO IDEA!
IT'S TRUE! WHEN I WAS IN MIDDLE SCHOOL, THERE WERE TIMES WHEN I CAME THIS CLOSE TO KILLING MY PARENTS.
COMING ROM YOU, SOMEHOW ' DOESN'T SOUND LIKE A JOKE.

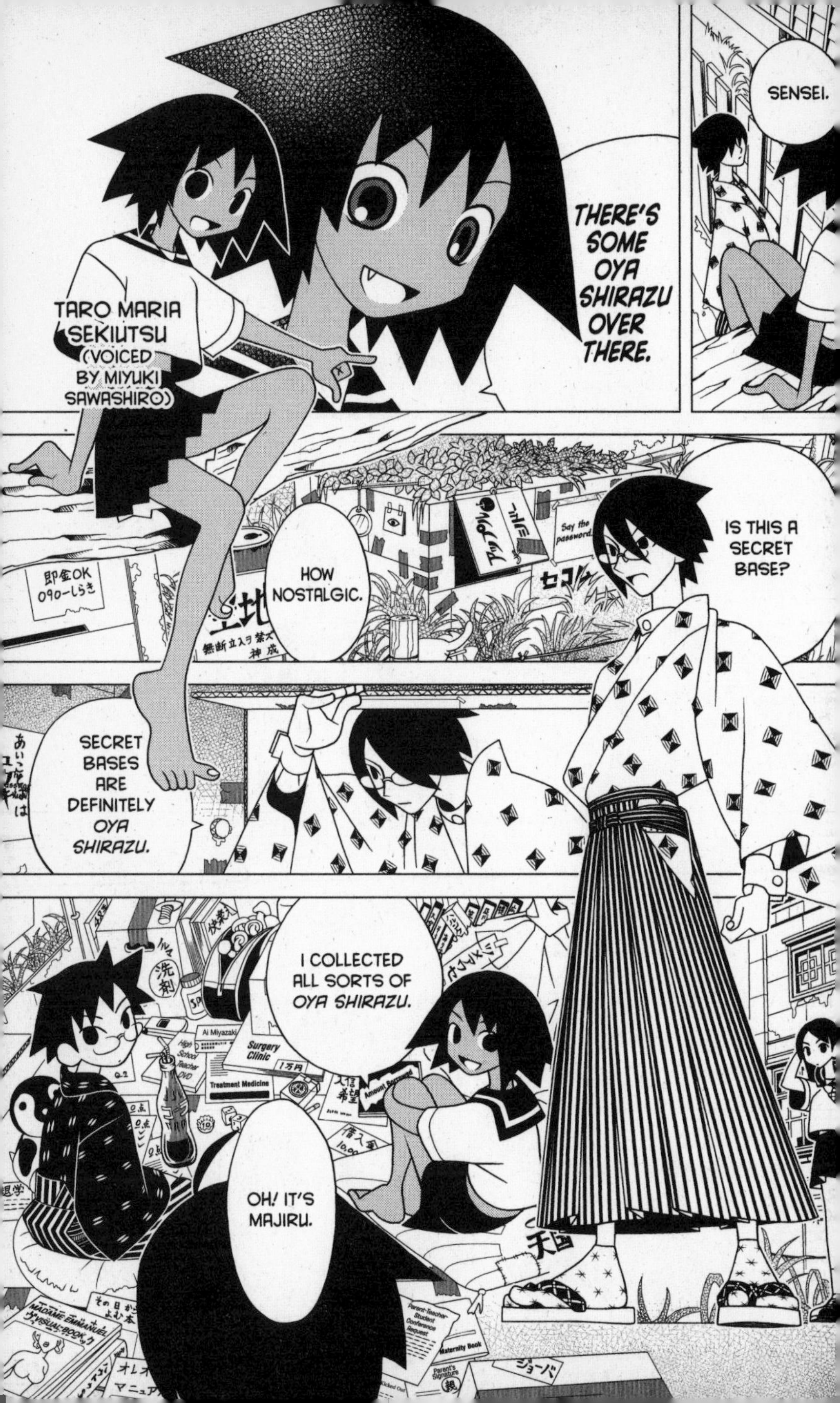
SENSEI.
THERE'S SOME OYA SHIRAZU OVER THERE.
TARO MARIA SEKIUTSU (VOICED BY MIYUKI SAWASHIRO)
IS THIS A SECRET BASE?
HOW NOSTALGIC.
Say the password.
即金OK 090-しらき
SECRET BASES ARE DEFINITELY OYA SHIRAZU.
I COLLECTED ALL SORTS OF OYA SHIRAZU.
OH! IT'S MAJIRU.
洗剤
Ai Miyazaki
High School Teacher DVD
Surgery Clinic
1万円
Treatment Medicine
Amount Borrowed
MADAME EMMANUEL VISUAL BOOK
Parent-Teacher-Student Conference Request
Maternity Book
Parent's Signature
ジョーバ

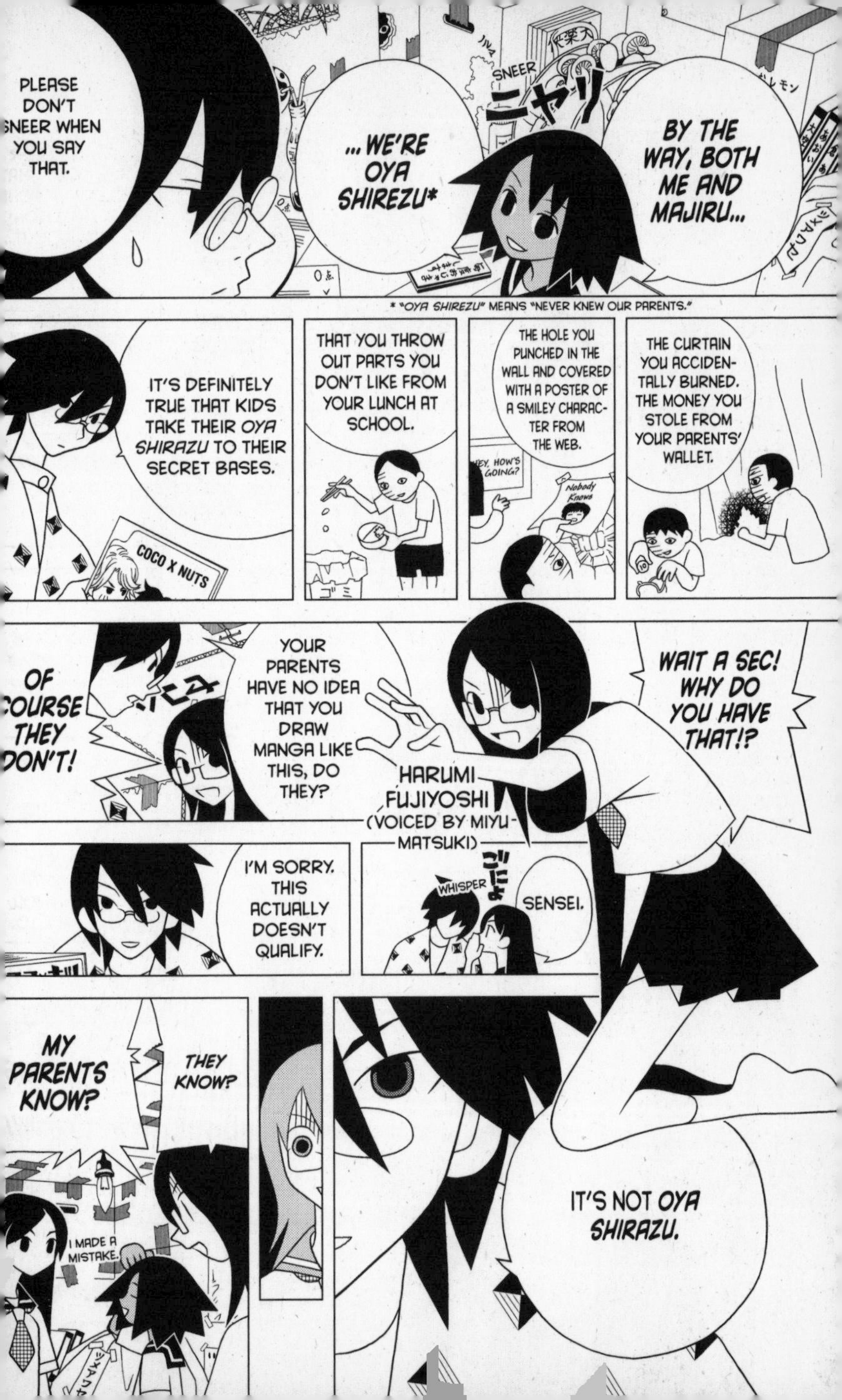
BY THE WAY, BOTH ME AND MAJIRU...
SNEER
...WE'RE OYA SHIREZU*
PLEASE DON'T SNEER WHEN YOU SAY THAT.
* "OYA SHIREZU" MEANS "NEVER KNEW OUR PARENTS."
THE CURTAIN YOU ACCIDENTALLY BURNED. THE MONEY YOU STOLE FROM YOUR PARENTS' WALLET.
THE HOLE YOU PUNCHED IN THE WALL AND COVERED WITH A POSTER OF A SMILEY CHARACTER FROM THE WEB.
Nobody Knows
THAT YOU THROW OUT PARTS YOU DON'T LIKE FROM YOUR LUNCH AT SCHOOL.
IT'S DEFINITELY TRUE THAT KIDS TAKE THEIR OYA SHIRAZU TO THEIR SECRET BASES.
COCO X NUTS
WAIT A SEC! WHY DO YOU HAVE THAT!?
YOUR PARENTS HAVE NO IDEA THAT YOU DRAW MANGA LIKE THIS, DO THEY?
HARUMI FUJIYOSHI (VOICED BY MIYU MATSUKI)
OF COURSE THEY DON'T!
WHISPER
SENSEI.
I'M SORRY. THIS ACTUALLY DOESN'T QUALIFY.
IT'S NOT OYA SHIRAZU.
THEY KNOW?
MY PARENTS KNOW?
I MADE A MISTAKE.

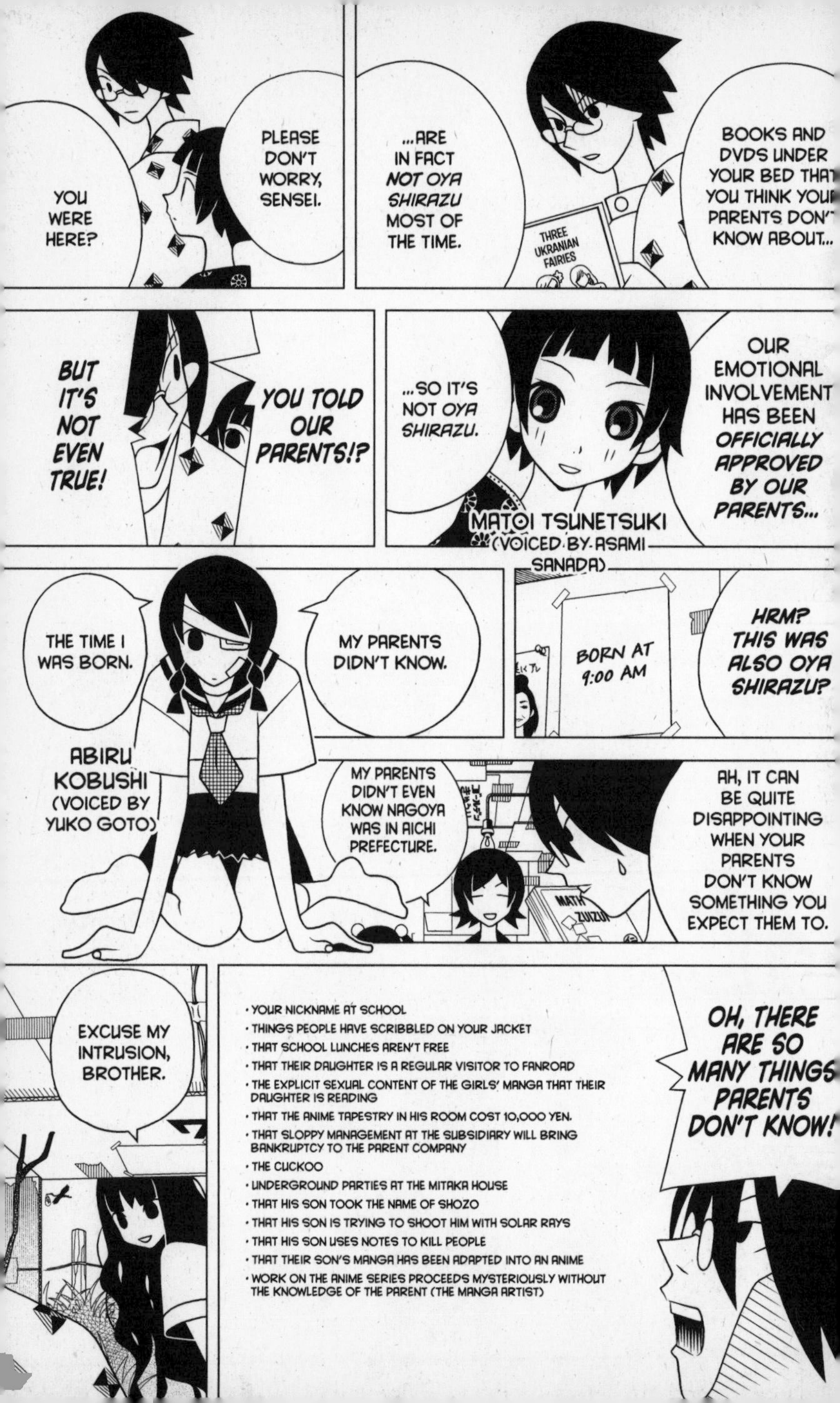
BOOKS AND DVDS UNDER YOUR BED THAT YOU THINK YOUR PARENTS DON'T KNOW ABOUT...
THREE UKRANIAN FAIRIES
...ARE IN FACT *NOT OYA SHIRAZU* MOST OF THE TIME.
PLEASE DON'T WORRY, SENSEI.
YOU WERE HERE?
OUR EMOTIONAL INVOLVEMENT HAS BEEN *OFFICIALLY APPROVED* BY OUR PARENTS...
...SO IT'S NOT *OYA SHIRAZU.*
MATOI TSUNETSUKI (VOICED BY ASAMI SANADA)
YOU TOLD OUR PARENTS!?
BUT IT'S NOT EVEN TRUE!
HRM? THIS WAS ALSO OYA SHIRAZU?
BORN AT 9:00 AM
AH, IT CAN BE QUITE DISAPPOINTING WHEN YOUR PARENTS DON'T KNOW SOMETHING YOU EXPECT THEM TO.
MY PARENTS DIDN'T EVEN KNOW NAGOYA WAS IN AICHI PREFECTURE.
MATH
MY PARENTS DIDN'T KNOW.
THE TIME I WAS BORN.
ABIRU KOBUSHI (VOICED BY YUKO GOTO)
OH, THERE ARE SO MANY THINGS PARENTS DON'T KNOW!
• YOUR NICKNAME AT SCHOOL
• THINGS PEOPLE HAVE SCRIBBLED ON YOUR JACKET
• THAT SCHOOL LUNCHES AREN'T FREE
• THAT THEIR DAUGHTER IS A REGULAR VISITOR TO FANROAD
• THE EXPLICIT SEXUAL CONTENT OF THE GIRLS' MANGA THAT THEIR DAUGHTER IS READING
• THAT THE ANIME TAPESTRY IN HIS ROOM COST 10,000 YEN.
• THAT SLOPPY MANAGEMENT AT THE SUBSIDIARY WILL BRING BANKRUPTCY TO THE PARENT COMPANY
• THE CUCKOO
• UNDERGROUND PARTIES AT THE MITAKA HOUSE
• THAT HIS SON TOOK THE NAME OF SHOZO
• THAT HIS SON IS TRYING TO SHOOT HIM WITH SOLAR RAYS
• THAT HIS SON USES NOTES TO KILL PEOPLE
• THAT THEIR SON'S MANGA HAS BEEN ADAPTED INTO AN ANIME
• WORK ON THE ANIME SERIES PROCEEDS MYSTERIOUSLY WITHOUT THE KNOWLEDGE OF THE PARENT (THE MANGA ARTIST)
EXCUSE MY INTRUSION, BROTHER.

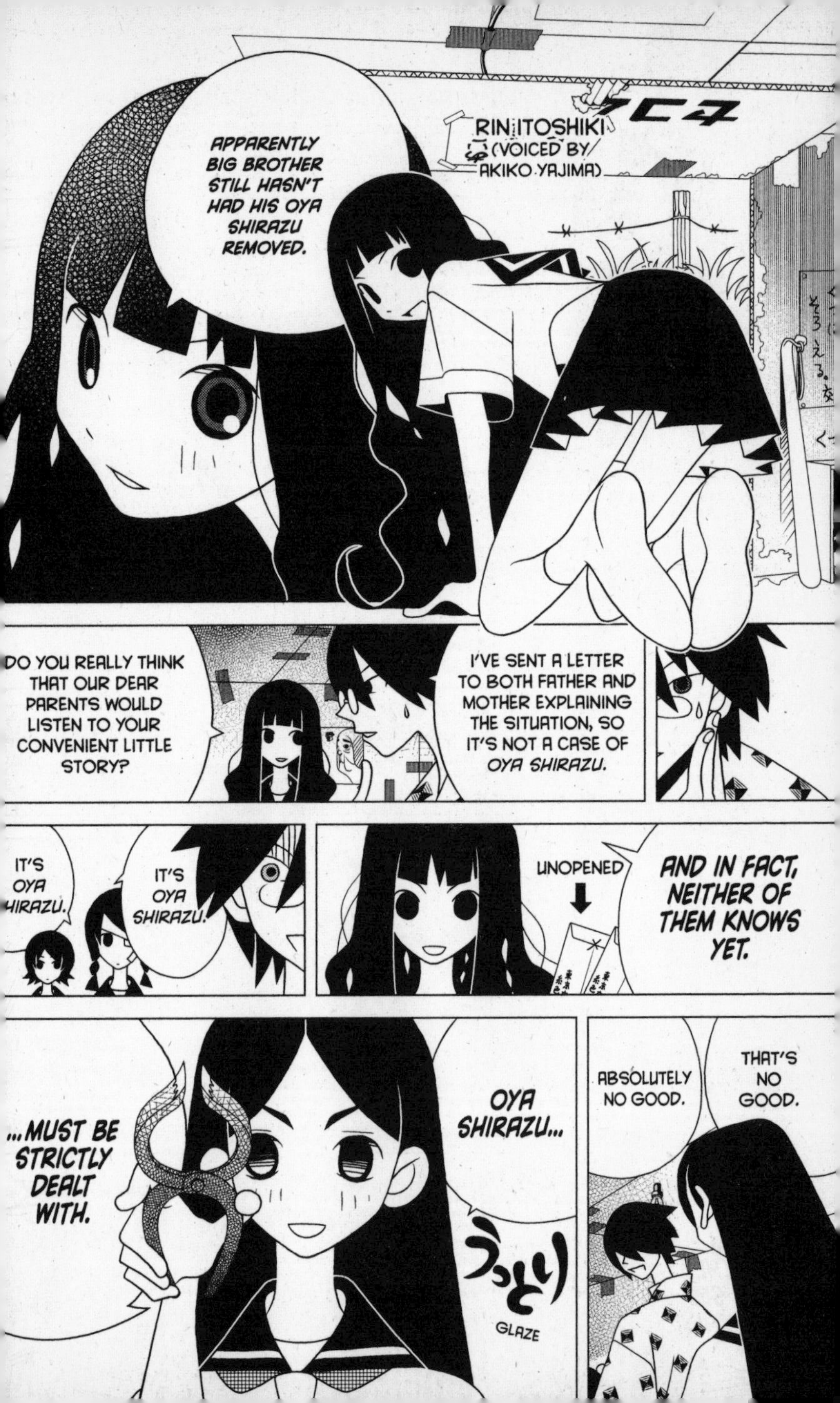

RIN ITOSHIKI (VOICED BY AKIKO YAJIMA)
APPARENTLY BIG BROTHER STILL HASN'T HAD HIS OYA SHIRAZU REMOVED.
I'VE SENT A LETTER TO BOTH FATHER AND MOTHER EXPLAINING THE SITUATION, SO IT'S NOT A CASE OF OYA SHIRAZU.
DO YOU REALLY THINK THAT OUR DEAR PARENTS WOULD LISTEN TO YOUR CONVENIENT LITTLE STORY?
AND IN FACT, NEITHER OF THEM KNOWS YET.
UNOPENED
IT'S OYA SHIRAZU.
IT'S OYA HIRAZU.
THAT'S NO GOOD.
ABSOLUTELY NO GOOD.
OYA SHIRAZU...
...MUST BE STRICTLY DEALT WITH.
うっとり
GLAZE

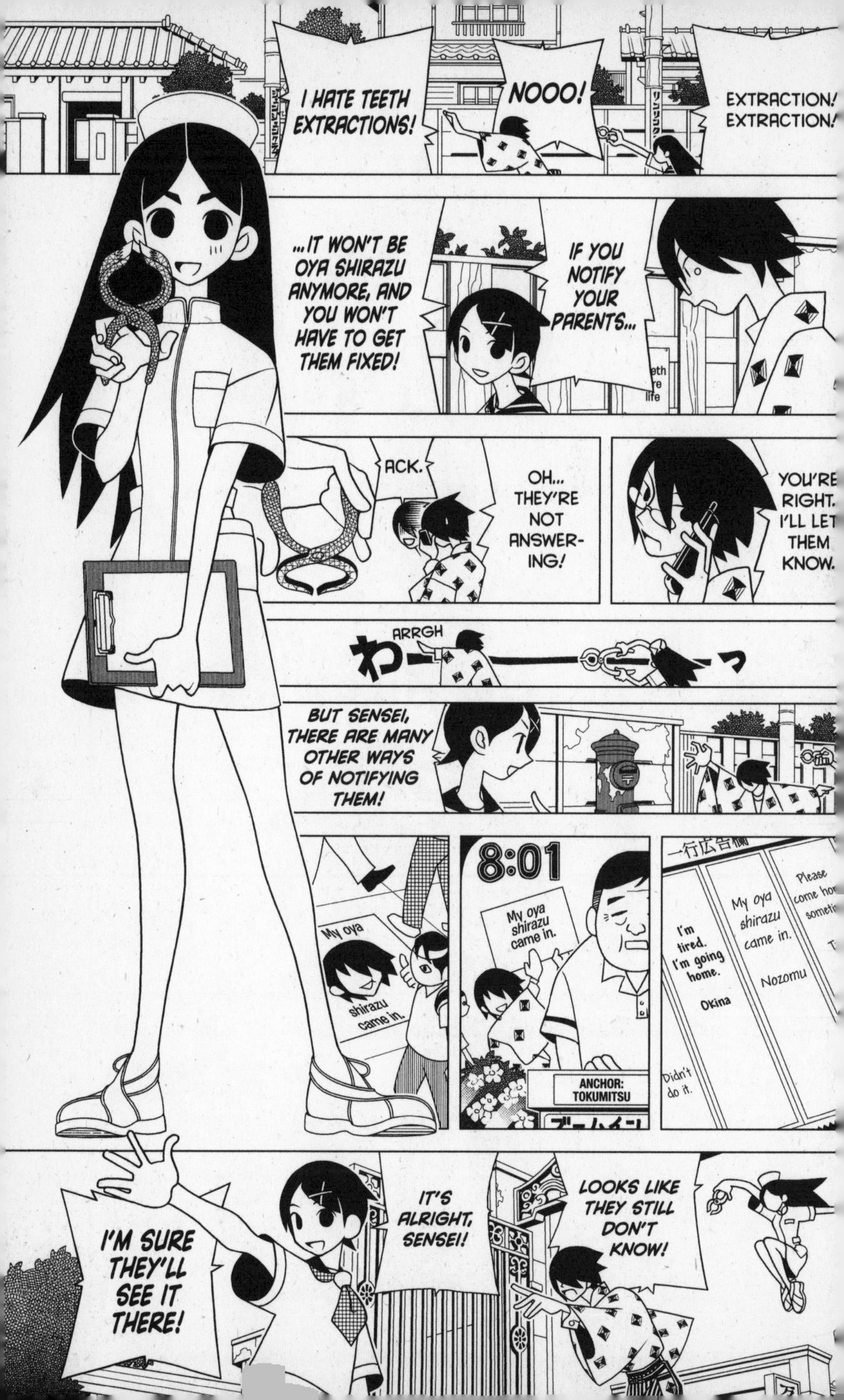

EXTRACTION! EXTRACTION!
NOOO!
I HATE TEETH EXTRACTIONS!
IF YOU NOTIFY YOUR PARENTS...
...IT WON'T BE OYA SHIRAZU ANYMORE, AND YOU WON'T HAVE TO GET THEM FIXED!
YOU'RE RIGHT. I'LL LET THEM KNOW.
OH... THEY'RE NOT ANSWERING!
ACK.
ARRGH
わーーっ
BUT SENSEI, THERE ARE MANY OTHER WAYS OF NOTIFYING THEM!
一行広告欄
Please come home
My oya shirazu came in.
Nozomu
I'm tired. I'm going home.
Okina
Didn't do it.
8:01
My oya shirazu came in.
ANCHOR: TOKUMITSU
My oya shirazu came in.
LOOKS LIKE THEY STILL DON'T KNOW!
IT'S ALRIGHT, SENSEI!
I'M SURE THEY'LL SEE IT THERE!

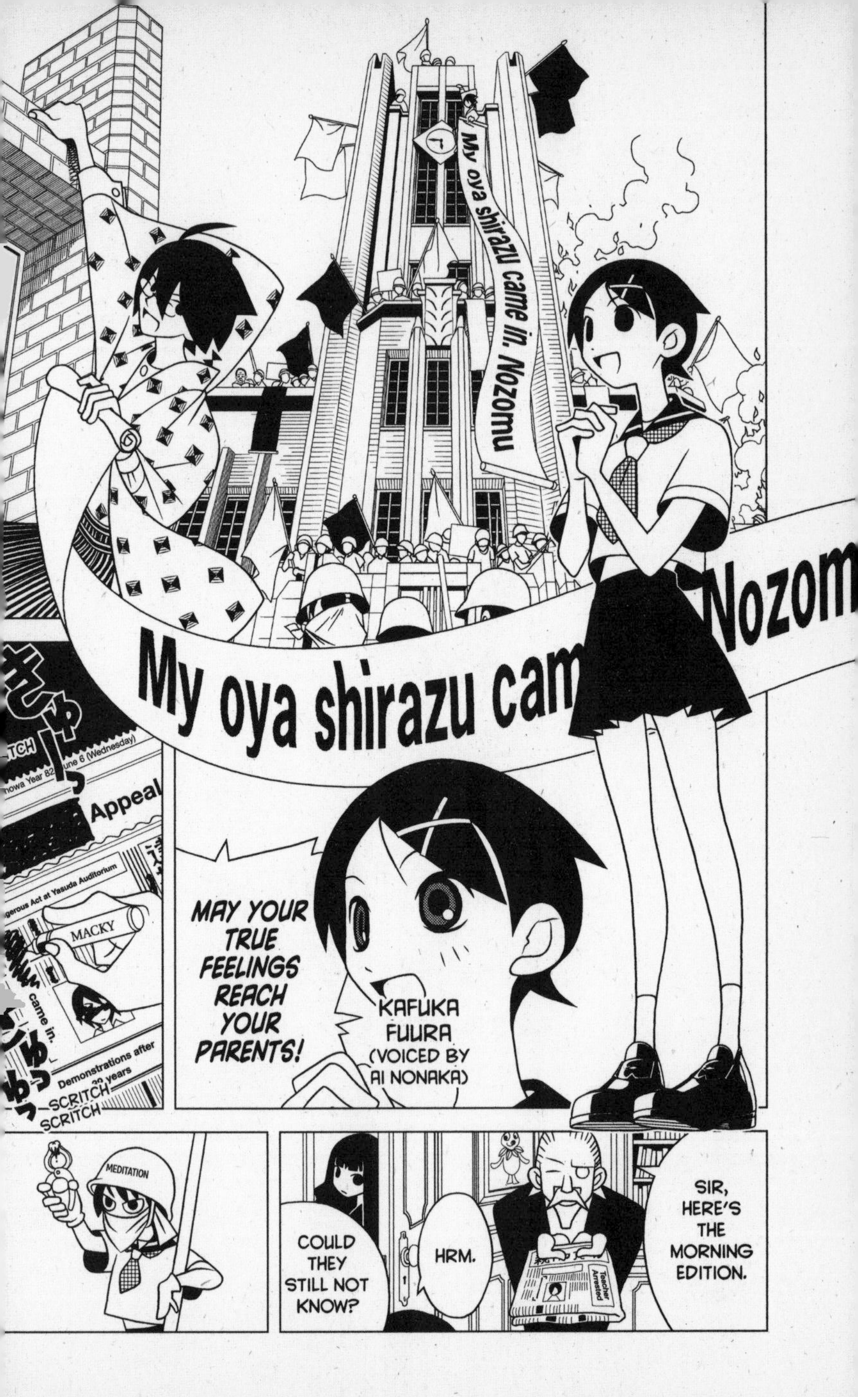
My oya shirazu came in. Nozomu
My oya shirazu cam
Nozom
MAY YOUR TRUE FEELINGS REACH YOUR PARENTS!
KAFUKA FUURA (VOICED BY AI NONAKA)
TCH
nowa Year 82 June 6 (Wednesday)
Appeal
gerous Act at Yasuda Auditorium
MACKY
came in.
Demonstrations after
years
SCRITCH
SCRITCH
SIR, HERE'S THE MORNING EDITION.
Teacher Arrested
HRM.
COULD THEY STILL NOT KNOW?
MEDITATION

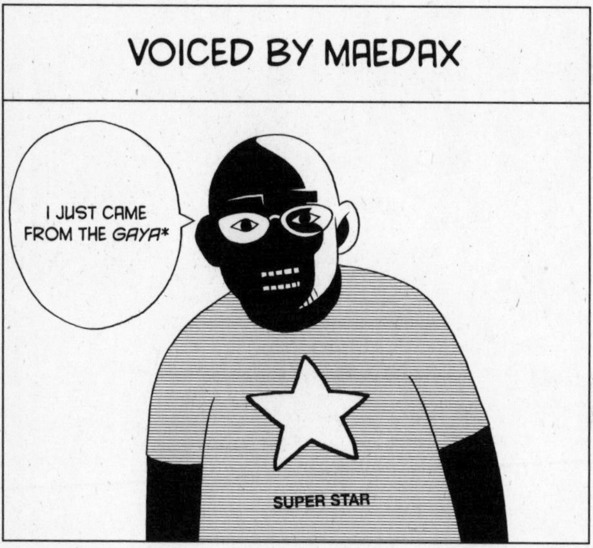

SUPER ANNOYING GUY

*A GAYA IS A RECORDING SESSION DURING WHICH ALL THE VOICE ACTORS COME TOGETHER TO RECORD THE BUSY NOISES OF CONVERSATION AND PEOPLE TALKING IN PUBLIC PLACES, CLASSROOMS, ETC.

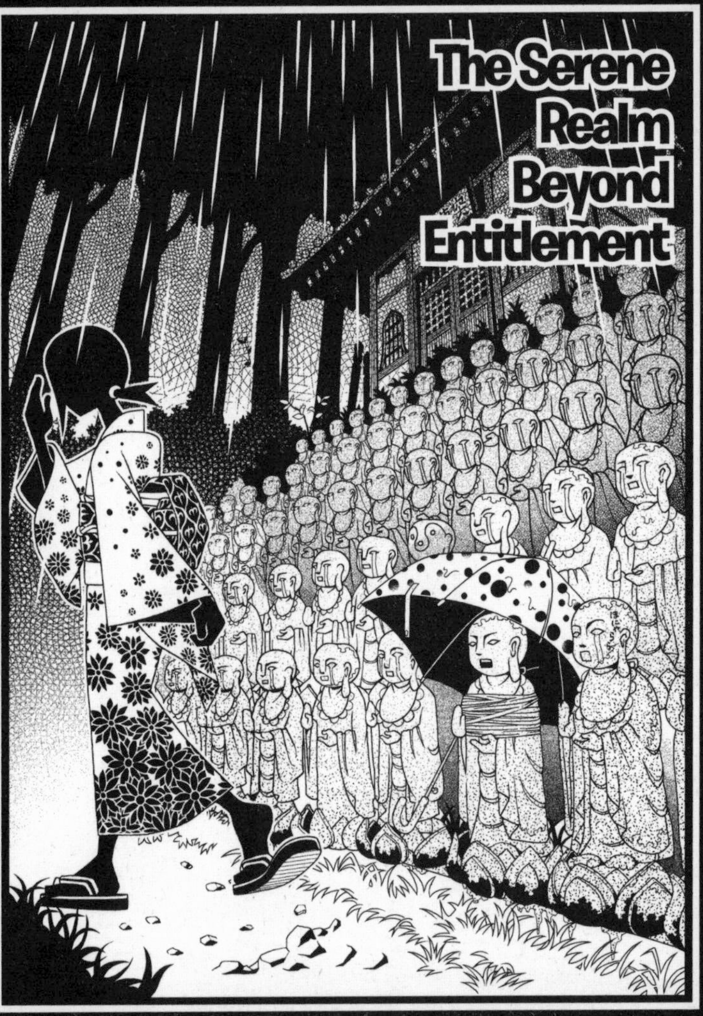
The Serene Realm Beyond Entitlement

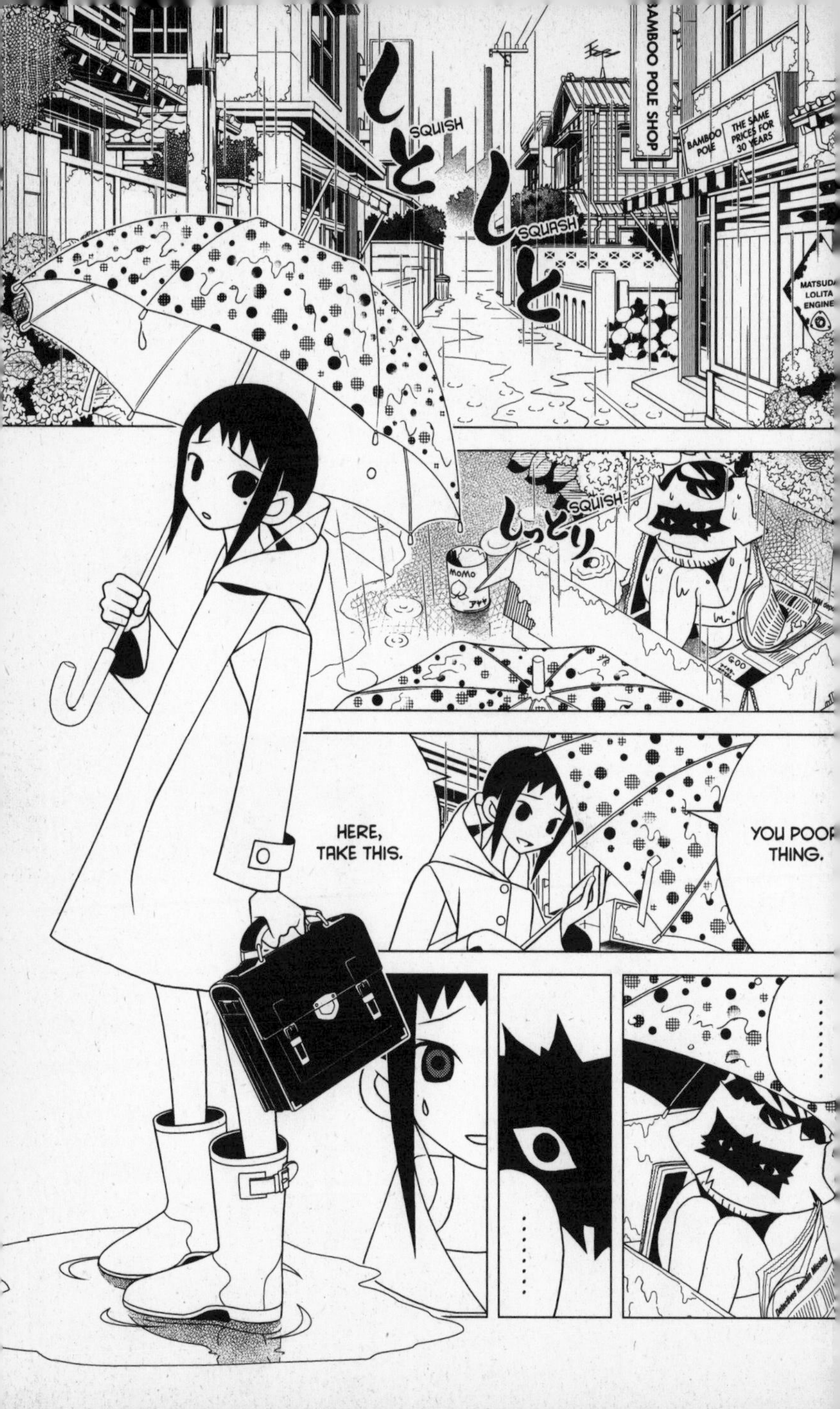
BAMBOO POLE SHOP
THE SAME PRICES FOR 30 YEARS
BAMBOO POLE
MATSUDA LOLITA ENGINE
しと
SQUISH
しと
SQUASH
しっとり
SQUISH
MOMO
GOO
YOU POOR THING.
HERE, TAKE THIS.
Detectives Remain Missing
......

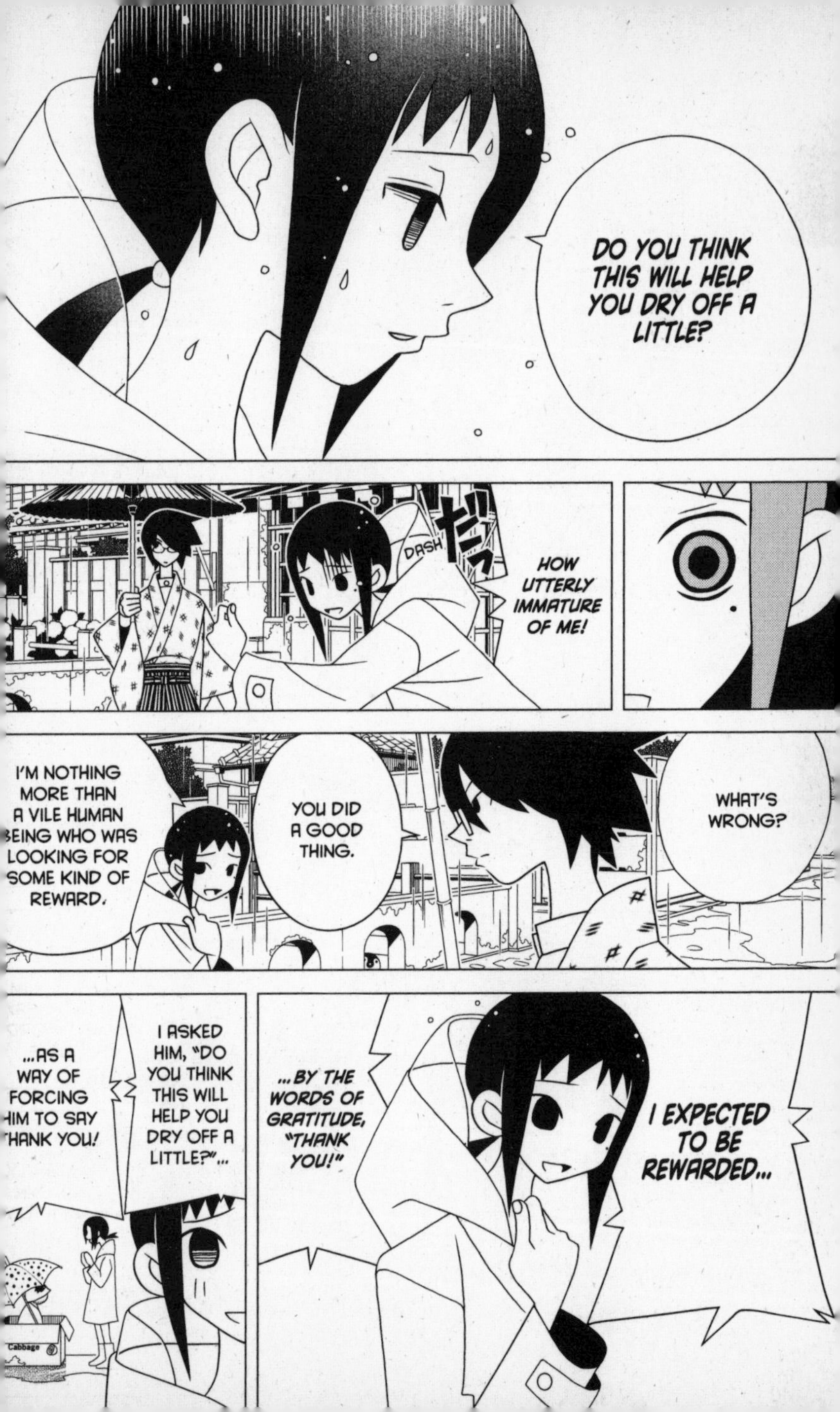
DO YOU THINK THIS WILL HELP YOU DRY OFF A LITTLE?
HOW UTTERLY IMMATURE OF ME!
DASH
WHAT'S WRONG?
YOU DID A GOOD THING.
I'M NOTHING MORE THAN A VILE HUMAN EING WHO WAS LOOKING FOR SOME KIND OF REWARD.
I EXPECTED TO BE REWARDED...
...BY THE WORDS OF GRATITUDE, "THANK YOU!"
I ASKED HIM, "DO YOU THINK THIS WILL HELP YOU DRY OFF A LITTLE?"...
...AS A WAY OF FORCING IM TO SAY HANK YOU!
Cabbage

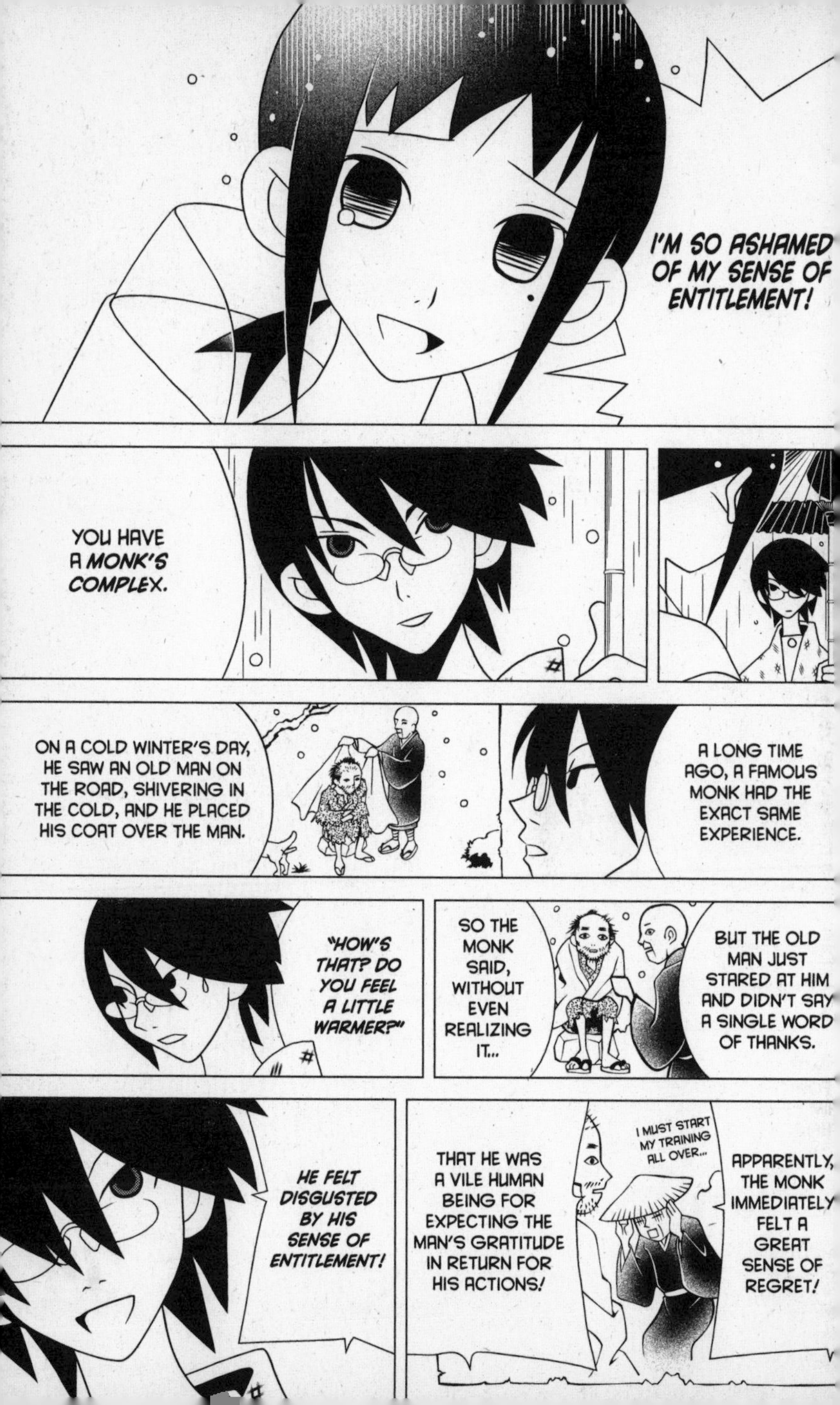

I'M SO ASHAMED OF MY SENSE OF ENTITLEMENT!
YOU HAVE A MONK'S COMPLEX.
A LONG TIME AGO, A FAMOUS MONK HAD THE EXACT SAME EXPERIENCE.
ON A COLD WINTER'S DAY, HE SAW AN OLD MAN ON THE ROAD, SHIVERING IN THE COLD, AND HE PLACED HIS COAT OVER THE MAN.
BUT THE OLD MAN JUST STARED AT HIM AND DIDN'T SAY A SINGLE WORD OF THANKS.
SO THE MONK SAID, WITHOUT EVEN REALIZING IT...
"HOW'S THAT? DO YOU FEEL A LITTLE WARMER?"
APPARENTLY, THE MONK IMMEDIATELY FELT A GREAT SENSE OF REGRET!
I MUST START MY TRAINING ALL OVER...
THAT HE WAS A VILE HUMAN BEING FOR EXPECTING THE MAN'S GRATITUDE IN RETURN FOR HIS ACTIONS!
HE FELT DISGUSTED BY HIS SENSE OF ENTITLEMENT!

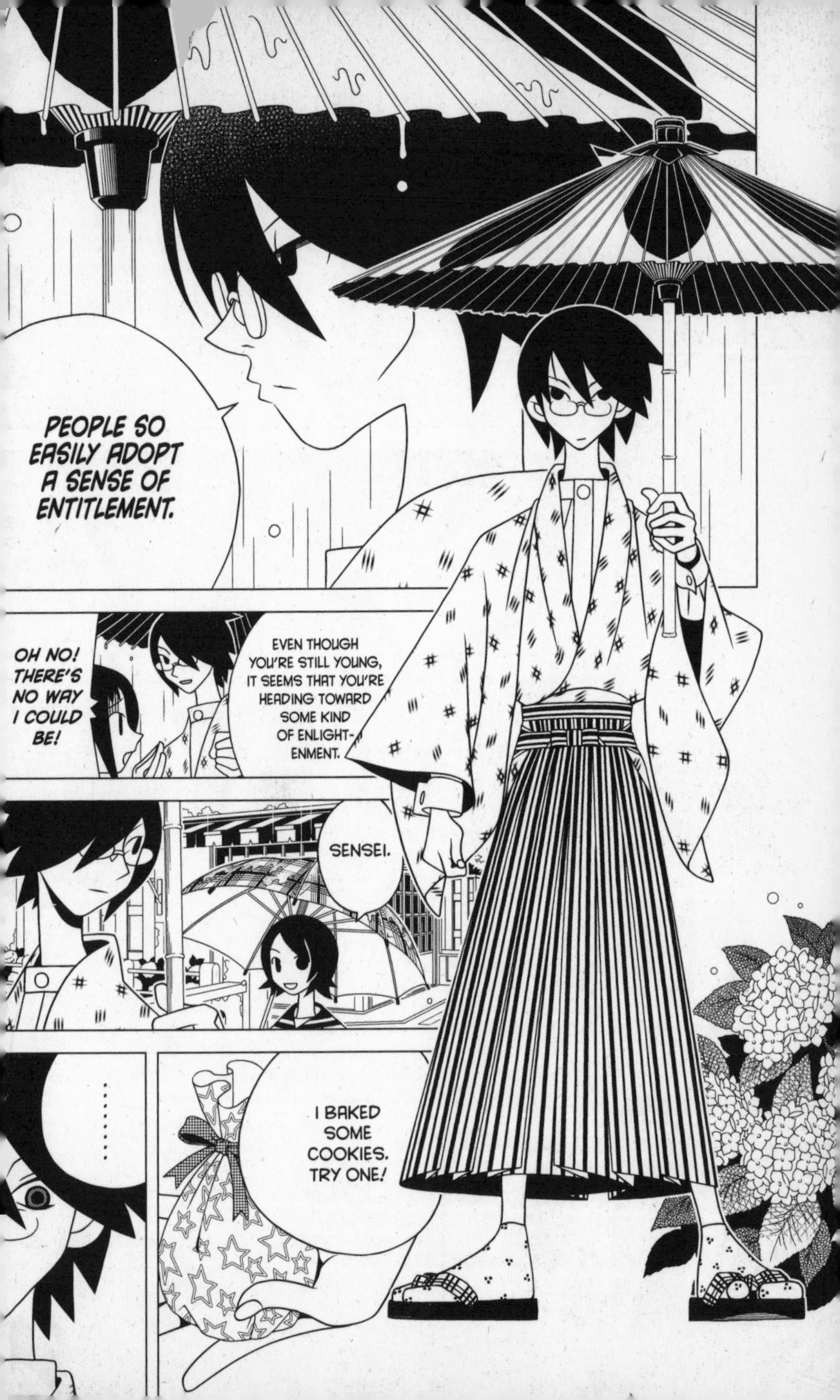
PEOPLE SO EASILY ADOPT A SENSE OF ENTITLEMENT.
EVEN THOUGH YOU'RE STILL YOUNG, IT SEEMS THAT YOU'RE HEADING TOWARD SOME KIND OF ENLIGHT-ENMENT.
OH NO! THERE'S NO WAY I COULD BE!
SENSEI.
I BAKED SOME COOKIES. TRY ONE!
......

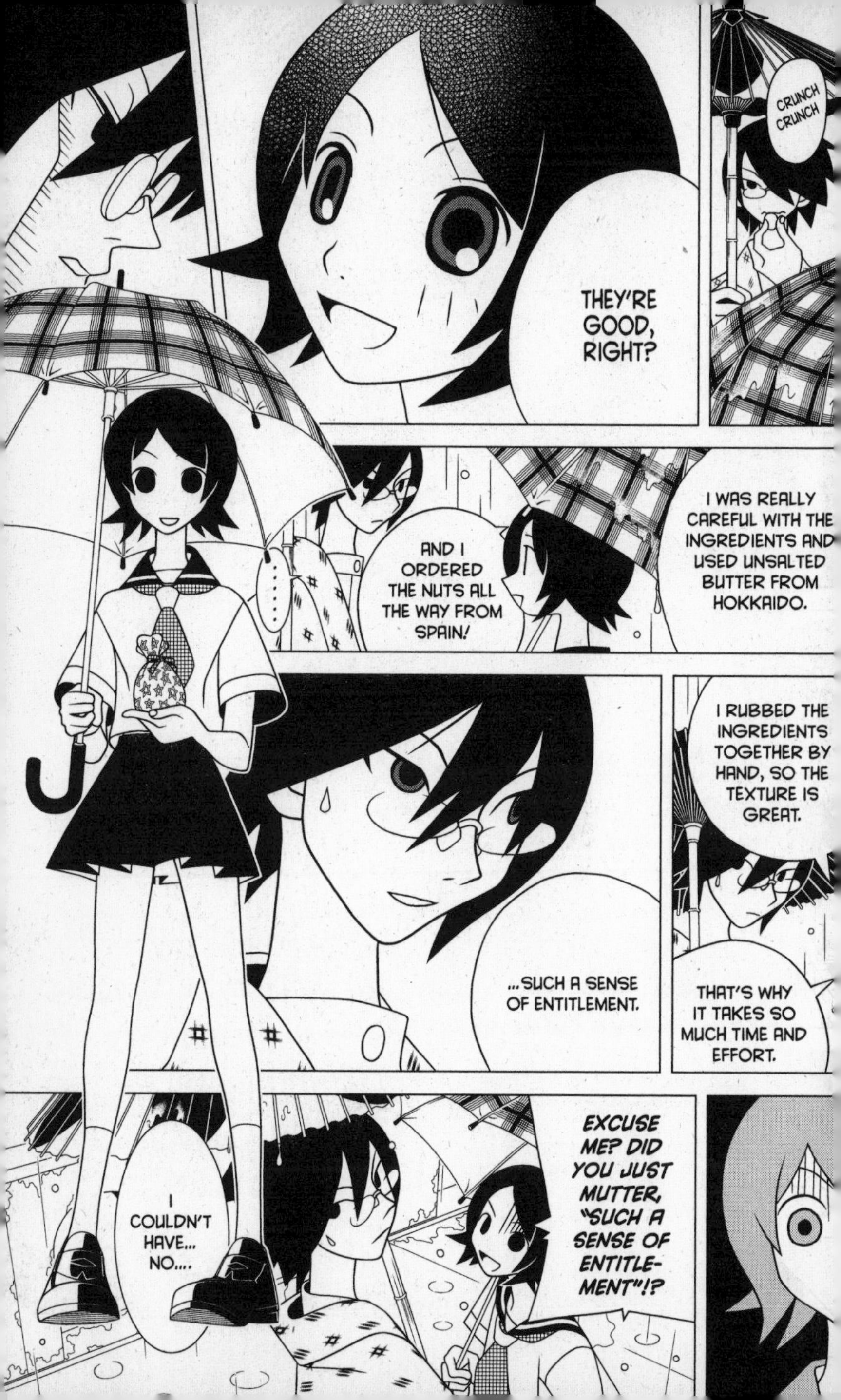
CRUNCH CRUNCH
THEY'RE GOOD, RIGHT?
I WAS REALLY CAREFUL WITH THE INGREDIENTS AND USED UNSALTED BUTTER FROM HOKKAIDO.
AND I ORDERED THE NUTS ALL THE WAY FROM SPAIN!
I RUBBED THE INGREDIENTS TOGETHER BY HAND, SO THE TEXTURE IS GREAT.
THAT'S WHY IT TAKES SO MUCH TIME AND EFFORT.
...SUCH A SENSE OF ENTITLEMENT.
EXCUSE ME? DID YOU JUST MUTTER, "SUCH A SENSE OF ENTITLE-MENT"!?
I COULDN'T HAVE... NO....

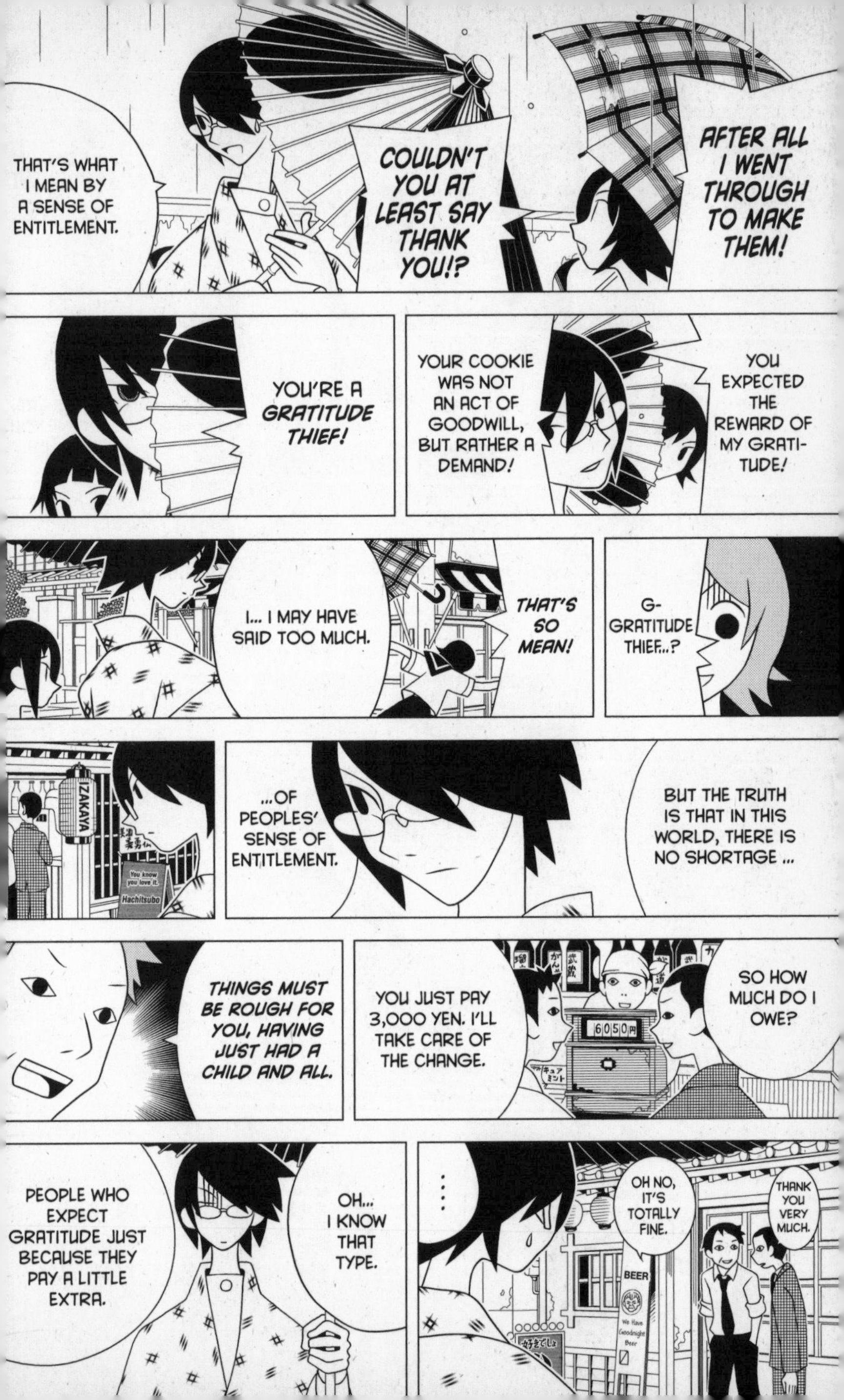
AFTER ALL I WENT THROUGH TO MAKE THEM!
COULDN'T YOU AT LEAST SAY THANK YOU!?
THAT'S WHAT I MEAN BY A SENSE OF ENTITLEMENT.
YOU EXPECTED THE REWARD OF MY GRATITUDE!
YOUR COOKIE WAS NOT AN ACT OF GOODWILL, BUT RATHER A DEMAND!
YOU'RE A GRATITUDE THIEF!
G- GRATITUDE THIEF...?
THAT'S SO MEAN!
I... I MAY HAVE SAID TOO MUCH.
BUT THE TRUTH IS THAT IN THIS WORLD, THERE IS NO SHORTAGE ...
...OF PEOPLES' SENSE OF ENTITLEMENT.
IZAKAYA
You know you love it.
Hachitsubo
SO HOW MUCH DO I OWE?
6050円
YOU JUST PAY 3,000 YEN. I'LL TAKE CARE OF THE CHANGE.
THINGS MUST BE ROUGH FOR YOU, HAVING JUST HAD A CHILD AND ALL.
THANK YOU VERY MUCH.
OH NO, IT'S TOTALLY FINE.
BEER
We Have Goodnight Beer
....
OH... I KNOW THAT TYPE.
PEOPLE WHO EXPECT GRATITUDE JUST BECAUSE THEY PAY A LITTLE EXTRA.

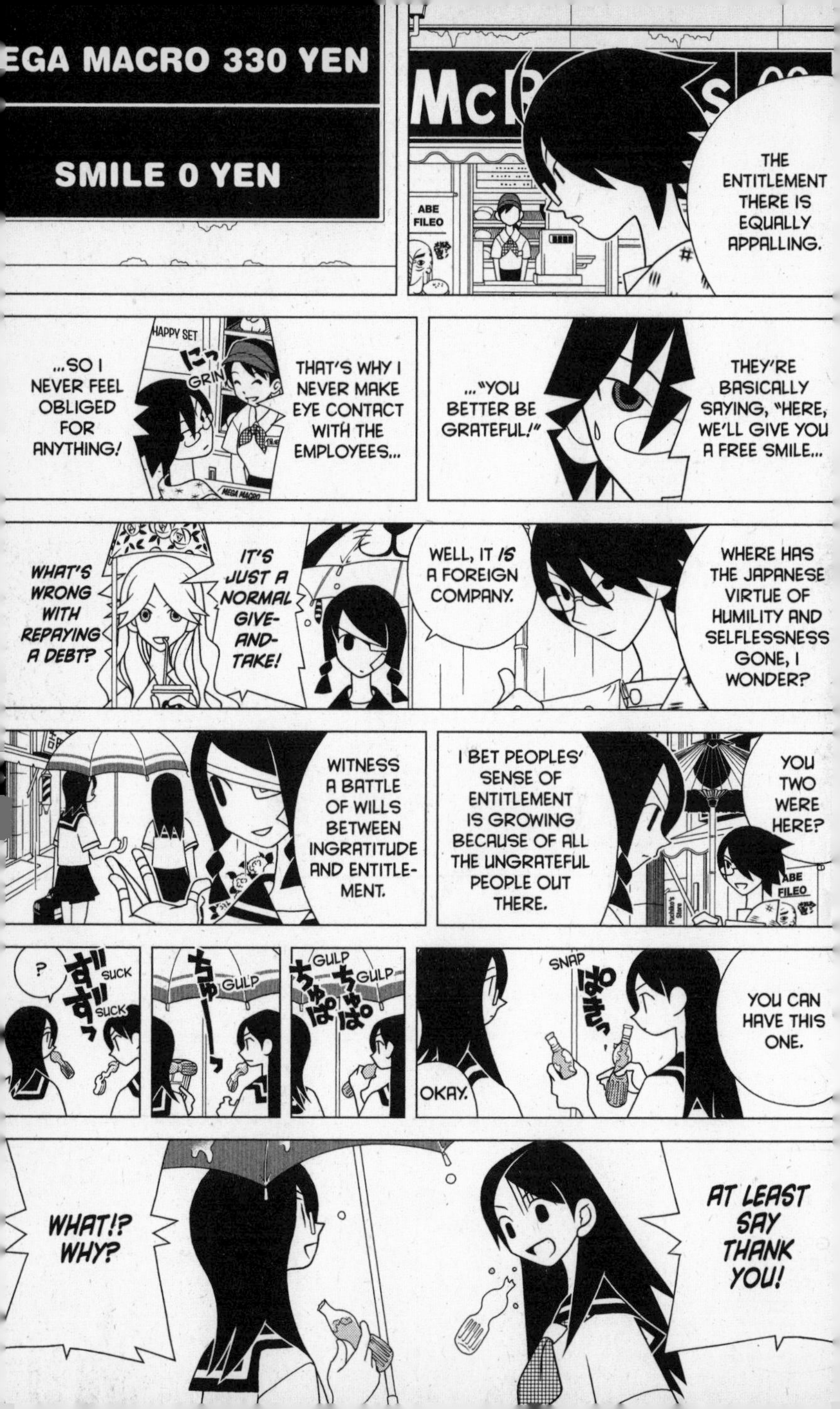
McR
S
ABE FILEO
THE ENTITLEMENT THERE IS EQUALLY APPALLING.
EGA MACRO 330 YEN
SMILE 0 YEN
THEY'RE BASICALLY SAYING, "HERE, WE'LL GIVE YOU A FREE SMILE...
..."YOU BETTER BE GRATEFUL!"
THAT'S WHY I NEVER MAKE EYE CONTACT WITH THE EMPLOYEES...
HAPPY SET
にっ
GRIN
...SO I NEVER FEEL OBLIGED FOR ANYTHING!
MEGA MACRO
WHERE HAS THE JAPANESE VIRTUE OF HUMILITY AND SELFLESSNESS GONE, I WONDER?
WELL, IT IS A FOREIGN COMPANY.
IT'S JUST A NORMAL GIVE-AND-TAKE!
WHAT'S WRONG WITH REPAYING A DEBT?
YOU TWO WERE HERE?
ABE FILEO
I BET PEOPLES' SENSE OF ENTITLEMENT IS GROWING BECAUSE OF ALL THE UNGRATEFUL PEOPLE OUT THERE.
WITNESS A BATTLE OF WILLS BETWEEN INGRATITUDE AND ENTITLE-MENT.
YOU CAN HAVE THIS ONE.
SNAP
ぱきっ
OKAY.
GULP
ちゅぱ
GULP
ちゅぱ
ちゅーっ
GULP
?
ずずっ
SUCK
SUCK
AT LEAST SAY THANK YOU!
WHAT!? WHY?

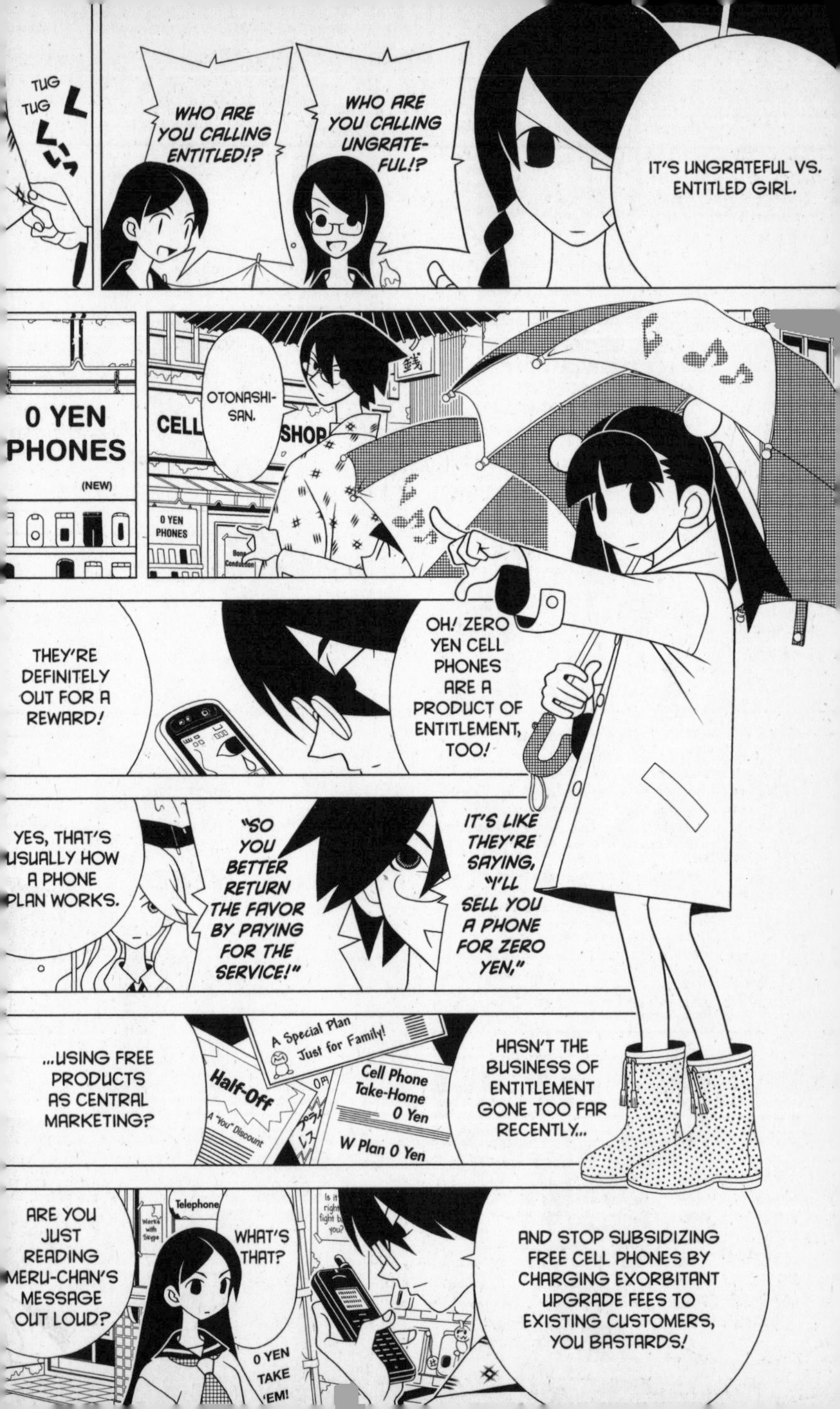
IT'S UNGRATEFUL VS. ENTITLED GIRL.
WHO ARE YOU CALLING UNGRATE-FUL!?
WHO ARE YOU CALLING ENTITLED!?
TUG TUG
OTONASHI-SAN.
CELL SHOP
0 YEN PHONES
Bone Conduction
0 YEN PHONES
(NEW)
OH! ZERO YEN CELL PHONES ARE A PRODUCT OF ENTITLEMENT, TOO!
THEY'RE DEFINITELY OUT FOR A REWARD!
IT'S LIKE THEY'RE SAYING, "I'LL SELL YOU A PHONE FOR ZERO YEN,"
"SO YOU BETTER RETURN THE FAVOR BY PAYING FOR THE SERVICE!"
YES, THAT'S USUALLY HOW A PHONE PLAN WORKS.
HASN'T THE BUSINESS OF ENTITLEMENT GONE TOO FAR RECENTLY...
A Special Plan Just for Family!
Cell Phone Take-Home 0 Yen
W Plan 0 Yen
Half-Off
A "You" Discount
...USING FREE PRODUCTS AS CENTRAL MARKETING?
AND STOP SUBSIDIZING FREE CELL PHONES BY CHARGING EXORBITANT UPGRADE FEES TO EXISTING CUSTOMERS, YOU BASTARDS!
WHAT'S THAT?
0 YEN TAKE 'EM!
Telephone
Works with Skype
ARE YOU JUST READING MERU-CHAN'S MESSAGE OUT LOUD?

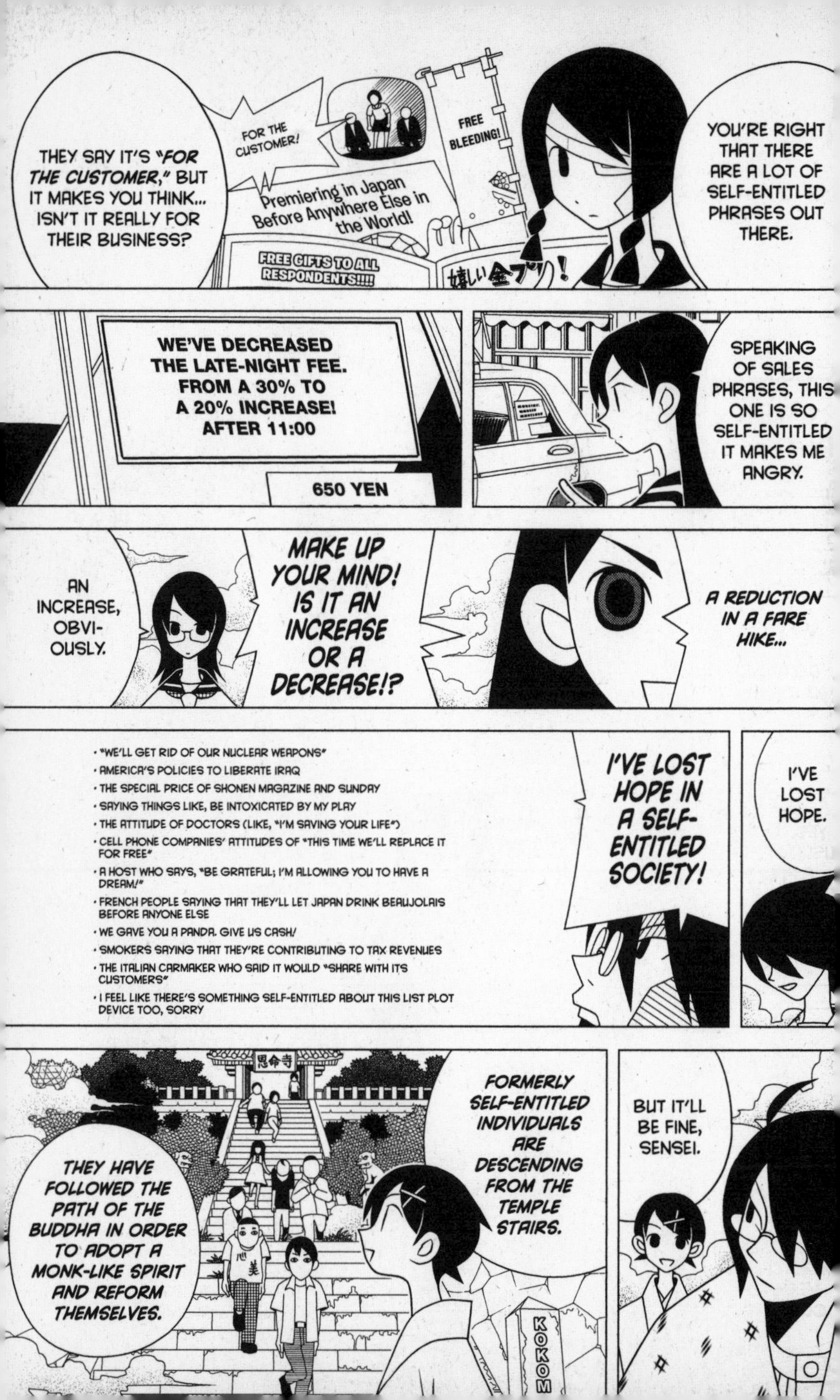

YOU'RE RIGHT THAT THERE ARE A LOT OF SELF-ENTITLED PHRASES OUT THERE.
FREE BLEEDING!
FOR THE CUSTOMER!
THEY SAY IT'S "FOR THE CUSTOMER," BUT IT MAKES YOU THINK... ISN'T IT REALLY FOR THEIR BUSINESS?
Premiering in Japan Before Anywhere Else in the World!
嬉しい金ブ
FREE GIFTS TO ALL RESPONDENTS!!!!
SPEAKING OF SALES PHRASES, THIS ONE IS SO SELF-ENTITLED IT MAKES ME ANGRY.
WE'VE DECREASED THE LATE-NIGHT FEE. FROM A 30% TO A 20% INCREASE! AFTER 11:00
650 YEN
A REDUCTION IN A FARE HIKE...
MAKE UP YOUR MIND! IS IT AN INCREASE OR A DECREASE!?
AN INCREASE, OBVIOUSLY.
I'VE LOST HOPE.
I'VE LOST HOPE IN A SELF-ENTITLED SOCIETY!
• "WE'LL GET RID OF OUR NUCLEAR WEAPONS"
• AMERICA'S POLICIES TO LIBERATE IRAQ
• THE SPECIAL PRICE OF SHONEN MAGAZINE AND SUNDAY
• SAYING THINGS LIKE, BE INTOXICATED BY MY PLAY
• THE ATTITUDE OF DOCTORS (LIKE, "I'M SAVING YOUR LIFE")
• CELL PHONE COMPANIES' ATTITUDES OF "THIS TIME WE'LL REPLACE IT FOR FREE"
• A HOST WHO SAYS, "BE GRATEFUL; I'M ALLOWING YOU TO HAVE A DREAM!"
• FRENCH PEOPLE SAYING THAT THEY'LL LET JAPAN DRINK BEAUJOLAIS BEFORE ANYONE ELSE
• WE GAVE YOU A PANDA. GIVE US CASH!
• SMOKERS SAYING THAT THEY'RE CONTRIBUTING TO TAX REVENUES
• THE ITALIAN CARMAKER WHO SAID IT WOULD "SHARE WITH ITS CUSTOMERS"
• I FEEL LIKE THERE'S SOMETHING SELF-ENTITLED ABOUT THIS LIST PLOT DEVICE TOO, SORRY
BUT IT'LL BE FINE, SENSEI.
KOKOM
FORMERLY SELF-ENTITLED INDIVIDUALS ARE DESCENDING FROM THE TEMPLE STAIRS.
思命寺
THEY HAVE FOLLOWED THE PATH OF THE BUDDHA IN ORDER TO ADOPT A MONK-LIKE SPIRIT AND REFORM THEMSELVES.

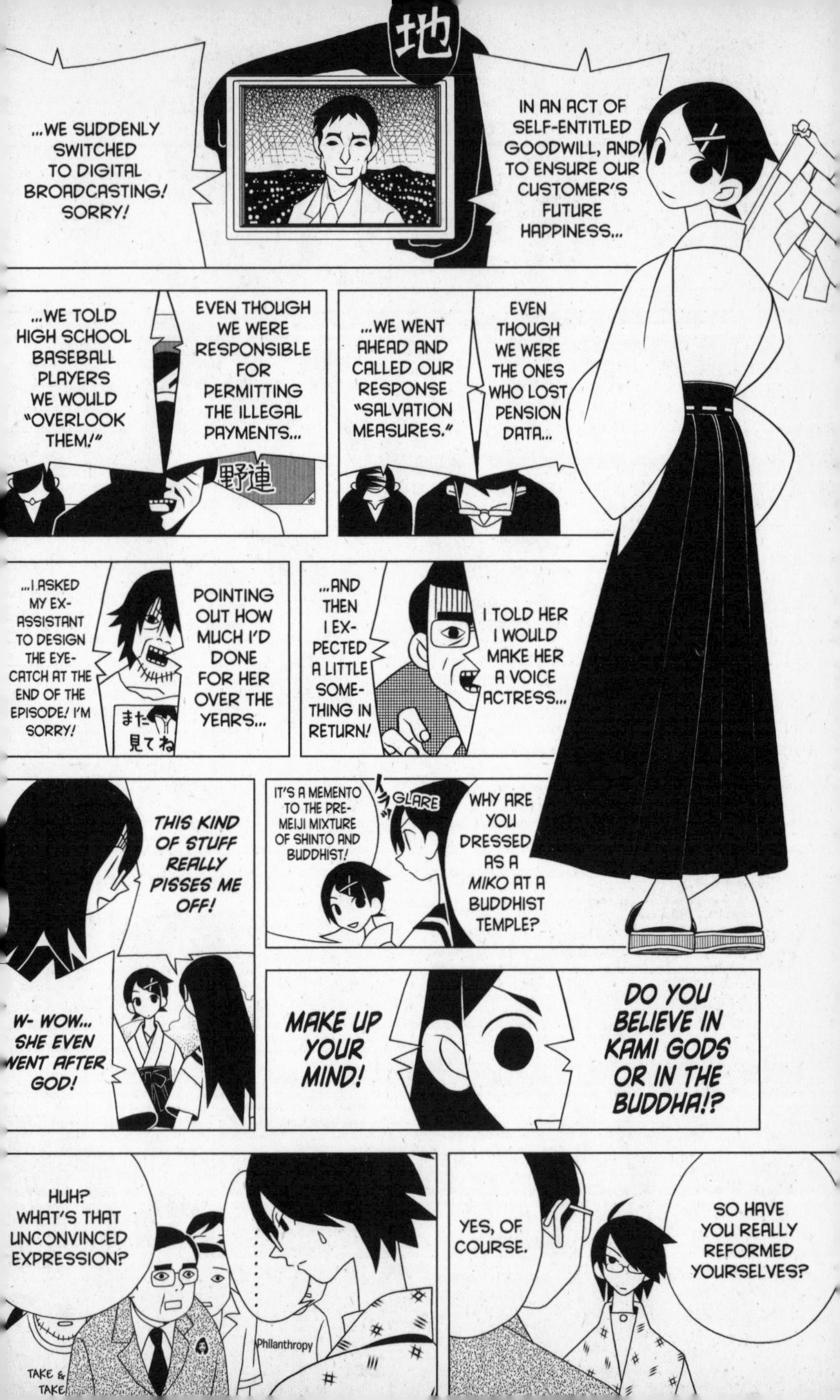
地
IN AN ACT OF SELF-ENTITLED GOODWILL, AND TO ENSURE OUR CUSTOMER'S FUTURE HAPPINESS...
...WE SUDDENLY SWITCHED TO DIGITAL BROADCASTING! SORRY!
EVEN THOUGH WE WERE THE ONES WHO LOST PENSION DATA...
...WE WENT AHEAD AND CALLED OUR RESPONSE "SALVATION MEASURES."
EVEN THOUGH WE WERE RESPONSIBLE FOR PERMITTING THE ILLEGAL PAYMENTS...
...WE TOLD HIGH SCHOOL BASEBALL PLAYERS WE WOULD "OVERLOOK THEM!"
野連
I TOLD HER I WOULD MAKE HER A VOICE ACTRESS...
...AND THEN I EXPECTED A LITTLE SOMETHING IN RETURN!
POINTING OUT HOW MUCH I'D DONE FOR HER OVER THE YEARS...
...I ASKED MY EX-ASSISTANT TO DESIGN THE EYE-CATCH AT THE END OF THE EPISODE! I'M SORRY!
WHY ARE YOU DRESSED AS A *MIKO* AT A BUDDHIST TEMPLE?
GLARE
IT'S A MEMENTO TO THE PRE-MEIJI MIXTURE OF SHINTO AND BUDDHIST!
DO YOU BELIEVE IN KAMI GODS OR IN THE BUDDHA!?
MAKE UP YOUR MIND!
THIS KIND OF STUFF REALLY PISSES ME OFF!
W- WOW... SHE EVEN WENT AFTER GOD!
SO HAVE YOU REALLY REFORMED YOURSELVES?
YES, OF COURSE.
HUH? WHAT'S THAT UNCONVINCED EXPRESSION?
Philanthropy
TAKE & TAKE

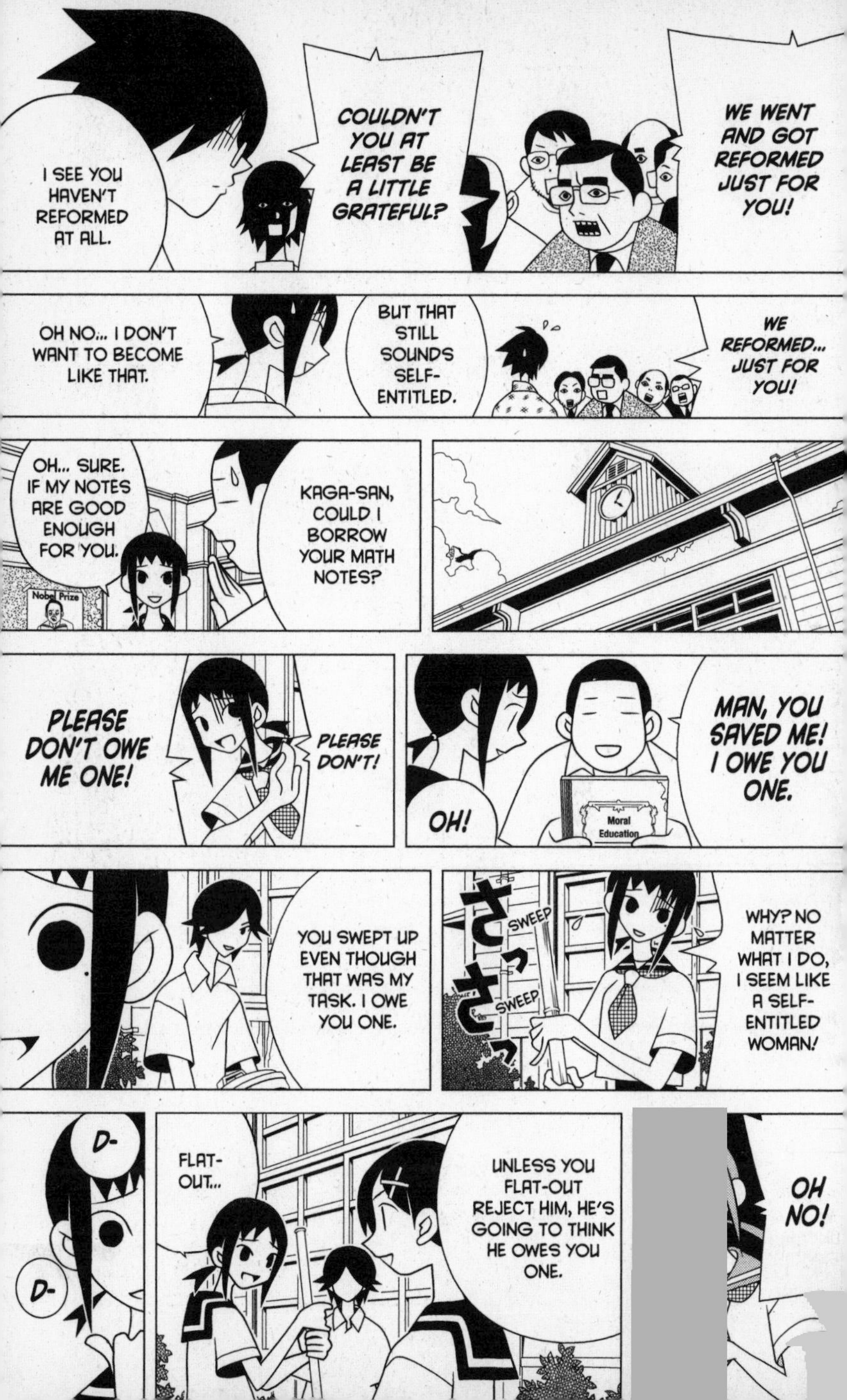
WE WENT AND GOT REFORMED JUST FOR YOU!
COULDN'T YOU AT LEAST BE A LITTLE GRATEFUL?
I SEE YOU HAVEN'T REFORMED AT ALL.
WE REFORMED... JUST FOR YOU!
BUT THAT STILL SOUNDS SELF-ENTITLED.
OH NO... I DON'T WANT TO BECOME LIKE THAT.
KAGA-SAN, COULD I BORROW YOUR MATH NOTES?
OH... SURE. IF MY NOTES ARE GOOD ENOUGH FOR YOU.
Nobel Prize
MAN, YOU SAVED ME! I OWE YOU ONE.
Moral Education
OH!
PLEASE DON'T!
PLEASE DON'T OWE ME ONE!
WHY? NO MATTER WHAT I DO, I SEEM LIKE A SELF-ENTITLED WOMAN!
SWEEP
SWEEP
さっさっ
YOU SWEPT UP EVEN THOUGH THAT WAS MY TASK. I OWE YOU ONE.
OH NO!
UNLESS YOU FLAT-OUT REJECT HIM, HE'S GOING TO THINK HE OWES YOU ONE.
FLAT-OUT...
D-
D-

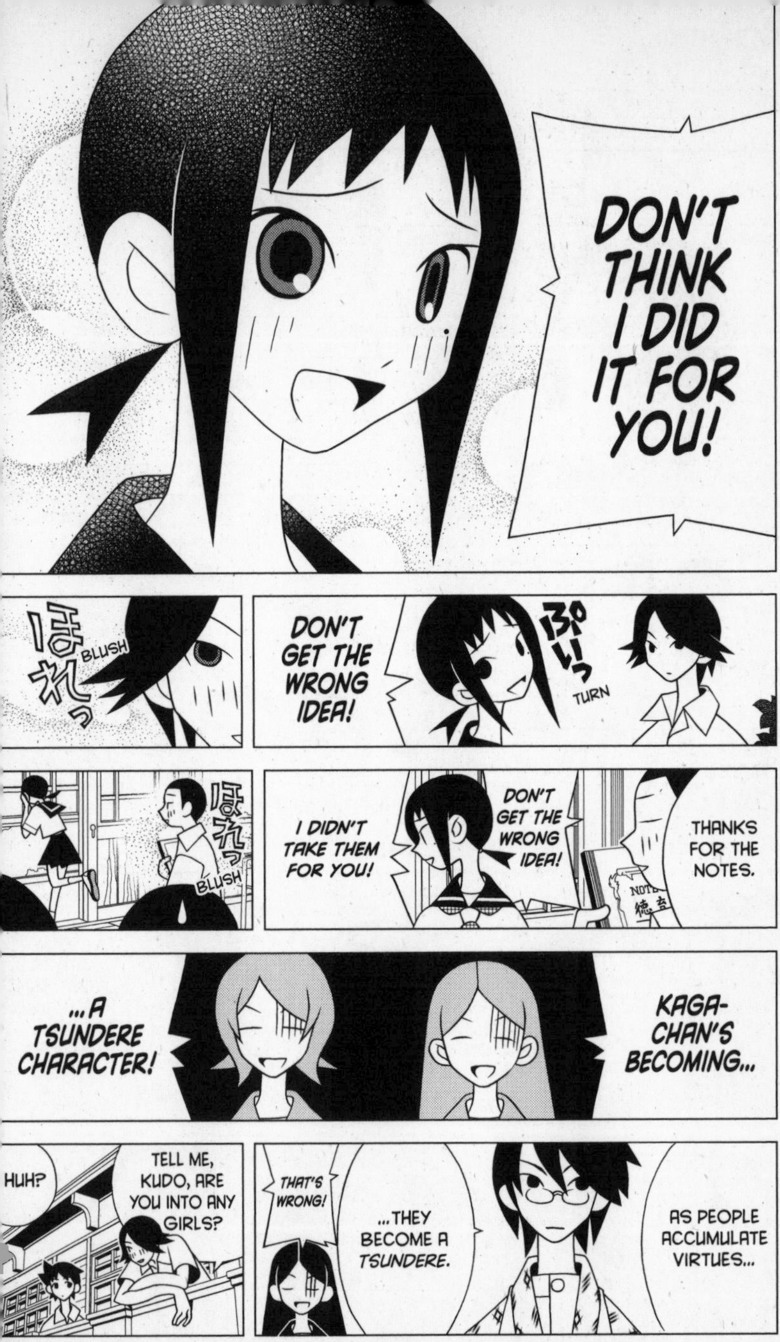

DON'T THINK I DID IT FOR YOU!
DON'T GET THE WRONG IDEA!
ぷいっ
TURN
ほれっ
BLUSH
THANKS FOR THE NOTES.
DON'T GET THE WRONG IDEA!
I DIDN'T TAKE THEM FOR YOU!
ほれっ
BLUSH
KAGA-CHAN'S BECOMING...
...A TSUNDERE CHARACTER!
AS PEOPLE ACCUMULATE VIRTUES...
...THEY BECOME A TSUNDERE.
THAT'S WRONG!
TELL ME, KUDO, ARE YOU INTO ANY GIRLS?
HUH?

UH... ER....
D-... DO-...
DON'T THINK I WANTED YOU TO BUY IT FOR ME!
OH... THAT'S NOT NICE. I'M SORRY! I'M SORRY!
MAYBE SHE'S A TSUNWABI?

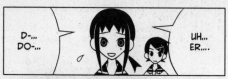

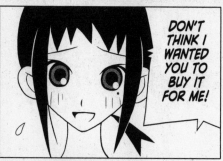

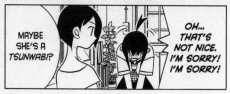

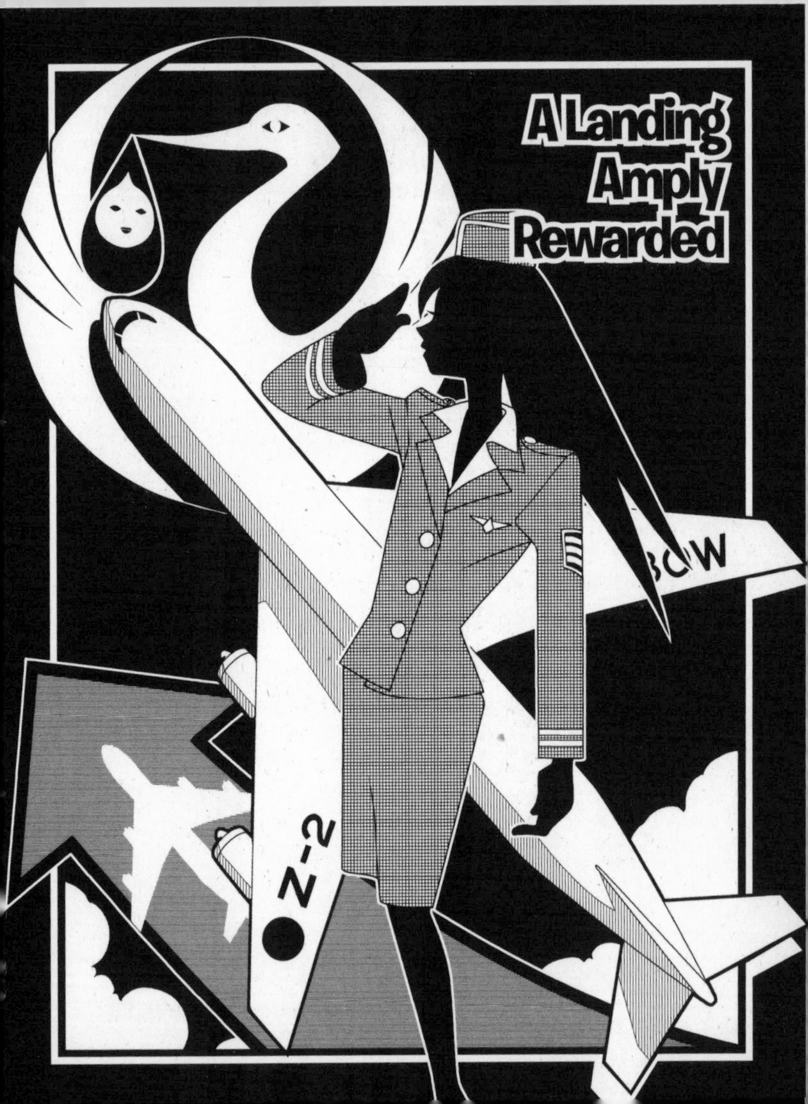
A Landing Amply Rewarded

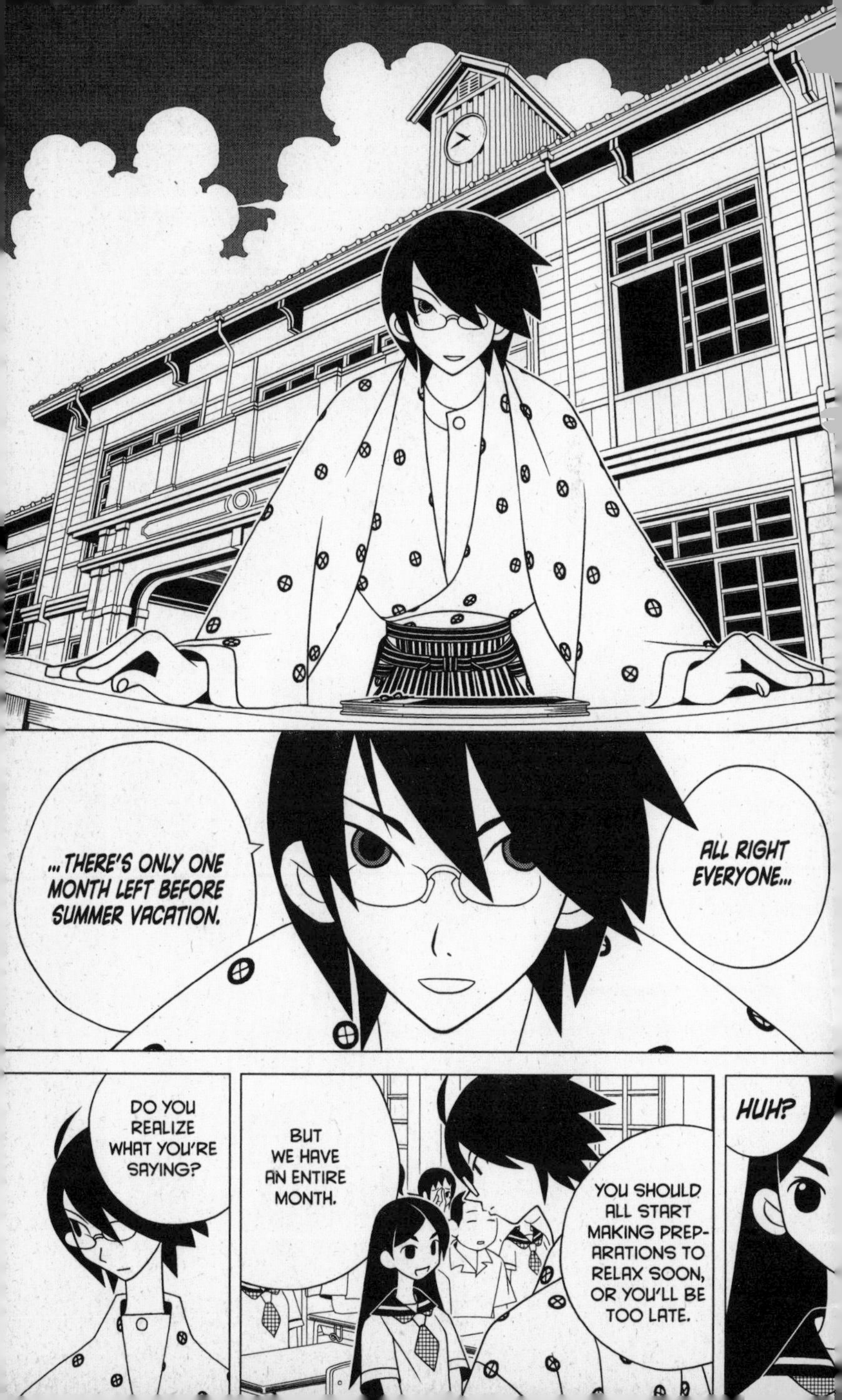
ALL RIGHT EVERYONE...
...THERE'S ONLY ONE MONTH LEFT BEFORE SUMMER VACATION.
HUH?
YOU SHOULD ALL START MAKING PREP-ARATIONS TO RELAX SOON, OR YOU'LL BE TOO LATE.
BUT WE HAVE AN ENTIRE MONTH.
DO YOU REALIZE WHAT YOU'RE SAYING?

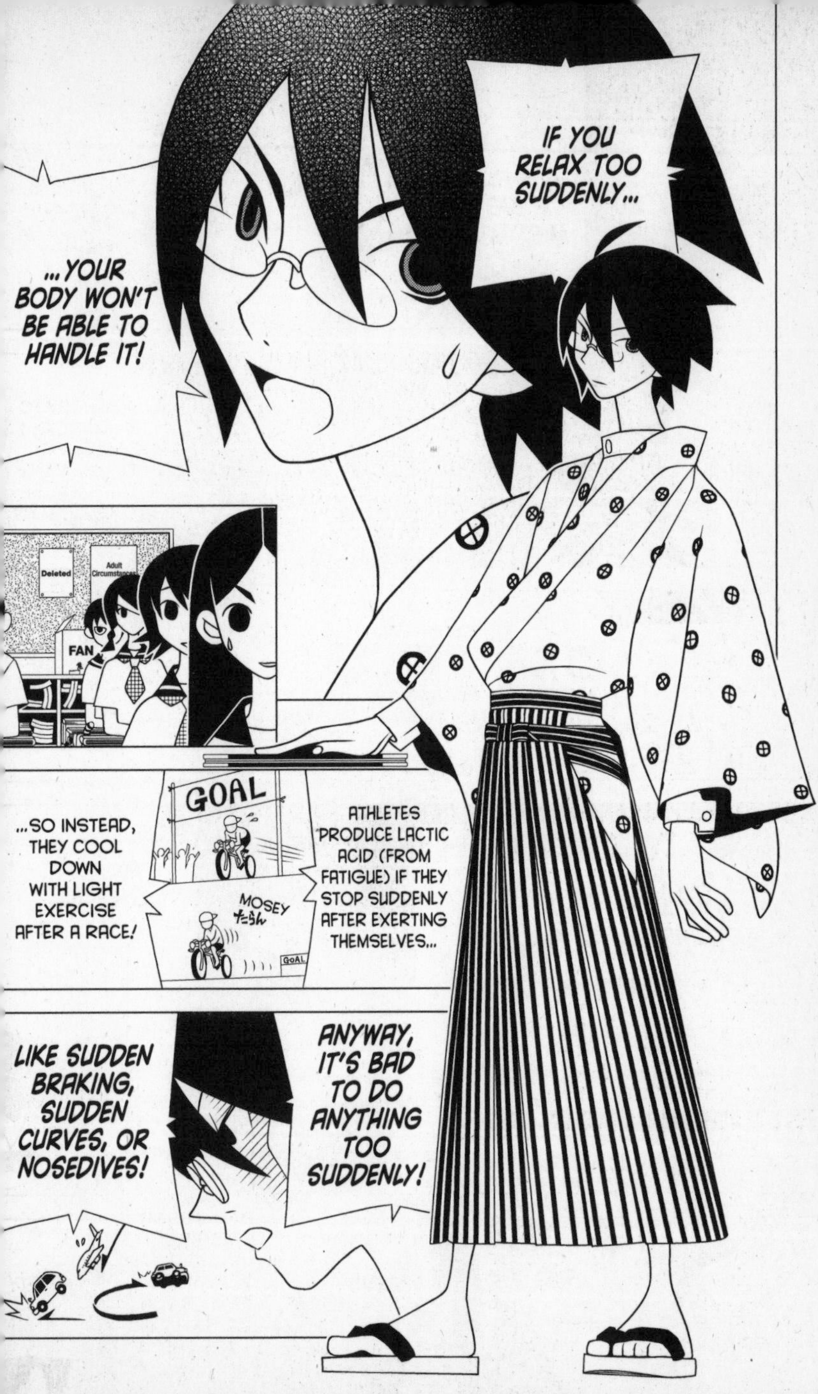
IF YOU RELAX TOO SUDDENLY...
...YOUR BODY WON'T BE ABLE TO HANDLE IT!
Deleted
Adult Circumstances
FAN
ATHLETES PRODUCE LACTIC ACID (FROM FATIGUE) IF THEY STOP SUDDENLY AFTER EXERTING THEMSELVES...
GOAL
MOSEY
たらん
GOAL
...SO INSTEAD, THEY COOL DOWN WITH LIGHT EXERCISE AFTER A RACE!
ANYWAY, IT'S BAD TO DO ANYTHING TOO SUDDENLY!
LIKE SUDDEN BRAKING, SUDDEN CURVES, OR NOSEDIVES!

IT'S LIKE MAKING A HARD LANDING.

IT'S ALL A BIG MISTAKE!

"DUE TO THE AUTHOR'S SUDDEN ILLNESS..."

IF YOU LAND GENTLY, THE SHOCK WON'T BE AS BIG.

Soft Landing

Hard Landing

Small Shock

Large Shock

IF YOU TRY TO LAND WITHOUT ENOUGH SPACE, YOU'LL EXPERIENCE A BIGGER SHOCK.

Class 2-F Pre-Su Vacation Plan

Tue	Wed	Thu
26	27	28
3	4	

THIS WILL HELP YOU UNDERSTAND.

YOU HAVE TO PREPARE YOUR BODIES FOR RELAXATION STARTING NOW!

IT WILL BE TOO LATE IF YOU START RELAXING IN JULY!

Class 2-F Pre-Summer Vacation Plan

	Sun	Mon	Tue	Wed	Thu	Sat
3 Days Off	OFF	6/25	26	27	28	OFF
4 Days Off	OFF	7/2	3	OFF	OFF	6
5 Days Off	OFF	OFF	10	OFF	OFF	13
6 Days Off	OFF	OFF	OFF	18	OFF	OFF
6.5 Days Off	OFF	23 Closing Day	OFF	OFF	OFF	OFF

THIS IS AN INCREMENTAL RELAXATION PLAN.

IS THIS GOING TO BE ALL RIGHT WITH THE SCHOOL?

HOLD ON!

AGREED!

AGREED!

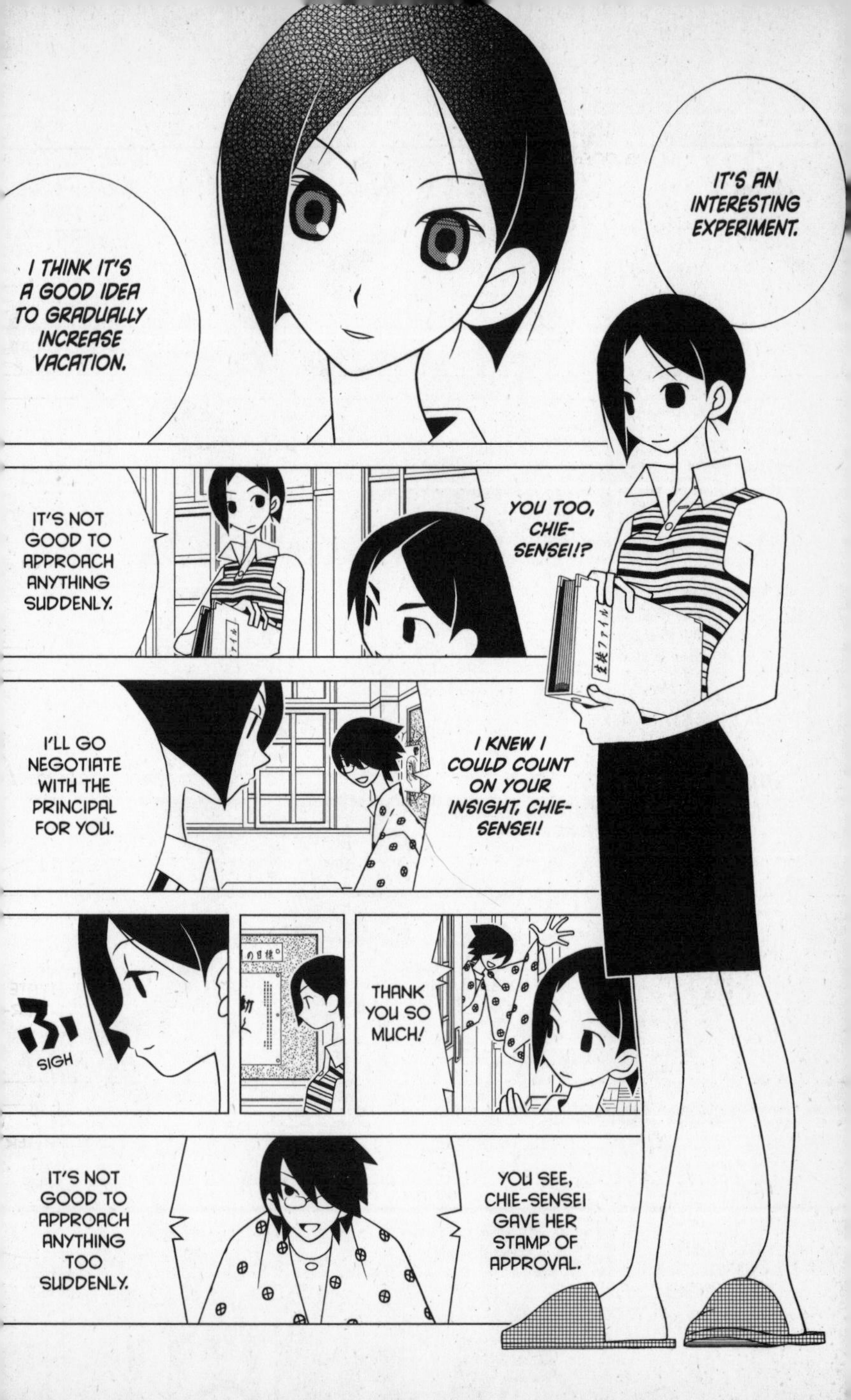
IT'S AN INTERESTING EXPERIMENT.
I THINK IT'S A GOOD IDEA TO GRADUALLY INCREASE VACATION.
生徒ファイル
YOU TOO, CHIE-SENSEI!?
IT'S NOT GOOD TO APPROACH ANYTHING SUDDENLY.
I KNEW I COULD COUNT ON YOUR INSIGHT, CHIE-SENSEI!
I'LL GO NEGOTIATE WITH THE PRINCIPAL FOR YOU.
THANK YOU SO MUCH!
ふ
SIGH
YOU SEE, CHIE-SENSEI GAVE HER STAMP OF APPROVAL.
IT'S NOT GOOD TO APPROACH ANYTHING TOO SUDDENLY.

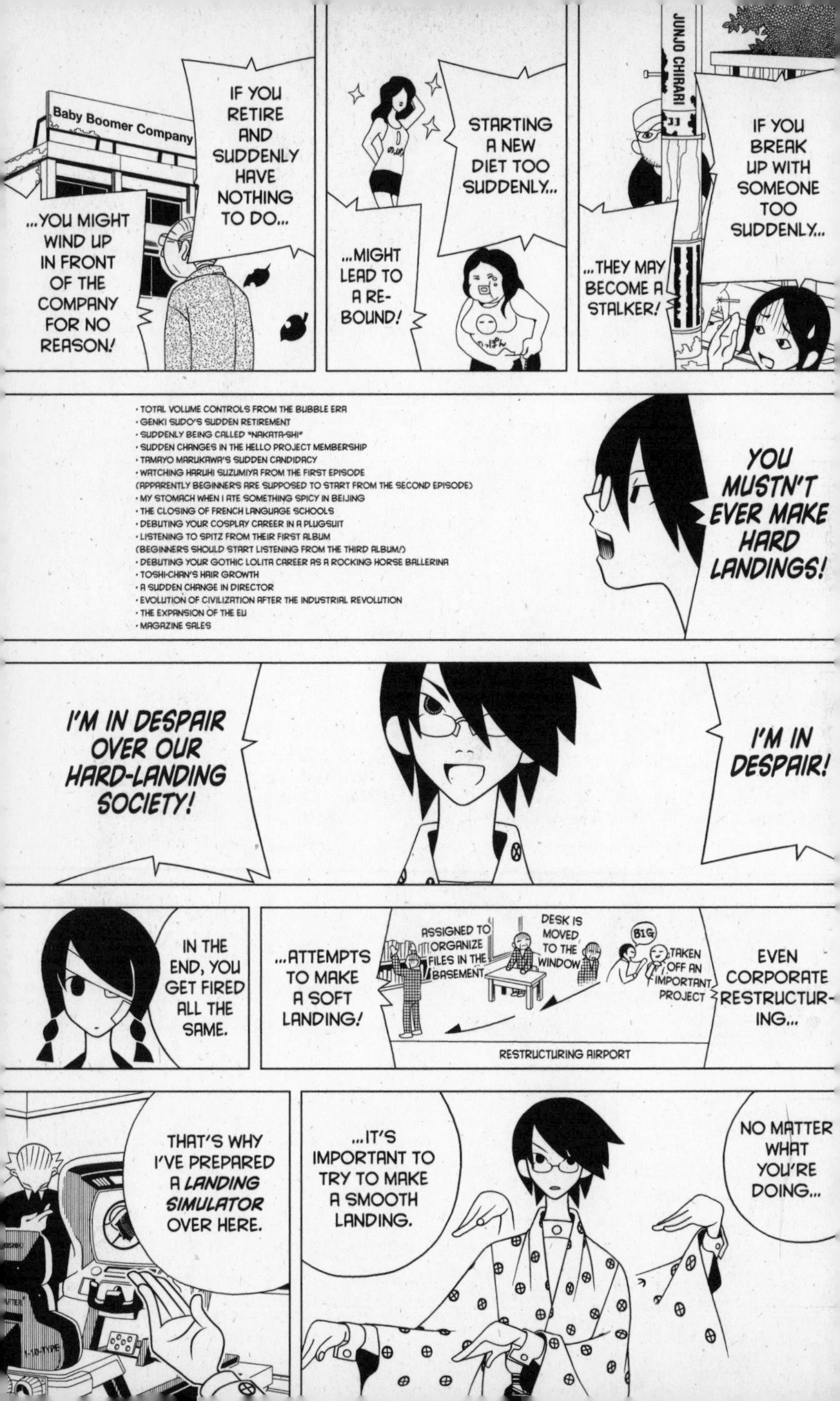
JUNJO CHIRARI
IF YOU BREAK UP WITH SOMEONE TOO SUDDENLY...
...THEY MAY BECOME A STALKER!
STARTING A NEW DIET TOO SUDDENLY...
...MIGHT LEAD TO A RE-BOUND!
Baby Boomer Company
IF YOU RETIRE AND SUDDENLY HAVE NOTHING TO DO...
...YOU MIGHT WIND UP IN FRONT OF THE COMPANY FOR NO REASON!
YOU MUSTN'T EVER MAKE HARD LANDINGS!
· TOTAL VOLUME CONTROLS FROM THE BUBBLE ERA
· GENKI SUDO'S SUDDEN RETIREMENT
· SUDDENLY BEING CALLED "NAKATA-SHI"
· SUDDEN CHANGES IN THE HELLO PROJECT MEMBERSHIP
· TAMAYO MARUKAWA'S SUDDEN CANDIDACY
· WATCHING HARUHI SUZUMIYA FROM THE FIRST EPISODE
(APPARENTLY BEGINNERS ARE SUPPOSED TO START FROM THE SECOND EPISODE)
· MY STOMACH WHEN I ATE SOMETHING SPICY IN BEIJING
· THE CLOSING OF FRENCH LANGUAGE SCHOOLS
· DEBUTING YOUR COSPLAY CAREER IN A PLUGSUIT
· LISTENING TO SPITZ FROM THEIR FIRST ALBUM
(BEGINNERS SHOULD START LISTENING FROM THE THIRD ALBUM!)
· DEBUTING YOUR GOTHIC LOLITA CAREER AS A ROCKING HORSE BALLERINA
· TOSHI-CHAN'S HAIR GROWTH
· A SUDDEN CHANGE IN DIRECTOR
· EVOLUTION OF CIVILIZATION AFTER THE INDUSTRIAL REVOLUTION
· THE EXPANSION OF THE EU
· MAGAZINE SALES
I'M IN DESPAIR!
I'M IN DESPAIR OVER OUR HARD-LANDING SOCIETY!
EVEN CORPORATE RESTRUCTUR-ING...
TAKEN OFF AN IMPORTANT PROJECT
BIG
DESK IS MOVED TO THE WINDOW
ASSIGNED TO ORGANIZE FILES IN THE BASEMENT
RESTRUCTURING AIRPORT
...ATTEMPTS TO MAKE A SOFT LANDING!
IN THE END, YOU GET FIRED ALL THE SAME.
NO MATTER WHAT YOU'RE DOING...
...IT'S IMPORTANT TO TRY TO MAKE A SMOOTH LANDING.
THAT'S WHY I'VE PREPARED A *LANDING SIMULATOR* OVER HERE.

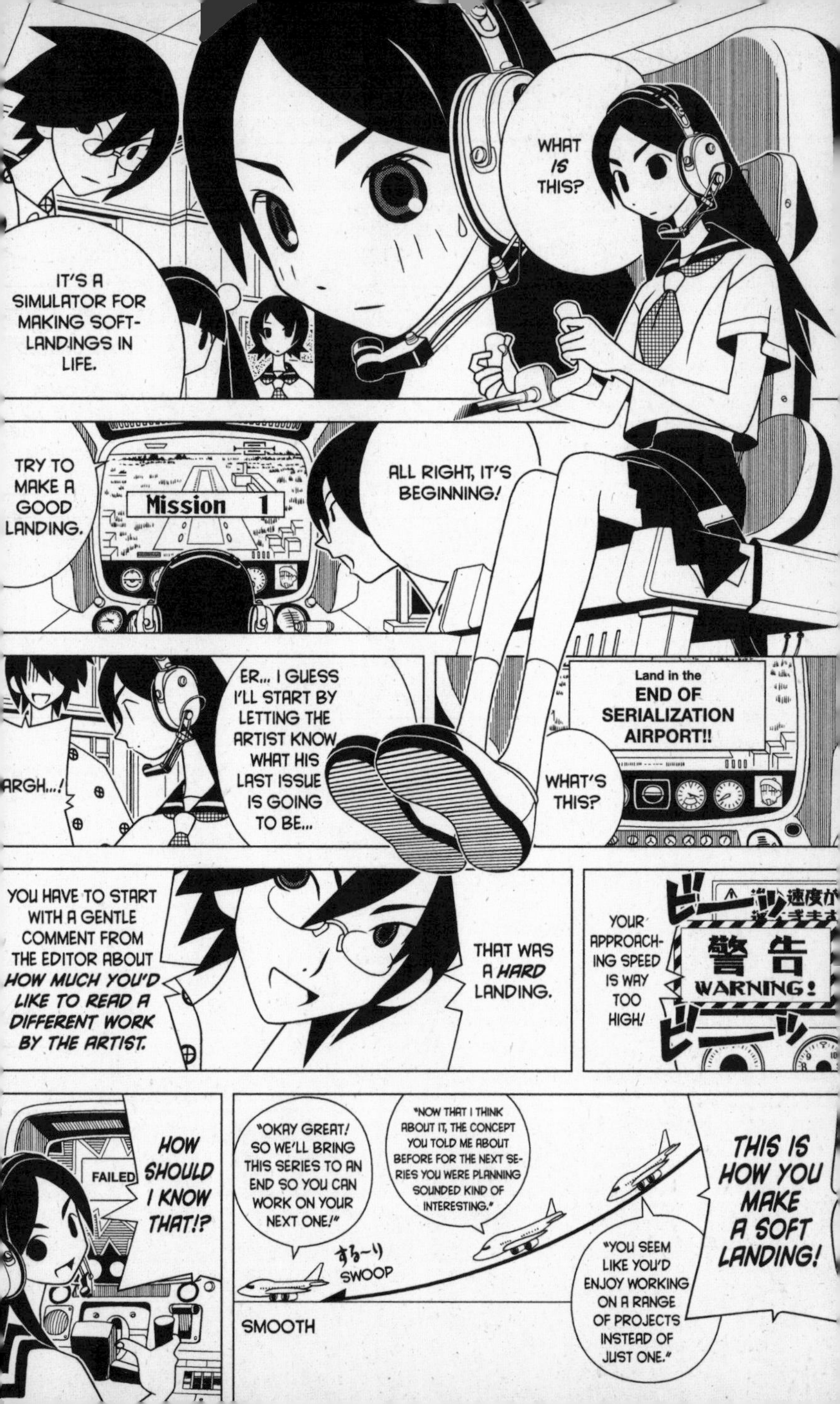
WHAT *IS* THIS?
IT'S A SIMULATOR FOR MAKING SOFT-LANDINGS IN LIFE.
ALL RIGHT, IT'S BEGINNING!
Mission 1
TRY TO MAKE A GOOD LANDING.
Land in the END OF SERIALIZATION AIRPORT!!
WHAT'S THIS?
ER... I GUESS I'LL START BY LETTING THE ARTIST KNOW WHAT HIS LAST ISSUE IS GOING TO BE...
ARGH...!
ビーッ
警告
WARNING!
ビーッ
YOUR APPROACHING SPEED IS WAY TOO HIGH!
THAT WAS A *HARD* LANDING.
YOU HAVE TO START WITH A GENTLE COMMENT FROM THE EDITOR ABOUT *HOW MUCH YOU'D LIKE TO READ A DIFFERENT WORK BY THE ARTIST.*
THIS IS HOW YOU MAKE A SOFT LANDING!
"YOU SEEM LIKE YOU'D ENJOY WORKING ON A RANGE OF PROJECTS INSTEAD OF JUST ONE."
"NOW THAT I THINK ABOUT IT, THE CONCEPT YOU TOLD ME ABOUT BEFORE FOR THE NEXT SERIES YOU WERE PLANNING SOUNDED KIND OF INTERESTING."
"OKAY GREAT! SO WE'LL BRING THIS SERIES TO AN END SO YOU CAN WORK ON YOUR NEXT ONE!"
するーり
SWOOP
SMOOTH
FAILED
HOW SHOULD I KNOW THAT!?

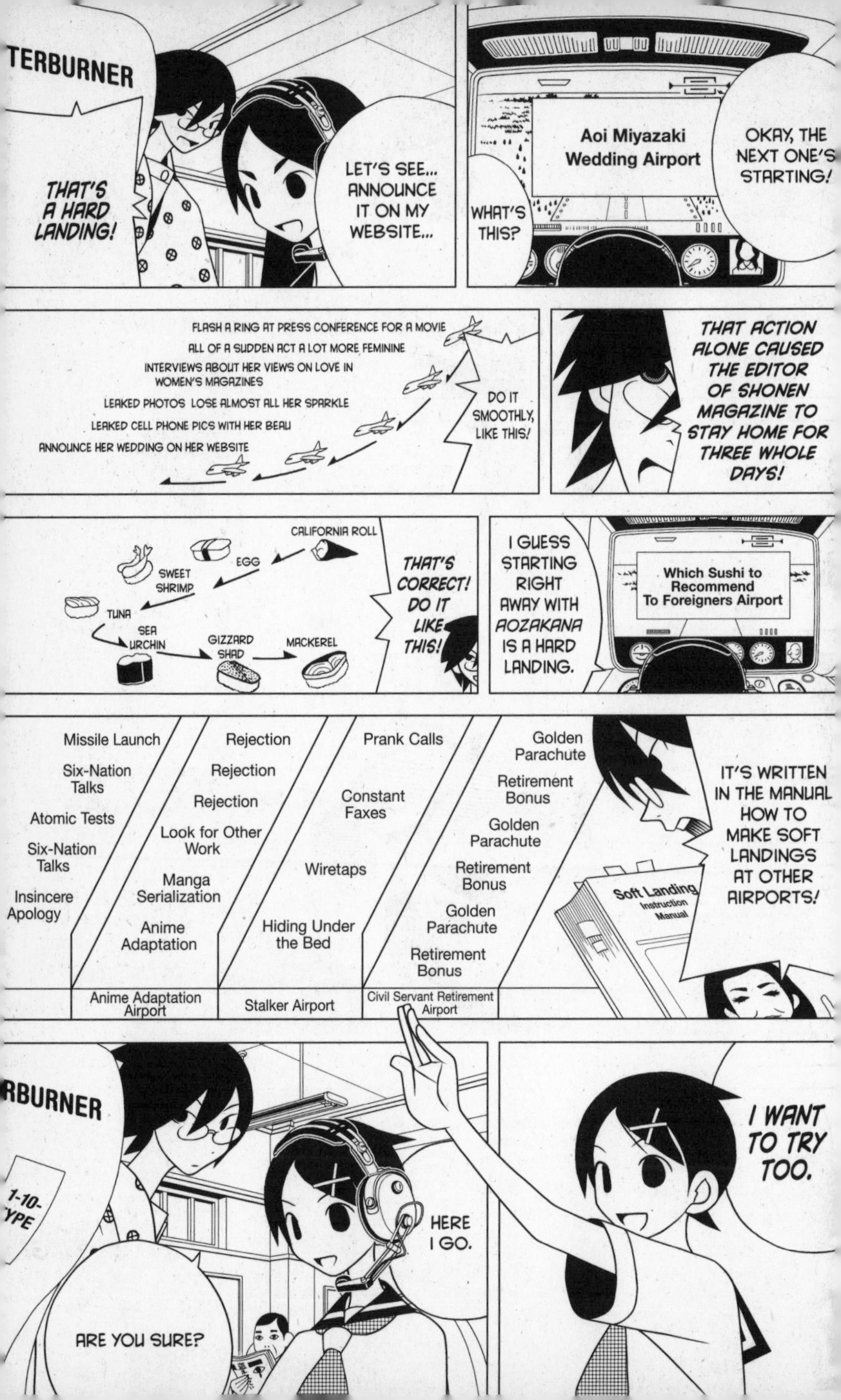
OKAY, THE NEXT ONE'S STARTING!
Aoi Miyazaki Wedding Airport
WHAT'S THIS?
LET'S SEE... ANNOUNCE IT ON MY WEBSITE...
TERBURNER
THAT'S A HARD LANDING!
THAT ACTION ALONE CAUSED THE EDITOR OF SHONEN MAGAZINE TO STAY HOME FOR THREE WHOLE DAYS!
DO IT SMOOTHLY, LIKE THIS!
FLASH A RING AT PRESS CONFERENCE FOR A MOVIE
ALL OF A SUDDEN ACT A LOT MORE FEMININE
INTERVIEWS ABOUT HER VIEWS ON LOVE IN WOMEN'S MAGAZINES
LEAKED PHOTOS LOSE ALMOST ALL HER SPARKLE
LEAKED CELL PHONE PICS WITH HER BEAU
ANNOUNCE HER WEDDING ON HER WEBSITE
Which Sushi to Recommend To Foreigners Airport
I GUESS STARTING RIGHT AWAY WITH AOZAKANA IS A HARD LANDING.
THAT'S CORRECT! DO IT LIKE THIS!
CALIFORNIA ROLL
EGG
SWEET SHRIMP
TUNA
SEA URCHIN
GIZZARD SHAD
MACKEREL
IT'S WRITTEN IN THE MANUAL HOW TO MAKE SOFT LANDINGS AT OTHER AIRPORTS!
Soft Landing Instruction Manual
Golden Parachute
Retirement Bonus
Golden Parachute
Retirement Bonus
Golden Parachute
Retirement Bonus
Civil Servant Retirement Airport
Prank Calls
Constant Faxes
Wiretaps
Hiding Under the Bed
Stalker Airport
Rejection
Rejection
Rejection
Look for Other Work
Manga Serialization
Anime Adaptation
Anime Adaptation Airport
Missile Launch
Six-Nation Talks
Atomic Tests
Six-Nation Talks
Insincere Apology
I WANT TO TRY TOO.
HERE I GO.
RBURNER
1-10-
YPE
ARE YOU SURE?

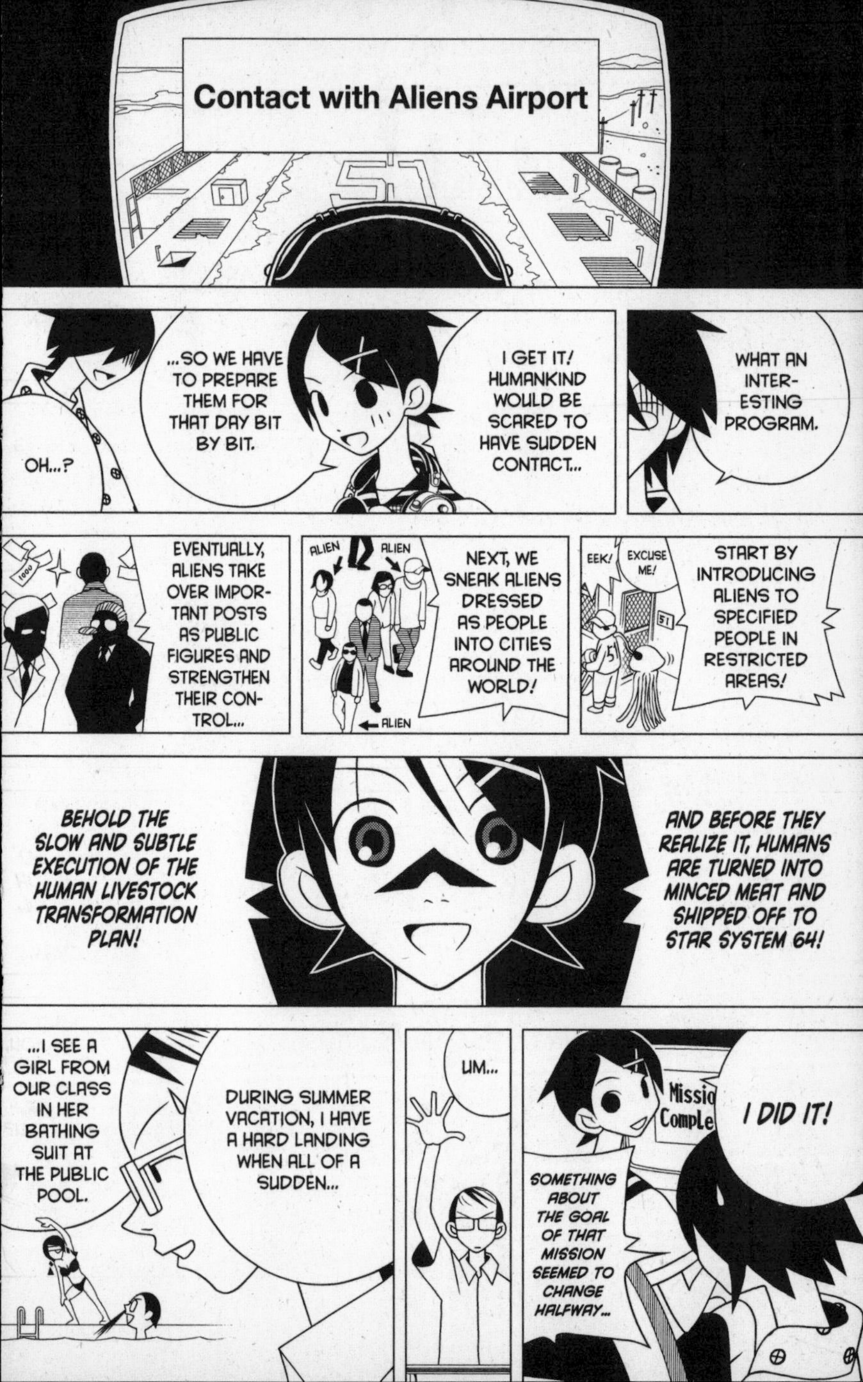

Contact with Aliens Airport
51
WHAT AN INTER-ESTING PROGRAM.
I GET IT! HUMANKIND WOULD BE SCARED TO HAVE SUDDEN CONTACT...
...SO WE HAVE TO PREPARE THEM FOR THAT DAY BIT BY BIT.
OH...?
START BY INTRODUCING ALIENS TO SPECIFIED PEOPLE IN RESTRICTED AREAS!
EXCUSE ME!
EEK!
51
NEXT, WE SNEAK ALIENS DRESSED AS PEOPLE INTO CITIES AROUND THE WORLD!
ALIEN
ALIEN
ALIEN
EVENTUALLY, ALIENS TAKE OVER IMPOR-TANT POSTS AS PUBLIC FIGURES AND STRENGTHEN THEIR CON-TROL...
1000
AND BEFORE THEY REALIZE IT, HUMANS ARE TURNED INTO MINCED MEAT AND SHIPPED OFF TO STAR SYSTEM 64!
BEHOLD THE SLOW AND SUBTLE EXECUTION OF THE HUMAN LIVESTOCK TRANSFORMATION PLAN!
I DID IT!
Missio Comple
SOMETHING ABOUT THE GOAL OF THAT MISSION SEEMED TO CHANGE HALFWAY...
UM...
DURING SUMMER VACATION, I HAVE A HARD LANDING WHEN ALL OF A SUDDEN...
...I SEE A GIRL FROM OUR CLASS IN HER BATHING SUIT AT THE PUBLIC POOL.

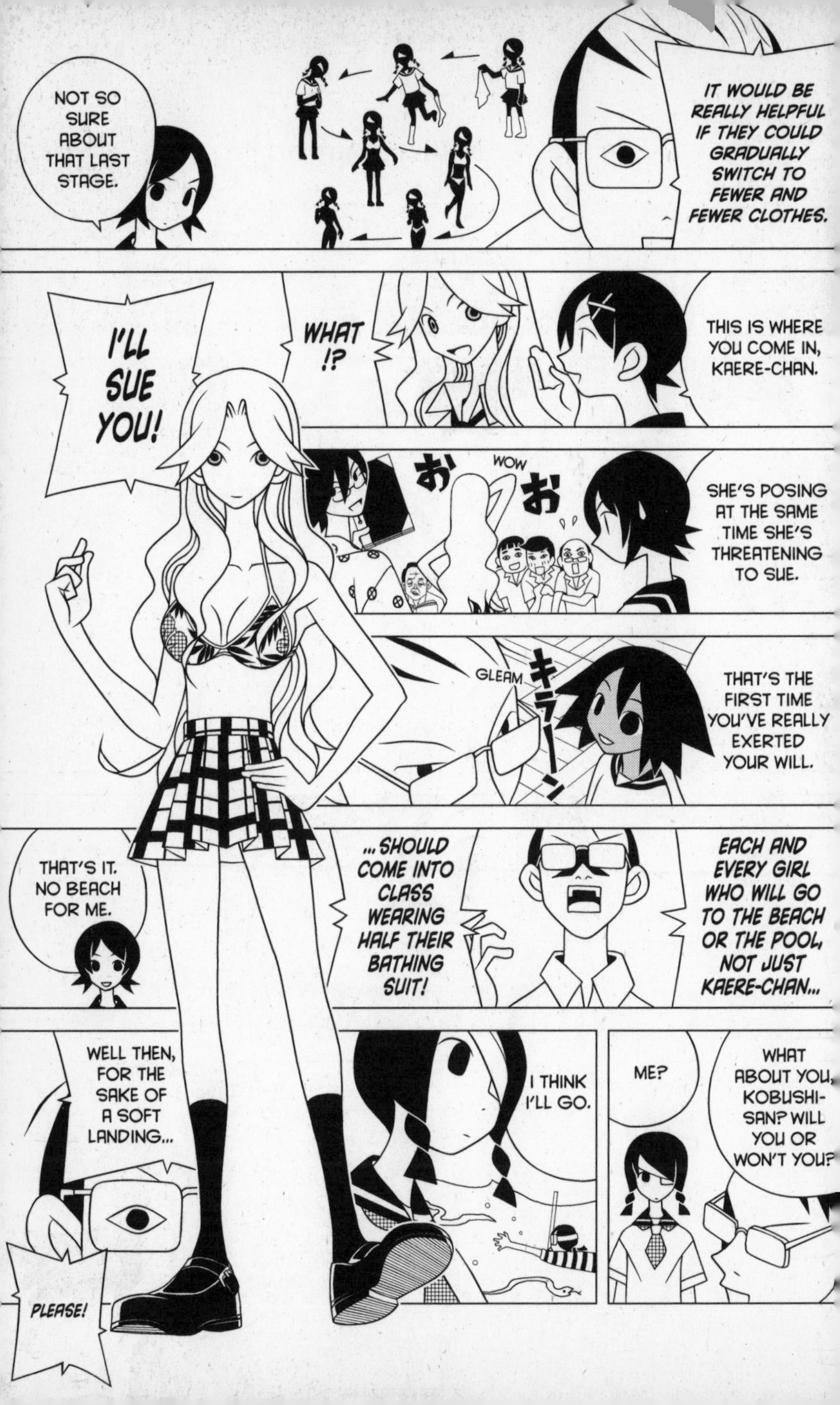
IT WOULD BE REALLY HELPFUL IF THEY COULD GRADUALLY SWITCH TO FEWER AND FEWER CLOTHES.
NOT SO SURE ABOUT THAT LAST STAGE.
THIS IS WHERE YOU COME IN, KAERE-CHAN.
WHAT !?
SHE'S POSING AT THE SAME TIME SHE'S THREATENING TO SUE.
お WOW お
THAT'S THE FIRST TIME YOU'VE REALLY EXERTED YOUR WILL.
GLEAM キラーン
I'LL SUE YOU!
EACH AND EVERY GIRL WHO WILL GO TO THE BEACH OR THE POOL, NOT JUST KAERE-CHAN...
...SHOULD COME INTO CLASS WEARING HALF THEIR BATHING SUIT!
THAT'S IT. NO BEACH FOR ME.
WHAT ABOUT YOU, KOBUSHI-SAN? WILL YOU OR WON'T YOU?
ME?
I THINK I'LL GO.
WELL THEN, FOR THE SAKE OF A SOFT LANDING...
PLEASE!

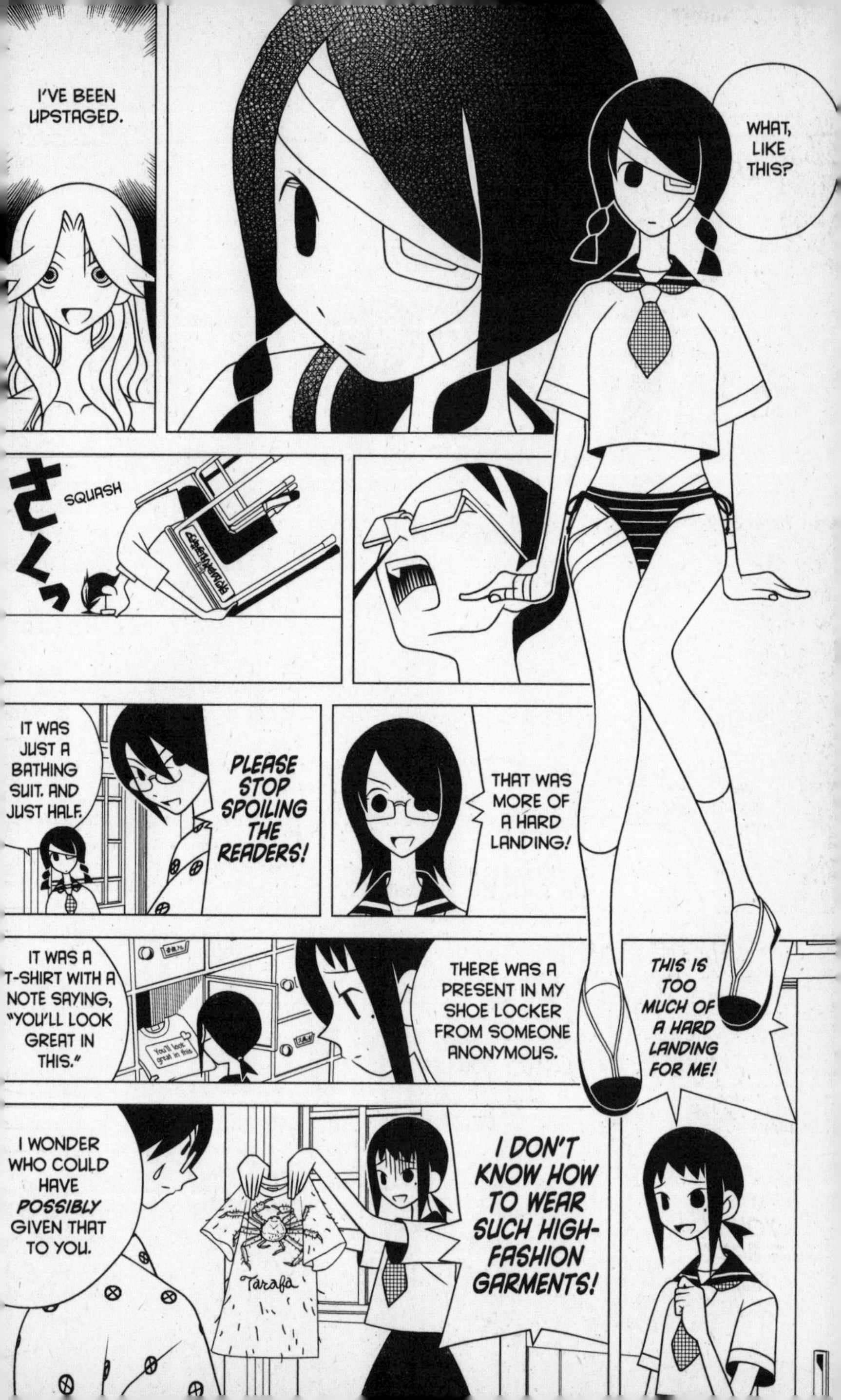
WHAT, LIKE THIS?
I'VE BEEN UPSTAGED.
さくっ
SQUASH
THAT WAS MORE OF A HARD LANDING!
PLEASE STOP SPOILING THE READERS!
IT WAS JUST A BATHING SUIT. AND JUST HALF.
THIS IS TOO MUCH OF A HARD LANDING FOR ME!
THERE WAS A PRESENT IN MY SHOE LOCKER FROM SOMEONE ANONYMOUS.
IT WAS A T-SHIRT WITH A NOTE SAYING, "YOU'LL LOOK GREAT IN THIS."
You'll look great in this
I DON'T KNOW HOW TO WEAR SUCH HIGH-FASHION GARMENTS!
Tarafa
I WONDER WHO COULD HAVE POSSIBLY GIVEN THAT TO YOU.

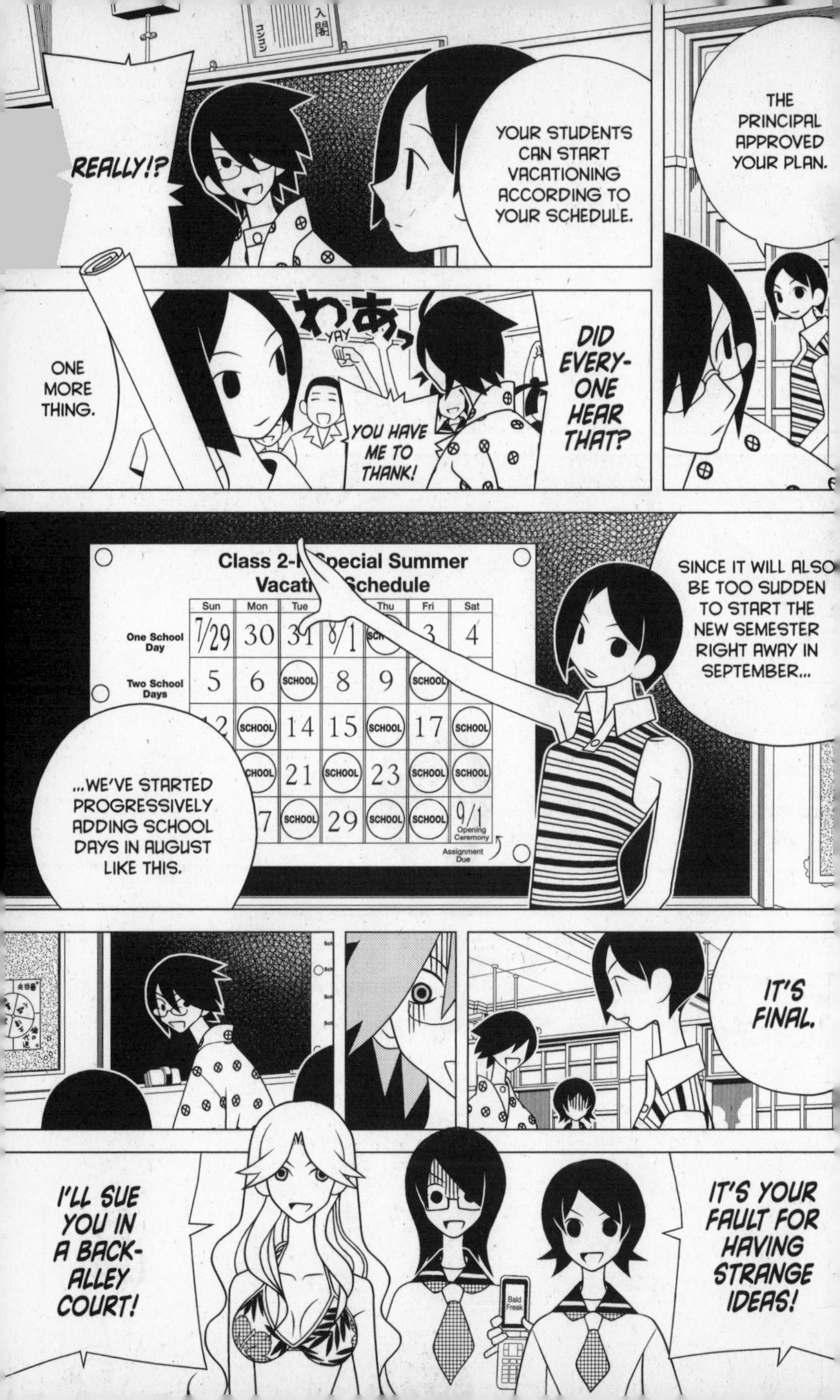
THE PRINCIPAL APPROVED YOUR PLAN.
YOUR STUDENTS CAN START VACATIONING ACCORDING TO YOUR SCHEDULE.
REALLY!?
DID EVERY-ONE HEAR THAT?
わあっ
YAY
YOU HAVE ME TO THANK!
ONE MORE THING.
SINCE IT WILL ALSO BE TOO SUDDEN TO START THE NEW SEMESTER RIGHT AWAY IN SEPTEMBER...
Class 2-H Special Summer Vacation Schedule
Sun Mon Tue Wed Thu Fri Sat
One School Day 7/29 30 31 8/1 SCHOOL 3 4
Two School Days 5 6 SCHOOL 8 9 SCHOOL
12 SCHOOL 14 15 SCHOOL 17 SCHOOL
SCHOOL 21 SCHOOL 23 SCHOOL SCHOOL
27 SCHOOL 29 SCHOOL SCHOOL 9/1 Opening Ceremony
Assignment Due
...WE'VE STARTED PROGRESSIVELY ADDING SCHOOL DAYS IN AUGUST LIKE THIS.
IT'S FINAL.
IT'S YOUR FAULT FOR HAVING STRANGE IDEAS!
Bald Freak
I'LL SUE YOU IN A BACK-ALLEY COURT!

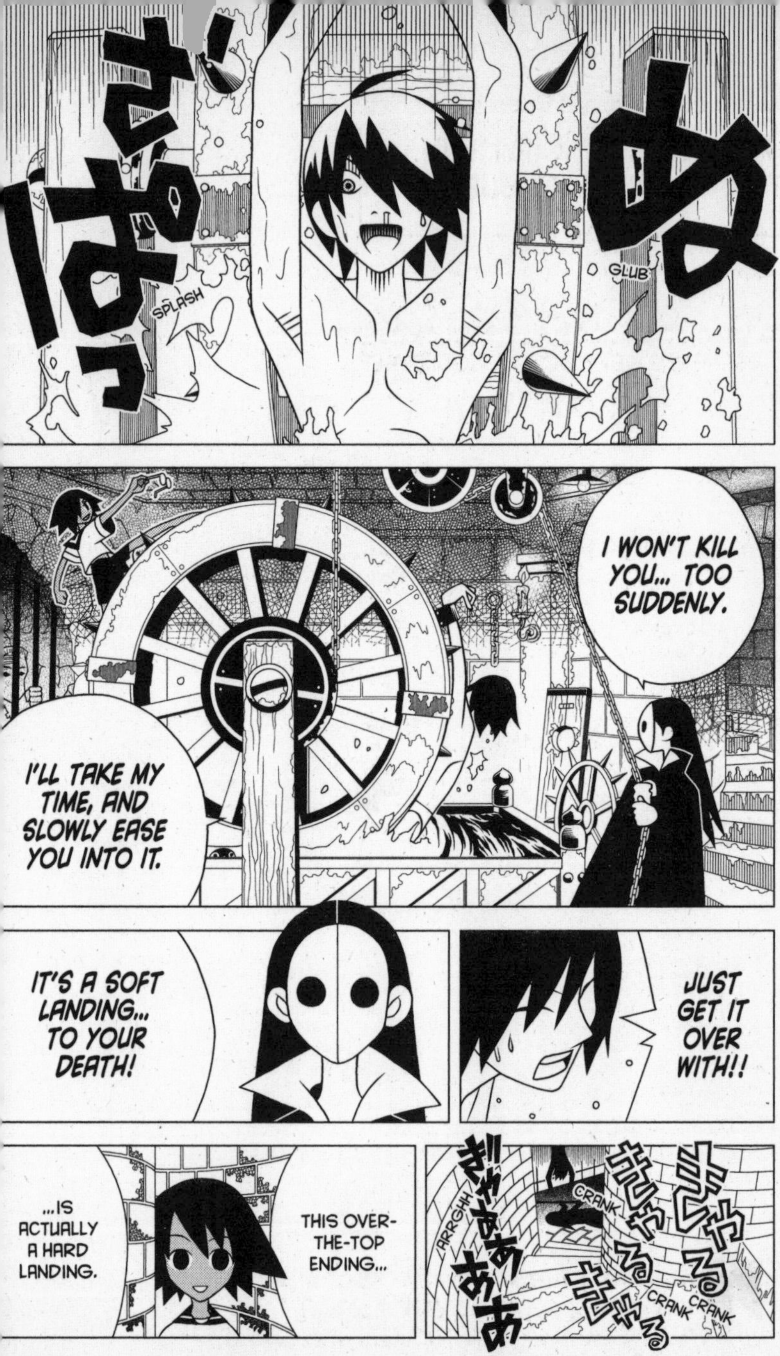
ぬ
GLUB
ざぱっ
SPLASH
I WON'T KILL YOU... TOO SUDDENLY.
I'LL TAKE MY TIME, AND SLOWLY EASE YOU INTO IT.
JUST GET IT OVER WITH!!
IT'S A SOFT LANDING... TO YOUR DEATH!
きゃるきゃる
きゃるきゃる
CRANK
CRANK
CRANK
ぎゃああああ!!
ARRGHH
THIS OVER-THE-TOP ENDING...
...IS ACTUALLY A HARD LANDING.

PLEASE PARTICIPATE IN A SOFT LANDING SURVEY

Q: WHICH GENRE DO YOU THINK KUMETA-SENSEI'S NEXT WORK SHOULD BE?

1) SPORTS (ENTIRELY SPORTS-ONLY)
2) LOVE COMEDY (WITHOUT INTERRUPTION)
3) FANTASY (VOLUMINOUS, SET ON EARTH)
4) A DRAMA ABOUT OVERCOMING ILLNESS
5) A STORY WHERE THE HEROINE DIES
6) A STORY WHERE THE HEROINE GETS PREGNANT
7) A BATTLE MANGA THAT ENDS AFTER 10 VOLUMES

MY EDITOR MR. TAKEDA ACTUALLY TOLD ME THAT HE THINKS I SHOULD DRAW A SOCCER MANGA. HE SAID THIS EVEN THOUGH HE HAS NO INTEREST IN READING IT!

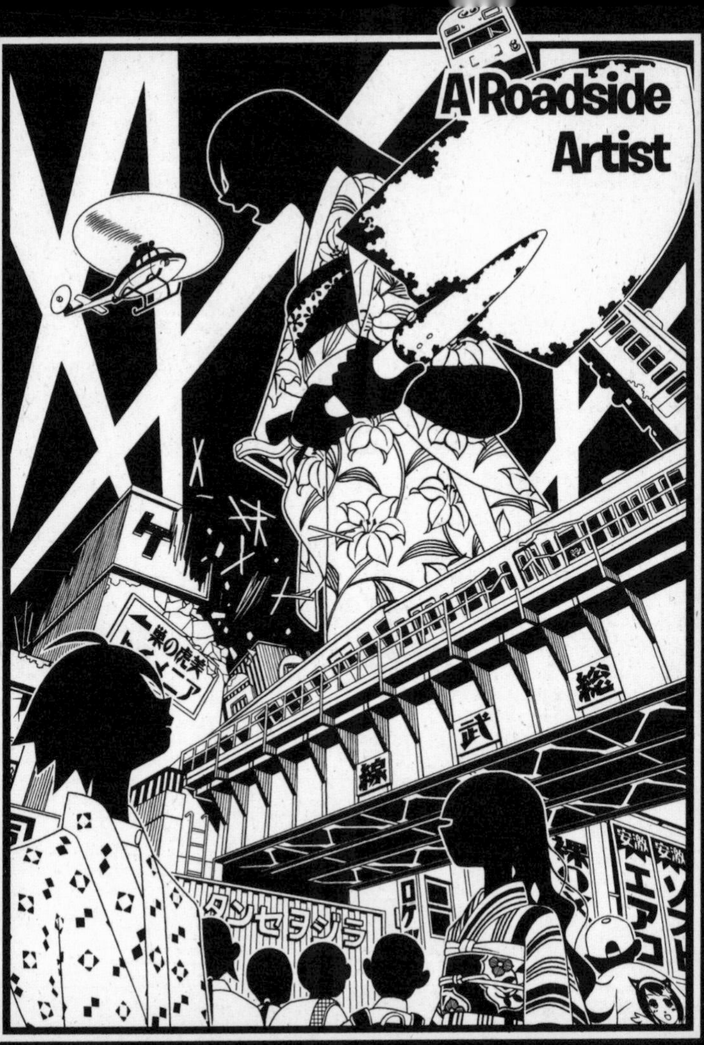
A Roadside Artist

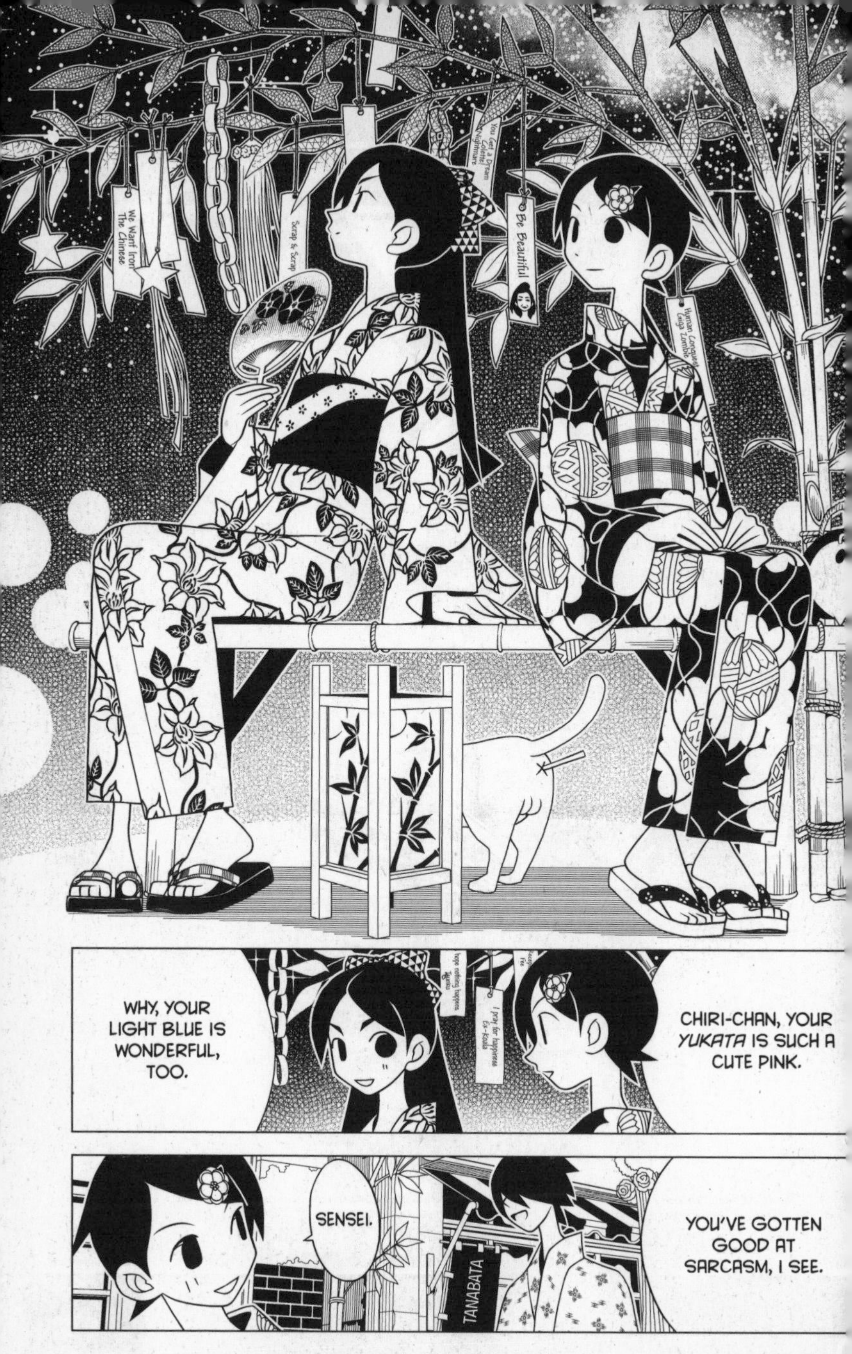
Be Beautiful
Scrap & Scrap
We Want Iron The Chinese
CHIRI-CHAN, YOUR *YUKATA* IS SUCH A CUTE PINK.
WHY, YOUR LIGHT BLUE IS WONDERFUL, TOO.
YOU'VE GOTTEN GOOD AT SARCASM, I SEE.
TANABATA
SENSEI.

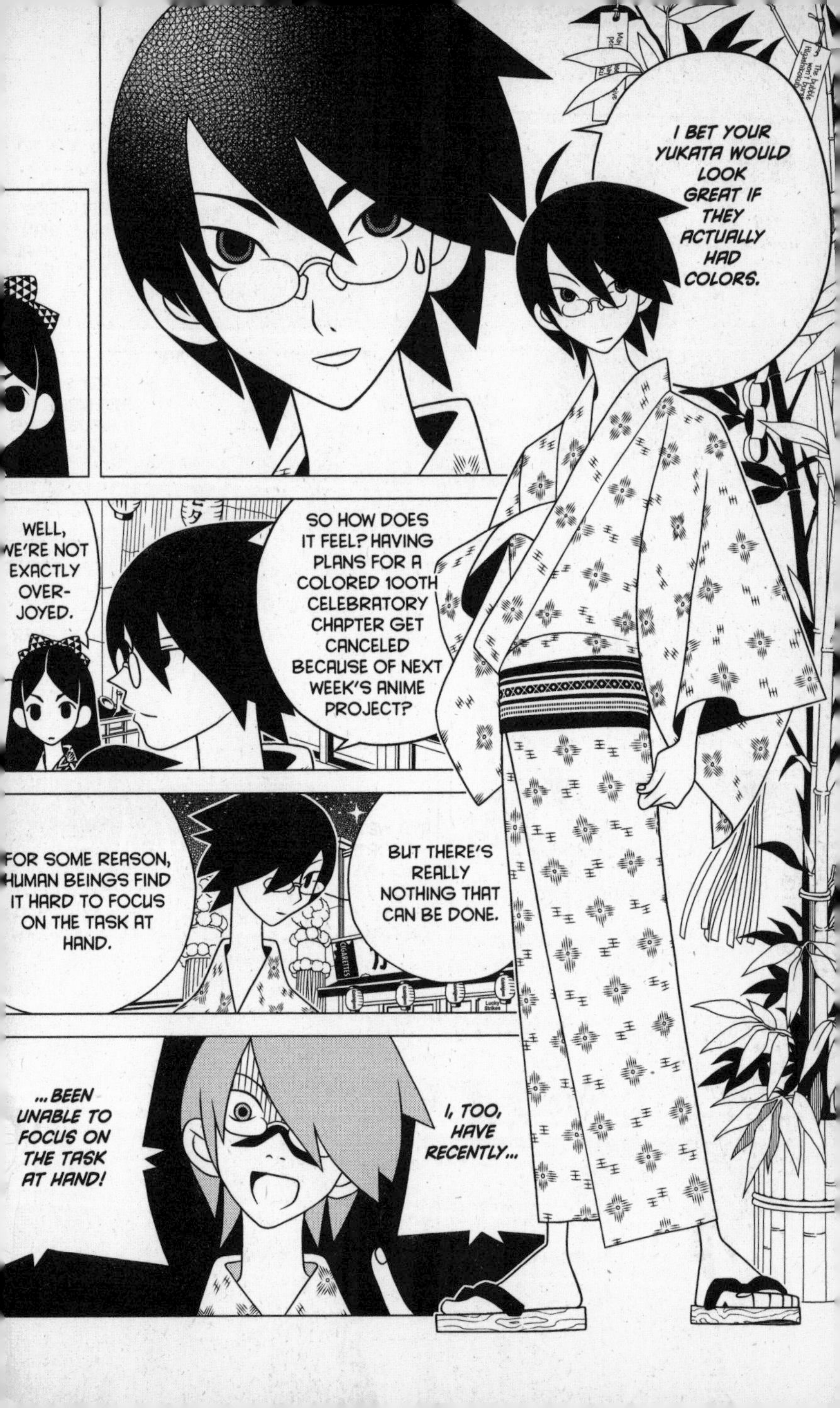
I BET YOUR YUKATA WOULD LOOK GREAT IF THEY ACTUALLY HAD COLORS.
SO HOW DOES IT FEEL? HAVING PLANS FOR A COLORED 100TH CELEBRATORY CHAPTER GET CANCELED BECAUSE OF NEXT WEEK'S ANIME PROJECT?
WELL, WE'RE NOT EXACTLY OVER-JOYED.
BUT THERE'S REALLY NOTHING THAT CAN BE DONE.
FOR SOME REASON, HUMAN BEINGS FIND IT HARD TO FOCUS ON THE TASK AT HAND.
CIGARETTES
I, TOO, HAVE RECENTLY...
...BEEN UNABLE TO FOCUS ON THE TASK AT HAND!

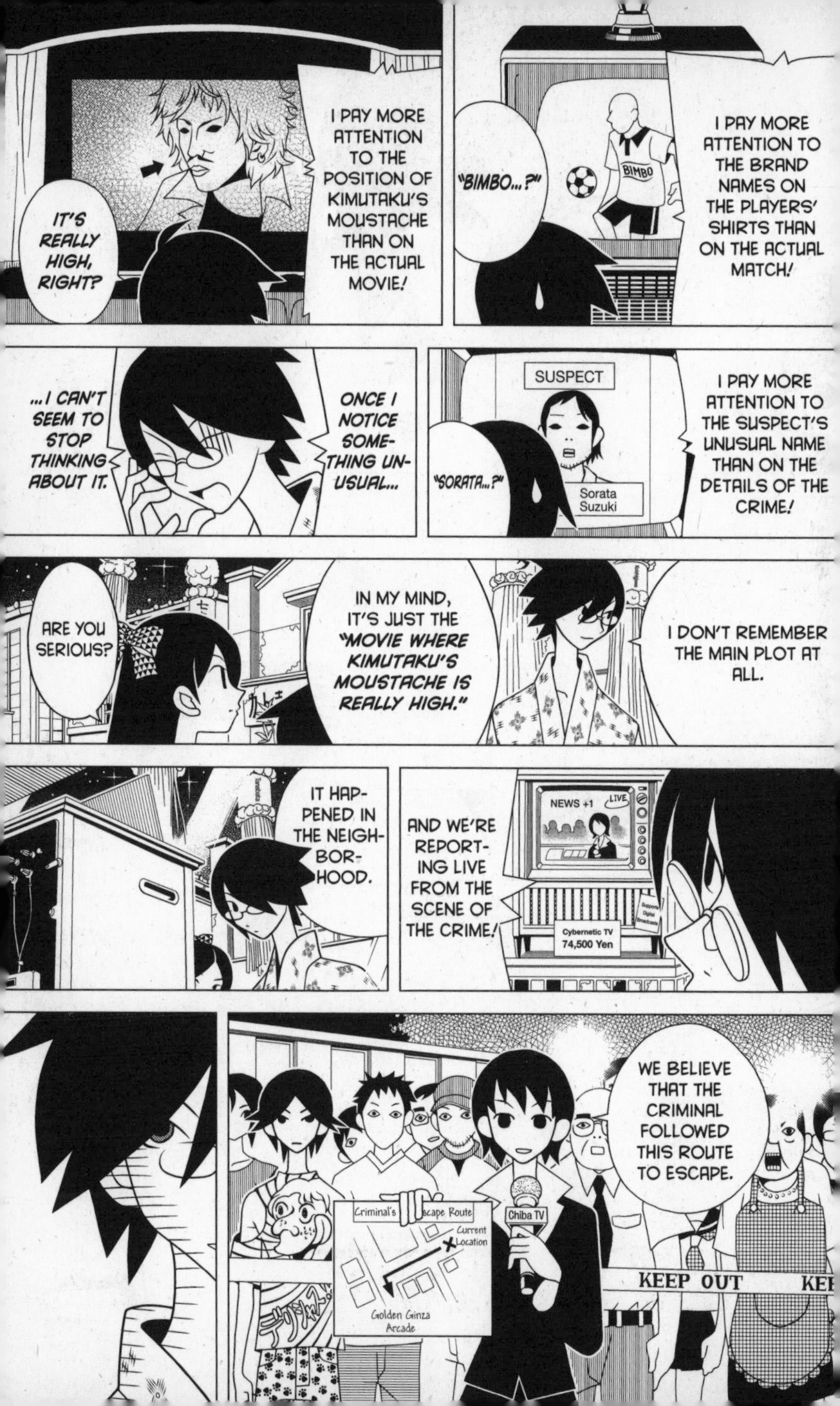
I PAY MORE ATTENTION TO THE BRAND NAMES ON THE PLAYERS' SHIRTS THAN ON THE ACTUAL MATCH!
BIMBO
"BIMBO...?"
I PAY MORE ATTENTION TO THE POSITION OF KIMUTAKU'S MOUSTACHE THAN ON THE ACTUAL MOVIE!
IT'S REALLY HIGH, RIGHT?
SUSPECT
I PAY MORE ATTENTION TO THE SUSPECT'S UNUSUAL NAME THAN ON THE DETAILS OF THE CRIME!
"SORATA...?"
Sorata Suzuki
ONCE I NOTICE SOMETHING UNUSUAL...
...I CAN'T SEEM TO STOP THINKING ABOUT IT.
I DON'T REMEMBER THE MAIN PLOT AT ALL.
IN MY MIND, IT'S JUST THE "MOVIE WHERE KIMUTAKU'S MOUSTACHE IS REALLY HIGH."
ARE YOU SERIOUS?
NEWS +1
LIVE
Cybernetic TV 74,500 Yen
AND WE'RE REPORTING LIVE FROM THE SCENE OF THE CRIME!
IT HAPPENED IN THE NEIGHBORHOOD.
WE BELIEVE THAT THE CRIMINAL FOLLOWED THIS ROUTE TO ESCAPE.
Chiba TV
Criminal's scape Route
Current Location
Golden Ginza Arcade
KEEP OUT

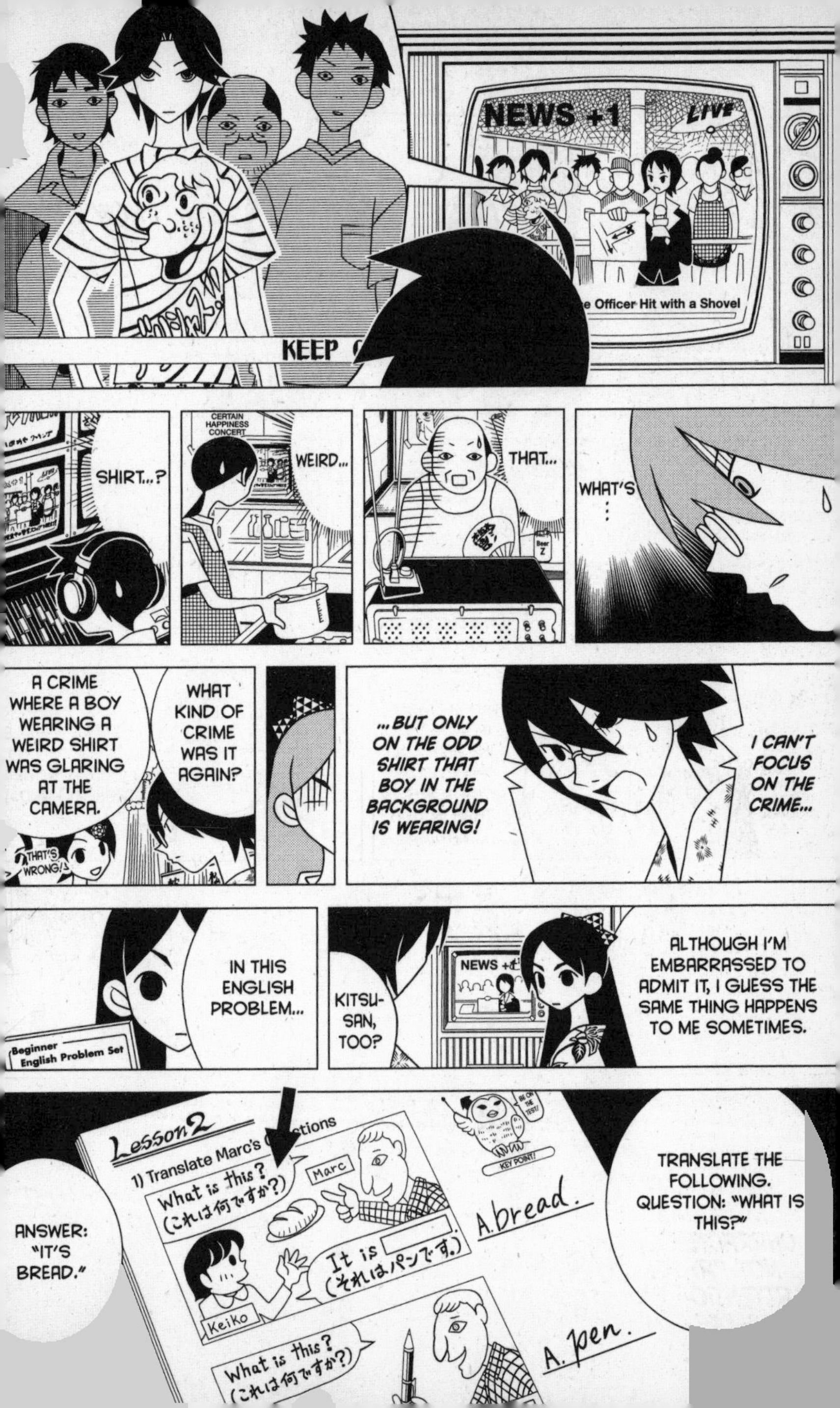

NEWS +1
LIVE
e Officer Hit with a Shovel
KEEP
WHAT'S
...
THAT...
WEIRD...
CERTAIN HAPPINESS CONCERT
SHIRT...?
I CAN'T FOCUS ON THE CRIME...
...BUT ONLY ON THE ODD SHIRT THAT BOY IN THE BACKGROUND IS WEARING!
WHAT KIND OF CRIME WAS IT AGAIN?
A CRIME WHERE A BOY WEARING A WEIRD SHIRT WAS GLARING AT THE CAMERA.
THAT'S WRONG!
ALTHOUGH I'M EMBARRASSED TO ADMIT IT, I GUESS THE SAME THING HAPPENS TO ME SOMETIMES.
NEWS +
KITSU-SAN, TOO?
IN THIS ENGLISH PROBLEM...
Beginner English Problem Set
TRANSLATE THE FOLLOWING. QUESTION: "WHAT IS THIS?"
BE ON THE TEST!
KEY POINT!
Lesson 2
1) Translate Marc's
tions
What is this? (これは何ですか?)
Marc
A. bread.
It is (それはパンです。)
Keiko
What is this? (これは何ですか?)
A. pen.
ANSWER: "IT'S BREAD."

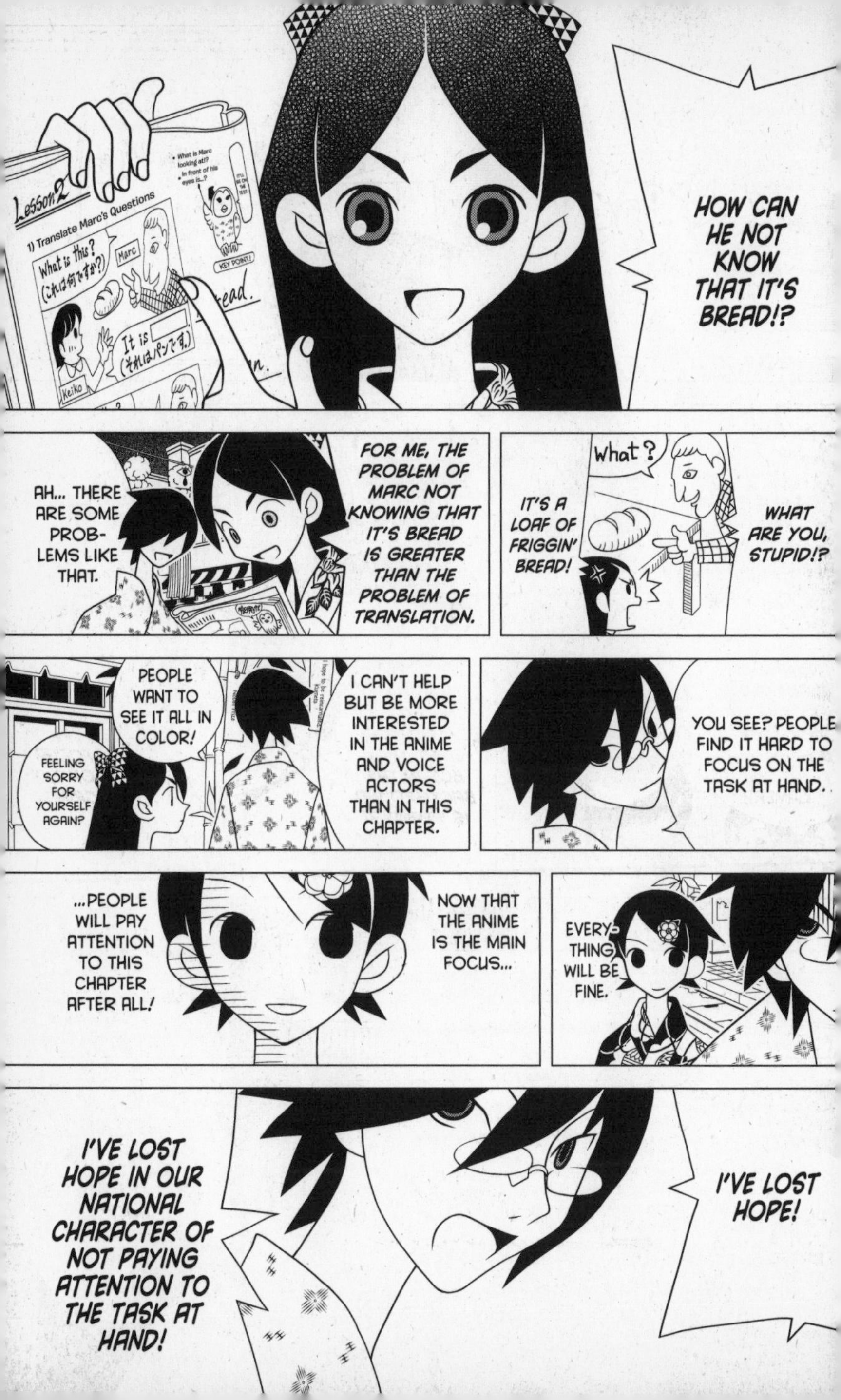
HOW CAN HE NOT KNOW THAT IT'S BREAD!?
Lesson 2
1) Translate Marc's Questions
What is Marc looking at!? In front of his eyes is...?
KEY POINT!
What is this? (これは何ですか?)
Marc
It is (それはパンです。)
Keiko
What?
WHAT ARE YOU, STUPID!?
IT'S A LOAF OF FRIGGIN' BREAD!
FOR ME, THE PROBLEM OF MARC NOT KNOWING THAT IT'S BREAD IS GREATER THAN THE PROBLEM OF TRANSLATION.
AH... THERE ARE SOME PROB-LEMS LIKE THAT.
YOU SEE? PEOPLE FIND IT HARD TO FOCUS ON THE TASK AT HAND.
I CAN'T HELP BUT BE MORE INTERESTED IN THE ANIME AND VOICE ACTORS THAN IN THIS CHAPTER.
PEOPLE WANT TO SEE IT ALL IN COLOR!
FEELING SORRY FOR YOURSELF AGAIN?
EVERY-THING WILL BE FINE.
NOW THAT THE ANIME IS THE MAIN FOCUS...
...PEOPLE WILL PAY ATTENTION TO THIS CHAPTER AFTER ALL!
I'VE LOST HOPE!
I'VE LOST HOPE IN OUR NATIONAL CHARACTER OF NOT PAYING ATTENTION TO THE TASK AT HAND!

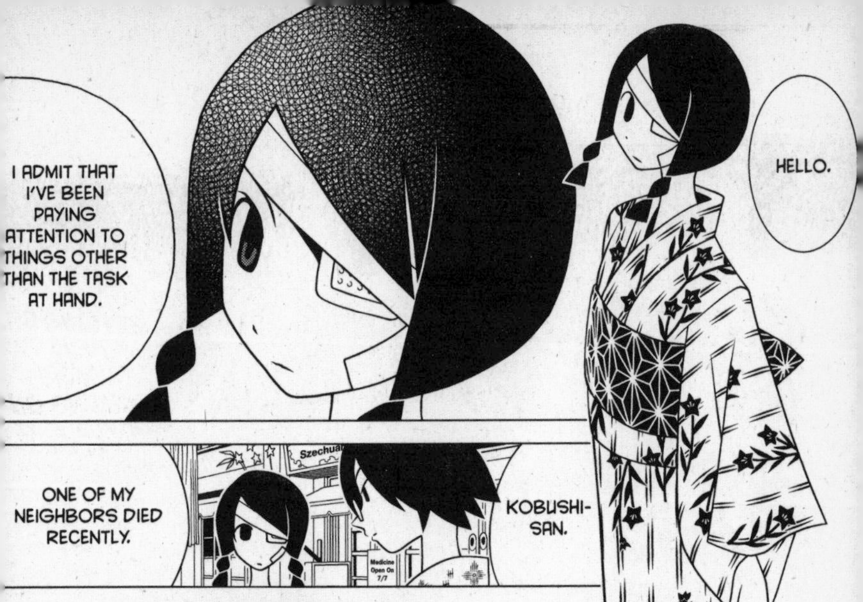
HELLO.
I ADMIT THAT I'VE BEEN PAYING ATTENTION TO THINGS OTHER THAN THE TASK AT HAND.
Szechuan
KOBUSHI-SAN.
Medicine Open On 7/7
ONE OF MY NEIGHBORS DIED RECENTLY.
AT THE FUNERAL, ALL I COULD THINK ABOUT...
I'M SURE MY HUSBAND IS HAPPY...
MIKA KANAI!?
SATOMI KOROGI!?
...WAS THE *AMAZING ANIME VOICE* OF THE CHIEF MOURNER!
EVEN THOUGH I FELT AWFUL THROUGHOUT THE WHOLE THING, I COULDN'T STOP THINKING ABOUT IT.
SHIDO LIQUOR
DON'T DRINK AND DRIVE
AH... I CAN SEE HOW THAT MIGHT HAPPEN.

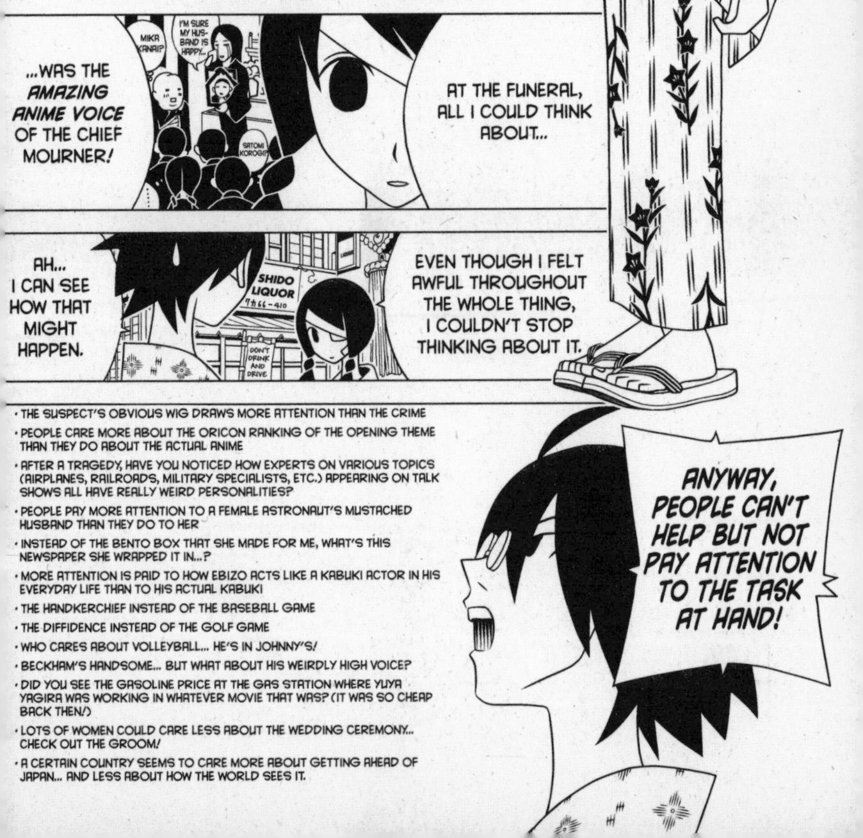
ANYWAY, PEOPLE CAN'T HELP BUT NOT PAY ATTENTION TO THE TASK AT HAND!

- THE SUSPECT'S OBVIOUS WIG DRAWS MORE ATTENTION THAN THE CRIME
- PEOPLE CARE MORE ABOUT THE ORICON RANKING OF THE OPENING THEME THAN THEY DO ABOUT THE ACTUAL ANIME
- AFTER A TRAGEDY, HAVE YOU NOTICED HOW EXPERTS ON VARIOUS TOPICS (AIRPLANES, RAILROADS, MILITARY SPECIALISTS, ETC.) APPEARING ON TALK SHOWS ALL HAVE REALLY WEIRD PERSONALITIES?
- PEOPLE PAY MORE ATTENTION TO A FEMALE ASTRONAUT'S MUSTACHED HUSBAND THAN THEY DO TO HER
- INSTEAD OF THE BENTO BOX THAT SHE MADE FOR ME, WHAT'S THIS NEWSPAPER SHE WRAPPED IT IN...?
- MORE ATTENTION IS PAID TO HOW EBIZO ACTS LIKE A KABUKI ACTOR IN HIS EVERYDAY LIFE THAN TO HIS ACTUAL KABUKI
- THE HANDKERCHIEF INSTEAD OF THE BASEBALL GAME
- THE DIFFIDENCE INSTEAD OF THE GOLF GAME
- WHO CARES ABOUT VOLLEYBALL... HE'S IN JOHNNY'S!
- BECKHAM'S HANDSOME... BUT WHAT ABOUT HIS WEIRDLY HIGH VOICE?
- DID YOU SEE THE GASOLINE PRICE AT THE GAS STATION WHERE YUYA YAGIRA WAS WORKING IN WHATEVER MOVIE THAT WAS? (IT WAS SO CHEAP BACK THEN!)
- LOTS OF WOMEN COULD CARE LESS ABOUT THE WEDDING CEREMONY... CHECK OUT THE GROOM!
- A CERTAIN COUNTRY SEEMS TO CARE MORE ABOUT GETTING AHEAD OF JAPAN... AND LESS ABOUT HOW THE WORLD SEES IT.

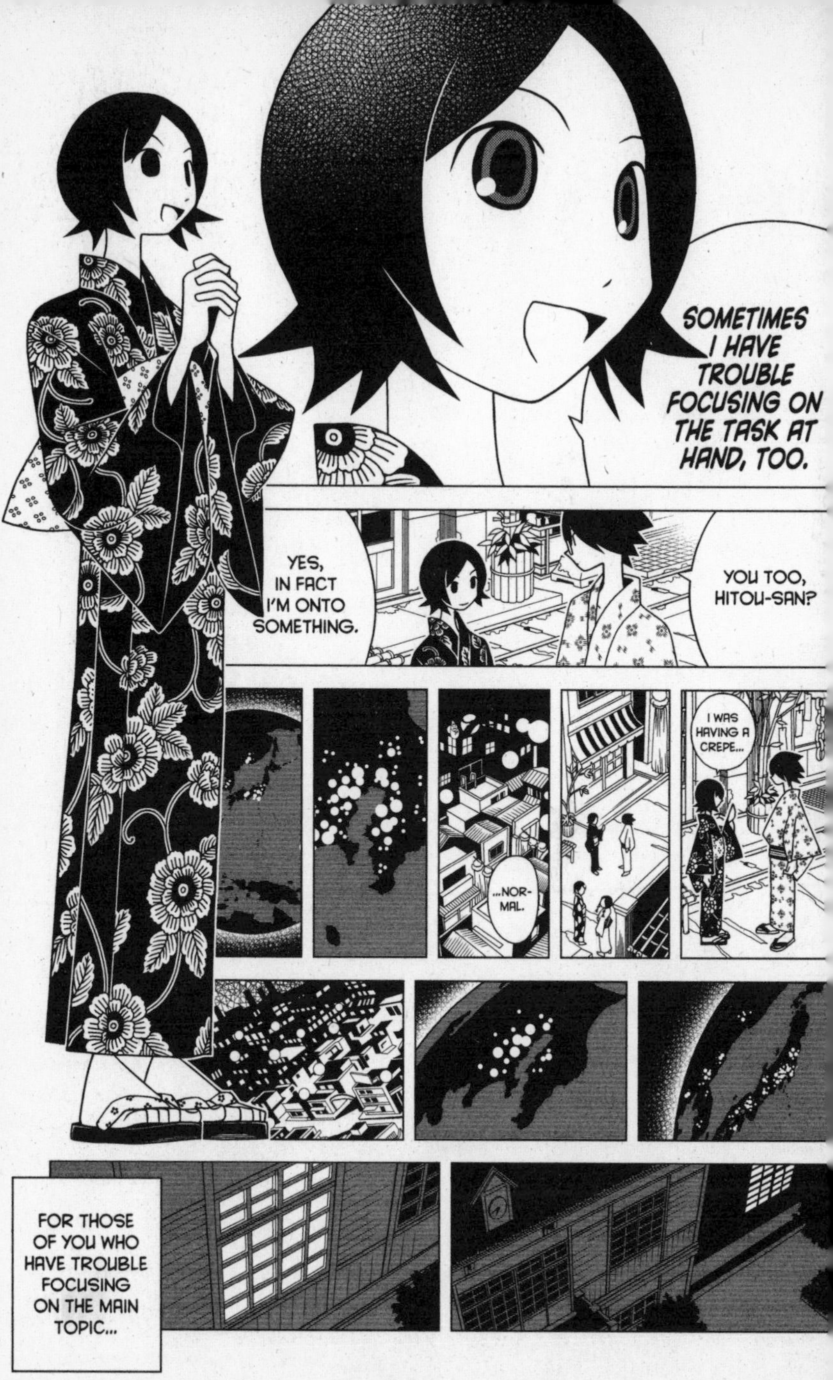
SOMETIMES I HAVE TROUBLE FOCUSING ON THE TASK AT HAND, TOO.
YOU TOO, HITOU-SAN?
YES, IN FACT I'M ONTO SOMETHING.
I WAS HAVING A CREPE...
...NOR-MAL.
FOR THOSE OF YOU WHO HAVE TROUBLE FOCUSING ON THE MAIN TOPIC...

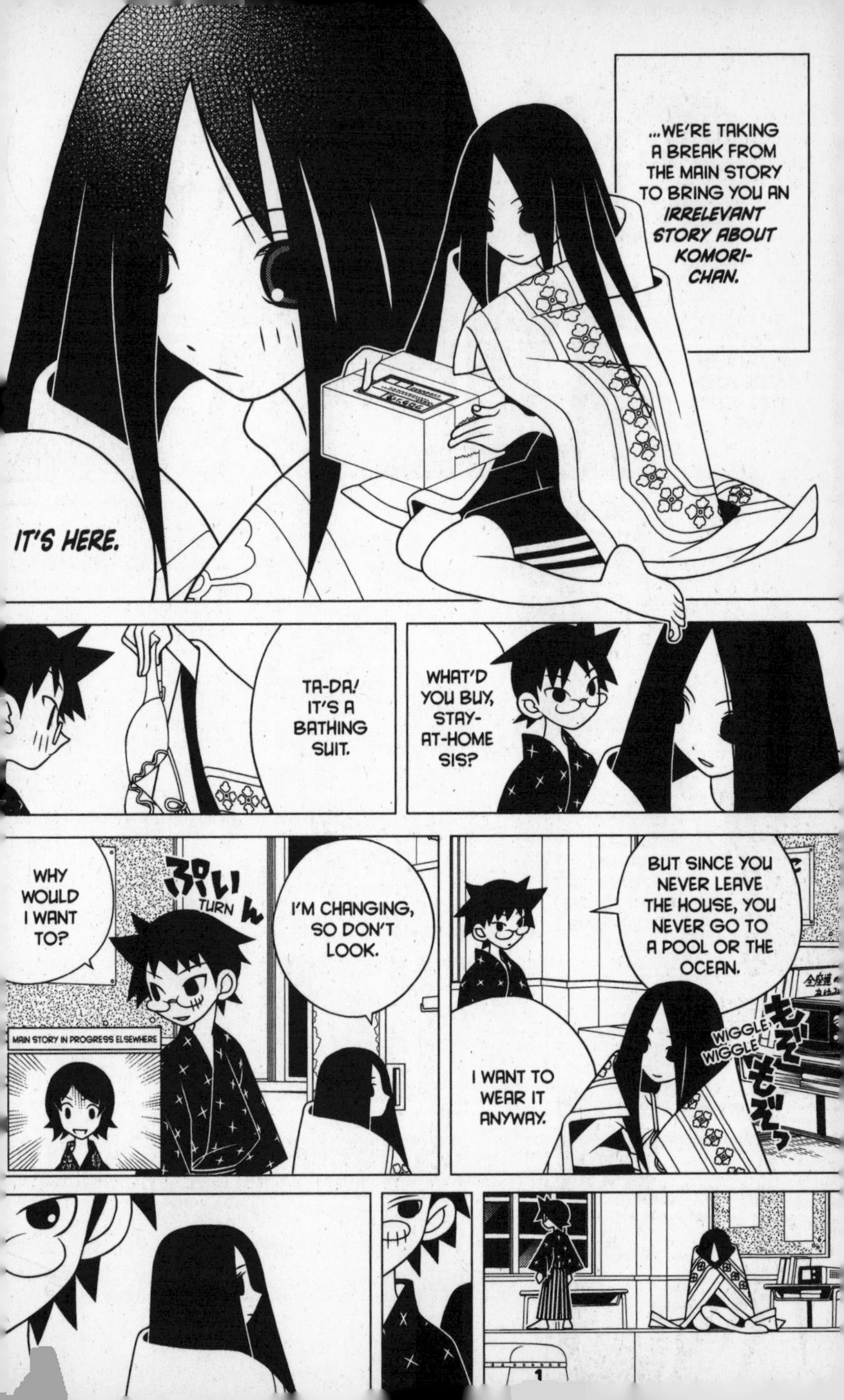
...WE'RE TAKING A BREAK FROM THE MAIN STORY TO BRING YOU AN *IRRELEVANT STORY ABOUT KOMORI-CHAN.*
IT'S HERE.
WHAT'D YOU BUY, STAY-AT-HOME SIS?
TA-DA! IT'S A BATHING SUIT.
BUT SINCE YOU NEVER LEAVE THE HOUSE, YOU NEVER GO TO A POOL OR THE OCEAN.
もぞもぞっ
WIGGLE WIGGLE
I WANT TO WEAR IT ANYWAY.
I'M CHANGING, SO DON'T LOOK.
ぷいん
TURN
WHY WOULD I WANT TO?
MAIN STORY IN PROGRESS ELSEWHERE

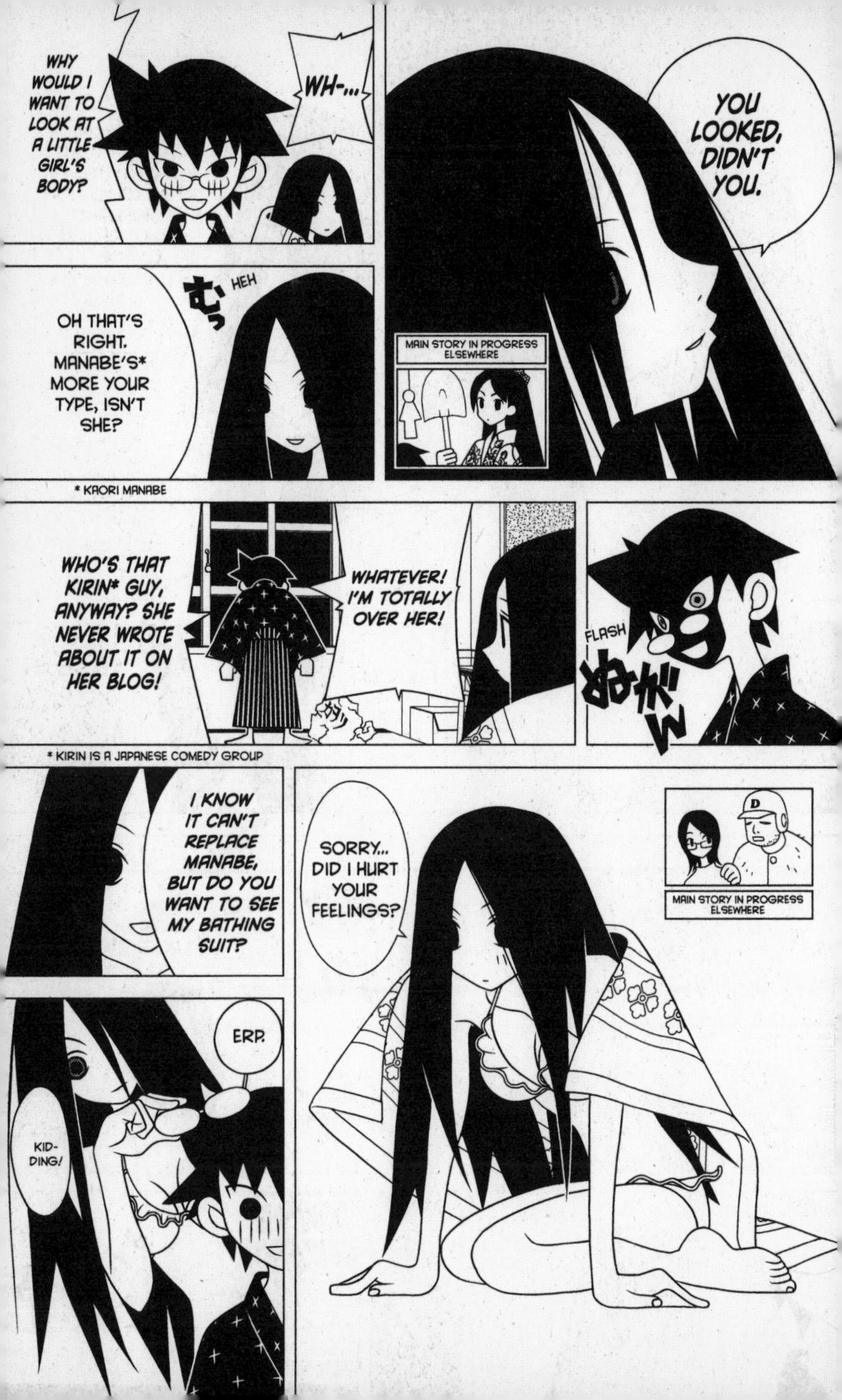
YOU LOOKED, DIDN'T YOU.
WH-...
WHY WOULD I WANT TO LOOK AT A LITTLE GIRL'S BODY?
MAIN STORY IN PROGRESS ELSEWHERE
HEH
OH THAT'S RIGHT. MANABE'S* MORE YOUR TYPE, ISN'T SHE?
* KAORI MANABE
FLASH
WHATEVER! I'M TOTALLY OVER HER!
WHO'S THAT KIRIN* GUY, ANYWAY? SHE NEVER WROTE ABOUT IT ON HER BLOG!
* KIRIN IS A JAPANESE COMEDY GROUP
MAIN STORY IN PROGRESS ELSEWHERE
SORRY... DID I HURT YOUR FEELINGS?
I KNOW IT CAN'T REPLACE MANABE, BUT DO YOU WANT TO SEE MY BATHING SUIT?
ERP.
KID-DING!

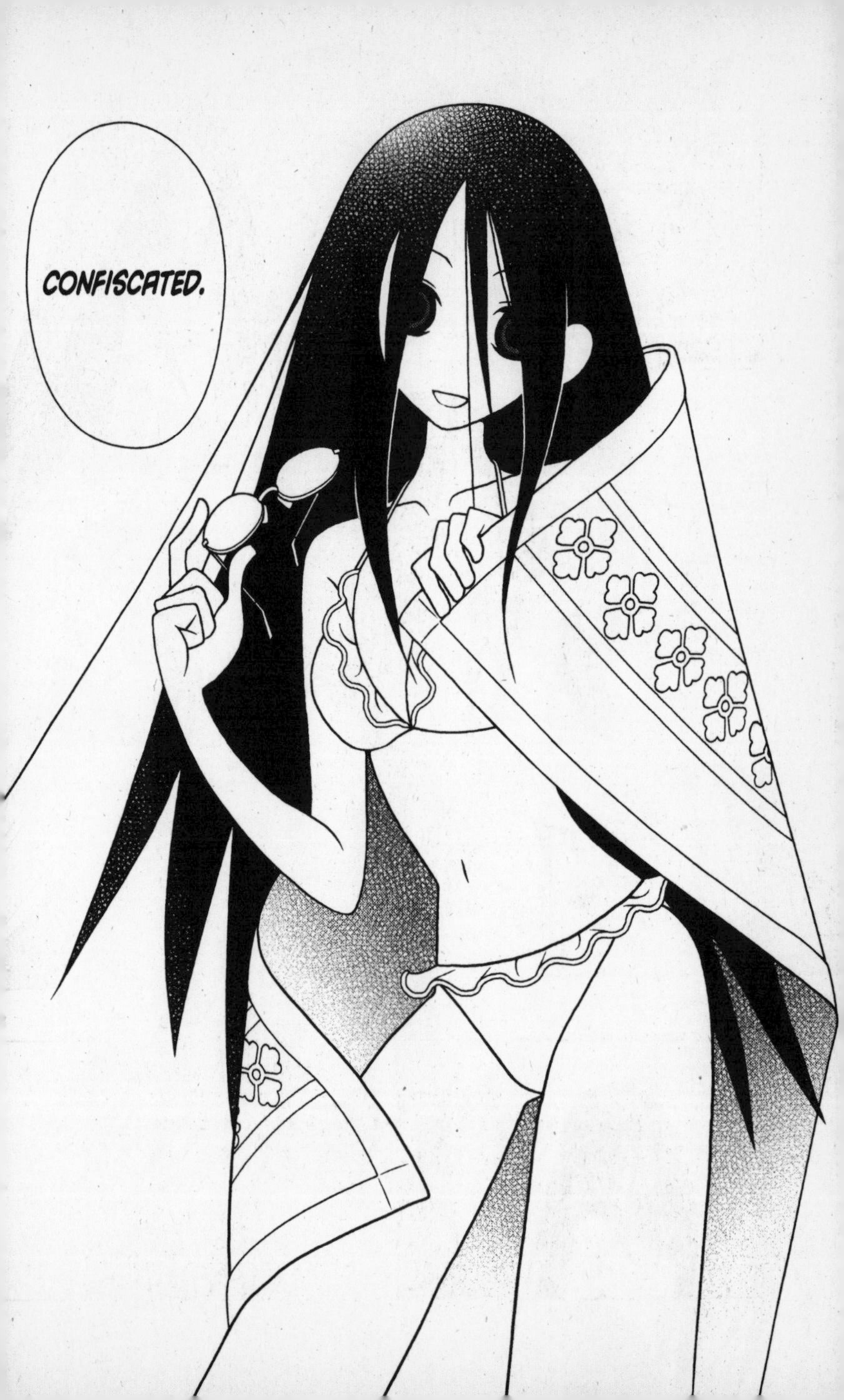
CONFISCATED.

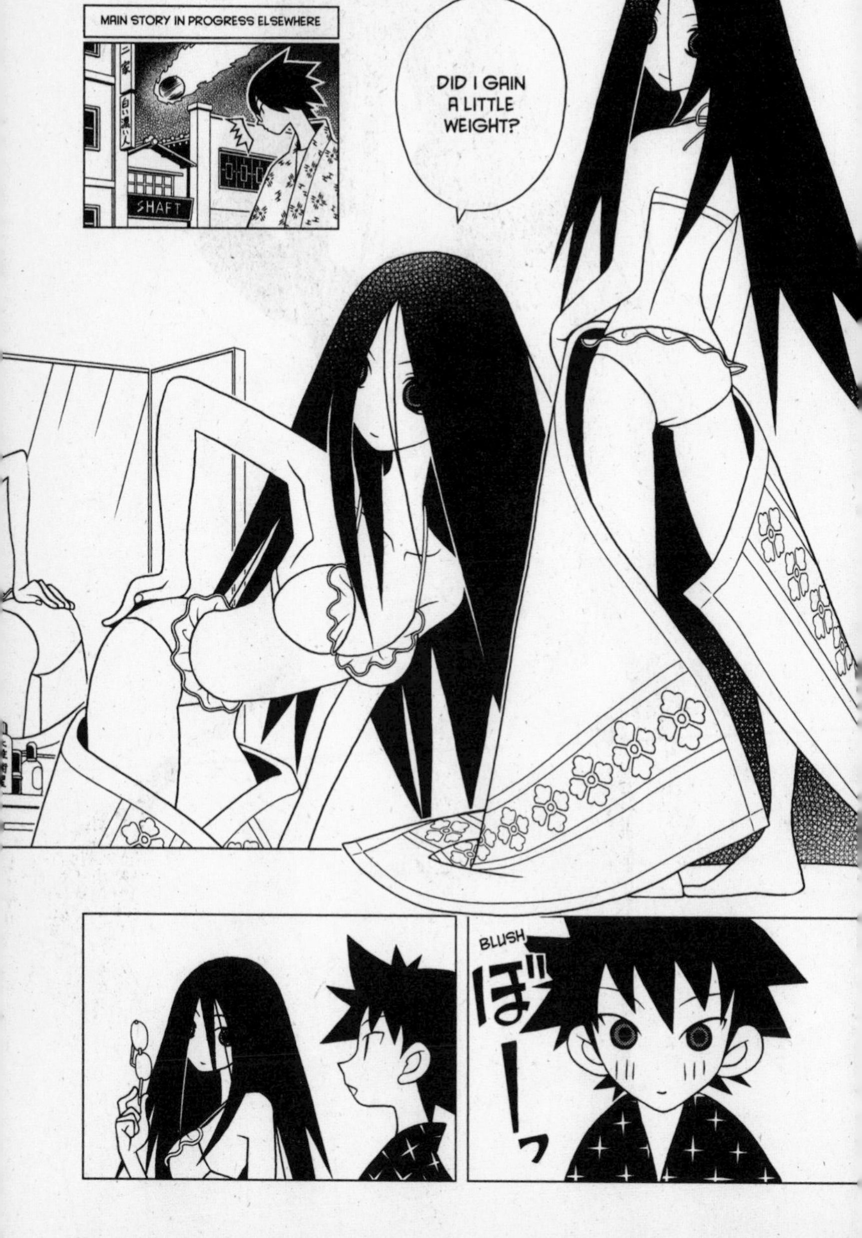
DID I GAIN A LITTLE WEIGHT?
MAIN STORY IN PROGRESS ELSEWHERE
SHAFT
BLUSH
ぼーっ

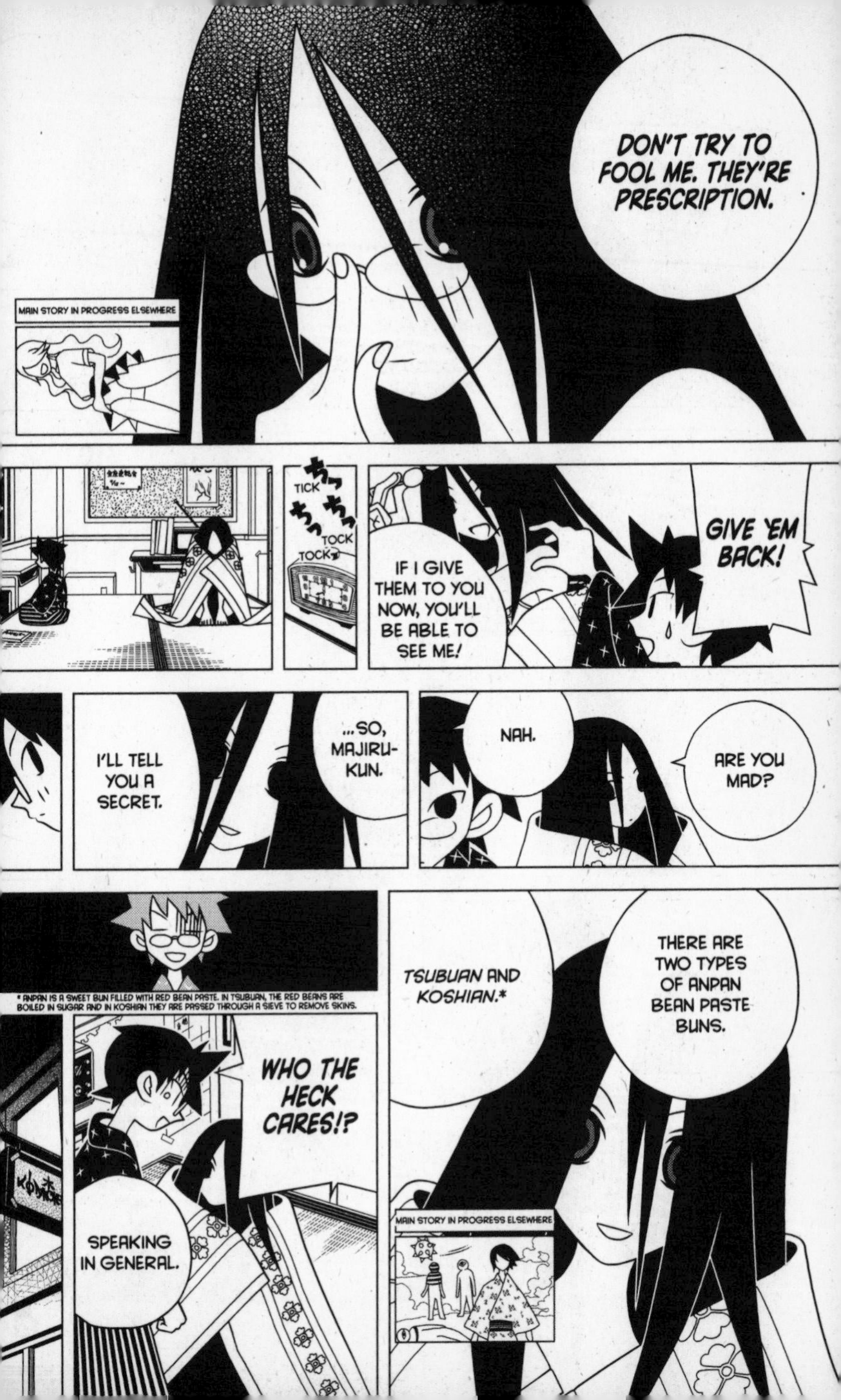
DON'T TRY TO FOOL ME. THEY'RE PRESCRIPTION.
MAIN STORY IN PROGRESS ELSEWHERE
GIVE 'EM BACK!
IF I GIVE THEM TO YOU NOW, YOU'LL BE ABLE TO SEE ME!
TICK
TOCK
TOCK
ARE YOU MAD?
NAH.
...SO, MAJIRU-KUN.
I'LL TELL YOU A SECRET.
THERE ARE TWO TYPES OF ANPAN BEAN PASTE BUNS.
TSUBUAN AND KOSHIAN.*
MAIN STORY IN PROGRESS ELSEWHERE
* ANPAN IS A SWEET BUN FILLED WITH RED BEAN PASTE. IN TSUBUAN, THE RED BEANS ARE BOILED IN SUGAR AND IN KOSHIAN THEY ARE PASSED THROUGH A SIEVE TO REMOVE SKINS.
WHO THE HECK CARES!?
SPEAKING IN GENERAL.

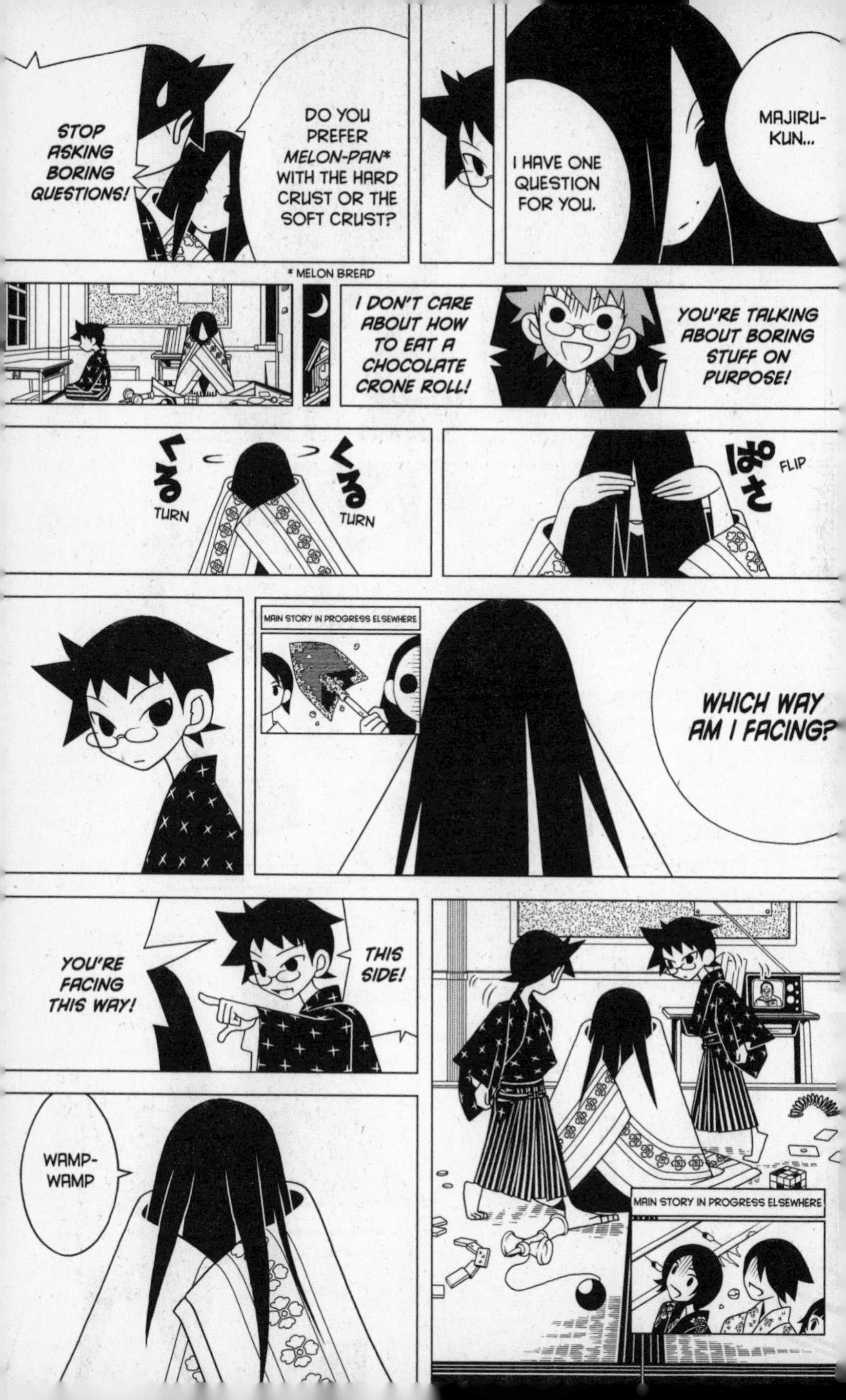
MAJIRU-KUN...
I HAVE ONE QUESTION FOR YOU.
DO YOU PREFER MELON-PAN* WITH THE HARD CRUST OR THE SOFT CRUST?
STOP ASKING BORING QUESTIONS!
* MELON BREAD
YOU'RE TALKING ABOUT BORING STUFF ON PURPOSE!
I DON'T CARE ABOUT HOW TO EAT A CHOCOLATE CRONE ROLL!
ぱさ
FLIP
くる
TURN
くる
TURN
WHICH WAY AM I FACING?
MAIN STORY IN PROGRESS ELSEWHERE
MAIN STORY IN PROGRESS ELSEWHERE
THIS SIDE!
YOU'RE FACING THIS WAY!
WAMP-WAMP

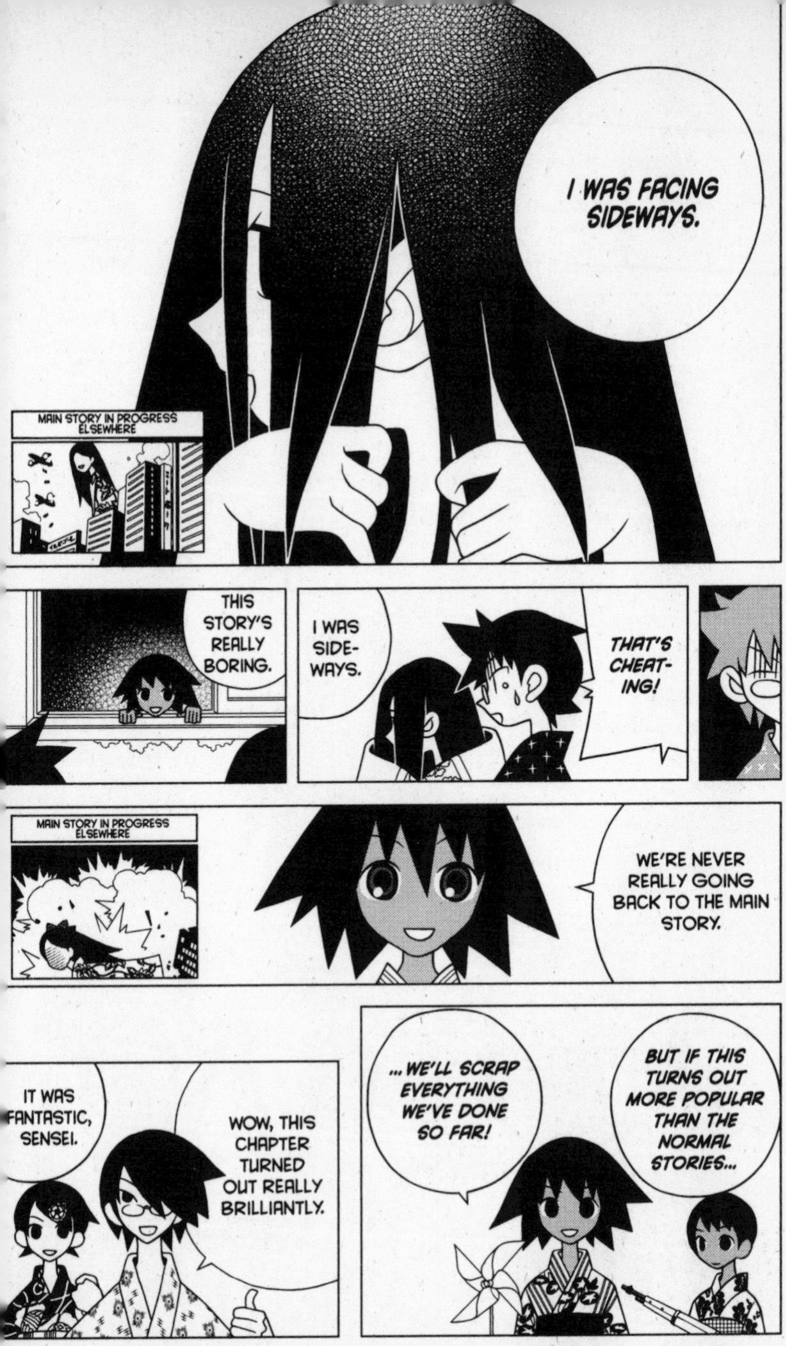
I WAS FACING SIDEWAYS.
MAIN STORY IN PROGRESS ELSEWHERE
THAT'S CHEATING!
I WAS SIDEWAYS.
THIS STORY'S REALLY BORING.
WE'RE NEVER REALLY GOING BACK TO THE MAIN STORY.
MAIN STORY IN PROGRESS ELSEWHERE
BUT IF THIS TURNS OUT MORE POPULAR THAN THE NORMAL STORIES...
...WE'LL SCRAP EVERYTHING WE'VE DONE SO FAR!
WOW, THIS CHAPTER TURNED OUT REALLY BRILLIANTLY.
IT WAS FANTASTIC, SENSEI.

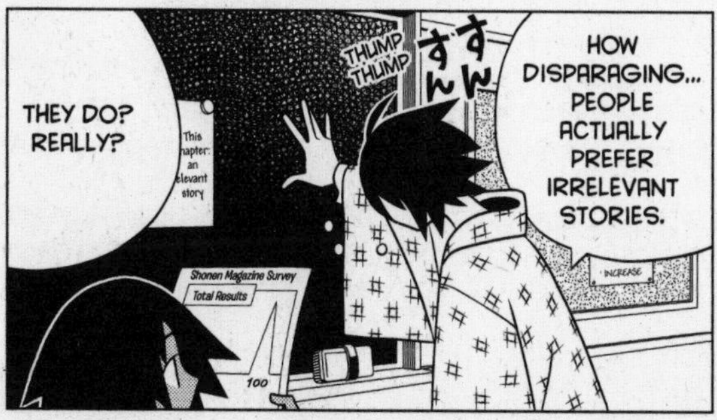
HOW DISPARAGING... PEOPLE ACTUALLY PREFER IRRELEVANT STORIES.
INCREASE
すん ずん
THUMP THUMP
This hapter: an elevant story
THEY DO? REALLY?
Shonen Magazine Survey
Total Results
100

CURRENT CHARGES FROM THIS ISSUE

LETTER OF ACCUSATION

PLAINTIFF:
OCCUPATION: STUDENT
NAMES: KAERE KIMURA

DEFENDANT: NOZOMU ITOSHIKI
OCCUPATION: HIGH SCHOOL TEACHER
NAME: NOZOMU ITOSHIKI

DATE: MAY 30
ATTN: SCHOOL BOARD

- PURPOSE OF ACCUSATION

THESE CHARGES ARE REGISTERED TO REQUEST THAT HARSH PUNISHMENT BE DEALT TO THE
DEFENDANT FOR HIS ACTIONS BELOW.

- FACTS OF THE ACCUSATION

THE DEFENDANT LED THE STUDENTS OF HIS CLASS, AROUND THE END OF MAY, TO A LOCATION
OUTSIDE OF SCHOOL FOR A LESSON. AS HE BECAME QUITE IMPASSIONED DURING THE DELIV-
ERY OF THIS LESSON, IT WENT OVER THE ALLOTTED TIME, AND THE STUDENTS WERE LED TO A
DESTINATION FURTHER AWAY THAN THEY HAD ORIGINALLY PLANNED FOR.
    AFTER THIS, THE DEFENDANT LOST HIS WAY BACK TO THE SCHOOL, AND WANDERED AROUND
DAISAN SENTAKU CITY FOR SEVERAL HOURS WITH HIS STUDENTS, LEAVING THE ENTIRE CLASS
WORN OUT AND IN A STATE OF DISTRESS.
    AS A RESULT, WHILE SEVERAL STUDENTS SUFFERED DAMAGES TO THEIR EMOTIONAL AND
PHYSICAL HEALTH DUE TO ANXIETY, THE DEFENDANT FAILED TO CONTACT THESE STUDENTS'
GUARDIANS AND REFUSED TO ADMIT RESPONSIBILITY FOR HAVING LED THEM INTO ANOTHER
PREFECTURE, AND SIMPLY RESPONDED TO PROTESTS FROM THE STUDENTS WITH VERBAL ME-
ANDERINGS.
    THIS INCIDENT HAS LED ME TO FEEL UNCERTAINTY AS TO THE DEFENDANT'S LEADERSHIP ABILI-
TIES AS AN EDUCATOR, AND I MUST FORMALLY REGISTER THIS COMPLAINT IN REGARDS TO HIS
PERSISTENT ATTITUDE OF AVOIDING RESPONSIBILITY, WHICH IS A FAR CRY FROM THE LOFTY
IDEAL OF AN EDUCATOR.
    IT IS WITH HOPES THAT THE SCHOOL BOARD WILL NOW CONDUCT A THOROUGH INVESTIGA-
TION OF THE DEFENDANT NOZOMU ITOSHIKI'S QUALIFICATIONS AS AN EDUCATOR, AND CLARIFY
ITS POSITION ON BOTH HIS ABILITIES AND PERSONALITY, THAT I HEREBY SUBMIT THIS COM-
PLAINT.

MEANS OF AUTHENTICATION
STANDBY OBSERVER CLASS 2-F

PAPER BLOGS

17 YEARS IN THE EARTH

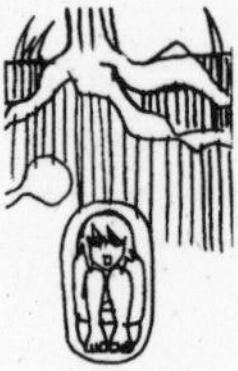

I CAN'T HELP BUT FEEL LIKE I'M LIVING LIKE A CICADA. CICADAS HAVE STINK BUG EYES. I HAVE GROUND BEETLE EYES.
CICADAS WERE IN THE GROUND FOR 17 YEARS AND I WAS THERE FOR SEVEN YEARS. I WAS IN CONSTANT REGRET ABOUT EVERY SERIES I WAS WORKING ON FOR DIFFERENT MAGAZINES. THE EARTH WAS MADE OF LAYERS OF REGRET UPON REGRET. I SPENT 17 YEARS THERE.
AFTER I CRAWLED OUT, THE SOIL WAS JUST AS POLLUTED. AFTER EMERGING, CICADAS LIVE FOR ONE WEEK AND THEN DIE... I'M LIKELY TO DIE ANY ONE OF THESE DAYS TOO.
THE SUMMER DAYS OF EXUBERANCE OVER THE ANIME ADAPTATION WILL SOON BE OVER. THE SUMMER DAYS WILL BE OVER, AND I'M SURE A LONG SUMMER VACATION WILL BEGIN.
IT'S ENOUGH ALREADY.
"HAVE I REACHED MY GOALS?"
COACH: "WE'LL TALK LATER."

ARTICLE URL | COMMENTS (0) | TRACKBACK (0)

DAILY WAGE 1,000 YEN

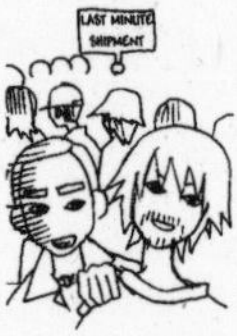
LAST MINUTE SHIPMENT

IT'S A PRACTICE RUN FOR MY LONG SUMMER VACATION. I FIND MYSELF SPACING OUT A LOT RECENTLY. THE OTHER DAY I WENT TO BIG CAMERA AND HUNG OUT IN THE VIDEO GAME AREA. SUDDENLY A STORE ATTENDANT YELLED, "WE GOT A LAST MINUTE SHIPMENT OF WIIS! IF YOU'D LIKE TO BUY ONE, LINE UP OVER HERE!" I WATCHED EVERYONE GET IN LINE.
SINCE I ACTUALLY BOUGHT A WII ON THE FIRST DAY IT CAME OUT (THIS IS THE ONLY ACCOMPLISHMENT I'M PROUD OF FROM LAST YEAR), I PUFFED MY CHEST WITH A SENSE OF SUPERIORITY AND CASUALLY WATCHED AS PEOPLE LINED UP. THEN, A CHINESE MAN CAME UP TO ME AND SAID IN BROKEN JAPANESE, "YOU'RE NOT GOING TO BUY A WII? IF YOU LINE UP AND BUY ONE FOR ME, I'LL BUY IT OFF YOU FOR AN EXTRA 1,000 YEN!"
...SO I CAME THIS CLOSE TO BEING HIRED OUT BY A CHINESE GUY FOR 1,000 YEN!
AHH... LOOKING CLOSELY, ALL THE PEOPLE IN LINE WERE ON THEIR LONG SUMMER VACATIONS. THAT'S WHY THE KIDS COULDN'T GET IN.

ARTICLE URL | COMMENTS (0) | TRACKBACK (0)

TSUNDEREI

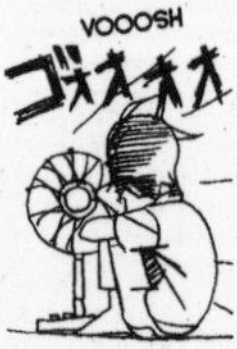
VOOOSH

I WAS SITTING STARING AT THE BLADES OF MY FAN WHEN I REMEMBERED SOMETHING. WHEN I WAS A KID WE HAD A FAN AT HOME CALLED "SUZUKAZE."
WHAT WOULD SUZUKAZE'S CHILD BE NAMED? THIS IS ALL I CAN THINK OF THESE DAYS. IT'S BECAUSE I HAVE THIS STRONG FEELING I'LL BE ASKED TO GIVE A NAME.
IF IT'S A GIRL... SUZUKA? ...SUZUKO? ...SUJIKA? HMM, I GUESS DEFINITELY NOT SUJIKA. SHE'D GET BULLIED.
BUT WAIT. EVEN IF I'M ASKED TO NAME THE CHILD, I HAVE TO THINK OF A NAME THAT SUZUKAZE WOULD HAVE PICKED. SINCE SUZUKAZE IS A GIRL WITH BIG DREAMS, SHE MIGHT ACTUALLY CHOOSE A CRINGE-WORTHY NAME.

SHE MIGHT FORCE SOME STRANGE READINGS FROM KANJI, LIKE READING "佳音" AS "CANNON" OR "摘日鈴" AS "TSUNDEREI," OR "紅蘭風" AS "CLAMP."
IF IT'S A BOY, PLEASE DON'T PLAY THE WHOLE WIND CONNECTION AND NAME HIM SOMETHING LIKE "疾風" (READ "HAYATE"). HE'LL GROW UP WITH NO MANNERS. I'M SURE OF IT. YES, I'M ABSOLUTELY SURE.
HALF A DAY WENT BY OF ME THINKING LIKE THIS. I'VE DECIDED TO TAKE THE NAME OF THE CHILD OF SUZUKAZE THAT I THOUGHT OF WITH ME TO THE GRAVE.

ARTICLE URL | COMMENTS (0) | TRACKBACK (0)

FOGGY VISION

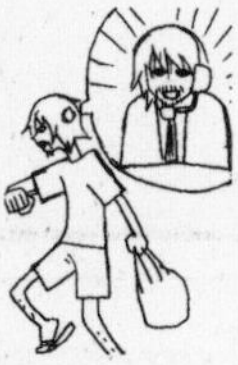

EVEN THOUGH I HAVEN'T ENTERED MY LONG SUMMER VACATION YET, I'M BEEN SPACING OUT WAY TOO MUCH.
I'M TALKING WITH PEOPLE AND CAN'T THINK OF THE WORDS FOR THINGS.
IT TOOK ME A HALF A DAY JUST TO REMEMBER MAEDA-KUN'S LAST NAME. IT'S SENILITY, I TELL YOU.
I'M WEARING OLD T-SHIRTS INSIDE OUT, DIFFERENT SHOES ON EACH FOOT, AND RIGHT WHEN I THOUGHT SOMETHING WAS WEIRD WITH MY VISION IT TURNED OUT ONE OF THE LENSES ON MY GLASSES HAD COME OUT.
I'VE COME OFF MY AXIS AS A HUMAN BEING.
I WAS ASKED AT A CONVENIENCE STORE, "DID A BOMB EXPLODE OR SOMETHING?"
APPARENTLY, AS A WAY OF AVOIDING COMING UP AT A LOSS FOR WORDS, TV ANNOUNCERS PRACTICE GIVING PLAY-BY-PLAYS OF THEIR EVERYDAY ACTIONS.
THAT'S IT!
I'VE DECIDED TO DO THE SAME THING TO STOP ME FROM SPACING OUT.
I'M BEGINNING MY PLAY-BY-PLAY.
KOJI KUMETA STANDS UP SLOWLY AND PUTS ON HIS SHOES. HE OPENS THE DOOR WITH HIS RIGHT HAND, AND LEAVES THE ROOM. KOJI KUMETA GOES INTO THE HALLWAY. HE TURNS TO THE RIGHT! HE GOES DOWN THE STAIRS! KOJI KUMETA GOES BACK TO HIS ROOM TO GET HIS WALLET. NOW HE HAS HIS WALLET. AND HE'S FORGOTTEN WHY HE LEFT IN THE FIRST PLACE. HE REMEMBERS THAT HE HAD WANTED TO GO TO THE CONVENIENCE STORE. HE ARRIVES AT THE STORE. HE FORGETS WHAT IT WAS HE WANTED TO BUY. FOR SOME REASON HE BUYS A SABLA. HE FORGETS TO BUY LUNCH.
UGH, I'M SICK OF THIS ALREADY. GOODBYE EVERYONE!
KOJI KUMETA GENTLY WAVES HIS RIGHT HAND AND DISAPPEARS INTO THE DARKNESS.
HE DISAPPEARS INTO THE DEEP, DEEP DARKNESS!
GOODBYE KOJI KUMETA! GOODBYE!

ARTICLE URL | COMMENTS (0) | TRACKBACK (0)

TO MYSELF AT 15

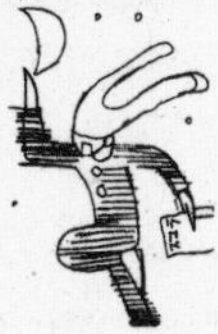

IN THE WORDS OF A CERTAIN WILDLY-SELLING JUMP ARTIST, "I'M ALWAYS MAKING MANGA WITH MYSELF AT 15 AS THE TARGET AUDIENCE."
IF I TRIED TO DRAW FOR MYSELF AT 15, WE'D BE IN BIG TROUBLE. ALL I THOUGHT ABOUT DAY AND NIGHT WHEN I WAS 15 WERE WOMEN'S BODIES. RUNNING AWAY WITH TIGHTS THAT I STOLE! RUNNING AWAY (EVEN THOUGH I DIDN'T STEAL THEM). THAT WAS HOW I SPENT MY NIGHTS WHEN I WAS 15.
IT WOULD BY NECESSITY BECOME A HUGE ADVENTURE EPIC ABOUT WOMEN'S BODIES.
"I'LL BE THE KING OF THE RED LIGHT DISTRICT!"
I WOULD GET A GOMUGOMU FRUIT FROM A GOMUGOMU VENDING MACHINE, THEN GET SCANDALOUS PHOTOS OF WOMEN'S BODIES MOSTLY FROM SWEDEN, THEN ENTER INTO THE "ABSOLUTE TERRITORY" KNOWN AS THE GRAND LINE (BETWEEN THE KNEE-HIGH SOCKS AND THE SKIRT), AND THEN GET THE HIDDEN JEWEL. I WOULD GET THE HIDDEN JEWEL!!
SO THE PARADOX WOULD BE THAT IF I DREW FOR MYSELF AT 15, IT WOULD END UP BEING AN OVER-18-ONLY SERIES. I'VE COME TO A POINT IN MY LIFE WHERE IT'S EVEN HARD FOR ME TO USE ADULT THEMES ANY MORE. BUT I'LL SHRUG OFF MY FAILURES, SO IF MS. KIKUKO WILL BE AN ETERNAL 17-YEAR-OLD, I'LL BE FOREVER OVER-18-ONLY! ♡

...SORRY BABY, I DON'T THINK I CAN DO IT.

ARTICLE URL | COMMENTS (0) | TRACKBACK (0)

ANIME UNIVERSITY. NIGHT CLASSES.

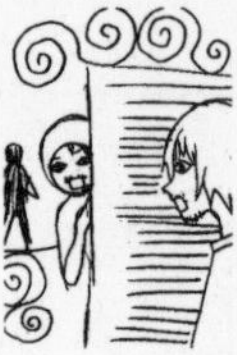

AFTER MY SERIES GOT ANIMATED, SOME PEOPLE HAVE SAID THAT I'VE BEEN "ACTING REALLY HAPPY." IN FACT, I HAVE. I KNOW, IT'S LUDICROUS, RIGHT? IT MIGHT BE LUDICROUS FROM THE PERSPECTIVE OF A MANGA ARTIST WHOSE FIRST SERIALIZED WORK GOT ANIMATED AND AIRED IN THE MAIN NETWORKS. FOR ME, IT'S LIKE FINALLY GETTING ACCEPTING INTO AN ANIME UNIVERSITY AFTER 17 YEARS OF RETAKING THE TEST.

AND STILL, I'M HAPPY. I'D BE HAPPY EVEN IF IT WAS A LOCAL ANIME UNIVERSITY AND I WAS GOING TO NIGHT CLASSES. HOWEVER, THIS HAS GIVEN RISE TO A MORE DANGEROUS SCENARIO. MY DEPRESSION HAS BECOME MANIC DEPRESSION. MY MOOD SWINGS HAVE GOTTEN LARGER. THEY'RE FLYING ALL OVER THE PLACE! THE LENGTH OF THE PENDULUM SWINGING BETWEEN DEPRESSION AND MANIA HAS BECOME LARGER, AND I CAN'T CONTROL MYSELF.

BACK IN THE DAY I WOULD HAVE JUST CONTEMPLATED SUICIDE, BUT NOW I SOMETIMES FEEL LIKE FLYING!

PEOPLE SAY THAT NOTHING CAN BE DONE ONCE YOU'VE SERVED OUT HEAVEN'S WILL. THEY SAY YOU CAN'T DO ANYTHING ABOUT DESTINY. IN THAT CASE, SUICIDE IS THE LIFETIME OF THE SOUL. I'VE SERVED OUT THE WILL OF MY SOUL. IT'S MY NATURAL LIFE. THE SOUL HAS IT'S OWN NATURAL LIFE.

PUT ANOTHER WAY, PEOPLE CAN'T LIVE WITHOUT ACTIVELY TRYING TO. IT TAKES EFFORT TO EAT FOOD AND DRINK WATER, AND THAT'S HOW WE LIVE. SLACKING OFF ON THESE EFFORTS LEADS US TO DIE.

I CAN SEE MY GAPPELDONGER (IT'S ME FROM MY DOPPELGANGER'S PERSPECTIVE). WHICH WILL BE STRONGER, THE GAPPELDONGER OR THE DOPPELGANGER?

WHICH CAME FROM THE FUTURE, THE GAPPELDONGER OR THE DOPPELGANGER? IS THE GAPPELDONGER "ACTING HAPPY?" WHAT ABOUT THE DOPPELGANGER?

MY BAGGELDONGER HAS APPEARED.

MY BAGGELDONGER SAID TO ME, "BOTH OF YOU ARE ACTING HAPPY."

"SO ARE YOU."

ARTICLE URL | COMMENTS (0) | TRACKBACK (0)

PORORO-PAIN

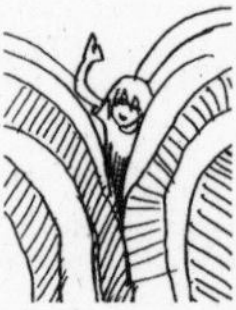

THERE ARE TOO MANY THINGS THAT DISAPPOINT ME WHEN I'M THIS HAPPY. WHEN PEOPLE SEND ME ANIMAGE MAGAZINE WITHOUT ANY REFERENCE TO ZETSUBOU-SENSEI, WHEN THERE'S A LONG INTERVIEW WITH GORO MIYAZAKI IN THAT ISSUE, WHEN PEOPLE WHO'VE POROROCA'ED FROM THE ANIME TELL ME THE "ORIGINAL MANGA IS BORING," OR WHEN PEOPLE WHO'VE POROROCA'ED FROM THE VOICE ACTORS TELL ME THAT "THE CHARACTER YOU DREW DOESN'T SOUND RIGHT VOICED BY ___," OR WHEN THAT VOICE ACTOR TELLS ME THAT "KAIZO WAS ACTUALLY FUNNIER."

WHEN LIFE THROWS YOU UP AND THEN PUSHES YOU DOWN, IT'S EASY TO BECOME MANIC-DEPRESSIVE. MY BEKKELDONGER APPEARS. HE PUSHES MY HAND. HE PUSHES THE HAND THAT DRAWS THIS MANGA.

I CAN'T DRAW STRAIGHT LINES. WHEN I DRAW STRAIGHT LINES, THE BEKKELDONGER APPEARS AND MESSES IT UP.

I FEEL LIKE I'M LIVING LIKE A CICADA. IT'S ALMOST THE END OF MY SOUL'S NATURAL LIFE. I'LL BE HIRED BY THE CHINESE FOR 1,000 YEN. I'LL TAKE SUZUKAZE'S DAUGHTER'S NAME WITH ME TO THE GRAVE. I CAN SEE MY GAPPELDONGER.

EARTH WHICH HAS BEEN COMPACTED BY REGRET UPON REGRET EVENTUALLY BECOMES AN ACTIVE FAULT ZONE, AND SUCKS ME UP IN ONE PIECE. GOODBYE, KOJI KUMETA! GOODBYE!

ARTICLE URL | COMMENTS (0) | TRACKBACK (0)

Since we were completely ignored by anime magazines, I made my own!

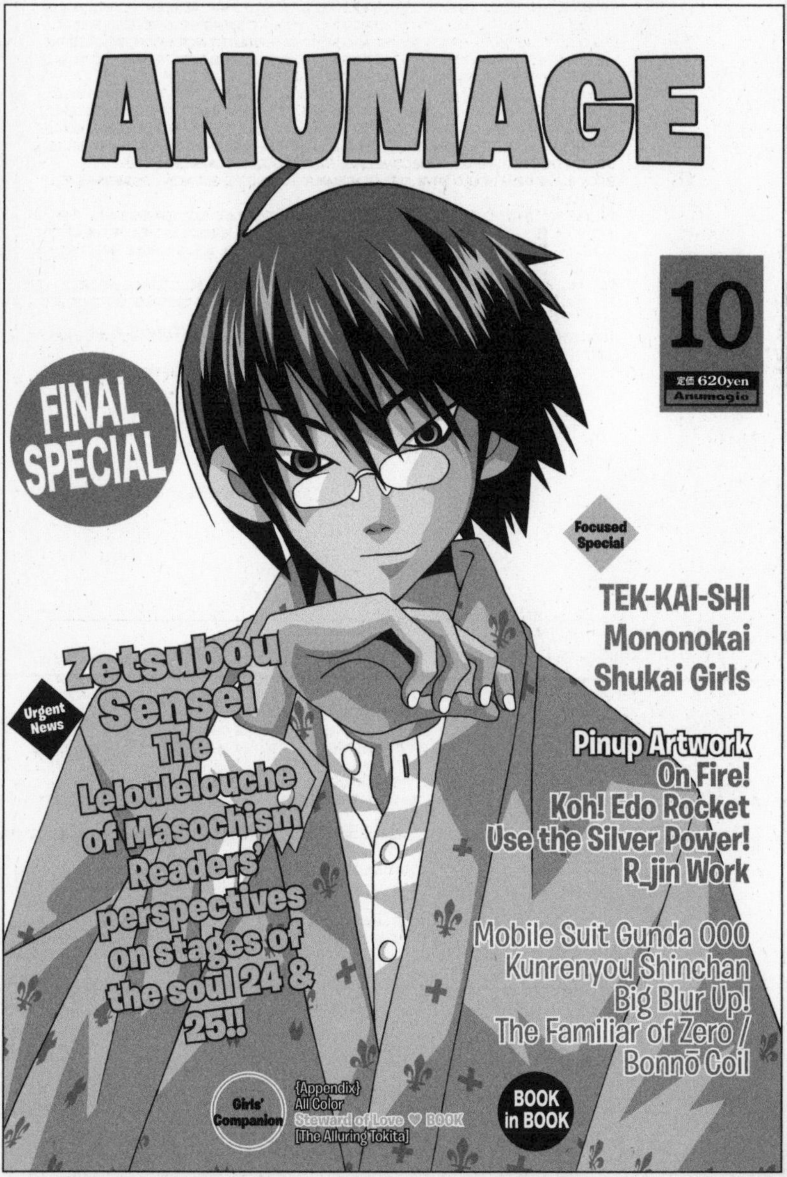
ANUMAGE
10
定価 620yen
Anumagio
FINAL SPECIAL
Focused Special
TEK-KAI-SHI
Mononokai
Shukai Girls
Urgent News
Zetsubou Sensei
The Leloulelouche of Masochism
Readers' perspectives on stages of the soul 24 & 25!!
Pinup Artwork
On Fire!
Koh! Edo Rocket
Use the Silver Power!
R_jin Work
Mobile Suit Gunda 000
Kunrenyou Shinchan
Big Blur Up!
The Familiar of Zero / Bonnō Coil
Girls' Companion
{Appendix}
All Color
Steward of Love ♥ BOOK
[The Alluring Tokita]
BOOK in BOOK

Kitchiri, Kafka, and Meru are three girls who are looking forward to their bright and dazzling new semester at school.

When "Masked Teacher Zetsubou" wall appears out of nowhere, they press their heads against him and ask him, "isn't there a medicine that works for despair?" In order to defeat the Masked Teacher who acts like he owns the place, the girls obtain the power to transform into the legendary earphone knights "Lillicure" ...all with generous doses of sophistry.

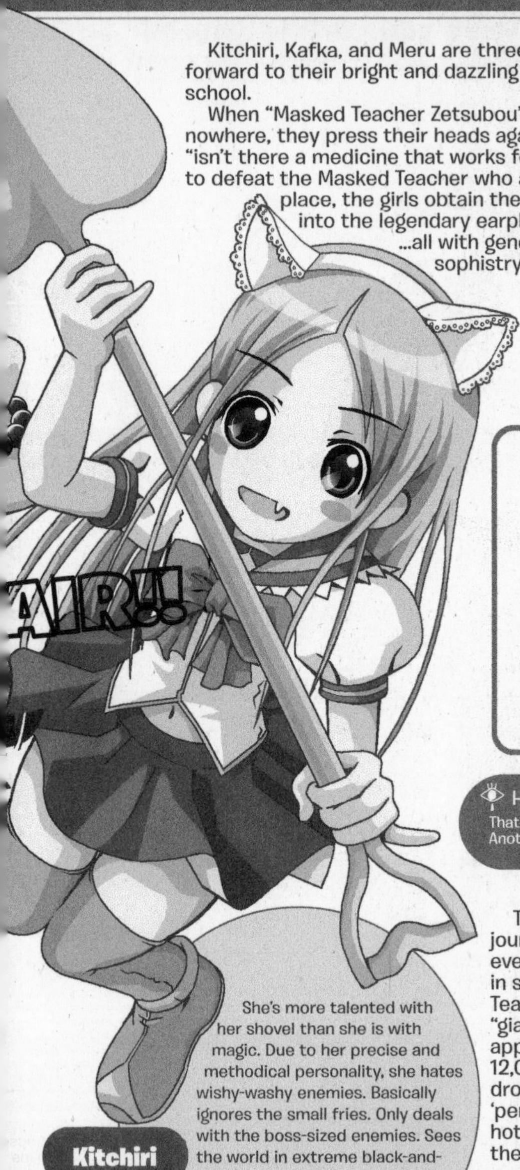
AIR!!

ZETSUBOU SENSEI

Late Nights on Depression Day Every Week
Chiba Inside-my-brain TV
TV God
TV Soul
Planet MX TV
Zun TV

HIGHLIGHT

That penguin actually becomes a man. Another one appears later, too.

The girls leave on a journey prowling around every corner of the town in search of the Masked Teacher's weakness, the "giant candy drop that appears if you collect 12,000 Jintan candy drops that the mysterious 'penguin who becomes a hot guy' dropped all over the place."

Kitchiri

She's more talented with her shovel than she is with magic. Due to her precise and methodical personality, she hates wishy-washy enemies. Basically ignores the small fries. Only deals with the boss-sized enemies. Sees the world in extreme black-and-white.

Things she hates: Late-evening sunshine

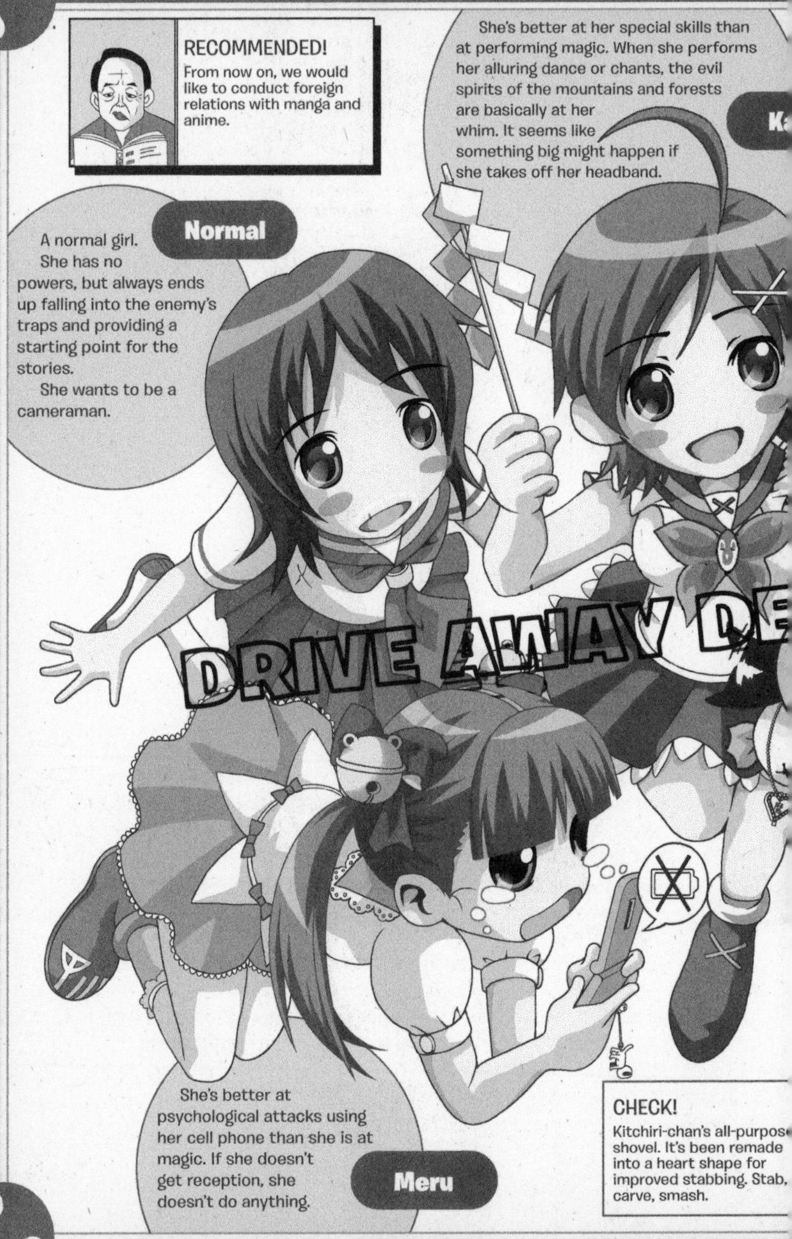
RECOMMENDED!
From now on, we would like to conduct foreign relations with manga and anime.
Ka
She's better at her special skills than at performing magic. When she performs her alluring dance or chants, the evil spirits of the mountains and forests are basically at her whim. It seems like something big might happen if she takes off her headband.
Normal
A normal girl.
She has no powers, but always ends up falling into the enemy's traps and providing a starting point for the stories.
She wants to be a cameraman.
DRIVE AWAY DE
Meru
She's better at psychological attacks using her cell phone than she is at magic. If she doesn't get reception, she doesn't do anything.
CHECK!
Kitchiri-chan's all-purpos shovel. It's been remade into a heart shape for improved stabbing. Stab, carve, smash.

ZETSUBOU LITERARY COMPILATION
CRIME AND REJECTION

People chosen at the top of lotteries have the right to disregard
morals, ethics, and publication codes. Even evil can be forgiven
to increase sales. People like this continue to rule the publishing
world. Manga artists outside of this world continue to create
their mediocre works, just barely managing to keep serialized.
How much longer will I have to be the latter? Knowing that it's
an unrealistic plan, I acknowledge my sin and brought my pen
to the paper. However, even the moe-e that I thought was very
well drawn met with rejection. The words of readers in front of
the Akihabara train station rung in my head. "Kiss the earth. And
scream to the people of the world... I've catered to you!" The
thing stuck in my heart became softer, and the tears poured out.

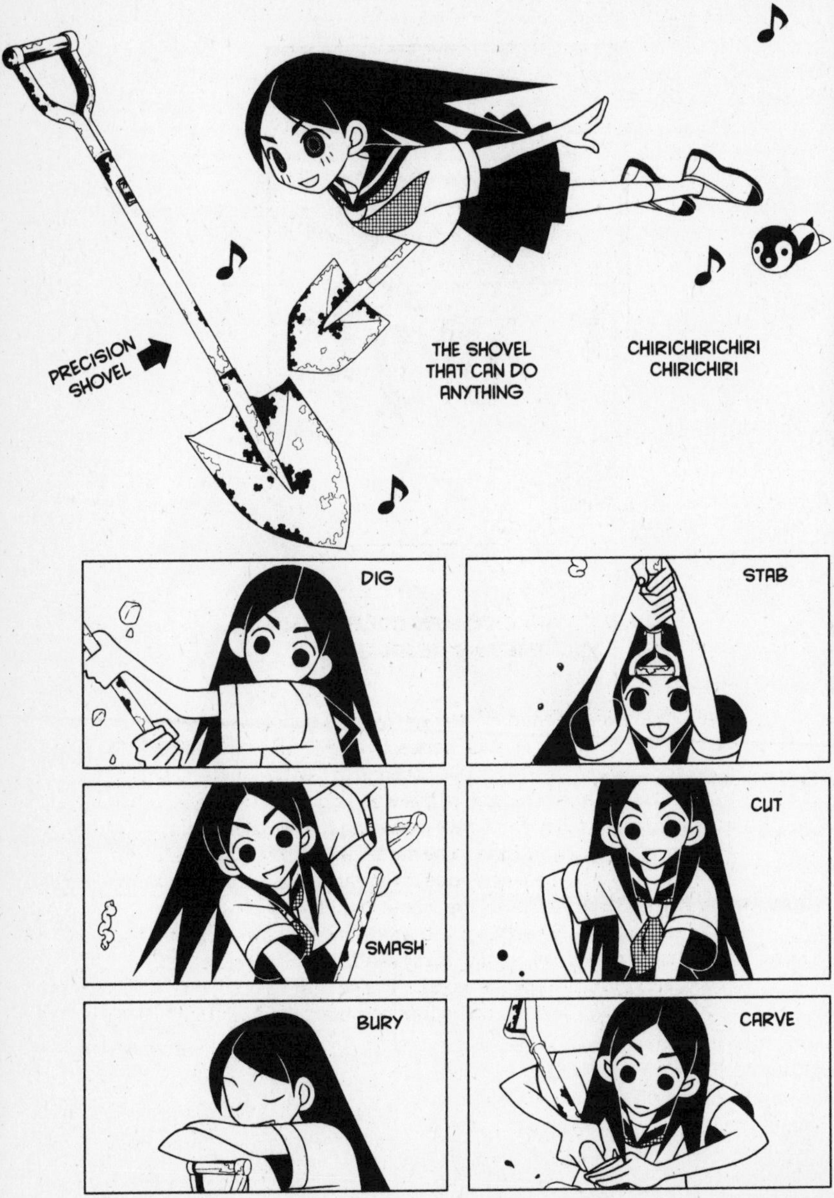
CHIRICHIRICHIRI CHIRICHIRI
THE SHOVEL THAT CAN DO ANYTHING
PRECISION SHOVEL
STAB
DIG
CUT
SMASH
CARVE
BURY

Translation Notes

Japanese is a tricky language for most Westerners, and translation is often more art than science. In the case of a text-dense manga like *Sayonara, Zetsubou-sensei*, it's a delicate art indeed. Although most of the jokes are universal, Koji Kumeta is famous for filling his manga with references to Japanese politics, entertainment, otaku culture, religion and sports. Unless you're a true Japanophile, it's difficult to understand it all without some serious background knowledge of current events at the time when the manga was running. Kumeta also uses references to foreign literature and politics, so even Japanese readers probably don't get all the humor. For your reading pleasure, here are notes on some of the more obscure references and difficult-to-translate jokes in *Sayonara, Zetsubou-Sensei*.

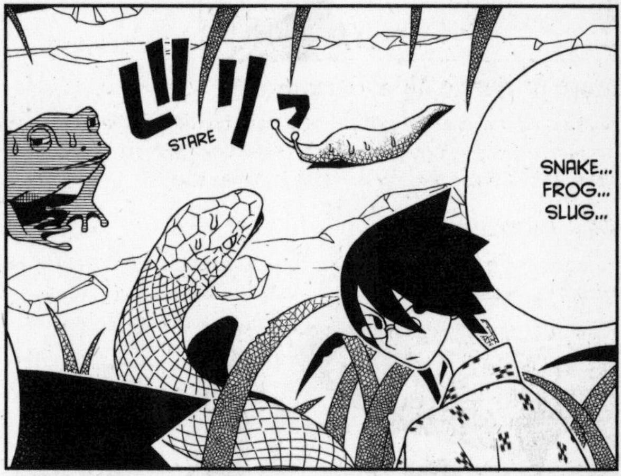
SNAKE...
FROG...
SLUG...
STARE

Kitsune-ken, page 8

Literally "fox-fist," kitsune-ken is a traditional game similar to rock-paper-scissors, but the three hand positions signify a fox, a hunter, and a village headman. The headman beats the hunter, whom he outranks; the hunter beats the fox, whom he shoots; the fox beats the headman, whom he bewitches.

Hikikomori, big-sister-for-rent, page 12

Literally "pulling away, being confined," hikikomori is a Japanese term to refer to people, often young adults, who have chosen to withdraw from social life and isolate themselves completely from society. As an initiative to help people suffering in this way, various private and public initiatives have started "sibling for rent" services where young people visit hikikomori and talk with them.

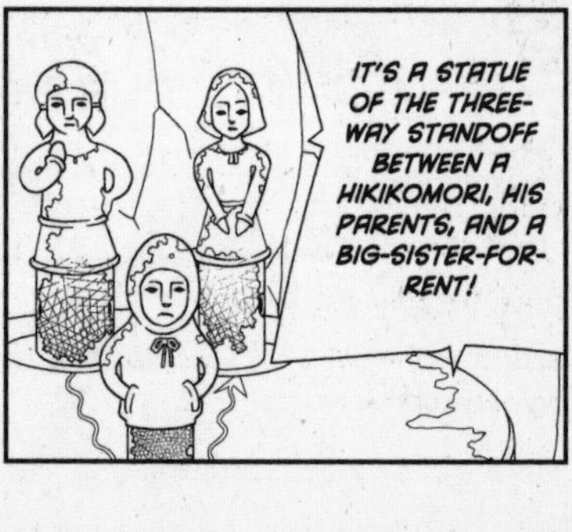
IT'S A STATUE OF THE THREE-WAY STANDOFF BETWEEN A HIKIKOMORI, HIS PARENTS, AND A BIG-SISTER-FOR-RENT!

Enka, page 26

Enka is a popular Japanese music genre considered to resemble traditional Japanese music stylistically. Modern enka, however, arose in the Postwar period and commonly contains expressions of modern Japanese nonmaterial nationalism.

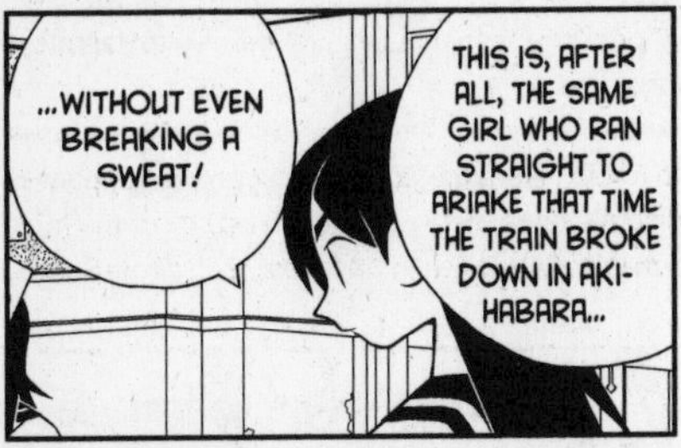
THIS IS, AFTER ALL, THE SAME GIRL WHO RAN STRAIGHT TO ARIAKE THAT TIME THE TRAIN BROKE DOWN IN AKI-HABARA...
...WITHOUT EVEN BREAKING A SWEAT!

From Ariake to Akihabara, page 27

Ariake is an area near Tokyo Bay where many conventions, including manga and anime conventions, are held. Akihabara is considered the "Otaku City" of Tokyo, and is also a hub for electronics shops. These two locations are approximately 5.3 miles apart.

New semester, page 51

In case you were wondering, the school year and fiscal year in Japan begin in April, hence all the references to new beginnings.

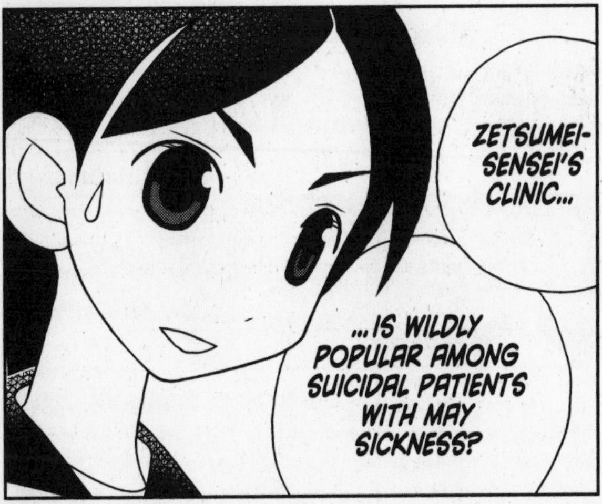
ZETSUMEI-SENSEI'S CLINIC...
...IS WILDLY POPULAR AMONG SUICIDAL PATIENTS WITH MAY SICKNESS?

May Sickness, page 65

Since the school year and fiscal year begin on April 1 in Japan, "May sickness" refers to people growing weary of their new routines.

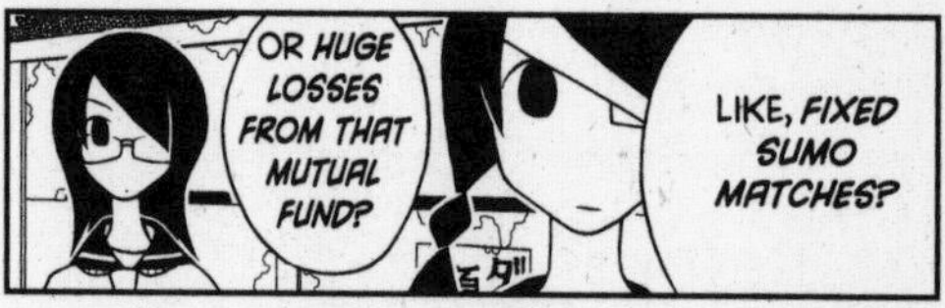
LIKE, FIXED SUMO MATCHES?
OR HUGE LOSSES FROM THAT MUTUAL FUND?

Fixed Sumo Matches, page 69

Scandal in the sumo world is of particular sensitivity to the Japanese because of the high status of sumo as a cultural heritage and national sport. Since 2007, when this manga was originally printed, to the present day several instances of fixed matches coming to light have rocked the sumo world.

Cliff-edge sensei, page 71

n November, 2006, the female dog Rinrin was discovered stuck on a cliff in Tokushima prefecture and made national news. Many people saw her story on TV and offered to adopt her.

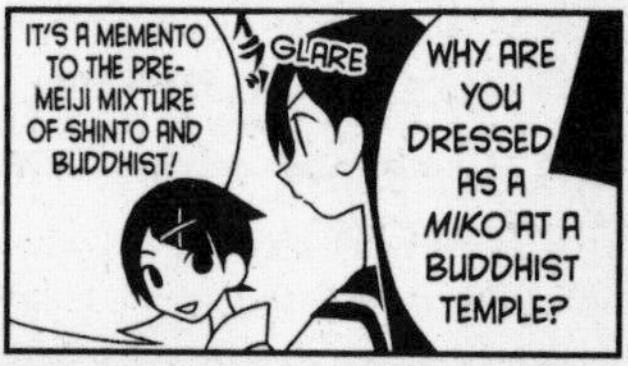
WHY ARE YOU DRESSED AS A MIKO AT A BUDDHIST TEMPLE?
GLARE
IT'S A MEMENTO TO THE PRE-MEIJI MIXTURE OF SHINTO AND BUDDHIST!

Miko at a Buddhist temple, kami page 114

Historically, miko meant a "female shaman, spirit medium" who conveyed oracles from kami ("spirits; gods"), and presently means a "shrine maiden; virgin consecrated to a deity" who serves at Shinto shrines. Since miko and kami are both Shinto terms, Chiri is angered that they appear in a Buddhist shrine.

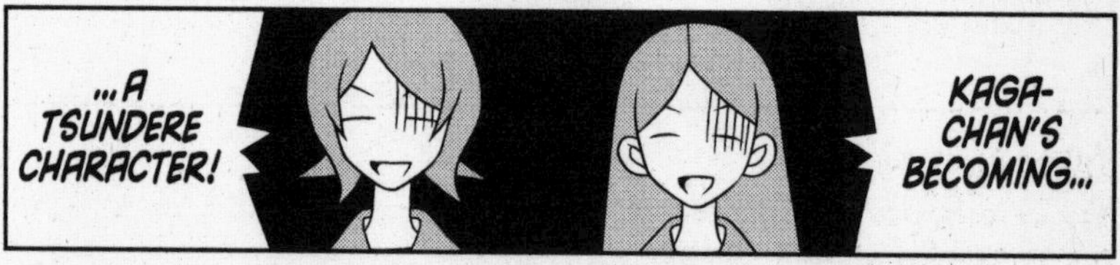
KAGA-CHAN'S BECOMING...
...A TSUNDERE CHARACTER!

Tsundere, tsunwabi, page 116

A Japanese character development process that describes a person who is initially cold and even stile towards another person before gradually showing their warm side over time. The word is derived from the terms tsun-tsun meaning to "turn away in disgust," and dere-dere, meaning "lovey dovey." Tsundere characters have a strong following among otaku.

Tsun-wabi" in this case is a pun combining tsundere and owabi, which means "apology" (so a person who is initially hostile, and then profusely apologetic).

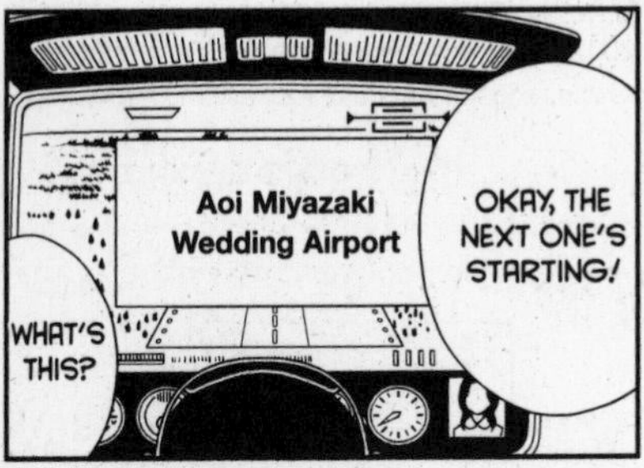
OKAY, THE NEXT ONE'S STARTING!
Aoi Miyazaki Wedding Airport
WHAT'S THIS?

Aoi Miyazaki, page 125

A Japanese actress best known for her pure image and roles such as in Nana and Virgin Snow. Because of this pure image, it caused great shock to her fans when she suddenly announced her marria
at the age of 22.

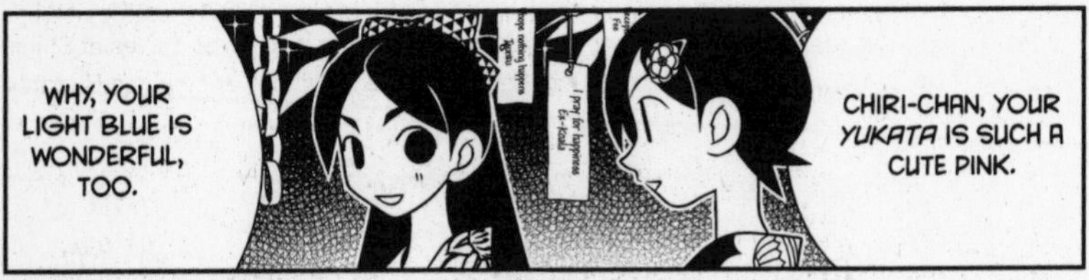
CHIRI-CHAN, YOUR *YUKATA* IS SUCH A CUTE PINK.
WHY, YOUR LIGHT BLUE IS WONDERFUL, TOO.

Yukata, page 133

A casual summer kimono usually made of cotton. People wearing yukata are a common sight in Japa
at fireworks displays, bon-odori festivals, and other summer events.

PREVIEW OF
SAYONARA, ZETSUBOU-SENSEI

The Power of Negative Thinking **11**

We're pleased to present you a preview from
Sayonara, Zetsubou-Sensei, volume 11. Please check
our website (www.kodanshacomics.com) to see when
this volume will be available in English. For now you'll
have to make do with Japanese!

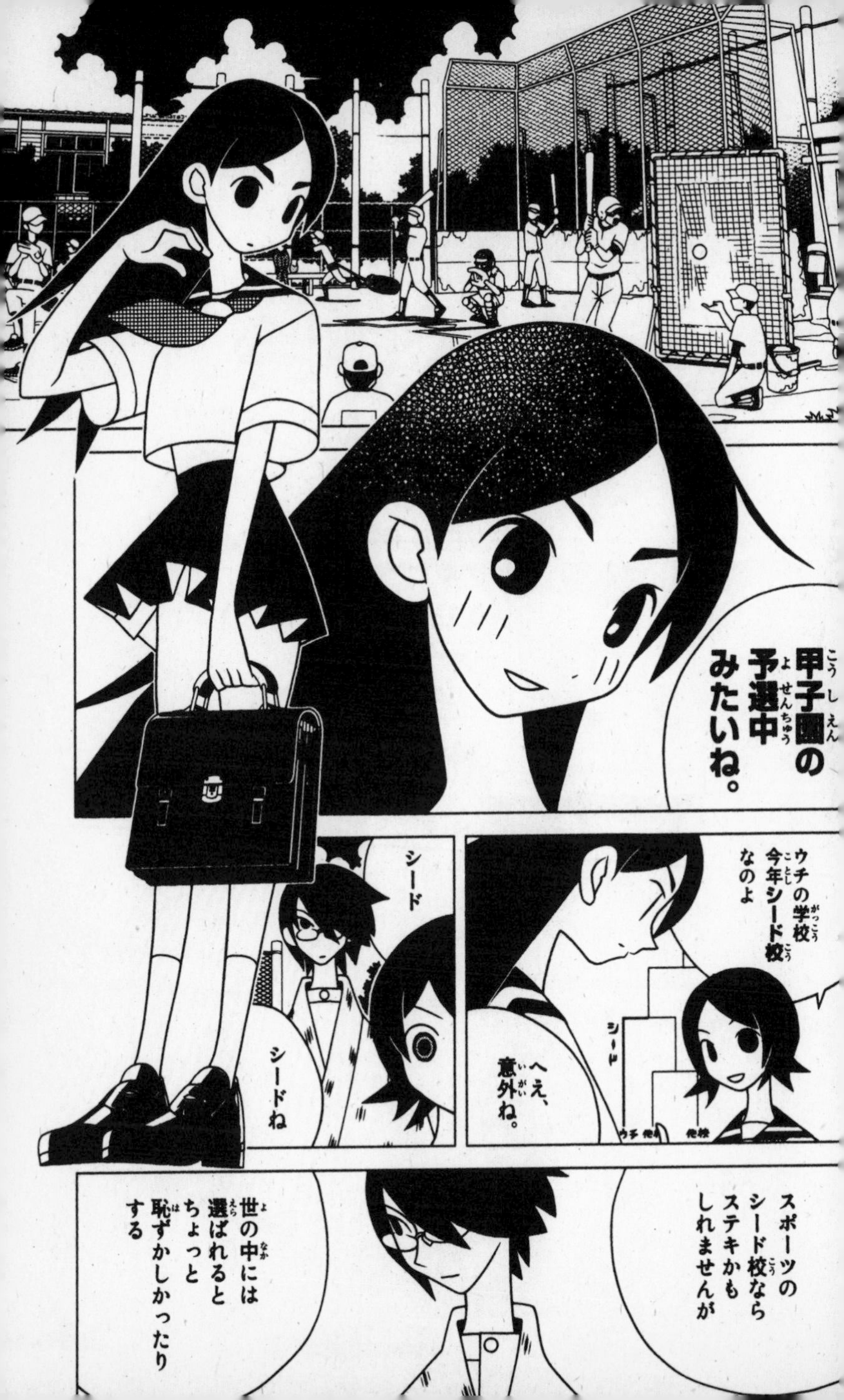
甲子園の予選中みたいね。
ウチの学校今年シード校なのよ
シード
へえ、意外ね。
ウチ
他校
シード
シードね
スポーツのシード校ならステキかもしれませんが
世の中には選ばれるとちょっと恥ずかしかったりする

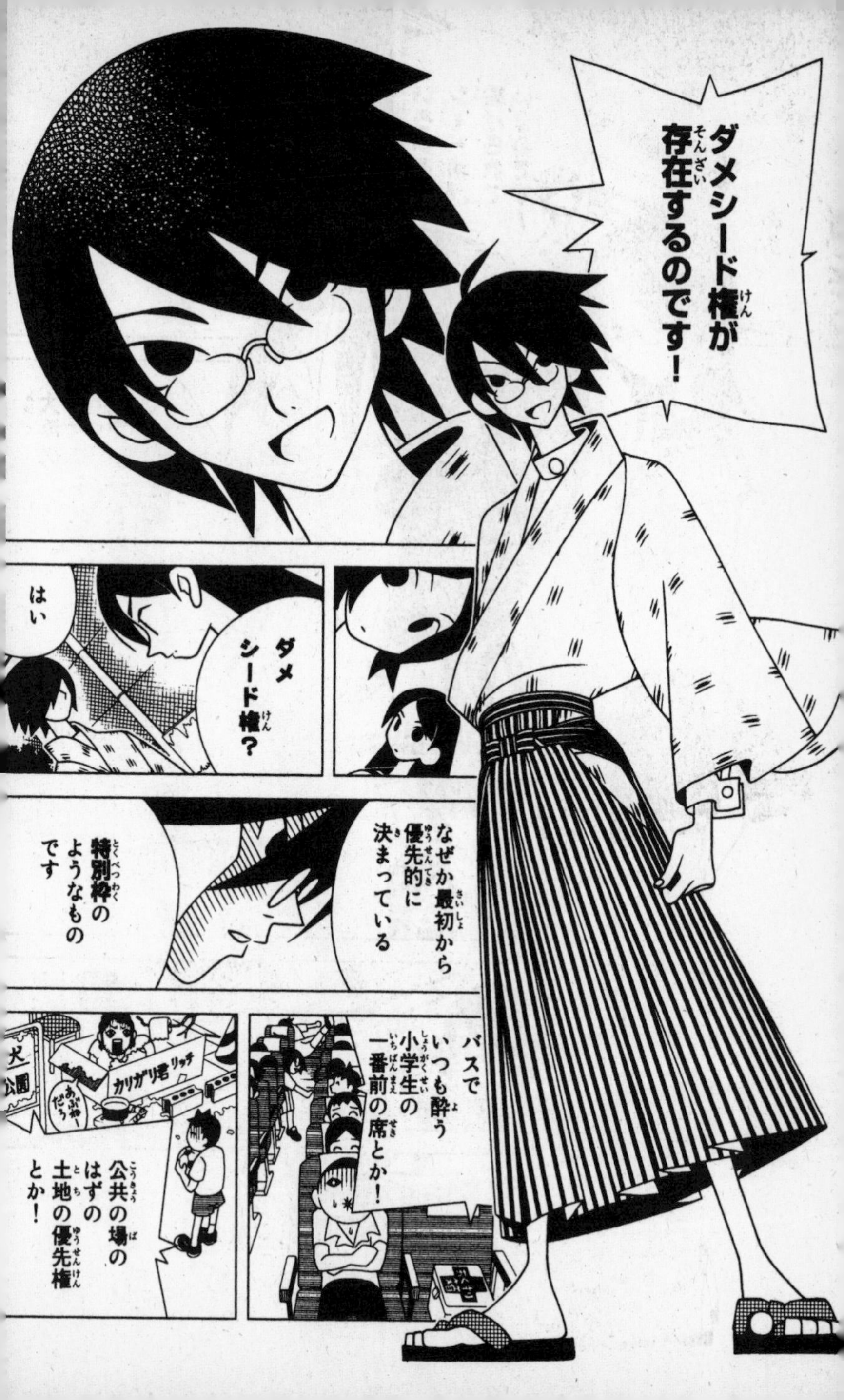
ダメシード権が存在するのです！
ダメシード権？
はい
なぜか最初から優先的に決まっている
特別枠のようなものです
バスでいつも酔う小学生の一番前の席とか！
カリガリ君 リッチ
公園
公共の場のはずの土地の優先権とか！

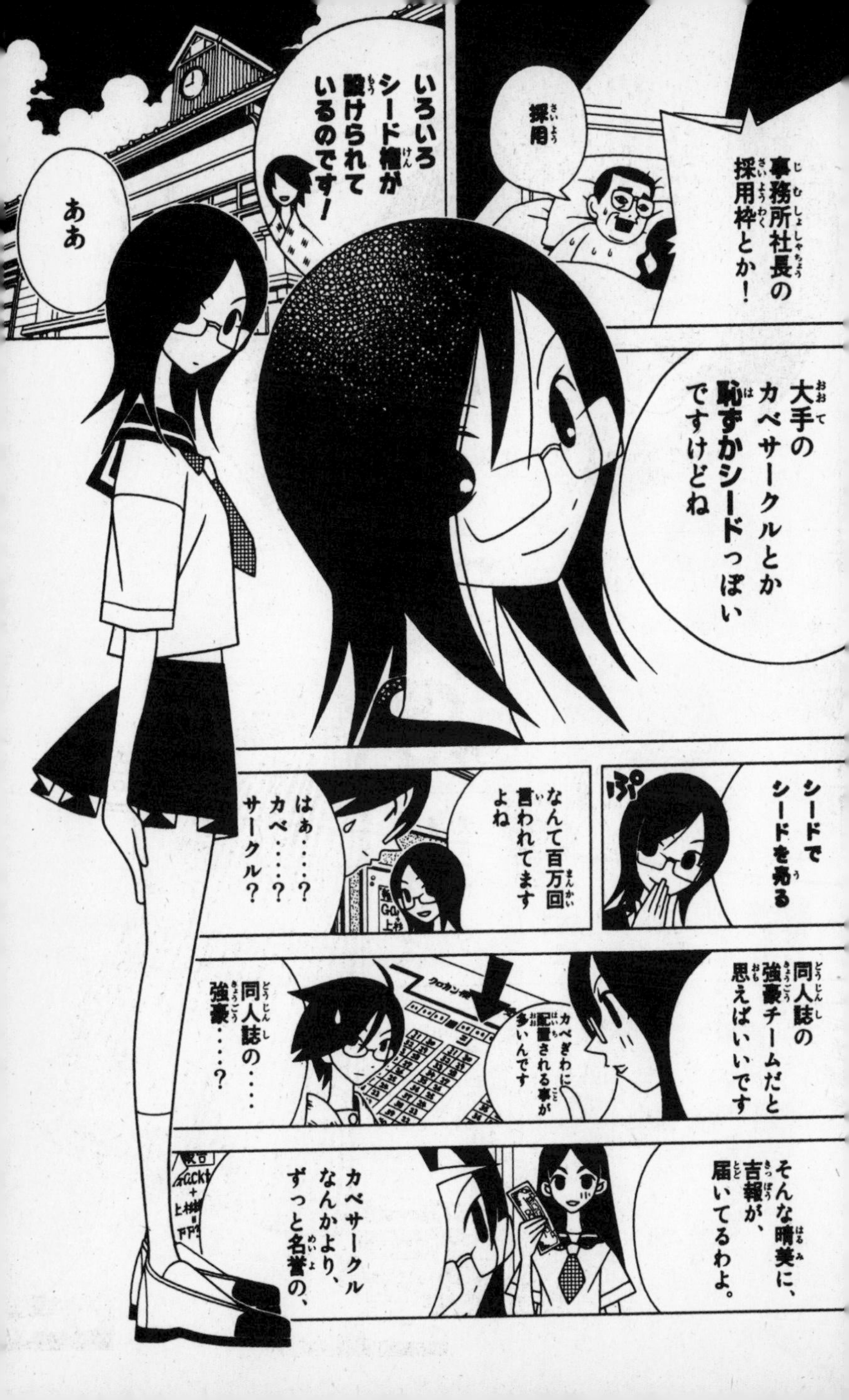
事務所社長の採用枠とか！
採用
いろいろシード権が設けられているのです！
ああ
大手のカベサークルとか恥ずかシードっぽいですけどね
シードでシードを売る
ぷ
なんて百万回言われてますよね
はぁ……？カベ……？サークル？
同人誌の強豪チームだと思えばいいです
カベぎわに配置される事が多いんです
同人誌の……強豪……？
そんな晴美に、吉報が、届いてるわよ。
カベサークルなんかより、ずっと名誉の、

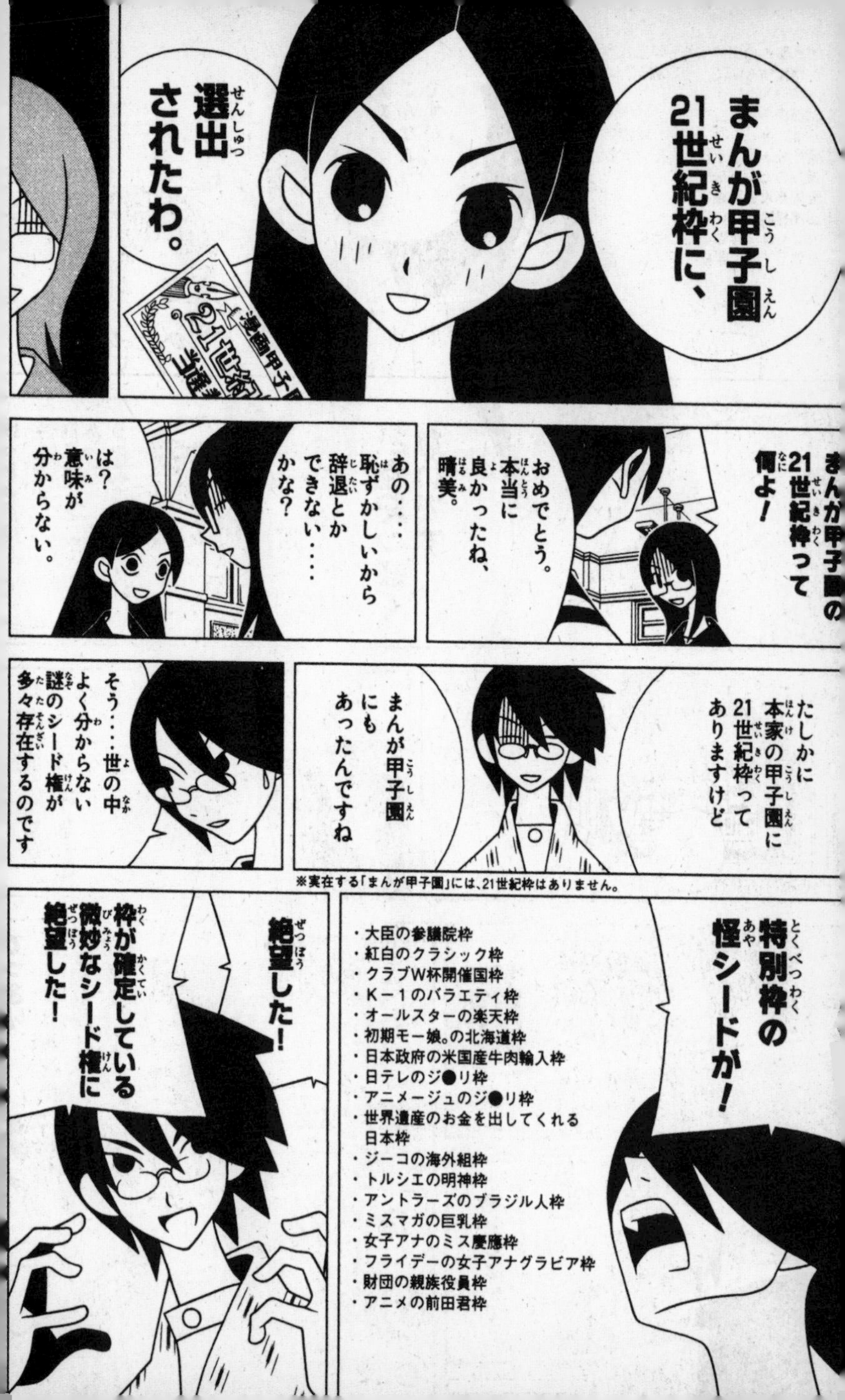

まんが甲子園21世紀枠に、
選出されたわ。
漫画甲子園 21世紀枠 当選
まんが甲子園の21世紀枠って何よ!
おめでとう。本当に良かったね、晴美。
あの……恥ずかしいから辞退とかできない……かな?
は?意味が分からない。
たしかに本家の甲子園に21世紀枠ってありますけど
まんが甲子園にもあったんですね
そう……世の中よく分からない謎のシード権が多々存在するのです
※実在する「まんが甲子園」には、21世紀枠はありません。
特別枠の怪シードが!
・大臣の参議院枠
・紅白のクラシック枠
・クラブW杯開催国枠
・K－1のバラエティ枠
・オールスターの楽天枠
・初期モー娘。の北海道枠
・日本政府の米国産牛肉輸入枠
・日テレのジ●リ枠
・アニメージュのジ●リ枠
・世界遺産のお金を出してくれる日本枠
・ジーコの海外組枠
・トルシエの明神枠
・アントラーズのブラジル人枠
・ミスマガの巨乳枠
・女子アナのミス慶應枠
・フライデーの女子アナグラビア枠
・財団の親族役員枠
・アニメの前田君枠
絶望した!
枠が確定している微妙なシード権に絶望した!

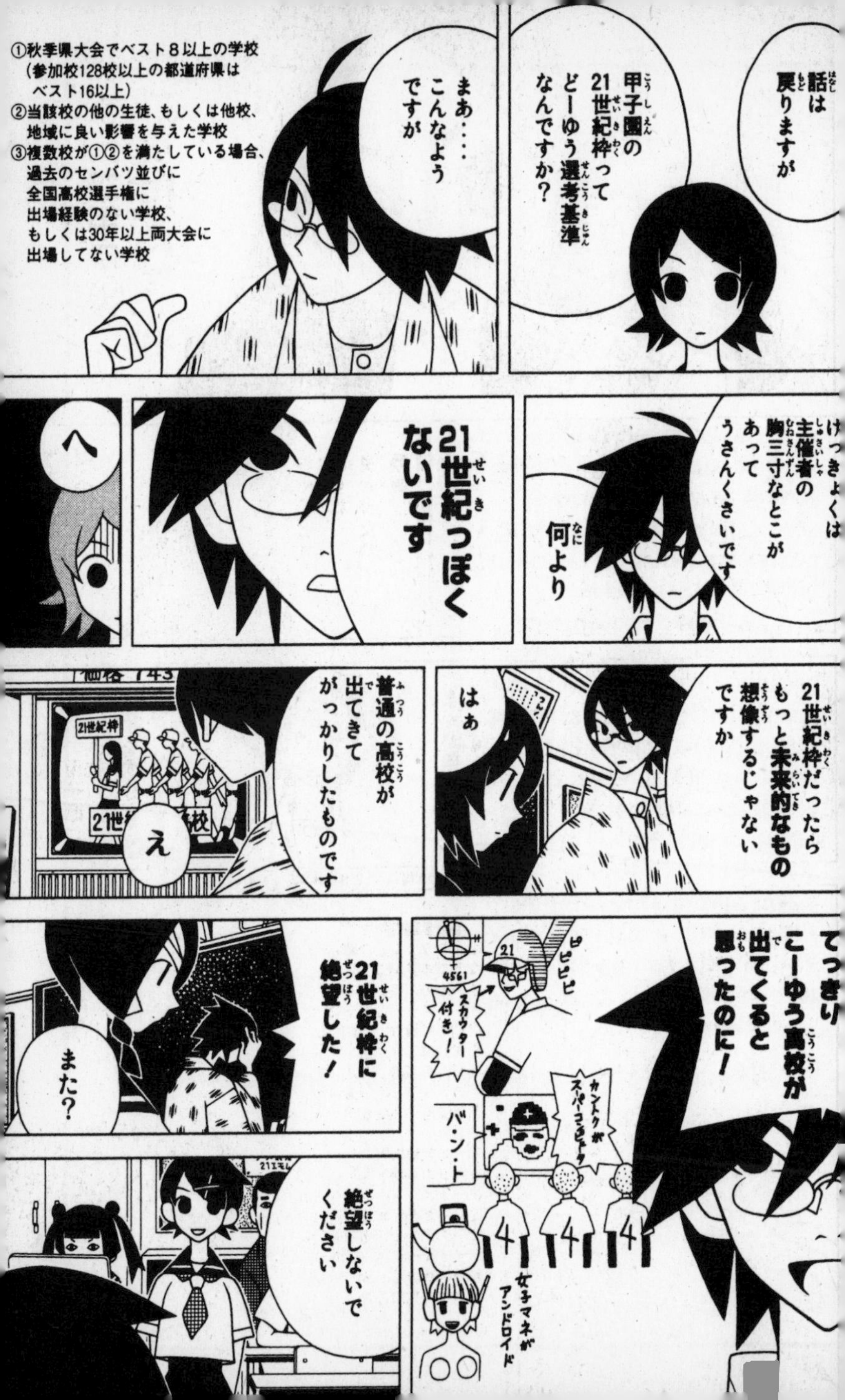

話は戻りますが
甲子園の21世紀枠ってどーゆう選考基準なんですか？
まあ…こんなようですが
①秋季県大会でベスト８以上の学校
（参加校128校以上の都道府県はベスト16以上）
②当該校の他の生徒、もしくは他校、地域に良い影響を与えた学校
③複数校が①②を満たしている場合、過去のセンバツ並びに全国高校選手権に出場経験のない学校、もしくは30年以上両大会に出場してない学校
けっきょくは主催者の胸三寸なとこがあってうさんくさいです
何より
21世紀っぽくないです
へ
21世紀枠だったらもっと未来的なもの想像するじゃないですか
はぁ
普通の高校が出てきてがっかりしたものです
21世紀枠
え
てっきりこーゆう高校が出てくると思ったのに！
4561
21
ピピピピ
スカウター付き！
カントクがスーパーコンピュータ
バ・ン・ト
女子マネがアンドロイド
21世紀枠に絶望した！
また？
絶望しないでください

BY KEN AKAMATSU

Negi Springfield is a ten-year-old wizard teaching English at an all-girls Japanese school. He dreams of becoming a master wizard like his legendary father, the Thousand Master. At first his biggest concern was concealing his magic powers, because if he's ever caught using them publicly, he thinks he'll be turned into an ermine! But in a world that gets stranger every day, it turns out that the strangest people of all are Negi's students! From a librarian with a magic book to a centuries-old vampire, from a robot to a ninja, Negi will risk his own life to protect the girls in his care!

Ages: 16+

Special extras in each volume! Read them all!

VISIT WWW.KODANSHACOMICS.COM TO:
• View release date calendars for upcoming volumes
• Find out the latest about new Kodansha Comics series

FROM HIRO MASHIMA,
CREATOR OF **RAVE MASTER**

Lucy has always dreamed of joining the Fairy Tail, a club for the most powerful sorcerers in the land. But once she becomes a member, the fun really starts!

Special extras in each volume! Read them all!

RATING T AGES 13+

TOMARE! STOP

You're going the wrong way!

MANGA IS A COMPLETELY DIFFERENT TYPE OF READING EXPERIENCE.

TO START AT THE **BEGINNING**, GO TO THE **END**!

That's right!

Authentic manga is read the traditional Japanese way—from right to left, exactly the *opposite* of how American books are read. It's easy to follow: Just go to the other end of the book and read each page—and each panel—from right side to left side, starting at the top right. Now you're experiencing manga as it was meant to be!